TWICE AS GOOD

"EDUCATIONAL EVANGELISTS": John Rice and Julia Head, Condoleezza Rice's great-grandparents (above), were born into slavery. Family lore says that a white plantation owner, not John Rice, fathered Julia's nine children. Julia's son John left the cotton fields of Eutaw, Alabama, to get "book learning" and then became a preacher, building church-schools for "Negroes." On her mother's side, Rice's grandparents didn't go to college, but they insisted that their five children should. Angelena Ray, Condoleezza's mother, attended Miles College. At Miles, she was a member of the women's cultural club—Harmonia (below, third from left, back row). Angelena went on to be a schoolteacher. Condoleezza's father, Rev. John Rice, named for his father and grandfather, eventually became the vice chancellor of the University of Denver.

IDYLLIC, BUT . . . Angelena and John had a conscious plan to make their daughter "special." And Rice enjoyed a surprisingly happy childhood for a girl growing up in segregated Birmingham. Her grandmother, Mattie Ray, started teaching Condoleezza to play piano when "Condo," as her father called her, was just three years old. Being middle-class helped the Rices shelter Condoleezza somewhat from Jim Crow—she never had to ride in the back of a bus, because her parents owned a car. In the picture to the left, Rice is sitting on top of her uncle Alto Ray's car. But John and Angelena couldn't protect Condo from everything. On Sept. 15, 1963, Rice's friend Denise McNair, seen below receiving her kindergarten "diploma" from Rev. Rice, was killed when the Ku Klux Klan dynamited the Sixteenth Street Baptist Church. Eight-year-old Condoleezza felt her father's church, two miles away from the blast, "rocking like an earthquake."

IN A HURRY: When Condoleezza was thirteen, the Rices moved to Denver. For the first time, she went to school with white children—at St. Mary's Academy. But all she cared about was skating. Other than skating, her social life was so limited that she attended her junior prom with her father's secretary's little brother (above, near right). Having skipped first and seventh grades, Rice graduated from St. Mary's when she was just sixteen (near right). More incredibly, the same year she was a senior, Rice was also a freshman at the University of Denver, where she joined a sorority (center right). She graduated as the most decorated woman in the Class of '74; Rice holds the Outstanding Senior Woman plaque (above, center right) with her parents. She went on to Notre Dame, where she dated linebacker Wayne Bullock (above, far right) while getting her master's before returning to DU to earn her PhD in 1981 at just 26 (far right).

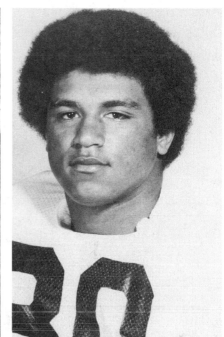

AT THE RIGHT HAND OF POWER: Stanford University hired Rice as a junior professor (left) in 1981 under their affirmative action program, impressed by her poise and self-confidence. The same qualities wowed Brent Scowcroft, and in 1988, the Republican national security expert invited Rice to work for him in the first George Bush administration. As the National Security Council's director for the Soviet Union, Rice was one of four people on the U.S. team that negotiated the reunification of Germany. With President Bush at a 1990 Superpower summit in Helsinki (below). In her last day at the White House on Mar. 1, 1991 (far below), with Bush, then-deputy national security adviser Robert Gates, and national security adviser Scowcroft.

When Rice returned to Stanford, president Gerhard Casper (above, left) shocked the university — and Rice — by naming the 38-year-old provost and vice president. Rice "had never managed anything," as she puts it, and her confrontational style and millions of dollars in budget cuts led to student protests and hunger strikes (above). But in six years as provost, she managed to close the budget gap and create freshman seminars so that senior faculty taught the youngest students (below).

THE CONFIDANTE: On Mar. 7, 1999, Condoleezza Rice was at George W. Bush's side when he officially launched his presidential exploratory committee (above). By then, Rice and Bush were so close they were "attached at the frontal lobe," says a longtime Rice friend. After Bush won the White House, Rice regularly joined the president and first lady for Sunday dinners and trips to the Bushes' ranch in Texas. As national security adviser, Rice became famous for her absolute defense of Bush and his foreign policy—and talents as a pianist. She played at Constitution Hall (below) with cellist Yo-Yo Ma on Apr. 2, 2002.

But Rice's role in the administration became increasingly controversial after the 9/11 attacks and the Iraq invasion. On Apr. 8, 2004, she testified before the 9/11 commission (above), answering charges the administration had been too slow to respond to the al-Qaeda threat. Despite the controversies of the first term, including the failure to find weapons of mass destruction in Iraq, the weekend after Bush was reelected in Nov. 2004, Bush asked Rice to become his secretary of state. Rice had told a friend, "No way, I don't want that job!" but took it, believing she had to help Bush rebuild the Middle East. Rice is seen at her ceremonial swearing-in (below) by Supreme Court Justice Ruth Bader Ginsburg on Jan. 28, 2005. Rice's closest aunt, Genoa "G" McPhatter, stands between Bush and Ginsburg as her uncle Alto Ray looks on.

LA SÉDUCTION: The week after she took office, Rice left on an offensive to Europe to repair alliances strained by the Iraq war. She is seen with French president Jacques Chirac (above) in Paris. Two months later, on Apr. 6, 2005, Rice prayed at the bier of Pope John Paul II (below) as part of a delegation that included three presidents. Washington insiders—and even some of Rice's aides—believed she was a weak national security adviser, outflanked by Secretary of Defense Donald Rumsfeld and Vice President Dick Cheney. But as secretary she wielded new power, moderating Bush's foreign policy and playing the go-between in the increasingly difficult war in Iraq.

On May 15, 2005, she met with Iraqi Kurdish leader Massoud Barzani (above) in northern Iraq to press for Sunni inclusion. While Iraq descended into civil war, the fundamentalist Taliban made a comeback in Afghanistan. Rice meets with Afghan president Hamid Karzai at right. But she was still by Bush's side. She rides with Bush and Russian leader Vladimir Putin before a G8 summit in St. Petersburg in July 2006. National security adviser Stephen Hadley is seen to the left of the golf cart (below).

INTERNATIONAL CELEBRITY: As the war in Iraq worsened, Rice was the only member of the Bush cabinet to maintain a positive approval rating. Children, local celebrities, and athletes met her on her arrivals in foreign capitals. In Indonesia, she attended an Islamic school (far left). And in Kyrgyzstan, Rice was greeted by a falconer (near left). *Vanity Fair* named her to its "Best-Dressed" list, noting the "*Matrix*-style" coat and leather boots she wore on a visit to the American army base in Wiesbaden, Germany (below, left). Her un-Washington style was apparent when she attended a state dinner in India in Mar. 2006 (right) and hosted the winners of the Kennedy Center Honors in December: Steven Spielberg, Dolly Parton, Smokey Robinson, Zubin Mehta, and Andrew Lloyd Webber (below).

LEGACY? But relative popularity isn't the same as being popular, and the world voiced its opposition to much of Bush's foreign policy—and to Rice—on her trips abroad: from the United Kingdom, where protestors condemned American abuses at Abu Ghraib and the alleged torture of terrorism suspects in 2005; to the Middle East, where Rice delayed calling for a ceasefire in the summer war between Israel and Hezbollah in 2006; to South Korea, where demonstrators protested Rice's refusal to hold one-on-one talks with North Korea over its nuclear program.

Disillusioned with the war in Iraq, voters handed Congress to the Democrats in Nov. 2006. Attempting to revive his foreign policy, Bush shook up his team (below), adding Robert Gates as defense secretary and Peter Pace as chairman of the joint chiefs. Then, the president announced a "surge" of troops into Iraq and that Rice would lead an effort to get Israelis and Palestinians to agree on a peace deal. In Feb. 2007, Rice met with Israeli prime minister Ehud Olmert and Palestinian president Mahmoud Abbas (above). Bush's legacy—and Rice's—will depend on whether the surge can rescue the mission in Iraq, and whether Condoleezza Rice can succeed where no other secretary of state has before.

TWICE AS GOOD

CONDOLEEZZA RICE

AND HER

PATH TO POWER

MARCUS MABRY

MODERN TIMES

Modern Times is a trademark of Rodale Inc.

Rodale books may be purchased for business or promotional use or for special sales. For information, please write to: Special Markets Department, Rodale Inc., 733 Third Avenue, New York, NY 10017.

Printed in the United States of America
Rodale Inc. makes every effort to use acid-free ⊗, recycled paper ◉

Photography credits appear on page 351.

Book design by Christopher Rhoads

Library of Congress Cataloging-in-Publication Data is on file with the publisher.

ISBN-13 978–1–59486–362–2 hardcover

ISBN-10 1–59486–362–8 hardcover

Distributed to the trade by Holtzbrinck Publishers

2   4   6   8   10   9   7   5   3   1   hardcover

To Chris

for his love, his humor, and his light

and

For Tiffani, Miracle, and Monet:

May you always be twice as good
—and may you someday not have to be

CONTENTS

PREFACE

I met Mattie Ray Bonds at Glory's just outside Birmingham in Fairfield, Alabama. The family-style soul food restaurant was just up the road from Miles College, which Miss Mattie and her sister Angelena had attended. She was the closest of the five children of Mattie Lula Ray and Albert Robinson Ray, from what Miss Mattie and others told me, to Angelena, mother of Condoleezza Rice. I had come to talk to Miss Mattie about her niece and the family that produced her. But Miss Mattie, an exuberantly independent eighty-four-year-old, told me that Saturday morning in September, "I can show you better than I can tell you."

She took me to a tiny clapboard church in Sayreton, north Birmingham, tucked at the end of a dead-end street behind a clutch of houses. St. Paul's, C.M.E.[1] bore no adornment, not even a cross. When Miss Mattie had first known St. Paul's, back when C.M.E. stood for Colored Methodist Episcopal, it was called Suggs Chapel. Before the Reverend John Rice married Angelena and converted a good part of the Ray family to the Rices' Presbyterianism, the Rays were all C.M.E. Miss Mattie made a point of saying she still was. Her eldest brother Albert had become a C.M.E. preacher when he was just seventeen: "As a little boy, every cat, every dog that would die in this neighborhood, he'd preach at their funeral," said Bonds.

When the Rays gathered for family reunions, which they hadn't done since Condoleezza went to Washington in 2001, they returned to St. Paul's. Miss Mattie and Condoleezza would play for Sunday services. (Condoleezza Rice said that after she leaves government service, she plans to buy the church a new piano because its current piano is missing a G.)

Later, Bonds would take me to the house where her mother and father raised their children, where Condoleezza first touched a piano as a two-year-old in the family room in the back. When the Rays moved to Hooper City, it was all woods. Their house, built by her father, was one of only three homes. An old board covered the well he dug so the family could have water close at hand. Albert Jr.'s graffiti was still etched into the back steps: *A.R.R. May 14, 1946.* But the front-porch swing was long gone, as was Daddy Ray's blacksmith shop out back, where Mattie had once heard her father tell a friend who asked, "'Albert, why you sending them girls of yours to school?' [Because] I don't know what's gonna happen in the future." [2]

"It was understood we would go to college," Miss Mattie told me. "Daddy told us, 'Get the feel of your *own* money.'" That Bonds took me first to a church, then to home and to school, said much about Ray family values.

Then she guided me farther away from the interstate, up a wooded hillside. She wanted me to see where her grandmother, Emma Parrom, Condoleezza's great-grandmother, was buried. Though Daddy Ray hadn't finished high school, Mattie Lula Parrom Ray had gone to finishing school and been taught classical piano by an Austrian, though she ended up teaching piano to neighborhood children for a nickel. Since Miss Mattie hadn't been up the hill herself in forty years, she had me stop one of the locals so she could ask directions. Theodette Juan Langford—who turned out to be a grandson of Emma Parrom's niece and therefore a distant relative—hopped into his car and started leading us farther up the hill to the old Negro cemetery. When he failed to find it, another local man, Andrew Kelly, abandoned his lawn mower and hopped in Langford's car to lead the way.

We drove out of the new development that topped Hayes Highlands, where spacious houses looked across the Jones Valley, past empty fields that still had the lot numbers posted on them, down an unpaved road by houses that had been smashed like Popsicle stick models in the tornado of '77. Known as the Smithfield Tornado, it lasted only fifteen minutes but took twenty-two lives and destroyed 167 homes. [3] Many of them still lay ruined twenty-nine years later. Finally, we came to an eight-foot-tall chain-link fence topped with barbed wire. Someone had scratched on the black and gray *No Trespassing* sign "Ala Power. For keys call 322-9979."

A jungle rose on the other side of the fence. On one side of the padlocked gate, the fencing had been pushed aside. The only "road" was two parallel tracks where tires had worn away the grass. I told my companions that I was going in to look for the graveyard. Langford and Kelly said they would come, too. I told Miss Mattie she could wait in the air-conditioned car. "No, baby. I'm going, too," she said.

Though we had known each other only a few hours, I understood there was no point in arguing with Mattie Ray Bonds. We squeezed through the narrow opening one after the other; Miss Mattie deigned to take our hosts' arms for support as she walked through upright. We were fifty yards down the tracks before I said, looking to each side, that this didn't look like a cemetery. It was a forest. The trees were thirty feet tall. The local men assured me this was the cemetery; then Langford spied two concrete slabs barely distinguishable in the underbrush. I crept through the tangle of trees and vines to one and pulled back the dense mat of roots that covered it. It was the thick concrete block used to cover a grave, but there was no headstone.

In fact, we could only find one:

ROBERT CROSS

PVT FIRST CLASS

SEPTEMBER 26, 1938

For a moment, we all stood silent in the thick late-summer air. Here lay hundreds, maybe thousands of ancestors of black Alabamans, including Emma Parrom, their last resting place reclaimed by nature.

Miss Mattie compared it with the Native American burial ground up in Moundville. Left unspoken was the fact that the prehistoric Native American burial mounds, a national historic landmark, received a measure of respect.

Any biography presents challenges, much like hunting for headstones in a forest. Before I started work on this book in March 2005, I sent a letter through trusted channels to Secretary of State Condoleezza Rice's office requesting her cooperation. I wanted to interview the secretary and, just as important, get a list of sources who could provide insight into who she was. Pending her decision, I got to work, approaching her biography as a writer would any historical figure. I scoured old documents—from the University of Denver's files on her father, John Rice, to Jefferson County, Alabama, birth and marriage records. I spoke with sources who didn't require Rice's approval—from neighbors in Birmingham and Tuscaloosa to classmates in Denver to members of the George H. W. Bush administration like George Shultz, James Baker, and Brent Scowcroft. I worked, I often thought, as if Rice were dead, as though there were no primary source I could speak with, which, in a sense, was true.

When I finally met with Condoleezza Rice in her seventh-floor offices at the State Department in May 2006, she agreed to cooperate, just as her friend and colleague Coit "Chip" Blacker had said she would. Blacker had been my International Relations adviser at Stanford. Like most student-professor relationships, ours had not been close. Other than one course I took with him, we saw each other only when he had to sign my course schedule and my graduation requirement sheet.

I had no relationship with Condi Rice, though she had taught at Stanford while I was a student there in the late 1980s, specifically in my I.R. concentration, the Soviet Union. She was on leave or fellowships for more than half my time at Stanford. I had not seen her, other than on television as a commentator on *ABC News* in the nineties, until our paths crossed at the Council on Foreign Relations in October 2000. I had just finished a year as a council fellow, and she was leading presidential candidate George W. Bush's foreign policy team. We were two of only a handful of African Americans at the event in an audience of hundreds. She spoke for half an hour with no notes and not one stutter. Afterward, she received a standing ovation.

We had only met face-to-face once before, at an editorial board meeting at *Newsweek* in 2005. But when we met in May 2006 for our brief introductory talk, Rice, radiating grace and warmth, made me feel as though we were old friends. As we sat together with her top communications advisers, I detailed the scope of my project. I wanted to discover the real Condoleezza Rice, I told her. I was a poor kid from Trenton, New Jersey, whose life had been transformed by education and who was the first Northerner born into a family of Southerners. Since Stanford, my career had been devoted to international relations as a foreign correspondent and then an editor. My extracurricular life was the Albert G. Oliver Program, a small New York City nonprofit that sent bright black and Latino kids to private schools, where their lives could be transformed by education, just like mine and hers had been. In other words, I told Rice, most of the subjects that touched her story animated my own: race, education, opportunity, and foreign affairs.

In the end, Rice agreed to furnish the telephone numbers of family and friends from a list I would submit to her office and to try to find time for me to interview her, though she couldn't guarantee that. But at the end of 2006, she accorded me two in-depth interviews totaling a little more than three hours.

Rice is famously private. She is also extraordinarily disciplined, the product of a generation of Southern African Americans who believed strongly in propriety and a stark separation between the public and the private.

Many of Rice's friends, and particularly her relatives, were initially reluctant to disclose personal details, especially details they thought could be misconstrued or embarrassing to the secretary. In the end, they were immensely forthcoming. They were motivated, I think, by a desire to paint a more nuanced picture than the two-dimensional image of Rice that often dominated the public view. She was much more than George W. Bush's confidante to them. Time and again, they told stories that illustrated a very different Condi Rice.

Many of the sources were, like Miss Mattie Ray Bonds, octogenarian black Southern women. Because they came of age in a time and a place where frank exchange between the races was rare if not nonexistent—especially in their private lives—they shared things with me that, to put it plainly, I do not believe they would have shared with a white biographer. That fact remains a reality in America today. It greatly helped me in writing this biography. (Rice's stepmother, Clara Rice, only in her sixties but also a Birmingham native, declared with obvious delight as she opened the door to me, "They didn't tell me that a *brother* would be interviewing me!")[4]

The older African American women told me they were sharing their stories because I was a "nice young man." In relaying some of that reporting, even after more than twenty years as a journalist, I have to admit to a certain measure of discomfort. But my professional charge supersedes my personal feelings. Something the Ray family and especially its most famous progeny are very familiar with—duty and discipline—were and are that family's watchwords.

I have endeavored to paint as complete a picture of my subject as possible. In doing so, I seek to answer the mundane questions of her personal life as well as the historic questions of our public life. For their help in furnishing details and analysis, I am forever indebted to the people of Condoleezza Rice's life who so generously shared their stories and bestowed on me their trust. I have paid particular attention to abiding by the wishes of the sources who spoke to me off the record or not for attribution. I hope that in the fullness of time, if not immediately, my sources will agree that I have been if not discreet, by virtue of the enterprise, then at least honorable and fair.

Marcus Mabry
Basket, New York
January 31, 2007

INTRODUCTION: ESSENCE

Ironically, it may have started in 1968, a year that was a crack in time. That was the year Bobby Kennedy and Martin Luther King were shot. But the event that really struck me was the Soviet invasion of Czechoslovakia. I can still feel the strong sense I had of remorse and regret that a brave people had been subdued.[1]

CONDOLEEZZA RICE
Campus Report
December 7, 1983

A virtual civil war had broken out at *Essence*. For the first time anyone could remember, the selection of a cover subject had led to threats of resignation.[2] The source of the angst? Dr. Condoleezza Rice. The most powerful black woman in 230 years of American government. Arguably the most powerful African American woman in the world. The only black woman ever to have been secretary of state—or national security adviser to the president of the United States, or provost of Stanford University. An unprecedented woman.

Such turmoil is not the usual fare of *Essence*. It's *the* magazine of the African American woman and typically dwells on more mundane matters, like the lives and loves of black celebrities.[3] But the monthly also explores—and for this it is cherished by millions of readers—the trials and tribulations of black women, that population who, as nineteenth-century educator Anna Julia Cooper observed, is the only group in America who can claim that "when and where I enter, in the quiet, undisputed dignity of my womanhood . . . [an entire] race enters with me."[4] *Essence* finds its voice and its vision in that fact: that as the black woman attains her full personhood in American society, her progeny, the entire black race, will gain it with her.

xxix

When the suggestion had been made in a meeting of senior editors, there had been no disagreement. The question at hand was who should grace the cover of *Essence*'s annual "power issue." Of course there was Oprah. But Winfrey had already been on the cover of a previous power issue,[5] and, according to *Essence* editors, she had made it clear that she wouldn't be able to appear on another because of obligations to her own magazine.[6]

And other than Winfrey, no other black woman could touch Condi Rice when it came to power. Rice had helped George W. Bush reach the White House—twice. She was the face of the United States to the entire world. And in that early summer of 2005, her public standing at home and abroad was growing by the day. She was the only member of the administration with a positive approval rating.[7] She had been the first person to inform the president that a plane had hit the World Trade Center on September 11.[8] "We're talking about a black woman who [as secretary of state] was two bullets away from the presidency," said Michaela Angela Davis, one of the highest-ranking editors at the magazine, misstating the line of presidential succession but only by one.[9]

Davis—named for the African American activist Angela Davis, who had grown up just a few miles north of Rice and had written of the terrors of living in "Bombingham," Alabama[10]—wanted to see Rice on the cover. But "half the staff wasn't having it."[11] The divide was not generational: Akiba Solomon, the young and politically conscious health editor, and Janice Bryant, a senior copy editor old enough to be her mother, both thought Rice shouldn't appear on the cover. Some of the dissidents said Rice was a murderer because she was "sending African Americans to die" in Iraq and, they argued, was directly responsible for the deaths of Iraqi civilians, "other people of color."[12] And fresh in the minds of many of the journalists was the magazine's recent eleven-hundred-word tribute to six African American servicewomen killed in Iraq and Afghanistan, "They Never Made It Home."[13] "How would the mothers, sisters, daughters, aunts, and cousins, *Essence*'s target audience, feel when they read what would inevitably be a fluff piece on Rice in *their* magazine?" asked Solomon.[14]

Almost as soon as the "center of the book" meeting ended, the uproar began. The women of *Essence* clustered in hallways and cubicles. "Did you hear? They want to make *her* the cover!" When executive editor Linda Villarosa came to work the following Monday, the women—smart, beautiful, educated, *black* women—like Condoleezza Rice—crowded into her office to voice their displeasure. Villarosa remembered someone using the word *sit in*.[15]

Villarosa didn't want Rice on the cover, either, but for different reasons. She thought Rice wouldn't appeal to the *Essence* newsstand buyer, a young woman more interested in Beyoncé than Condi. Besides, Villarosa thought, Rice wasn't making any particular news at the moment: She had been secretary of state for months; she wasn't about to announce for the presidency. Villarosa told the staffers that if they felt this strongly, they should plead their case to editorial director Susan Taylor.

Taylor invited the petitioners in, along with those who supported a Rice cover. About twenty-two staffers gathered, and the arguments instantly became heated. Women who had never uttered a word at an editorial meeting found their voices. One of the magazine's few white staffers said Rice wasn't worthy of the cover. An African copy editor said she was hurt and confounded by both the lack of solidarity and the naïveté of her colleagues, who clearly didn't understand how lucky they were to live in a country where an African American woman could rise to such heights; where she came from, women were abused and humiliated.

The other side argued that for millions of black women, the cover of *Essence* signified the highest praise. "Being on the cover would have been her entrée into the hearts of black women," said Solomon. "And she doesn't belong there. Just because you're born black and female doesn't mean we should love you."[16]

It was the Condi conundrum. Later in 2005, *Washington Post* columnist Eugene Robinson framed the question at the heart of the *Essence* debate more whimsically: "Like a lot of African Americans, I've long wondered what the deal was with Condoleezza Rice."[17]

It was fitting that Condoleezza had chosen as her vocation the study of the Soviet Union, a nation Winston Churchill called "a riddle wrapped in a mystery inside an enigma."[18] For most Americans, Rice could be described the same way.

As a public figure, she is one of a kind: influential, attractive, intelligent, charming, and tough. *Forbes* dubbed her the most powerful woman in the world twice (far ahead of Oprah).[19] A black woman in a white man's world, she gives no hint of feeling out of place or ever in doubt. Even before George W. Bush was elected president in 2000, she was his most articulate promoter—his "secret weapon," said the press.[20] And as criticism mounted at the end of Bush's first term and intensified during his second—over issues from Iraq to Katrina to domestic spying—Rice became the president's most ardent defender and simultaneously rose to become the most popular member of the cabinet, the steely yet stylish avatar of American power. She made *Vanity Fair*'s "Best-Dressed List 2006."[21] Pulitzer Prize–winning fashion writer Robin Givhan of the *Washington Post* even called her "sexy."[22]

But despite her high profile, few can say they *know* Condoleezza Rice. For most of her public life, she has jealously guarded her privacy. She claims a small circle of very close friends. She refuses to discuss her romantic life. A suspected grind, she typically rises shortly after 4:30 each morning to work out and is in her State Department office before 7. She mostly avoids the Washington party circuit and is in bed most nights by 10. While she does not shy away from the details of her biography—her childhood in the segregated South, her strong religious faith, her historic rise—she does not relish talking about herself, which in Washington may be the most exceptional thing about her.

During her tenure as head of the National Security Council, she seemed to delight in official Washington's confusion over the question, "What does Condi think?" While other administration officials fed the media and the rumor mill with their agendas, Rice mostly kept her own counsel and kept her counsel to the president to herself. As one former administration official who has known Rice for almost twenty years put it, "To write her biography is such a challenge because her American story is so powerful, and she has *such* enormous discipline so that getting underneath it—wowie zowie!"[23]

And yet her personal history provides both a lens through which to view the most important developments of our times and an opportunity to plumb their impact. Few American lives have so touched the great events of the last half century, both in the United States and on the global stage, and been so touched by them as has the life of Condoleezza Rice. Born in 1954, she was personally affected by segregation, then by integration, by affirmative action, and also by the women's movement. She has played key roles in the reunification of Europe and the fall of the Soviet Union, the response to September 11, the rise of American hegemony and the advent of George W. Bush's "transformational" foreign policy, and the war in Iraq. The challenge of writing about Rice is compounded by her contradictions. To her detractors, she is obtuse, obstinate, and remote. To her supporters, she is clear-minded and determined. And to some of them, their choice to be the first woman and the first African American president of the United States. She is a survivor of segregation who became one of the most recognizable members of a party that rose to national dominance in part through a "Southern strategy" that exploited white resentment over black civil rights gains. She is a beneficiary of both the civil rights movement and affirmative action who changed her party registration from Democrat to Republican in 1982.[24] She has never gone in for identity politics; she is an evangelical for the power of individual will. Is her story, then, the culmination of the civil rights movement, or did her success unfold parallel to it, even in spite of it? Is she an example to millions of minorities and women (as well as white men), or is her path so unique that it doesn't provide a road map for anyone else's?

As I discovered in years of interviews with the people who know her best, there is much more to Condi Rice than the political brawler who stares down Senate committees. Her friends and family paint a portrait of a woman the public has never known: a relaxed and funny woman who puts her family before even the president she serves. Who waited outside an NFL locker room in Cincinnati with her girlfriend when she was a young college professor to glimpse her heroes. Who prefers to date "bad boys" and athletes. Who called a hospital in Alabama from the Middle East to make sure the staff knew she was looking out for her twenty-eight-year-old cousin who was in their care, dying of a terminal illness. Who never wanted to be secretary of state.

I was surprised to learn that many of Rice's loved ones disapproved of and, in some cases, even disdained President Bush and his policies, policies that they feared have unfairly tainted Rice. They worry about her legacy. Her best friend is gay. Her best girlfriend is "left of Lenin" and describes herself as "an emotional mess."

And yet, Rice's public life is about nothing if not self-contained discipline and the will to power.

That's what her six years in Washington have shown. From the very beginning, she played a far larger role in George Bush's presidential career than her foreign policy portfolio suggested. First, she was the then Texas governor's schoolmaster in international relations. By all accounts, the candidate needed it;

he had rarely left North America. He had little knowledge of the world, with the exception of Mexico. But according to what Rice told friends and family, he was a quick study. Under her guidance, Bush was able to present himself credibly as the potential leader of the free world.

But in the process, Rice became much more than George W.'s tutor. She and Bush developed a personal affinity; "attached at the frontal lobe," as one of her closest friends put it. Bush came to trust her, and she believed in his vision and his values. He brought parts of Rice to the fore that had always been there but had seldom been dominant. Once Bush won, Rice was well placed to become the fulcrum on which the new president depended to balance his quarrelsome national security team. She was a veteran of Bush's father's National Security Council, famous for its moderation and its discipline.

Only Rice never saw her role as a referee between hawks and moderates; she believed her primary duty was to advise the president. Just as after 9/11, she came to believe that in order for America to be truly safe, the Middle East had to be transformed. As long as the aspirations of everyday Muslims, "the Arab street," could not be channeled into democratic institutions like elections, they would fester and turn to rage, a rage that would fuel a jihad against the West.

It was the pursuit of that transformation that motivated Rice's actions in the run-up to the war in Iraq. In the months before the 2003 invasion, she became the administration's strongest witness for "regime change." More articulate than her boss, more likeable than the vice president, more committed to the goal than the secretary of state, and less abrasive than the secretary of defense, Rice was for many the impassioned voice of reason—though, in hindsight, she may have also been a master of hyperbole.

On television and in editorial pages, she detailed Saddam Hussein's crimes against humanity, his links to al-Qaeda, and his nuclear ambitions. When critics protested that the administration lacked solid evidence that Hussein possessed stockpiles of weapons of mass destruction, it was Rice who shot back, "We don't want the smoking gun to be a mushroom cloud."[25] And when the war turned ugly and critics began to call for a timetable for U.S. forces to withdraw from Iraq, Rice compared them to Northerners who wanted to end the Civil War before the slaves were free.[26]

Despite her steely presence in public, many observers judge her tenure as national security adviser to have been a failure in at least one crucial aspect: She did not ensure that the president received and acted on the best objective intelligence before deciding to take the country to a costly "preemptive war" in Iraq. She did not ensure that the American project in Iraq was subjected to critical skepticism. Many critics also argue that as national security adviser, Rice failed to prioritize the terrorist threat before September 11. The 9/11 commission cited the lack of information-sharing between the CIA and the FBI as a structural flaw of the intelligence system, not the fault of Condi Rice. But, as I learned, even many of Rice's supporters—those inside and outside Washington who believe she did all she could have been expected to do before 9/11 and during the run-up to war in Iraq—often wonder how such an intelligent and capable woman could have allowed so much of American foreign policy years to go so terribly wrong.

And yet, while the administration faces its toughest domestic criticism and a Democratic Congress, Rice has grown more powerful than ever. By the end of the first Bush term, after being "rolled" by Secretary of Defense Donald Rumsfeld, according to even her supporters inside the administration, she learned to outmaneuver him. In the second term, from her perch at the State Department, she convinced Bush to pursue a more realist foreign policy—offering to talk to Iran for the first time in more than twenty years. Then, in February 2007, she convinced Bush to cut a deal with North Korea to end its nuclear weapons program but, so far at least, keep the arms it already has. The neoconservatives charged Rice had persuaded Bush to reward North Korea's "bad behavior." But Washington insiders were just impressed that she had seemingly outfoxed Vice President Dick Cheney, who with Rumsfeld had scuttled previous attempts to cut similar deals.

For those who know her, Rice's increasing power comes as no surprise. "She would have no problem taking down Don Rumsfeld," her best friend scoffed more than a year before Rumsfeld was forced to resign. And now, it seemed, she could take on even Dick Cheney. Since Rice first discovered the world of international relations as a nineteen-year-old former piano major searching for a new discipline, she has been fascinated by power. Over her years in Bush's White House, she has learned to use it.

So does Rice have a political future? As the Bush presidency limps toward its final year, under the constraints of a divided government and overwhelming public disapproval of the war in Iraq (Bush's approval rating sank to the lowest of any president in a generation in January 2007),[27] Rice's political prospects appear dim. But given her will, her relative youth, and the passage of time, they may not always seem so. She has never believed in limits. Even as a nine-year-old, according to her father, Condoleezza stood in front of the White House—at a time when blacks in Birmingham couldn't eat a hamburger at a lunch counter—and vowed, "One day I'll be in that house."[28]

Because Rice's domestic politics are largely unknown, conservative Republicans have taken her hawkish foreign policy views and loyalty to the president to mean she agrees with his social agenda. Yet some moderate Democrats and Independents have suggested, perhaps in an act of political transference, that she must be a social moderate, a Trojan horse waiting to expose her true colors once she has "real power."

Rice's die-hard political boosters have dubbed themselves "Condinistas," committed to getting her to run for office: whether vice president, senator, or governor. They have dismissed her repeated denials of plans to ever seek her party's nomination, pointing out that she has always left the door cracked to being "drafted."[29] For a while, the press enthusiastically participated. Less than two months after being confirmed as secretary of state, Rice met with the editors of the *Washington Times*. In an interview centered on foreign policy, she refused to take the journalists' invitation to reprise the General William T. Sherman pledge that "If nominated, I will not run; if elected, I will not serve,"[30] igniting what was the most titillating weekend of political speculation since the 2004 elections.

By Sunday morning, she jousted with NBC's Tim Russert, over and over, about what constituted a denial. In feigned exasperation, Rice finally chuckled, "I don't want to run for president of the United States. I have no intention of doing so. I don't think I'll be president of the United States ever. Is that good enough?"

But it wasn't. Russert followed up, "And you'll never run?"

"I don't intend to run."

"But it's different . . . " Russert insisted, boyishly apologetic.

"I *won't* run."

"Oh, we got it," Russert smiled.

"All right, there you go," Rice smiled back.

"Thanks very much."

But as often happens in politics, trumpeting her unwillingness to run became proof of exactly the opposite: As *Time* magazine wrote of potential 2008 presidential candidates in August 2005, "At this early stage, part of the trick to lead-ing the pack is insisting that you aren't part of it."[31]

Since Hurricane Katrina in 2005 and the congressional midterms in 2006, Rice has defended an embattled administration. And yet, her association with President Bush and his policies has not eliminated the possibility that she could appear on a Republican ticket in 2008. By December 2006, while Rice no longer enjoyed high approval ratings among Democrats and Independents, she still boasted a fifty-seven percent approval rating overall (compared with Bush's thirty-six percent).[32] In a Gallup Poll that month, Republicans ranked her as the woman they most admired, ahead of Laura Bush. Independents and Democrats ranked her third, behind only Hillary Clinton and Oprah Winfrey, and men overall ranked her second, just one point behind Clinton.[33] Rice's greatest asset as secretary of state has been her relationship with the president. Their connec-tion goes beyond mere politics; Bush and Rice are virtual soul mates. Once Rice reportedly started at a Washington dinner party, "As I was telling my husb—" before she quickly corrected herself: "As I was telling President Bush."[34] Rice told me she doesn't believe she ever made the slip. But she's so close to President Bush that he tells other world leaders that she's like his "sister." But like many of Rice's attributes, that closeness may also have been a tragic flaw that contributed to many of the administration's foreign policy blunders.

While Rice began as Bush's tutor, she became his pupil. They fed off each other: two people from opposite worlds, he the scion who rebelled against his father's politics of moderation, and she the daughter of black strivers whose dictates she followed with surpassing discipline. But in crucial ways, they are more similar than different, both accustomed to a world where even as they enjoyed privilege, they saw themselves as outsiders going against the grain. For very different reasons, each developed a herculean ability to see the world as they wanted to see it—or as they needed to see it—regardless of the circum-stances outside.

If the North Korea deal holds—a big if—it will be a considerable legacy, but what history will ultimately judge her on will be Iraq. Will Rice be looked upon as an architect of international freedom and a new Middle East or the drafts-woman of a foreign policy that began America's decline on the world stage? What has she done, and what can she still do as secretary of state to tip the led-ger one way or the other? Over the next eighteen months, Rice will work to make sure Bush's vision of a transformed Middle East does not end with his presidency. She will attempt to lay the groundwork for a Palestinian state and peace with Israel. She will try to bring a diplomatic end to Iran's nuclear ambitions. But as a Rice colleague and friend told me, the "correlation of forces" is against her.

In the face of long odds, Rice will rely on the determination and confidence that have become her trademarks—the legacies of her deceased parents, Angelena and John. For generations, the Rices and the Rays believed that while segregation kept blacks from doing, it should not keep them from dreaming. When the civil rights protests exploded onto the streets of their hometown (and, thereby, into the national consciousness), with children marching against dogs and fire hoses, Rev. John Rice wanted no part of it. He believed in education, not protest. While his friend, civil rights activist Rev. Fred Shuttlesworth, and the Reverend Dr. Martin Luther King were catapulting Birmingham to the forefront of the greatest social revolution since the Civil War, Rev. Rice was fighting for Negroes to overcome the way his family always had—through hard work and a stubborn refusal to be denied.

Condoleezza Rice learned those lessons well. As a result, she has accomplished great historic firsts. But in interviews, her friends and family presented ample evidence that her success—and her family's philosophy of individual empowerment—has also come at a price. In the coming pages, we will explore those costs, for Condoleezza Rice and for the world.

PART I
ALABAMA STEEL

CHAPTER ONE

DEBUT

I spend a lot of time thinking about how best to defend America against threats to her values, threats to her society, but sometimes my greatest fear is that when we finish paying for and thinking about how to defend ourselves with military forces, we will have very little left to defend.[1]

CONDOLEEZZA RICE
Class Day Speech
Stanford University
June 1985

She stood out for what she was not. As a little girl, she didn't fidget. "She never had to go to the bathroom like children do."[2] When Brent Scowcroft, President George H. W. Bush's future national security adviser, visited Stanford in 1984 for a talk with arms control experts, she stood out because she wasn't old. "More than [being] attractive and black, it was that she was young—and a comer," said Scowcroft twenty years later.[3] In 2000, Condoleezza Rice stood out at the Republican National Convention in Philadelphia, at least at first, because out of 2,022 delegates, she was one of eighty-five African Americans.[4]

Governor George W. Bush and Vice President Al Gore had been locked in a brutal race for the White House. Bush's challenge was to get the country to cast off Democratic leadership after eight relatively halcyon years of Bill Clinton. The governor had two principal strategies. One was to constantly highlight the differences between Gore, the political heir to Clinton—a philanderer who had had sex with an intern in the White House—and Bush's own upright character. Bush promised a new age of moral certitude—not preachy but plainspoken—a time of optimism and honor, in contrast to the Clinton years that he portrayed, economic prosperity aside, as a long nightmare of national disgrace.

Bush's other theme was aimed at voters who weren't convinced Clinton's moral failings should affect their vote in 2000. They were centrists less persuaded by appeals based on Bush's rectitude alone; Clinton was leaving anyway. To reach them, the Bush campaign heralded a new era of "compassionate conservatism," a middle ground between the Democrats' reliance on big government to solve the woes of individuals and the Republican tendency, Bush's slogan implied, to uncompassionately blame the unfortunates' problems on themselves.[5]

Compassionate conservatism was making inroads with the moderates that the governor needed to take the White House.[6] But his political strategists were taking nothing for granted; Bush wanted to not only reinvigorate the Republican Party but build the foundation for a permanent majority,[7] one that would unite moderates and conservatives, including minorities.[8]

Gore's message was aimed at the same middle-class, middle-of-the-road voter Bush so coveted. The voter who even after the sordid Monica Lewinsky scandal was still more concerned about her own affairs than Bill Clinton's. Gore hammered away at the Republicans for being ideologically extremist *men* determined to abolish "a woman's right to choose," removed from the concerns of everyday Americans.

But by the summer of 2000, it still wasn't clear who would capture the middle-class moderates.[9] Then onto the stage of the First Union Center in Philadelphia stepped Condoleezza Rice.

Convention chairman Andy Card had been promising "a different kind of convention for a different kind of Republican." In contrast to 1992, when conservative culture warriors had scared moderates away from Bush's father's candidacy, Card guaranteed "an upbeat message that highlights citizens who personify the ideas and principles of the Republican Party."[10] He couldn't have hoped for a better exemplar than Condi Rice: a black woman who had been a National Security Council staffer under President Bush, the former provost and vice president of Stanford University, and now W.'s chief foreign policy adviser.

With regal bearing, Rice took the stage in an exquisitely tailored suit, smiling broadly. She waved to the crowd and patiently waited for the applause to subside. Then, with the fluency of a college professor and the assurance of a woman accustomed to briefing the most powerful man in the world, she began.

> Thank you for that warm welcome. Thank you, Governor, for . . . that . . . generous introduction. [Governor Bush had introduced Rice remotely on a giant video screen.]
>
> Ladies and gentlemen, distinguished guests, fellow delegates from the G-o-o-olden State of California [cheers] . . . fellow delegates from across the country. Tonight, we gather to reflect on America's unique opportunity to lead the forward march of freedom and to fortify the peace.[11]

Rice rushed through "to lead the forward march of freedom," robbing the phrase of its accelerating tempo—whether because she was nervous at the start of the most important speech of her life, which was unlikely; or because she was famously a proponent of Realpolitik, which argued that interests, not ideals, drove international relations.

> We offer special thanks to all those Private Ryans who served over the decades—so that tyranny . . . would . . . not . . . stand. [applause]
>
> We remember those great Republican presidents who sustained American leadership through the decades, ended the Cold War, and lifted our nuclear nightmare. Thank you, Gerald Ford, thank you, Ronald Reagan, thank you, George—Herbert—Walker—Bush. [applause]
>
> And tonight, we gather to acknowledge this remarkable truth: The future belongs to liberty—fueled by markets and trade, protected by the rule of law, and propelled by the fundamental rights of the individual. Information and knowledge can no longer be bottled up by the state. Prosperity flows to those who can tap the genius of their people. [light applause]
>
> We have, ladies and gentlemen, a presidential nominee who knows what America must do to fulfill the promise of this new century. We have a nominee who knows the power of truth and honor.

With the last phrase, spoken with her eyes narrowed into a searing gaze as though in judgment of Bill Clinton, the country received a taste of the steeliness it would come to know in Condi Rice.

Over hoots and hollers, she continued, "We have a nominee . . . we have a nominee who will be the next great president of the United States of America—Texas Governor George W. Bush." The convention boilerplate led to sixteen seconds of sustained applause. But it was followed, less than two and a half minutes into her speech, with a story that had never been told on "national security night" from the rostrum of a Republican National Convention.

> It is fitting that I stand before you to talk about Governor Bush's commitment to America's principled leadership in the world, because that is the legacy and tradition of our party—because our party's principles made me a Republican. [applause]
>
> The first Republican that I knew was my father, John Rice, and he is still the Republican I admire most. My father joined our party because the Democrats in Jim Crow Alabama of 1952 would not register him to vote. The Republicans did.

The line was delivered with a flatness and a force that claimed retribution, as if this night in Philadelphia was payback time. Then, whether to be heard above the din or in a rare moment of personal anguish—Rice was known for her perpetual poise—she almost yelled, "I want you to know . . . I want you to know that my father has never forgotten that day, and neither have I!"

The crowd erupted. It was the sound of chains clanking to the stadium floor. The Republican Party, which had been saddled for two generations with the smear that it was the party of whites and the rich, was watching an articulate and appealing black woman not only sing its praises on national television but contrast it favorably to a racist Democratic Party.

Dropping her voice back to its normal register, Rice continued.

> I joined the party for different reasons. I found a party that sees me as an individual, not as part of a group.
>
> I found a party that puts family first. I found a party . . . I found a party that has love of liberty at its core. And I found a party that believes that peace begins with strength.

Then she described Bush's character and the impact it would have on American foreign policy: "It all begins with integrity in the Oval Office . . . Friend and foe—friend and foe—will know that he keeps his word and tells the truth."

George W. Bush believes that America has a special responsibility to keep the peace—that the fair cause of freedom depends on our strength and purpose.

He recognizes that the magnificent men and women of America's armed forces are not a global police force. They are not the world's 911. [applause]

. . . And I want to assure you if the time ever comes to use military force, President George W. Bush will do so to win—because for him, victory is . . . not . . . a . . . dirty . . . word. [During a fourteen-second ovation, she stared intensely over the crowd.]

. . . But most importantly, George W. Bush, the George W. Bush that I know, is a man of uncommonly good judgment. He is focused and consistent. He believes that we Americans are at our best when we exercise power without fanfare and arrogance. He speaks plainly and with a positive spirit.

Nine minutes into her speech, Rice returned to the theme of race.

In America, with education and hard work, it really does not matter where you came from—it matters only where you are going. [She would use the same phrase when referring to her father at his memorial ceremony four months later.] But that truth cannot be sustained if it is not renewed in each generation—as it was with my grandfather.

George W. Bush would have liked Granddaddy Rice. He was the son of a-a-a . . . farmer in rural Alabama . . . [she stutters for the first time in the speech, perhaps over the change from the released text, which included a description of her great-grandfather as "poor"], but he recognized the importance of education. Around 1918, he decided he was going to get book learning [The distributed copies of the speech read "he decided it was time to get book learning"; the spoken version eliminates the passive voice, conferring greater agency on Granddaddy Rice], and so he asked, in the language of the day, where a colored man could go to college. He was told about little Stillman College, a school about fifty miles away. So Granddaddy saved his cotton for tuition, and he went off to Tuscaloosa.

> After the first year, he ran out of cotton, and he needed a way to pay for college. Praise be—as he often does, God gave him an answer. My grandfather asked how those . . . other . . . boys were staying in school. And he was told that "they had what was called a scholarship," and they said, "If you wanted to be a Presbyterian minister, then you could have one, too." Granddaddy Rice said, "That's just what I had in mind." [light laughter and applause] And my family has been Presbyterian and college educated ever since.

Rice received the longest ovation of her speech: a full nineteen seconds of applause and cheers. Notably, it was not in appreciation for anything she had said about candidate Bush or the promise of a Bush presidency but for a story she told about the Rice family.

> But you know, that's not just my grandfather's story—that's an American story. The search for hope. The search for opportunity. The skill of good hard work.
>
> My friends, George W. Bush challenges us to call upon our better selves—to be compassionate toward those who are less fortunate; to cherish and educate every child, descendants of slaves and immigrants alike, and to thereby affirm the American dream for us all. [light applause]
>
> On that firm foundation, confident of what we are defending, confident of who we are, we will go forth, we will go forth, to extend peace, prosperity, and liberty beyond our blessed shores.
>
> Thank you.
>
> Let's go out and elect George W. Bush and Dick Cheney!
>
> Good night. God bless you, and God bless America.

The speech lasted just over thirteen minutes. Without applause, Rice had spoken for about ten minutes, devoting almost a third of that time to her family history and, both subtly and not, to race.

The media loathed Bush's contention-free coronation. Through every grudging minute of network airtime and for hundreds of column inches, journalists complained about the lack of discord inside and outside the arena:[12] the high level of orchestration that eliminated what little spontaneity could be hoped for in a modern political convention[13] and, especially, the diversity "window dressing."[14]

But Condoleezza Rice had enthralled even the gimlet-eyed journalists. A reporter for the *San Francisco Chronicle* summed her up as simply "a class act."[15] The *Philadelphia Inquirer* decreed her "the most important of the new GOP stars."[16] Wrote a minister and political rhetorician in the *Dallas Morning News*, "It may have been John McCain's evening, but it was Ms. Rice's moment." Conservative columnist George Will called her address "noble" and "deftly written (that 'Praise be' sentence is particularly masterful), drily funny, devoid of claims to victim status."[17]

Discussion of Rice's race and what it said about the Republicans generated far more ink than her foreign policy views. "Ms. Rice, an African American preacher's kid from Alabama and a former provost and professor from Stanford, epitomized personally and rhetorically what the whole Republican convention has been trying to present to the world—we're diverse, we care, we're smart, and we're on top of things," read one column. "She rocked the place."[18] The editorial page of the *Atlanta Journal-Constitution* exclaimed, "We challenge critics to ask Powell or [Rice] . . . if they feel as if they were paraded before the cameras merely to fool the public about the GOP's attitudes about minorities. That suggestion is an incredible insult to these two intelligent, accomplished African Americans."[19] And noting Rice and Colin Powell's prominence both at the convention and as potential high-level administration officials, Richard Cohen of the *Washington Post* observed it was "both striking and ironic that the Democrats can manage nothing similar."[20]

More important, Bush's "brainy African American adviser" had done her job. The needle started to move more resolutely in the direction of Bush among moderates and centrists.[21] So much so that some of the Republican faithful complained about the "sweetness and light" convention.[22] They said the party had worked so hard to be inclusive that it had hidden its conservative values. "There must be some contrast [with the Democrats], otherwise it is hard for people to become passionate," said a frustrated Iowa delegate.[23]

That lack of passion—and a last-minute revelation that Bush had been arrested on drunk-driving charges when he was thirty years old[24]—would lead many true believers to stay home on election day,[25] costing Bush the popular vote and nearly the election.

But one thing was certain: The loss of the popular vote had nothing to do with Condi Rice. Through her intensive tutoring and coaching sessions, she had transformed the ill-traveled governor into a credible leader of the free world. In her convention address, she had laid out the foundations of a Bush foreign policy (to the unexacting standards of political conventions at least), explaining what would distinguish it from a Gore or, more accurately, a Clinton foreign policy: not using the military as "the world's 911" to solve humanitarian problems; the unapologetic exercise of American power; close cooperation with Congress; a prohibition against using foreign policy for "partisan political gain"; and the embrace of the Powell Doctrine, which dictated that when you go to war, you go to win with overwhelming force and then get out.

Rice had described in soaring rhetoric a foreign policy that mixed idealism with realism, avoiding both Clinton's international meddling and the isolationism preached by some congressional Republicans.[26]

But Rice had something far more important that night in Philadelphia—international issues, after all, were literally at the bottom of voters' concerns in 2000.[27] She had made George Bush look smart. In poll after poll, Bush's Achilles heel had been that voters believed Gore was smarter than the Texas governor.[28] By association, Rice lent her candidate her aura of intelligence.

Her other principal triumph was the message her presence and presentation sent to white moderates. Rice had not only given flesh to the idea of the Republican "big tent," she had intimated that the Democrats, both historically and today, were the truly racist party: In 1952, they wouldn't register her father to vote; nowadays, they saw her as "part of a group," not an individual. It was the very definition of prejudice. The message to white centrists was that this *was* a different Republican Party; they didn't need to fear that a vote for Bush would be vote for intolerance . . . and maybe if they voted for the Democrats, they did. Rice was so convincing, along with Powell, that even skeptics like Richard Cohen conceded a Bush administration wouldn't be "your old man's GOP."[29] Some pundits speculated that African Americans could turn to the GOP in unprecedented numbers, predicting Bush's percentage of black support could reach into the high teens.[30]

It was a dramatic turnabout in perceptions of Bush and race. Just six months earlier, during the winter primary season, as Senator John McCain closed in on front-runner Bush, winning New Hampshire, a whispering campaign had infected the now all-important fight for South Carolina: McCain had a "black child."[31]

Governor Bush's team denied any part in the race baiting, but Bush's very first stop[32] after his loss in New Hampshire had been a visit to Bob Jones University, a school that banned interracial dating[33] and whose founder had called Catholicism "a cult."[34] McCain had labeled Bush a Falwell and Robertson Republican and had charged him with running an uninclusive campaign.[35] By the convention, Powell's and Rice's roles in resuscitating Bush's image as a tolerant centrist were crucial.

The rhetoric that Rice wielded to do it was surprisingly strident, especially given her biography. For a woman who had never been considered highly partisan, she had delivered a highly partisan address. But Condoleezza Rice had traveled a long road from Birmingham to the podium of the Republican National Convention, longer than most people watching inside or outside the hall knew. And she had come to win.

As a young professor at Stanford, Rice had been so moderate that many of her colleagues didn't believe she was a Republican at all. Others assumed she was a "foreign policy Republican," devoted to the tough line that Ronald Reagan pursued toward the Soviet Union, but on social issues, like them a Democrat or at least a libertarian.

It was true that her speeches in the eighties suggested a very different philosophy than the one Rice espoused in Philadelphia. She was so popular at Stanford that four times graduating seniors asked her to be their Class Day speaker,[36] the professor from whom they wanted to hear one last lecture before leaving "the Farm."[37] In one Class Day address in June 1985, she said, "I hope that we've taught you . . . there are other cultures to be accommodated and understood and that America herself could do with a bit less arrogance . . . [I hope] that you will remember that our institutions are very, very fragile . . . that even today, it makes a great deal of difference whether you were born in [affluent] Menlo Park or [impoverished] East Palo Alto, and [the] American dream is going to have to be delivered to all if we are going to be a country worth the paper on which our Declaration of Independence and our Bill of Rights are written."[38]

In her Class Day speech three years later—her face a little less rounded, her hair taking on the more sophisticated look of a grown-up—Rice spoke even more resolutely and at even greater length about the importance of diversity: "No set of experiences could be more important for your entry into the world out there than . . . acceptance of and respect for diversity . . . Look back on what you have learned to see that dominance is not a license to exploit because it is not a gift from God. Dominance is a matter of circumstance."[39]

Then, speaking overtly to the minorities in the audience ("I would like now to say a word to those of you who by matter of race, gender, religious belief, physical disability, or sexual orientation find yourselves in the minority"), Rice delivered perhaps the most powerful and personal part of any speech she has given. In it, the beginnings of the message she would deliver to the GOP twelve years later were plainly visible.

> I feel certain that we have taught you to call prejudice and bigotry by name and to challenge it in our institutional structures . . . But have we equipped you to deal with bigotry in your daily lives? Do you understand that prejudice is not an impenetrable force field that cannot be overcome? The will to succeed may be your most potent weapon against the prejudice that is still deeply ingrained in [the] fabric of our country and our world.
>
> Prejudice and bigotry are brought down . . . by the sheer force of determination of individuals to succeed and the refusal of a human being to let prejudice define the parameters of the possible.
>
> If your first reaction to failure is that prejudice is to blame—if your first thought when you or another minority succeeds is that race or gender or physical disability must have been the patron—if when someone disagrees with you or stands in your way, you immediately suspect that that person is a bigot . . . bigotry and prejudice are winning because their mere existence has begun to define your successes, your failures, and your relationship to others. You have become a part of the pernicious dismissal of individual will. You are sanctioning the belittlement of the efforts of generations of nameless minorities—women who scrubbed floors to send children to college, men who were spat upon but kept their dignity—people who suffered and sacrificed so that step by step, victory by victory, the walls of prejudice would be brought down, and one and then two and then many minorities could pass through and achieve.[40]

At the Republican National Convention, of course, Rice played a different role—it was a political convention, after all. Still, her partisan fervor was so pronounced that some commentators questioned whether it was "unseemly" for someone who could possibly occupy a diplomatic post in the near future.[41]

Moreover, the speech's impact was magnified because Rice was not just another partisan. She was a black woman and a product of the segregated South. And because of that background, she held a privileged place as a judge of racial rights and wrongs. No one with that pedigree and Rice's combination of prominence and promise had graced the stage of a national political convention in a generation.[42] In less than a quarter hour, Rice had inverted the conventional wisdom about race and politics in America, casting the GOP as the defenders of black equality and the Democrats as racist.

Had Rice's perspective evolved since she first registered as a Democrat before the 1976 election, the first presidential contest she was old enough to vote in? Had she only subsequently decided that the other party saw her as a color and not an individual? Was she ignoring her own personal history in service of a political goal? After all, Democratic president Lyndon Johnson had been a hero in the Rice household after he signed the Voting Rights Act in 1965.[43]

Certainly Rice liked to flex her rhetorical muscle; she was a champion debater. Nearly three years after Philadelphia, when the September 11 commission would fail to wrench from her any acknowledgment that Bush administration oversights or mistakes had contributed to the likelihood of the terror attacks on New York and Washington, Rice would tell her Palo Alto hairdresser, Brenda Hamberry-Green, who was proud of how well Rice had withstood hours of interrogation, "I can outtalk anybody. Nobody is going to beat me talking."[44]

As politics, the address was masterful: It painted sharp contrasts with the opposition, laid out broad philosophies, and even offered a few specifics. Its tone was personal yet reasoned, passionate yet logical. But in the end, it may have said more about Condoleezza Rice than it did about George W. Bush or the Democrats. That night, the exotic-sounding name of Condoleezza Rice rolled off the tongue of every political commentator in America as if they had been born to speak it. And two days later, at the conclusion of Bush's wildly successful convention, Rice joined the newly minted nominee onstage for his postacceptance celebration. As the cameras rolled and the balloons danced around them, Rice was the aide closest to the man who would soon assume leadership of the most powerful nation in human history.[45]

CHAPTER TWO

PERFECT

No matter what their particular status, most Negroes doubtlessly feel that there must be many things worse than being a Negro in Birmingham, for there are some whose lives and achievements have proved without doubt that a person can do almost anything he wants to do if his faith in God, in man, and in himself is strong enough. There are hundreds whose lives are exemplary of the eternal truth that our greatest strengths are often born of adversity.[1]

GERALDINE MOORE
Behind the Ebony Mask
1961

The city sat like a broad scab deep in the Jones Valley, gouged between the Shades and Red mountains of central Alabama. When the civil engineer first came upon the site of what would become Birmingham, it was "just an old cornfield, filled with stumps."[2] But above the limestone valley rose a mountain of iron ore overlooking three ogre-size fields of coal[3]—one of the only places in the world where the raw materials of steel and iron were found in such proximity and such abundance. With such God-given bounty, Birmingham was supposed to become the broad-shouldered city of industry and progress that would give the lie to Northern views of Southern indolence, the capital of the New South.[4]

On June 1, 1871, the Elyton Land Company, a group of investors turned real estate promoters,[5] founded their city at the point where two great railroads, the

Alabama & Chattanooga and the South & North, were destined to meet. Ever since that time, Birmingham had seemed to be eternally on the way to becoming—only it never got there. First a cholera outbreak and then the Wall Street crash of 1873 stopped the boom.[6] In the first half of the twentieth century, Birmingham rebounded: By 1910, nine railroads fed the swelling town; by the twenties, it boasted thirteen skyscrapers, hence its nicknames: the "Magic City," the "Largest City of Its Age in the World," "Youngest of the World's Great Cities."

Then came the Great Depression, which shuttered factories and choked the blast-furnace smokestacks that dotted Jones Valley. Supplying steel to the American war effort brought a new boom. In the postwar, with an American empire abroad and a rapidly expanding middle class at home, Birmingham thought the Promised Land was finally at hand. Then came the troubles.

For many white residents, this peculiar set of circumstances became a bitter joke. A large proportion of the population came from somewhere else, sent by home offices to the burgeoning backwater. They languished there, the city a metaphor for their own professional and social purgatory. *Harper's* magazine captured the spirit best with its headline to a profile of Birmingham: "The City of Perpetual Promise."[7]

For most African Americans—Negroes, in the parlance of the day—Birmingham was something else altogether. Their circumstances had slid right past purgatory and straight into hell, and nothing illustrated this better than segregation: Jim Crow may have been the law of much of the land by the 1950s and '60s, but Birmingham's Jim Crow was unlike anywhere else's. In her 1961 book, *Behind the Ebony Mask: What American Negroes Really Think*, Geraldine Moore, a Negro columnist for the mainstream *Birmingham News*, painted in achingly mundane language the life of Negro Birmingham in the days before the city became the center of the civil rights universe. Written in the tenor of the time—black-and-white newsreel erudition and civic boosterism—the book is seditiously understated.

"Chapter I: Birmingham" is divided into classic guidebook headings: Brief History, Other Interesting Facts, Some Scenic Spots, Some General Observations on Birmingham and Its People. But after extolling her town's many fine parks and generous civic-mindedness, in the closing section of the first chapter, Moore writes:

Negroes have the privilege of making purchases from almost all
of the retail establishments in the city, but the number of such establishments owned by Negroes is so negligible as to be altogether insig-
nificant. Likewise, Negroes do not own and cannot use the large hotels
in which the city takes so much pride. In retail establishments, they
cannot expect to be hired as salesmen, salesladies, or in any other
capacity which would put them on an equal footing with whites who
work. In industry, Negroes own no share of any consequence. They do
not expect to be hired as foremen or skilled laborers to any appreciable
degree, if at all. There are golf courses, clubs, restaurants, and other
facilities from which Negroes are barred.[8]

At the conclusion of the book, Moore provides a less prosaic, but chillingly
matter-of-fact description of a seemingly intransigent system of humiliation and
oppression.

There are no Negro policemen, bus operators, or firemen in Birmingham . . . There are no Negroes employed as cashiers or clerks in
the banks of Birmingham . . . Negro secretaries do not work in office
buildings that are occupied by white people.
. . . In Birmingham there are probably more reminders of segregation than in many other cities. On almost all drinking fountains are signs
which read "colored" and "white." In many public buildings, Negroes
still use special elevators. Negroes and whites have separate liquor stores.
In large department stores, separate toilet facilities are maintained for
white and colored. In most places, lunch counters are provided for white
people only . . . It is illegal for Negroes and whites to participate in any
kind of recreational activity together. Segregated seating is required at all
public meetings. There are segregated medical facilities. In most hospi-
tals, facilities for Negroes are located on basement floors. There are many
cities in America in which segregation is a general practice, but such
extreme actions are not taken to keep the races separated.[9]

At the dawn of the civil rights movement's most eventful period, Moore
quoted fellow *News* contributor Walling Keith, who wrote in his December 11,

1960, column: "Knowing the people of Alabama as I do, if I were directing this 'crusade' [for integration], this state would be the last—or next to last—against which to unleash the judicial whip. And Birmingham would be the last citadel to invade."[10]

Moore summed up the standoff with characteristic understatement: "Since there seems to be strong insistence upon more freedom and equality for Negroes, and equally strong resistance to the changes necessary for the realization of this objective, it is very difficult to predict what the future holds for the residents of Birmingham. Obviously, a showdown must come at some time, and just what will happen when it does comes, remains to be seen."[11]

Not for long. Shortly after Moore penned those words, a paroxysm of violence gripped much of the Deep South and Birmingham in particular. Segregation's roughneck brother, terror, joined it in the waking nightmares of the city's Negroes. Together, they would bring first the glare of the American media and then the eyes of the world.

The fuse had been lit at 12:52 p.m. on Monday, May 17, 1954. Without ceremony, Earl Warren, chief justice of the United States Supreme Court, read from the bench: "We conclude, unanimously, that in the field of public education, the doctrine of 'separate but equal' has no place . . . Separate educational facilities are inherently unequal."[12] Sitting to his right, as the senior associate justice, Birmingham native Hugo Black, who had spent a decade searching for a case to overturn *Plessy v. Ferguson* betrayed no emotion as his "long-plotted coup" saw the light of day.[13]

Though the *Brown* decision prompted some sporadic violence against "Negro interests," for the most part, the city avoided the immediate panic that set in many areas of the South.[14] One reason may have been the court's directive to implement integration "with all deliberate speed." Integration's opponents decided it would take them a good long while to deliberate.

In fact, the fear that the momentum from *Brown* was dying would lead Martin Luther King six years later to decide it was time to take "a calculated leap over the cliff." Sharing his idea—a massive series of nonviolent protests against Jim Crow—King would tell a coterie of lieutenants that "some of the people sitting here today will not come back alive from this campaign."[15] The cliff he had decided on was Birmingham.

When the *Brown* decision was handed down, Angelena Rice, a quiet but self-possessed Birmingham schoolteacher, was preparing for the birth of her first child. Twenty-nine-year-old Rice was demure, petite, light-skinned, and elegant. And in almost every way, she was the opposite of her husband, John, who was a Presbyterian minister. John Rice was a "mountain of a man,"[16] brown-skinned and warm, with a smile that seemed to reflect God's own love and a laugh that could shake the trees. A lover of big-band jazz,[17] he was jovial and gregarious and often played the merry prankster.

They seemed an unlikely pair: John who collected people and Angelena (Ann, to her friends) who kept mostly to her family, her church, and her school.[18] But the most important difference, given the times, may have been that John's skin was dark while Ann's was light.[19] Negroes placed as much store by skin color as whites, if not more.[20]

John Rice was an activist minister of sorts, heavily engaged in his community. He had big plans for his little church, Westminster Presbyterian, a modest brown-brick building at the meeting of Sixth Avenue and Center Place in the southwest corner of Birmingham. Rice wanted to create a youth fellowship that would instruct young people not just in academics but in life. Conscious of what racism could do to a young mind, Rice wanted to arm Negro children with the weapons that would make them, if not impervious to oppression, then at least resistant to the debilitating bitterness and self-doubt it could produce. He wanted them to learn different lessons in the dark heart of Jim Crow.[21]

John Wesley Rice Jr. had educational evangelism in his blood. His father and his mother had traveled the South, founding churches and schools. Granddaddy Rice, whom Condoleezza would immortalize in her speech to the Republican National Convention as a man "George W. Bush would have liked," had grown up picking cotton in the Black Belt,[22] named for the rich soil that made south-central Alabama the agricultural heartland of the state as well as home to the highest proportion of its Negro population.

Granddaddy Rice's parents had been born into slavery. His mother, Julia Head, was the daughter of a white plantation owner and one of his chattel[23] and had been a house slave in Greene County.[24] During the advance of the Union Army, according to family lore, Julia had hid the plantation's horses from the Union soldiers.[25] After Freedom, Julia married John Wesley Rice, a former slave from South Carolina.[26] According to another story passed from generation to generation, the father of Julia's nine children was actually the white slave owner, though John Rice raised them as his own. ("That's what I've been told," said Condoleezza Rice. "I don't know for sure.")[27]

Julia and John worked as tenant farmers[28] in the western Black Belt, raising their children as Methodists.[29] No one knows what gave their eldest child, John, the mind to leave the cotton fields of Eutaw, Alabama, to pursue book learning.[30] Maybe it was the backbreaking, finger-slicing business of picking cotton. Maybe it was the virtual servitude that he and his family lived under as farmers tending someone else's land. Or perhaps it was the random violence that could reach out like the hand of God and smite a young colored man in the rural South for no reason.[31]

Whatever his spark, in 1918, John Rice took the money he had saved and headed for Stillman Institute, thirty-five miles north in Tuscaloosa. Originally unaccredited, Stillman had been built by the Presbyterian Church to train Negroes to become ministers.[32] When Rice ran out of cotton money and learned he could get a scholarship if he agreed to become a Presbyterian preacher, he converted.

Granddaddy Rice's pioneering individualism had led him to Stillman, but he saw it as his mission to share the blessing of education. After finishing at Stillman in 1922, he married Theresa Hardnett, a half-Creole woman from Louisiana.[33] Together, they traveled throughout the Deep South building schools and churches,[34] Rice literally walking the streets to find young people to educate.[35] A lover of books, at the height of the Depression, John bought seven leather-bound, gold-embossed volumes—the complete works of Alexandre Dumas—for ninety dollars, a fortune at the time. Theresa was furious. "We can pay for them on time," said her husband.[36]

John and Theresa's only son, John Wesley Jr., was born in Baton Rouge on November 3, 1923,[37] while his father was ministering there.[38] Rice graduated from McKinley High in Baton Rouge, a Negro school of twelve hundred students, before following his father's path to Stillman Institute. When Rice arrived in Tuscaloosa in 1942, Stillman was teaching a Christian-inspired curriculum that went beyond preparing Negroes for the ministry. By now, the school was accredited, but only as a two-year junior college.[39] So in 1944, Rice set off for Johnson C. Smith College in Charlotte, North Carolina, a Presbyterian school that had a full four-year program.

Although most Smith students hailed from the Carolinas and Virginia, there was a large contingent of Stillman graduates, too. The student body represented a cross section of Negro society, from both well-off and working-class families.[40] Unassuming and friendly,[41] John Rice fit right in, joining the Young Men's Christian Association and the Alpha Phi Alpha fraternity.

After earning his B.A. in history in 1946,[42] true to his family heritage, Rice set out for his own educational frontier by becoming the director of the Petersburg Presbyterian Mission in Burlington, North Carolina. But then Rice's life took an unexpected turn. While Rice was leading the mission and also working toward his second degree, a bachelor's in divinity from Smith, Gloria Marie Goins of the class of 1948 reportedly told Rice that she was pregnant with his baby.[43]

John did the honorable thing and married Gloria. Only the marriage didn't last long. First, "they didn't see eye to eye on a lot of things," said the Reverend Dr. Clarence Thomas (Smith class of 1947), who had known both Rice and Goins; "she didn't help him much in his first pastorate" at the Petersburg Mission. More important, after several months, it became apparent that Goins wasn't pregnant. John Rice was furious. "Every time he would think about it, he said it would make him angry that she told that lie," remembered Rice's third wife, Clara.[44]

In the end, Goins would be erased from official Rice family history; when John Rice died in 2000, obituaries would report that he had been married twice: to Angelena and Clara.[45]

After getting his divinity degree in 1949, Rice moved to Birmingham. His father had started one of his mission churches in the city's Titusville neighborhood (pronounced *Tit*-is-ville). The church, Westminster Presbyterian,[46] was thriving and had recently moved from a two-story house into a proper church building on Sixth Avenue. In 1951, John Rice Jr. became Westminster's director of religious education. To earn money, he took a job as director of physical education and football coach at Industrial High in the relatively well-off Negro suburb of Fairfield.[47] Twenty-seven-year-old Rice had two college degrees, but he lived with his parents in the small three-room apartment at the back of the church.[48,49]

But he was handsome, and the female faculty at Fairfield Industrial High were widely enamored of him.[50] But it was the beautiful Angelena Ray, who taught music, math, science, and oratory, who won him.[51]

Like John Rice, Angelena Ray was from a family of strivers, too. Her father, Albert Robinson Ray III, was a miner, blacksmith, and homebuilder. Her mother, Mattie, taught piano to local children in their north Birmingham home.

Forty years after his death, a certain amount of mystery still surrounds the life of Albert Ray.[52] He was born June 30, 1893, to Angelena Davie, a favored black servant to a white family.[53-55] That was about the only thing that Angelena and her siblings knew for sure about their father's history. Ray told his children that he had run away from home when he was just thirteen years old, fearing for his life.[56] As the story goes, a white boy had ripped an earring from his sister's ear, and Ray taught the boy a lesson by beating him, a potentially fatal transgression. But according to Angelena's sister Mattie Bonds, her father ran away from Union Springs in rural Bullock County, Alabama, after his father or his stepfather—she wasn't certain which—had hit Ray's sister: "Daddy hit him with a two-by-four and tried to kill him and ran."[57]

What's known for certain is that when he ran away, Ray made his way to Birmingham. Alternate versions of the story have him being picked up on the side of the road or in a train station, with just a token in his pocket, by a white businessman named Wheeler and his family. "I think Daddy told a story," said Bonds. "Nobody would just pick you up on the side of the road, especially a white family, especially back then."

But the Wheelers raised Ray, and he worked at the family's Wheeler Dam Mine before moving to larger mines like Republic Iron and Steel.[58] In the years that followed, he learned to blacksmith and build houses. Eventually, he married Mattie Lula Parrom, the daughter of a Birmingham seamstress and an African Methodist Episcopal bishop from Columbus, Ohio. The bishop (Condoleezza Rice's great-grandfather) moved back up North,[59] but he made sure Mattie went to finishing school and received instruction in classical piano.[60]

Together, Mattie and Albert built a simple but comfortable life. Albert was industrious. He built their nine-room house in the mostly undeveloped Hooper City section of north Birmingham, dug a well so the family wouldn't have to haul water, and built a blacksmith shop for himself behind the house. He worked in the mines during the week, built houses on Saturday, and ran his blacksmith shop on nights and weekends. Mattie gave piano lessons, and her mother made all the clothes for the five Ray children.[61] On Sundays, the family attended Suggs Chapel, a Colored Methodist Episcopalian church in nearby Sayreton.

When the Great Depression hit, Mattie surprised her husband by revealing buckets of cash she had been saving. They used the money to buy property and send their children to college.[62] Four would become teachers—Angelena, Mattie, Genoa, and Alto—and Albert IV would become a minister. "Daddy and Mother instilled something in us," said Mattie Bonds. "It was just understood that we could go to college."[63] When a friend asked Ray why he was sending his daughters to school he replied, "I don't know what's gonna happen in the future." And whatever happened, he wanted his girls to be prepared. "Daddy told us, 'Get the feel of your *own* money. He didn't want you to have to take anything from somebody else," said Bonds.

Indeed, Albert and Mattie infused all their children with a dignity uncommon for the times. Daddy Ray wouldn't allow them to use colored water fountains or restrooms or ride segregated buses;[64] and he refused to let them work, as many Negro children did, performing chores in the homes of white people.[65] As a result, the Rays were singularly proud (some would say haughty), evincing not the class to which they were born—the children of a miner—but the one to which they aspired.

Ann graduated from Hooper City High School in 1941. She went on to earn her teaching degree at struggling all-Negro Miles College outside Birmingham. Mattie was also a Miles student, and the two seemed to their classmates to spend most of their waking hours together; they even dressed alike.[66] They attended cotillions dressed in flowing gowns and long white gloves, wearing movie-star hairdos. It was a rarefied existence in the midst of segregation.

By the time they had graduated from college, their educational attainment alone set the Rays apart. In 1950 in Alabama, just 1.4 percent of Negroes over twenty five years old had bachelor's degrees[67]—only 7.2 percent had high school diplomas.[68] And the Rays were not just well educated for their race; only 4.9 percent of whites had bachelor's degrees.[69] John Rice's family was even better educated than Angelena's. John had two bachelor's degrees and his only sibling, Theresa Rice, earned a PhD in English literature in 1953 from the University of Wisconsin. She would go on to become a college professor and do work in Africa for the State Department.

The Rays came from less-educated stock than the Rices, said Mattie Bonds. But they were at least as cultured. At Miles, Ann was a member of the Harmonia Club, a cultural group for young women. Though they had to sit in the coloreds-only section of the balcony, they attended symphonies and operas at the Birmingham Civic Center. And because three generations of Ray women played piano, music lessons had been de rigueur for all the Ray children.

When John Rice met Ann Ray in 1951, Ann was a petite, light-skinned beauty. Though she was quiet, she had a reputation for having a sharp tongue and a quick temper. One day, when Industrial High's principal challenged her in the middle of the main office for coming in late, Ann turned on him and asked, "How would you know, since you're always late?"[70] If the principal entered her classroom while she was teaching, she would tell him to get out.[71]

John Rice was no doubt attracted by both Angelena's beauty and her independent spirit. The two courted for three years, with John becoming practically a member of the Ray family, spending time looking after Genoa and Alto, who were a decade younger than their siblings. Angelena, almost thirty, didn't think she would ever get married, she would later tell her daughter. But on February 14, 1954, in the family room at the back of the Ray home in Hooper City, John and Ann wed in a small ceremony, said the Ray sisters, Mattie and Genoa.[72]

Condoleezza was born exactly nine months later. "As my mother said, it's a good thing I wasn't early," laughed Rice.[73] Of course, it was peculiar that the couple didn't have a church wedding, especially since John's father was the minister of Westminster Presbyterian, and John lived and worked in the church. But Mattie Bonds insisted her sister wasn't pregnant when she married John Rice, though she also admitted she couldn't know for sure. Condoleezza Rice had no doubt: "Knowing my mother, it was not an issue."[74]

Granddaddy Rice had died two months before Condoleezza was born, and John had taken over the Westminster flock. Ann had been helping her husband build the church's youth fellowship, but after Condoleezza was born, she couldn't stomach taking time away from her daughter to spend it with other children. "She had to spend her time with Condoleezza!" said church member Julia Emma Smith.[75]

Angelena had wanted to name her daughter Condolcezza (pronounced Condul-CHET-za), Italian for "with sweetness," but she was afraid Americans would mispronounce it. She had considered Andantino, but that meant "slowly," and Allegro, but that meant "fast"—which had negative connotations when applied to a young lady. So Ann altered the ending of *con dolcezza* to create Condoleezza.

Condo, as her father called his daughter, to her mother's chagrin, became her parents' everything. Ann and John—but particularly Ann—doted on her fiercely. For instance, Annye-Marie Downing, a neighbor of the Rices, was shocked to notice Ann ironing the tiny frills on Condoleezza's socks one day. "What in the world are you doing?" asked Downing.[76]

"I just love her so much," Downing recalled Ann replying.

"Why don't you [have] another child? You've got enough love [to give]," Downing said.

"I can't take this love from [Condoleezza]," Rice reportedly responded.

In her 1961 book profiling Negro Birmingham, *Behind the Ebony Mask*, journalist Geraldine Moore would report that among the things Birmingham Negroes were most proud of was their "quiet, stable, Christian family life."[77] The Rices were definitely among that number. Outside of tending to their daughter, their world consisted mostly of family, church, and school. John had his community activities, like his nascent youth fellowship, and Angelena had her shopping, a passion she would pass on to Condoleezza.

But the world outside their Christian home was becoming increasingly less quiet. Six months before Condoleezza's birth, the Supreme Court had handed down the *Brown v. Board of Education* decision outlawing segregation. John's friend,[78] the Baptist minister Fred Shuttlesworth, had launched a campaign to get Birmingham to obey the high court's ruling. After years of being ignored by the city fathers, in 1956, Shuttlesworth formed the Alabama Christian Movement for Human Rights (ACMHR). John, like most ministers, supported his friend's goals but didn't have much faith that he would succeed; instead, he invested his time in preaching to young people that they could overcome segregation by getting an education.

On December 26, 1956, Shuttlesworth held his first demonstration against Jim Crow. The day before, someone had thrown a bomb at his home, injuring his children, but Shuttlesworth was undeterred. From the pulpit of his Bethel Baptist Church, he testified that the Lord had spared him so he could lead his people to freedom. "That bomb had my name on it, but God erased it off,"[79] he proclaimed before leading 250 Negro protesters onto the whites-only sections of Birmingham's buses. More than 200 ACMHR volunteers were arrested that day.[80]

Most of the members of Shuttlesworth's organization were working and lower-middle-class people who had gained significantly less under segregation than the professional Negro class of teachers and preachers. Middle-class enclaves like the Rices' Titusville neighborhood weren't ready for revolution. Educated Negroes had lived under Jim Crow for generations and, like the Rices and the Rays, had managed to make the best of an intolerable situation. They were not oblivious to the civil rights tumult gradually building across the South, but they kept their distance, uncertain what it could achieve in the face of white intransigence. Rather than agitating for the overthrow of the system, middle- and upper-class leaders continued the tradition of carving out what freedom they could under segregation.[81] When it came to the masses, the middle class, with rare exception, was happy to let them fend for themselves or to suggest, often paternalistically, that they should follow the dictates of A. G. Gaston, Birmingham's self-made Negro business magnate, and his hero, Booker T. Washington, and devote themselves to their individual betterment. Besides, many members of the middle class felt—as Condoleezza Rice would argue forty-five years later—segregation was "collapsing of its own weight."[82]

The middle class didn't respond to Shuttlesworth's nonviolent protests, but segregation's most violent defenders did. One Labor Day evening, just five and a half miles away from where Mattie Ray was teaching the children of Hooper City to play piano and babysitting her two-year-old granddaughter, Condoleezza, Edward "Judge" Aaron was walking with his girlfriend when six men set upon him and threw him into the back of their car. The abductors were members of the resurrected Ku Klux Klan of the Confederacy. After pistol-whipping Aaron, they took him to their lair, a cinderblock shed in nearby Chalkville, where one of the Klansmen told Aaron to "make like a dog" and led him by the nape of the neck crawling into the shed.[83]

Inside, the Klansmen barraged their terrified captive with questions:

"You think any nigger is as good as a white man?"

"You got any children? You think nigger kids should go to school with my kids?"

"You think you got a right to vote?"

"Or eat where I eat?"

"Or use the same toilet I use?"

As Diane McWhorter wrote in *Carry Me Home: Birmingham, Alabama, The Climatic Battle of the Civil Rights Movement*, reconstructing the scene: "Finally, the rat court got to the point. 'Do you know Fred Shuttlesworth?'"

Aaron said he didn't. Then, with an order that he tell Shuttlesworth that this is what would happen to him or any nigger who tried to integrate Birmingham schools, one of the Klansmen took out a razor and sliced off Aaron's scrotum. As the men passed around the souvenir, one poured turpentine on Aaron's bloodied groin. In the process, he cauterized the wound and probably saved his victim's life. They put the souvenir in a paper cup to take home and dumped Aaron on the roadside. He was retrieved by policemen and survived.

Unsettling events seemed to be continually roiling the American landscape that fall of 1957. The morning after Aaron's mutilation, nine Negro teenagers arrived in starched shirts to desegregate Central High in Little Rock, Arkansas. National Guardsmen turned them back. Six days later, President Dwight D. Eisenhower signed the first federal civil rights legislation since Reconstruction, in spite of a record-breaking filibuster in the United States Senate by Dixiecrat Strom Thurmond. The same day, despite the warning the Klansmen had delivered in Aaron's blood, Fred Shuttlesworth took his kids to school—a white school.

Shuttlesworth had grown weary of the excuses of the local board of education over the lack of integration. He, his wife, his two daughters—Ruby Fredricka, twelve, and Patricia Ann, fourteen—and two seventeen-year-old boys who had also petitioned to attend white schools drove to all-white Phillips High School.[84] Their car was met by a mob. As Shuttlesworth stepped from the vehicle, white men kicked him and pounded him with brass knuckles, clubs, and chains. A woman from the nearby cheering section reportedly yelled, "Kill the motherfucking nigger, and it will be all over."[85] After several minutes, the police materialized. Shuttlesworth scrambled into his car and sped away. Someone in the crowd had stabbed his wife in the leg. His daughters had been so traumatized that they would never speak of the incident to each other.[86]

John Rice couldn't understand why Shuttlesworth would put his children in harm's way; he concentrated on making his own daughter's world idyllic. In 1958, when Condo was three years old, Rice received a little help from his congregation when Westminster church moved the Rices from the tiny apartment

they occupied behind the pulpit into a new house the congregation built at 929
Center Way, snug in the bosom of South Titusville. The manse, as Presbyterians
call the pastor's home, was modest by white folks' standards, but with its big
front porch and two bedrooms, it was a sight better than the Rices' living quar-
ters in the church's "west annex," where Condoleezza and her parents had shared
one small bedroom.

Their new, dark gray ranch house was in Titusville's brand-new subdivision
called Honeysuckle Circle, a set of concentric and overlapping ovals that sat in a
shallow valley south of Sixth Avenue and the church. Inside Honeysuckle Circle's
knot of streets, broad brick homes with large picture windows rose above neat
lawns. Children played and rode bicycles, their voices the only sound to break
the air other than the soft distant hum of Interstate 65. It was as idyllic a setting
as any Negro child could hope to grow up in in 1950s America.

Even geographically, South Titusville was isolated from the upheaval of the
city outside. Sixth Avenue formed a natural barrier to the north. To the west,
only Goldwire Street provided access to the neighborhood. Greensprings Avenue
acted as a southern buffer, and to the east, just blocks away from the University
of Alabama–Birmingham's campus, the tracks of the vaunted Louisville and
Nashville Railroad, the first great railroad empire of the South,[87] barred the way.
From Red Mountain and the statue of Vulcan, the god of the forge cast in Alabama iron, South Titusville lay completely camouflaged beneath a canopy of
green.

It was in that sanctuary of a neighborhood that Ann dressed Condoleezza in
the finest clothes from the best stores where white people shopped and instilled
in her all the refinement and elegance that made Ann herself a standout even
among the residents of Titusville. Angelena's contained reserve stood in sharp
contrast to John's boisterousness. His booming laugh and hulking body made
him impossible to miss—that and his habit of arriving late wherever he went. He
would launch his old Dodge screaming out of the driveway, apologizing to his
neighbors for the torrent of noise and energy. Except when Condo was on his
lap;[88] her father took his "little star" everywhere.[89] He was a busy, whirling
leader in the community. "Rev. Rice got around," said neighbor George "Third"
Hunter III, the older brother of Condoleezza's most frequent playmate in those
years. "Mrs. Rice wouldn't move much. But they'd go to the church—fifteen
minutes late, driving sixty miles an hour," Hunter laughed.

The relative placidity of the Rices' family life compared to the world slowly imploding outside allowed John and Ann to notice almost immediately the glimmer of promise in their little girl. She was smart. She was verbal at any early age, but unlike some precocious children, she didn't incessantly ask "how come?" in a high-pitched prattle. Westminster church members said her eyes showed she was "an old soul."

It was her grandmother Mattie Ray who realized that Condoleezza liked to play at playing the piano. Between the lessons Mattie gave for twenty-five cents a session to the neighborhood children of Hooper City,[90] Condoleezza would go over to the piano and tap the keys. Mrs. Ray decreed that her granddaughter should be taught to play. At first, Ann balked; her daughter was too young. But Mattie Ray was not easily deterred. Books were brought, and the little girl was placed on top of them.[91] Grandmother Ray herself would teach her to play.

Till now, Condoleezza's world had been bound by a chain of protective sanctuaries that, like stations on the underground railroad, offered refuge from the Birmingham the world knew: tiny Westminster Presbyterian, whose twenty-two polished pews echoed with breezy detachment; her cozy home on Center Way where she, her mother, and her father made up their own little society; and Mattie's house on Fourth Street in Hooper City, where she would hear older children murdering the piano all day. Now, like her tight-knit family, the piano would serve as a refuge.

Three-year-old Condoleezza Rice began her musical studies.[92] John promised that if she learned to play her grandmother's piano, he would buy her her own. She relentlessly practiced "What a Friend We Have in Jesus" until she conquered it.[93] John borrowed the money to fulfill his promise.[94] Before Condoleezza could read, she could read music.

Though they were educators, John and Angelena Rice were considerably less concerned about integration than Fred Shuttlesworth was. They had their own educational battles to wage: In the summer of 1959, the superintendent of Negro schools ruled that Condo's mid-November birthday meant she would be too young to start first grade in September. Determined that her daughter would not be penalized by an accident of birth, Angelena took a leave of absence to home-school her child. Condoleezza's friends found it strange that she didn't go to school with them, but Angelena knew what was best. And what was best was a serious education, especially for a girl who could read fluently by age five[95]— even if it added to the aura of otherness that was starting to surround her, from her serious demeanor to her remarkable discipline. "She seemed different from the other little girls. She was smarter and more reserved, more polished. You heard her playing the piano all the time. I mean *seriously* [playing]. For hours!" remembered Third Hunter, the Rices' across-the-street neighbor and the big brother of Condo's playmate Vanessa.

Condoleezza's school-day ritual didn't help her seem any more normal. At the beginning of the day, the chubby little girl, her thick hair divided into pig-tails, would put on her coat, leave her front door, walk to the end of the walk, and then turn around and come back inside the house.[96] Then she'd have a full day of classes—reading, writing, math—just like any other student. Only she was the only pupil, and her mother was the only teacher. At the appointed times, Ann and Condoleezza would break for lunch and recess, then go back to their studies.[97] "They didn't play. They did school," said Westminster member Julia Emma Smith.

Angelena taught Condoleezza until she started public school in 1961 in the second grade. Up to that point, Condoleezza's life had been extraordinarily sheltered, even for a middle-class girl in Titusville. She had school with her mother and spent most of her time with her extended family, which was both close-knit and close at hand. (When her uncle Alto Ray returned from the military and married, he moved just a few doors down from his parents.)[98] Once she left home, relatives said Ann moved Condoleezza from school to school to ensure that she had a diverse experience.[99] But one former school official speculated that her mother moved Condoleezza so she would always be in a school where her mother or Alto taught. That way, there was always a Ray nearby.[100]

Condoleezza did have friends. She played with Vanessa Hunter from across the street and other girls from their corner, like Margaret Wright and Carol Catlin. Like little girls everywhere, they played hopscotch, drawing the boxes on their driveways in chalk, dolls on Condoleezza's porch, and school on the black-board Vanessa's father had built in the Hunters' garage. (The dolls would go to school, too.) The girls took turns playing teacher, but Condoleezza was the teacher more often than anyone else.[101]

But even in their little girl world, the games were about advancement. In one, "Alabama Hit the Hammer," a girl would stand on the uppermost step and hold out her fists. One hand held a pebble; the other, nothing. She placed one hand above the other, then chanted in a sing song, "a-LA-ba-ma-HIT-the-ham-mer-HIGH-or-LOW?" alternating which was the upper hand with each syllable. The girls at the bottom of the steps guessed which hand held the rock. Whoever guessed correctly would get to advance one step. Each step represented a higher grade. Whoever reached the top, graduating first, won. The girls liked to play on Condoleezza's steps because they were the tallest.

The game suited Condoleezza. She was fiercely competitive, and she wasn't shy about performing—or outperforming. When another little girl got the lead role in a talent show, Condoleezza fumed that the part should have been hers. When the lead, just five years old and paralyzed by stage fright, couldn't sing her solo, Condoleezza brushed her aside and sang the song.[102]

The Rices were raising their little girl to believe that she was extraordinary—smart, talented, and beautiful—and to believe that she was capable of anything. Her strong will, which was becoming a running joke among her relatives, grew in part from the fiercely protective bubble that Angelena especially surrounded her with. Other children were allowed to ride their bikes lazily along the shaded streets of Honeysuckle Circle. Not Condoleezza. Other children played ball or jumped rope in the lightly trafficked streets, but not Condo.[103] She didn't stay at friends' houses for sleepovers either, or roam the neighborhood at Halloween with the other children.[104] Rev. Rice had to escort her trick-or-treating, and even then, only to the homes of church members.[105] Ann bought all her Girl Scout cookies.[106]

Her mother's distrust didn't extend only to strangers. Years later, Condoleezza told her stepmother, Clara, that no one was allowed to babysit her except her grandparents, Mattie and Daddy Ray. John's sister Theresa was only permitted to take her niece out once, and John remembered Angelena keeping a vigil until Condoleezza returned.[107] The Hunters' was the only house where Condoleezza was regularly allowed to play, and even just across the street, Angelena stood watching at her kitchen window.[108] One sweltering summer day, Mrs. Hunter went to close the garage door to keep out the heat and flies. But Condoleezza stopped her. "Miss Hunter, if you close the door, I'll have to go home," said the little girl.

"Why, honey?"

"Because my mother won't be able to see me."

"Then you gonna have to go home," said Hunter. "It's hot!"

Ann's protectiveness struck many of the Rices' neighbors and even some of Rev. Rice's flock as excessive. They still debate whether her mother's attachment to Condoleezza was healthy. "If her mama was still living, I don't think Condoleezza would even be out of her grasp," said George Hunter Jr., Vanessa's father, imitating a suffocating hug. "Mrs. Rice was just like that"—he wrapped his arms even more tightly around himself—"tight. And Condoleezza was just like that, too."

Angelena herself was conspicuously reserved. "She wasn't social at all; [Rev. Rice] was," said Paiszelle Cooleby, who lived next door to the Rices and whose son Raymond spent a lot of time with John. While Rev. Rice's burgeoning youth fellowship was embarking on all kinds of adventures—to Ullman High School football games, to the Birmingham Museum of Art, even to a synagogue to see a Torah—Angelena would be at home.[109] She only left the house to go to Westminster and help John with his pastoral mission, to go to school, to visit her family, or to shop. The Rices rarely received callers. And Ann had few friends of her own outside her brothers and sisters. Searching for the mot juste to describe her, Julia Emma Smith finally said with a shrug, "Just kind of sedate," though Smith found nothing strange in either her reserve or her protectiveness toward Condoleezza: "People always said, 'They sho' did love that child.' But you supposed to love 'em!"[110]

Much of Ann's demeanor (well mannered but distant) and her character (polite but discriminating) could be traced to the Ray family heritage. "They were likable people but . . . close-knit," said Smith. "They would socialize with you but [were] really always together." That was by design. Albert and Mattie's children had been raised with a sense of collective unity. Intense solidarity—some might say clannishness—was part of their family identity. "Our family is suspicious of outsiders and their motives," said Condoleezza Rice's first cousin Yvonne German.[111] One could have friends, but family came first. Independence and strength were the rules. As Condoleezza's grandfather Daddy Ray always said, "If you ever need help, the first and last place you should go is to your family."[112]

Ray instilled in Condoleezza's generation, as he had in Angelena and her siblings, the belief that being a Ray made you part of an elected elite. "Remember, you're a Ray," he preached to his grandchildren; and the Ray name carried with it responsibility, not just for your own actions but also for your kin. "Even as little children, Daddy Ray told us, 'If one of you doesn't have that means, none of you has, and if one of you has, then all of you have,'" said German.[113] Ray would line up his six grandchildren outside his house and wait for people to drive by so he could say, "These are my grandchildren." Eventually, neighbors started taking alternate routes, German said.

As insular as the Rays were, John Rice was outgoing—though he was so close to Ann's family that he was like another sibling. "[Pastor Rice] was a church and community man," said neighbor George Hunter with obvious pride.[114] John Rice was magnetic; he attracted friends and converts to Presbyterianism, including all the Rays except Ann's sister Mattie; but he had a particular pied piper effect on the children of Titusville. He didn't have a son, so it seemed all the young men in the neighborhood became his boys. They would follow him wherever he went, piling into the old Dodge. It was a tight fit, but there was nowhere else the gangly boys would have rather been.

Third Hunter, George Hunter's son, first met "Rev" when the Hunters moved to the new neighborhood. The then thirteen-year-old boy immediately took to the affable giant, and for the next eight years, Rice would be like a second father to him, helping him along his path to manhood, a journey made rougher still by being a young Negro male in the capital of segregation. Third mowed the Rices' lawn and washed their car. He spent hours discussing sports with Rev as they tested each other on obscure baseball stats. When Third entered Ullman High, where Rice was now working as a guidance counselor, he and Ray Goolsby asked if the reverend would drive them to school. But Hunter soon came to regret Rice's generosity; they rarely arrived at school on time. "Man, Rev. Rice messed us up," he laughed. "Rev. Rice was never nowhere on time!"[115]

Despite the Calvinistic dictates of Presbyterianism, Rice wasn't a paragon of discipline when it came to neatness either. The Dodge was a wastebasket of old candy wrappers, crumpled clothes, and scattered papers. Passengers had to "scoop" themselves a seat out of the trash that littered the back. Every two or three months, Rev would hand Third a bag to clear it out. Third Hunter was also one of the few people who crossed the threshold of the Rices' immaculate, if modestly furnished, home. "Mrs. Rice was friendly with me," remembered Hunter, "but she wasn't the kind to start up a thirty-minute conversation."

Though he was less solitary than his wife, Rev. Rice could be just as single-minded. For instance, when many of the members of his well-heeled congregation objected to the reverend inviting young people from nearby Loveman Village, a public housing project, to join Westminster's youth group, telling Rice, "These kids won't know how to behave!" Rice replied, "These kids could be [just] like yours" if given the opportunity.[116] Time would prove him right.

New Year's Day 1962 was a day of divided sentiments in the Rice household. Almost exactly six weeks after Condoleezza's seventh birthday, coach Bear Bryant's Alabama Crimson Tide rolled all the way to Bryant's first national championship. It was a fitting belated birthday present. In addition to rooting for the Cleveland Browns, whose games were broadcast in Birmingham,[117] John Rice and the daughter he had molded into a football fanatic cheered for 'Bama—the all-white university's segregation notwithstanding.[118]

But events in the world of politics conspired against a sports fan's ecstasy. The same weekend that the Tide beat Arkansas 10–3, commissioner Bull Connor, Bryant's famed "biggest fan," had Birmingham's 1,500 acres of parks posted with "No Trespassing" signs.

Fred Shuttlesworth had filed suit against the city's segregated parks three years earlier, citing the federal courts' antidiscrimination rulings. The previous fall, the suit finally reached a Republican federal judge who struck down the Jim Crow parks statutes and commanded that by January 16, 1962, the parks had to be integrated, including Kiddieland amusement park. *Time* magazine's December 22, 1961, issue reported Birmingham mayor Art Hanes telling a town meeting, "I don't think any of you want a nigger mayor or a nigger police chief. But I tell you that's what'll happen if we play dead on this park integration."[119] Shortly after Connor's desperate (and widely despised) move, Birmingham was hit by a rare snowstorm. It was as if God had decided to make the entire city a playground. Condoleezza Rice and Vanessa Hunter took the opportunity to build their first snowman—actually more of a snow mound, his body a single triangular mass.[120]

Condoleezza knew something of Connor. Though she couldn't grasp the full meaning of segregation, she had been discussing politics with adults since she was five.[121] She would telephone Julia Emma Smith, the codirector of her father's youth fellowship, and ask, "'Miss Smith, did you see what Bull Connor did?' I had to read the newspaper to keep up," said the Westminster parishioner. Added fellowship member Eva Carter, "You would just look at this child and think, *Is she real?*"[122]

Condoleezza was in her first year of public school, and as she was growing up, segregation was getting harder to ignore, even at the finest stores where she and Angelena shopped. It had reared its ugly head during a recent holiday shopping outing.[123] After choosing an appropriately exquisite dress, Ann and Condoleezza headed for the changing rooms. A saleswoman threw up a defensive block; Negroes were to try clothes on on the sales floor or not at all; dressing rooms were for whites. The saleswoman snatched the dress from Condoleezza and, in what she may have thought was a gracious gesture, told Angelena her daughter could try the dress on in a nearby storeroom.

True to her Ray upbringing and her quick temper, Angelena Rice held her ground: "My daughter will try on this dress in a dressing room, or I'm not spending my money here." Stunned by her defiance, the slack-jawed saleswoman led them to the farthest dressing room she could find. "I remember the woman standing there guarding the door, worried to death she was going to lose her job," said Condoleezza Rice.[124] On another shopping outing, a saleslady would scold the child for putting her black hands on the pretty hats. Angelena reportedly told the hired help, "I buy more in this store than you are paid, and you will not talk to my daughter that way . . . [Condoleezza,] you touch every hat in the place." Condo gladly obliged.[125]

In a similar incident of shopping while black as an adult, Rice would be at the Stanford Shopping Center during another holiday season with her friend Chip Blacker. At a Macy's counter, she asked to see the fine-jewelry earrings. Instead, the saleswoman pulled out the cheap stuff. "I didn't ask to see the costume jewelry. I asked to see the good jewelry," Rice corrected. "The young woman said something she thought we couldn't hear," said Blacker, "but Condi heard it. Let's say it started with a *B*.[126]

"Condi said, 'Excuse me?' The young woman didn't answer. And Condi said, 'Let's get one thing straight. You're behind the counter because you have to work for $6 an hour. I'm on this side asking to see the good jewelry because I make considerably more. And I'm asking to see the good jewelry.'" The store manager appeared, apologizing profusely, and showed Rice the expensive earrings.

But there were some prejudices from which John and Angelena could not shield Condoleezza—no matter how much love they gave her or how high the walls they built around her—dangers much more menacing than racism injecting itself into an afternoon shopping trip. Like when the Ku Klux Klan marched down Sixth Avenue in broad daylight right past Westminster Presbyterian. Or when Williams grocery store across the street from the church was dynamited.[127]

Like her grandfather, her parents imbued Condoleezza with a supreme sense of self for just such occasions. They told her that no one was better than she was. And they strategically filtered what they revealed about the world outside Titusville, particularly about racism.[128] But they didn't lie, unlike many parents who fibbed to their children to protect them from the reality of Jim Crow. The stories could be simple or elaborate, depending on the child's age and the depth of curiosity—or pain.

Kiddieland was a particular thorn in the side of Negro parents. Some told their children that Birmingham's only amusement park wasn't fun, though the colorful lights and shrieks of joy emanating from inside suggested otherwise. Some parents sent their children to visit relatives every summer so they wouldn't have to tell them they couldn't go to Kiddieland. Whatever the Jim Crow humiliation, parents did what they could to insulate their children; they made certain children used the bathroom before they left home so they wouldn't confront a segregated restroom. They packed lunches for long trips to avoid eating at dingy colored-only lunch counters or having to retrieve their food from the back door of a restaurant.

Like the rest of the middle class, money made it easier for the Rices to skirt at least some of the daily indignities. But whenever a Negro family mixed with white people, they ran the risk of their children encountering racism. Decades later, Carolyn Hunter still feels the sting. "At Fair Park, if they were standing in line, a little white child could come up and cut. They could be near the front but would have to let the white child go," said Hunter, her eyes heavy with pain. "God turned that thing around. Thank God for Martin Luther King."[129]

One way the Rices dealt with Birmingham's limits was to set Condoleezza's sites on the possibilities of the larger world. They wouldn't stoop to going to the State Fair on Negro day; instead they took Condo to Coney Island in New York when John was studying at Columbia one summer.[130] They explained that though she couldn't eat a hamburger at a restaurant or a downtown lunch counter, she could become president of the United States.[131] "They explained to me carefully what was going on, and they did so without any bitterness," Rice said in 1984.[132] It was an astounding feat. Most African Americans of Rice's age, and many in Birmingham, still speak with anger about the times they suffered discrimination. But Rice never has, perhaps because her parents never suggested the status quo was permanent.

You see, John and Angelena had had a plan, a conscious design from the time their daughter was very young.[133] She was going to be the best-prepared child in the world. There were lessons in violin, glockenspiel, and flute; tutoring in French and Spanish; ballet classes; Girl Scouts; and every book club her parents could sign her up for—so many, in fact, that Rice would never be able to bring herself to read for pleasure.[134] There was a full calendar of church activities and schooling in the social graces: speech, manners, dress, decorum. All that instruction led to a happy coincidence, or perhaps it was part of their plan, too: Condoleezza's life was so full of activities, so scheduled that her grasping mind had little room for thoughts of injustice or self-doubt.

Most of all, there was music. Angelena played the Westminster organ and from the time she was four years old, Condoleezza accompanied her on the piano. Condo also played for the Sunday school and the church choir. When she was six, her mother bought her a recording of *Aida*.[135] She played it over and over, losing herself in the music.[136] As an adult, she would tell a music critic, "It's not exactly relaxing if you are struggling to play Brahms. But it is transporting. When you're playing, there is only room for Brahms or Shostakovich."[137] It wasn't uncommon for middle-class families to have pianos at home; Condoleezza's friends Vanessa and Margaret did, too. What was different about Condoleezza was what she could do with the instrument. At age four, she had already given her first recital: At a meeting for new schoolteachers, wearing a taffeta dress and a fuzzy tam, Rice played a Tchaikovsky-inspired piece called "A Doll's Funeral."[138]

Condo's regimented world left little space for reflection on the Negro condition, but also little time for childish pursuits like purposeless play. The ordinary gave way to activities that would make her exceptional. So when Condoleezza wanted to perform as the Supremes with two other girls in a school talent show in the eighth grade, her father forbade it. It was "undignified."[139] Instead, she would do a tap routine by herself—though she had never learned to tap. Rev. Rice stood in front of the stage to make sure no one laughed at her sequined outfit. She was being trained to be a soloist.

When Condoleezza was about ten, she told her mother she was bored with the endless hours at the piano and wanted to quit. Angelena told her she was too young to make that decision.[140] Her daughter responded as any good Calvinist would and returned to her practicing. "It was amazing that she was [not] spoiled, with all the attention they gave her," said Julia Emma Smith.[141] But the attention the Rices gave, like the Rays, was not indulgent or coddling; it was an affection of expectation.

If otherworldly perfection wore on Condoleezza, she didn't show it. On the contrary, she lacked the mood swings common in children her age; as an adult, she would be aboundingly optimistic.[142] Perhaps she never bristled under the strict regimen of classes and lessons because it was all she knew. And spending most of her time with adults may have encouraged the development of her preternatural maturity, which in turn allowed her to shoulder great expectations without complaint. The religious faith in which she was steeped virtually from birth also demanded discipline and diligence; productive work is central to Presbyterianism. And, finally, neither the Rices nor the Rays fretted over circumstances; they confronted them or they went around them.

Then as now, many African American parents told their children, "You have to be twice as good." Meaning, they had to be twice as good as a white person to receive the same level of respect, opportunity, or status. "You were taught that you were good enough, but you might have to be twice as good given you're black," Condoleezza Rice often recalled. "It wasn't 'You have to be twice as good and that's unfair.' It was 'You might have to be twice as good,' end of story."[143] Complaining may have been the only vocabulary young Condoleezza lacked.

When the signs went up placing the children's parks under the guillotine of protecting "Our Way of Life," much of white Birmingham had had enough; they finally spoke out. More than twelve hundred of what author Diane McWhorter called, with some irony, the city's "most impressive decent citizenry" brought Bull Connor a petition entitled "Plea for Courage and Common Sense," quoting his campaign promise to expand the number of playgrounds in the city.[144] For these whites, the cost of protecting segregation in the face of the federal government's determination to dismantle it, statute by statute, was indeed getting too high.

Only Connor wasn't impressed. He told the decent citizens what they could do with their petition and kept the parks shuttered. The delusion that the good men and women of Birmingham were working fruitfully, in their own way, on their own timetable, to bury Jim Crow was getting harder and harder to sustain. Between 9 and 10 p.m. on January 16, the day the parks were supposed to be integrated, three churches were bombed.[145]

The intransigence of white leaders and the fear of segregationist violence drove a few more Negro leaders to Fred Shuttlesworth's cause over the course of 1962. Miles College president Lucius Pitts orchestrated a downtown department-store boycott for Easter weekend—to skirt authorities, it was called a selective buying campaign. It worked for a time, but not enough Negroes were selective in their buying, and by the summer, the boycott had failed. In retaliation, Newberry's and Woolworth's fired their Negro employees.[146] In September, the Southern Christian Leadership Council, headed by Martin Luther King Jr., held its annual convention in Birmingham, marking, as McWhorter called it, "the beginning of a new season in the history of civil rights, the Year of Birmingham."[147]

King's mere presence added fire to fellow SCLC leader Shuttlesworth's long-smoldering crusade. To keep King from marching, the department-store magnates agreed to integrate their toilets, water fountains, and elevators, but not the lunch counters. More than three hundred activists from all over the Southeast turned out for the convention.[148] It went off mostly without incident. Once the SCLC was gone, however, the "Whites Only" signs went back up.[149]

But it wasn't the resilience of Jim Crow that concerned young Condoleezza. On October 22, President Kennedy went on national television to say that Soviet nuclear missiles had been discovered in Cuba, ninety miles from U.S. shores. For seven excruciating days, the world feared that World War III was about to begin. Condoleezza followed the crisis closely with her parents.[150] On TV news reports of the threat to the Southeast, "you'd see these red arrows coming at Birmingham. I remember thinking that was something that maybe my father couldn't handle."[151]

A public pledge that the United States would never invade Cuba and a secret deal to remove American missiles aimed at the Soviet Union from Turkey put the nuclear boogeyman to bed, at least for a little while. On October 28, Secretary of State Dean Rusk told Kennedy, "We were eyeball to eyeball, and the other fellow just blinked." Condo was relieved.

Segregation would take considerably longer to vanquish.

CHAPTER THREE

RESISTANCE

As an educated person, you have tools to change your own circumstances for the bet-
ter whenever you find them stifling and along the way to change the lives of others, too.
But you have to believe—like many who had less reason to have faith in tomorrow but
nonetheless did—that the locomotive of human progress is individual will. And then
you have only to act on it, confident that you will succeed.[1]

CONDOLEEZZA RICE
University of Alabama General Commencement
May 15, 1994

First came the explosion. Brick, glass, steel, and mortar flew through the air. Closed doors were blown open, a passing driver was thrown from his car, and the air filled with acrid smoke. Those who were left stunned but still alive thought the Russians had attacked downtown Birmingham.[2]

The bomb had been left under the steps of the east door of the Sixteenth Street Baptist Church, concealed by a magnolia bush; when it exploded on Sunday, September 15, 1963, the clock inside the church sanctuary froze at 10:22.[3,4] Four little girls had been in the basement women's lounge, which was literally on the other side of the church's eastern wall.

Denise McNair was eleven years old. Addie Mae Collins, Cynthia Wesley, and Carole Robertson were fourteen and dressed in white for their roles as ushers that Sunday, part of the church's Youth Day celebration. Sunday school had ended, and they were fixing themselves up for the main service when the explosion tore a seven-by-seven-foot hole in the side of the church, leaving their bodies stacked like firewood in the demolished ladies' room. All their clothes were blown off by the blast; Denise McNair's grandfather, who ran a dry-cleaning shop across the street, had to identify his granddaughter by her shoes.[5]

Two miles south of Sixteenth Street, eight-year-old Condoleezza Rice was sitting in a pew at her father's church when she felt the building "rocking like an earthquake."[6] The bomb's tremors touched every Negro in Birmingham either literally or figuratively. Condoleezza and Denise had both attended Westminster Presbyterian's kindergarten, though Condo was three years younger than Denise.[7] Cynthia Wesley had participated in Rev. Rice's youth fellowship.[8] And Angelena's brother Alto taught social studies to Addie Mae Collins—four decades later, he still cries when he talks about the bombing. When they heard the explosion, folks thought there'd been an industrial accident at one of the mines. The Westminster Presbyterian congregation was shocked to learn the truth. After church, Condoleezza sat with her friends on the curb outside her house and asked, "Why? Why?"[9]

Segregation's henchmen were striking closer to home in 1963: That summer, a firebomb had been tossed into South Titusville but failed to explode. When John Rice went to the police to demand an investigation, they did nothing.[10] Another bomb had destroyed a store across Sixth Avenue from Westminster Presbyterian. A second bomb, intended to hurt anyone who came to investigate the blast, turned out to be dud.[11] Then, ten days after the church bombing, a shrapnel bomb exploded at the corner of Center Street and Sixteenth Avenue South, just four blocks from the Rice home.[12] The next attack was even closer: A gas bomb was thrown through the window of one of the Rices' neighbors; its stench choked the neighborhood. After John took Condo and Angelena to Angelena's parents in North Birmingham, he organized local men to patrol South Titusville with their shotguns.[13] Because night riders drove through Negro areas after dark—shooting guns, planting dynamite, and throwing firebombs—the South Titusville men set up roadblocks at dusk at each of the four entrances to the neighborhood,[14] which was pretty well cut off from the rest of the city already. And they instructed their neighbors to leave their front and back porch lights burning all night.

That fear was exactly what the Klansmen who had planted the Sixteenth Street bomb had been trying to instill. Just weeks before the bombing, a federal court had approved a Birmingham City Council school desegregation plan,[15] and

Fred Shuttlesworth had been on the verge of scoring his greatest victory. Only Alabama governor George Wallace was determined as he said in his inauguration address earlier that year to defend "Segregation now! Segregation tomorrow! Segregation forever!"[16]

After the court approved Birmingham's plan, Wallace forced the city's superintendent to close schools rather than allow them to be integrated. On Monday, September 9, Wallace reopened the schools under executive order but forbade black students to enter any school that had previously been all-white. In response, President Kennedy federalized the Alabama National Guard and, on September 10, used them to protect Birmingham's schools as they were finally integrated— by less than a half dozen Negro students.[17] That Saturday, Klansmen stashed the dynamite under the steps of Sixteenth Street Baptist Church.

While the world fumed in the aftermath of the bombing, America's homegrown terrorists were unapologetic. At a rally in Florida, Klan leader Rev. Connie Lynch told a cheering crowd that the victims were no more human or innocent than "rattlesnakes . . . And if it's four less niggers tonight, then good for whoever planted the bomb."[18]

Even the ostensibly respectable white mainstream did not find enlightenment in the slaughter of innocents. As Martin Luther King biographer Taylor Branch wrote in *Pillar of Fire*, the executive committee of the Southern Baptist convention rejected "a resolution of sympathy" for the Sixteenth Street congregation and sealed their records for thirty years to hide their "fitful consideration" of the proposal. And the doyens of Birmingham's business community in a White House meeting with Kennedy told the president they suspected the four girls had accidentally set off a store of dynamite the Negroes themselves had been storing in the church basement.[19]

If the official moves to kill Jim Crow sparked the wave of terror sweeping Birmingham, their impetus in turn had been the demonstrations that Martin Luther King had led that spring. Summoned by Shuttlesworth, King had arrived on April 3.[20] Earlier that day, the Alabama Christian Movement for Human Rights had launched an Easter protest campaign.[21]

The white establishment's response was to accuse the outsiders of stirring up "interracial discord."[22] The Negro establishment was just as caustic; the Negro newspaper, the *Birmingham World*, called the protests "both wasteful and worthless." And Negro ministers, in particular, assailed King for launching a protest campaign just as a new mayor promised to sideline the intractable public safety commissioner Bull Connor.

In the face of near universal opposition, King and Shuttlesworth went ahead anyway. The goal of their campaign was to fill the jails with nonviolent demonstrators until the national media had no choice but to notice. Media attention would force Birmingham to rescind legal segregation, King and Shuttlesworth reasoned, something nearly a decade of federal court decisions had failed to accomplish. With King himself in Birmingham, his men hoped to bring hundreds of Negroes out to protest. But dozens was the best they could do. On April 5, the *New York Times* reported—on page sixteen—"Integration Drive Slows/Sit-ins and Demonstration Plan Fails to Materialize."[23] Desperate to save the campaign, King decided to march himself. He was arrested on April 12, Good Friday.[24]

That day, the mainstream *Birmingham News* broke its usual news blackout of civil rights protests to run a small item headlined "White Clergymen Urge Local Negroes to Withdraw from Demonstrations." All the signatories, led by Episcopal Bishop C. C. J. Carpenter, were on record as being at least somewhat critical of segregation. The clergymen called King's campaign "unwise and untimely." King responded with his famous "letter from a Birmingham city jail."[25] As much an answer to the ministers, it was an anguished justification to himself for why he was sitting in a jail in Birmingham, Alabama.[26]

In the letter, King first denied that he was an "outsider"; he was president of the SCLC, and Shuttlesworth's ACMHR was an SCLC affiliate. "I am in Birmingham because injustice is here," King wrote. "Injustice anywhere is a threat to justice everywhere . . . "

> Birmingham is probably the most thoroughly segregated city in the United States. Its ugly record of brutality is widely known. Negroes have experienced grossly unjust treatment in the courts. There have been more unsolved bombings of Negro homes and churches in Birmingham than in any other city in the nation. These are the hard, brutal facts of the case. On the basis of these conditions, Negro leaders sought to negotiate with the city fathers. But the latter consistently refused to engage in good-faith negotiation . . .

Then King answered the perpetual lament of white moderates, much of the Negro middle class, and, according to a *Newsweek* poll later that year, seventy-four percent of white Americans: Why did civil rights leaders have to insist on equal rights for Negroes so immediately?

> We have waited for more than 340 years for our constitutional and God-given rights.
> . . . When you see the vast majority of your twenty million Negro brothers smothering in an airtight cage of poverty in the midst of an affluent society; when you suddenly find your tongue twisted and your speech stammering as you seek to explain to your six-year-old daughter why she can't go to the public amusement park that has just been advertised on television, and see tears welling up in her eyes when she is told that Funtown is closed to colored children, and see ominous clouds of inferiority beginning to form in her little mental sky, and see her beginning to distort her personality by developing an unconscious bitterness toward white people . . . when you are humiliated day in and day out by nagging signs reading "white" and "colored"; when your first name becomes "nigger," your middle name becomes "boy" (however old you are), and your last name becomes "John," and your wife and mother are never given the respected title "Mrs."; when you are harried by day and haunted by night by the fact that you are a Negro, living constantly at tiptoe stance, never quite knowing what to expect next, and are plagued with inner fears and outer resentments; when you no [sic] forever fighting a degenerating sense of "nobodiness" then you will understand why we find it difficult to wait. There comes a time when the cup of endurance runs over . . .

But even King's arrest and letter—which only one newspaper, a Quaker journal, showed any interest in printing—didn't attract media attention, at least not the kind that movement leaders wanted. When the mainstream press mentioned King or what his planners had code-named Project C, for confrontation, they criticized both; *Time* and the *New York Times*, for instance, blamed King for "inflamed tensions" in Birmingham.[27]

In the shadow of the marches and arrests downtown, John Rice continued to do what he had always done: to work to save as many young Negro lives as he could from ignorance and anger. "Most people were not boat rockers. They were not pronouncing publicly against the establishment," said Odessa Woolfolk, a former Titusville teacher and a historian of the black middle class who knew both Rev. Rices well. "The emphasis was on preparing our children for a better life."[28]

And few did that as assiduously as John Rice. He had spent the years since his daughter's birth, as Voltaire said, tending his garden.[29] He had built Westminster from the nascent former mission he had inherited from his father into a thriving congregation. After the Rices moved out of the pastor's apartment behind the pulpit, Rev. Rice had converted part of the suite of rooms into a daycare center for church members. He installed a dentist's chair to the left of the altar and brought in a white dentist to provide free checkups and care.[30]

But the heart of the dynamic church was the youth fellowship. Long before most churches discovered they could use Christian rock and hip-hop to connect the young to God, Rice held "flop nights" once or twice a month at Westminster, where adolescents and teenagers came to eat, play records, and dance. "That was [unheard of] in a black church," said Third Hunter, Rice's neighbor who joined the youth group even though he belonged to another church. "If you were able to get to Rev. Rice and talk to him, you'd latch on to him. He just made you feel comfortable."[31]

For Rice, it was educational evangelism by other means. There were religious parts of the youth fellowship, of course; for example, its regular Sunday-afternoon meetings introduced young people to the tenets of Presbyterianism—godliness, faith, hard work, and predestination—and the group attended religious conferences at Presbyterian colleges and the Church's Covenant Mountain retreat. But Rice also brought in teachers from Ullman High School to give the kids help in English, French, math, science, and chess. And because Rice was a former athlete and coach, there were always sports: baseball, volleyball, basketball, and, once a week, a trip to Honey Bowl, the segregated bowling alley down the street from the church. "The church provided an alternative [to the world outside]," said Julia Emma Smith, the youth group's codirector. "We had more fun than anyone! And Condoleezza would be at everything."[32]

Just eight years old, Condoleezza was much younger than the youth group members who were preteens and teenagers, but John took Condo everywhere. And fitting in with older children was becoming a necessity anyway; Condoleezza had skipped the first grade and in a few years, she'd skip the seventh.

Her parents had already shown Condoleezza the world beyond Birmingham. The family had spent the summers of 1960 and '61 in Colorado while Rev. Rice studied for his master's degree in education at the University of Denver.[33] And while other families went on vacations to national monuments, the Rices visited college campuses, once driving a hundred miles out of their way just to visit Ohio State.[34] Now John was leading a whole gaggle of young men and women on field trips to expand their world: to other houses of worship and, because he believed education would be their earthly salvation, to Atlanta's Clark College and other historically black schools.[35] And as his father had done before him, he helped any child he could get a scholarship to a Presbyterian college.[36]

The reputation of Rice's youth fellowship spread beyond Westminster Presbyterian, and even young people who didn't belong to the church were flocking to John's mini-movement. He was drawing so many children from other congregations and denominations that at least one minister protested to his parishioners that they had better start their own youth group.[37] "[Baptist, Methodist] Episcopal, every denomination would come to our church for youth group," said Julia Emma Smith. "We had one B'nai Brith girl."[38]

But while Rice was working to rescue the children of Birmingham from the realities of segregation, Martin Luther King's lieutenants had decided that the children would rescue Birmingham instead.

The Rices' seventeen-year-old neighbor, Third Hunter, had glommed onto a charismatic movement preacher from Mississippi named James Bevel. "We were his entourage," said Hunter.[39] At the movement's separate mass meetings for youth, Bevel preached about the meaning of what was happening in Birmingham. The teenagers sang movement songs and watched an NBC News documentary on the 1960 demonstrations in Nashville, where four thousand Negro students had forced the integration of libraries and lunch counters.[40] But civil rights wasn't the only thing on their minds: "It was a real nice atmosphere," said Hunter. "I went down there to chase girls. We became mass meeting hoppers. Every time they had one, we were there."

The meetings became so popular that by the time King posted bail and was released from jail, the youth meetings were drawing larger crowds than the adult meetings were. If anything, the adult movement seemed to be petering out as the youth movement grew. One reason was that fewer and fewer adults were willing to march in King's demonstrations, fearful that their white employers would fire them or that white banks would call in their loans. With some of King's aides proposing giving up on trying to change Birmingham, Bevel made an unorthodox suggestion: Let the children march. King's men were scandalized at the very thought of it—children demonstrating in the streets, going to jail. But King himself was noncommittal; he didn't say no, but he didn't sign off on Bevel's idea for a children's crusade either.[41]

Nonetheless, on May 2, fifty young people emerged two by two singing from the portals of the Sixteenth Street Baptist Church. In neat rows, they marched into the waiting police wagons.[42] Then came a second phalanx, also singing. Once they were hauled away, a third. And on and on and on—a seemingly inexhaustible multitude of teenagers, adolescents, and children. Nearly eight hundred Negro public school students had missed roll call that Thursday morning. More than one thousand people, ages six to twenty, filled Sixteenth Street Baptist. At least four columns headed in different directions from the church, a mix of falsettos, sopranos, tenors, and baritones that Birmingham had never heard before.[43] An elderly woman ran shouting along the arrest line, "Sing, children, sing!"[44]

As Diane McWhorter, a daughter of white Birmingham, recounted in *Carry Me Home*:

> . . . A policeman leaned down to address a demonstrator of no more than eight [the same age as Condoleezza] and said in the tenderly stern tone that southern daddies take with their daughters, "What do you want?"
>
> White people had high affection for colored children, even if the axiom that "pickaninnies are so cute" contained the unspoken corollary "Too bad they have to grow up." There was a white conviction that black adults had somehow "earned" their oppression, but the little girl's reply—"F'eedom"—defined as if for the first time the idea of "innocent victim."[45]

Third Hunter had been in one of the first lines. Hunter had decided to march—over the sobs of his mother, who feared he'd be expelled from school, as white administrators had promised. "Was that Third I saw getting into that paddy wagon on the news?" asked his father that night from a business trip to Atlanta,[46] before telling Carolyn Hunter they should let Third march, making the Hunters one of the rare middle-class families that supported the children's crusade.

Hunter's group's assignment was to act as decoys: Exit the church, cross at the traffic light, and start singing "We Shall Overcome." After two blocks, a policeman stopped the children and told them they were parading without a permit. He read them a city ordinance and said into his walkie-talkie, "Call the paddy wagon." Mostly for effect, said Hunter, since the police wagon was parked across the street.[47] The students were hauled off to the city jail. By early afternoon, the cells were so full there was no place to sit down. "At night, you had to claim your spot or sleep standing up," said Hunter.[48]

The next day, Friday, May 3, fifteen hundred Negro students missed school to participate in the marches. At 1 p.m., three hundred walked out of Sixteenth Street Church. After just two blocks, public safety commissioner Bull Connor ordered the young people to stop. Firemen stood ready with hoses. When the students proceeded, the firemen opened up the hoses. Children were splayed across the sidewalk, some turned end over end by the percussion of the stream. One little girl had a bloody nose and scratches on her face; one man's shirt was torn from his back.

Then Connor sent in the K-9 detail to clear Kelly Ingram Park catty-corner from the church, where hundreds of Negro spectators had gathered. One of the dogs lunged at teenager Walter Gadsden. The moment was caught on film by Bill Hudson, a photographer for the Associated Press.

That night across America, the scene of children being charged by German shepherds and mowed down by fire hoses dominated the evening news. The next day, Hudson's photo of Gadsden ran at three columns across the front page of the *New York Times* above the caption "Dogs and Hoses Repulse Negroes at Birmingham."[49]

But the Negroes kept coming. By Monday, thousands of demonstrators filled the Birmingham jail—not just children but adults, too,[50] so many that Connor had to open the fairgrounds to hold them. The children's crusade had turned around the Negro establishment; business magnate A. G. Gaston and preachers rallied to the cause. In fact, many adults, ashamed to see kids fighting their battles, converted. Those who felt they couldn't afford to put their jobs at risk donated money for bail funds for the demonstrators. Pilloried nationally and internationally, white Birmingham decided to negotiate an end to Jim Crow.

John Rice "detested" the children's crusade, he opposed sending children into harm's way, and he said he would never put his daughter in such danger—but he watched as his students plunged headlong into the gale. When the Board of Education ordered the doors and gates of Negro schools locked during school hours, the students went out the windows and pulled down the fences. Negro teachers and principals had been told that if they let students march, they would be fired.

It's difficult to believe, but Julia Emma Smith said Rice never addressed the marches in Westminster's youth group meetings.[51] Third Hunter couldn't remember what Rice said about the demonstrations: "He wasn't very political." But youth fellowship member Eva Carter remembered Rice advising group members not to take part. He told them, "There's a better way. I want you to fight with your mind," Carter told a reporter.[52]

Though Rice opposed King's methods, he drove Condoleezza to witness the downtown demonstrations—from a safe distance in their car.[53] Then he carried her on his shoulders through the makeshift detainment camp at the fairgrounds. He wanted to check in on his students and give Condo a glimpse of history in the making. "He was supportive of the civil rights movement, like everybody," says Condoleezza Rice today, "[but] my father was a very strong man, and the idea of a nonviolent response where people are beating up on you was not his cup of tea. He told my mother at one point, if somebody does that to me, then I'm going to end up in jail, and Condoleezza won't have a father. . . . His style was much more 'go take your shotgun and defend the community.'"[54]

On May 10, Shuttlesworth announced Birmingham's "accord with its conscience."[55] Within three days, downtown department stores would integrate their fitting rooms; within thirty days, their restrooms and water fountains; within sixty days, their lunch counters; and "one [Negro] salesperson or cashier" would be hired—it wasn't clear whether the deal stipulated one employee at each store or one collectively, which would later become a point of contention.

The Birmingham effect was felt across the nation. In the ten weeks following the children's crusade, more than seven hundred civil rights demonstrations took place in more than 180 towns and cities.[56] In the most history-changing consequence of Birmingham's 1963 protests, President Kennedy went on national television on June 11, 1963, to announce that he would send a bill to Congress outlawing segregation.[57] "This nation, for all its hopes and all its boasts, will not be fully free until all its citizens are free," said Kennedy.[58]

Kennedy's bill became the Civil Rights Act of 1964, which President Lyndon Johnson hustled and bullied through Congress—in part as the legacy of his predecessor, assassinated the previous November in Dallas. On July 2, 1964, Johnson signed H.R. 7152 into law, outlawing segregation in schools, restaurants, hotels, and other public accommodations and federally assisted programs, as well as racial and sexual discrimination in employment.[59]

The Rice family watched the signing ceremony on television, and a few days later, John, Angelena, and Condoleezza went to dinner at a fancy restaurant downtown. Condoleezza would describe the scene thirty-seven years later: White people looked up from their dinner plates in shock as the family was led to their table, then, said Rice, "they all went back to eating. And that was it."[60] But a few weeks later, the Rices went through a fast-food drive-thru window and after they drove off, nine-year-old Condoleezza bit into her hamburger to discover it was all onions.[61]

Of course, real equality didn't come overnight. In January 1966, for example, following another month of marches to protest the slow pace of Negro voter registration, twenty-three federal registrars set up shop under the authority of the Voting Rights Act, which outlawed barriers to voting anywhere in the United States. In their first day on the job, the federal registrars processed more than one thousand new voters,[62] and by the end of their campaign, an additional fifty thousand Negro voters were added to the rolls.[63]

Later that year, John Rice was appointed dean of students at his alma mater, Stillman College in Tuscaloosa. That summer, the Rices moved. John packed the Bibles, and Ann boxed up the sheet music. In the backseat of their Dodge, Condoleezza made a game of reading license plates as they left Birmingham behind.[64]

Despite the gains of the civil rights movement, Birmingham would once again fail to live up to its "perpetual promise." True integration didn't come until the end of the 1960s. And just as blacks were gaining access to the higher-paying jobs in the city's steel mills in the seventies, Big Steel drastically downsized, hit by stronger environmental standards and increased foreign competition.

Blacks did gain political power; the city started electing black mayors and city councillors beginning in the 1970s, including Condoleezza's childhood friend and Westminster youth fellowship member Carole Smitherman. But with integration, white and black middle-class flight sapped Birmingham of its tax base, making it a study in urban decay.[65] The fully integrated department stores moved to the suburbs or went out of business, leaving hulking shells behind downtown. Today, African American men litter the city that, as the saying goes, has a church or a liquor store on every other corner.[66] Even once-proud Titusville has succumbed to gangs and drugs; today, large patches of the neighborhood are run-down and dangerous.

Westminster Presbyterian has dwindled to less than one hundred mostly elderly parishioners, including Julia Emma Smith and Angelena's brother, Alto Ray, and his wife, Connie. The members of the congregation say John Rice's pastorship is still the high point of the church's history.

The former members of the church's youth fellowship group have fared much better than the church itself. Freeman Hrabowski, for example, is the president of the University of Maryland at Baltimore County. Eva Carter is a dean at Lawson State College near Birmingham. Mary Bush, who was the first black governor of the International Monetary Fund, is an international business consultant. Sheryl McCarthy is a newspaper columnist up north. Other John Rice protégés are doctors, professors, engineers, and lawyers, and many of them credit Rev. Rice's gospel of education and the values of self-confidence and determination he taught them at youth group for much of their success.

Predictably, Condoleezza Rice would learn her father's lessons better than anyone else, and in part thanks to them, she would go on to amass a record of historic achievement. Her years in Birmingham played a formative role in Rice's development, investing her with many of the traits that she carries today, yet it also played a complicated role, as complicated as Condoleezza's relationship to the history that swirled around her as a little girl.

Rice provides little help in understanding the effect Birmingham had on her either as a child or later in life, perhaps in part because she was only eleven years old when she left the Magic City, though she returned often over the next two years. And partly because, as Rice told me, "I don't find it all that useful to spend a lot of time analyzing myself. I'll let other people do that. It's just not something that's very productive."[67] Finally, decoding Birmingham's influence on Rice is complicated by her bifurcated view of reality: the life she lived inside the bubble her parents created for her—comfortable, supportive and loving—and the horrors of the world outside from which even John and Angelena could not completely shelter their daughter.

Condoleezza has sought, inevitably, to compose a single narrative from the two conflicting stories of Birmingham, the one inside her bubble—with music and ballet—and the one outside—with night riders and dynamited children. She often succeeded, constructing a coherent plotline that neatly explains what must have seemed inexplicable to a child. And sometimes she failed, the contradictions simply too great to be reconciled. Just two examples are Rice's perspectives on the role of class distinctions in Negro Birmingham and the extent of her parents' power and freedom.

Rice's detailed recollections of her childhood are often puzzling. In fact, in decades of interviews as an adult, Rice has offered conflicting testimony, whether because her understanding of the events in Birmingham has evolved or merely because she has refined how she describes them.

In the most striking example, for years Rice seemed to minimize—or even deny—experiencing fear or racism as a child. So it wasn't surprising when CBS's Katie Couric in a 2006 interview suggested, "In a way, not only geographically but psychologically, you were a bit shielded from some of the uglier things that were going on in terms of the civil rights movement." But then Rice responded with what sounded like a hint of condescension, "Well, yes, until bombs started going off in our neighborhood. You couldn't be shielded in Birmingham, you couldn't be."[68] But Couric's deduction grew from years of Rice saying exactly that: that she had been shielded from the ugliest parts of Birmingham's racial history.

In 1983, for example, Rice said the events and marches of 1963 "burned in [her] consciousness" but that she didn't remember being afraid.[69] In 2002, she told *Newsweek* the same thing—she said she did remember, however, exactly how many days of school she missed because of the unrest in 1963: thirty one.[70] And in an interview with *George* magazine in 2000, it was only after the reporter peppered her with questions—"But what about when Denise and Addie got killed? What about when the bomb went off in your own backyard? What about when your daddy took his gun and went out into the dark to protect the community? Weren't you afraid?"—did Rice concede, "I was kind of scared by

the [Sixteenth Street] church bombing."[71] But in a *Vogue* interview the following year, Rice was back to downplaying any memories of being terrorized. In
fact, she volunteered, she was more frightened by Fidel Castro than she was by
night riders: "I'll tell you, funnily enough, what scared me more was the Cuban
missile crisis. We all lived within range [of the Soviet missiles based in
Cuba]."[72]

Perhaps Rice was composing her personal historical narrative as she went
along, writing it in hindsight. Or perhaps she was changing emphasis in each
interview to illustrate whatever point she wanted to make. Since *Newsweek* was
reporting on how her childhood in Birmingham influenced how she became an
overachiever, she recalled how many days of school she missed, emphasizing the
steeliness and the dedication to achievement that her parents had instilled in her.
On the other hand, Katie Couric was interviewing her in the midst of the harshest criticism the Bush administration had endured over its increasingly unpopu-
lar Iraq policy. Hence, Rice emphasized the terror of her youth. And in the
interview, Condoleezza connected it to both the terrorists the Iraqis were living
with and the terror Americans could face if the United States withdrew from Iraq
before the country was stabilized.

Introducing herself to the Stanford University community as a young professor new to the university in 1983, Condoleezza told the faculty–staff weekly,
Campus Report, "I was in the heart of the political struggle all through my
childhood," emphasizing her connection to the historic events in Birmingham
and her origins as a black Southerner. In the same interview she said,
"1968 . . . was a crack in time. That was the year Bobby Kennedy and Martin
Luther King were shot. But the event that really struck me was the Soviet invasion of Czechoslovakia. I can still feel the strong sense I had of remorse and
regret that a brave people had been subdued."[73] In saying this, she was constructing her professional myth of creation, emphasizing her early and surprising interest in the Soviet Union and Eastern Europe.

In one of our interviews at the end of 2006, Rice explained the comments
she had made over the years. She said she had not meant to convey in her *Campus Report* interview, for instance, that she was more affected by the oppression
of the Czechs during the Soviet invasion than she was by the assassinations of
King, who had marched in Birmingham just five years before he was killed, and
Robert Kennedy. "Of course, the assassination of Bobby Kennedy, you'd have an

emotional response. Of course, the assassination of Martin Luther King, you would have an emotional response. [But] why would I have an emotional response to Prague Spring?. . . But I just remember feeling really bad for this man, [Czech leader Alexander] Dubček, faced by [Soviet] tanks rolling through the streets and wanting to know more about that."[74]

She also attempted to clarify the inconsistencies over whether she felt fear in Birmingham: She did, but not until 1963, when the bombs started going off closer to home. "Before '63, racism is there. You can't go to restaurants. You can't go to Kiddieland. Your parents try to explain to you why there are never any people on television that look like you . . . [Then comes] '63, which is violent and frightening, and there isn't any level of protection. . . . You know you're not safe at home. You're not safe in the streets."[75]

"You couldn't be protected from the—really, terror—of that year, because bombs were going off and there were night riders in neighborhoods and my little friend [Denise McNair] was killed. And you couldn't be protected from that."

It was a cogent argument, and it avoided the incredulous reaction that Rice's more frequent testimony—that she had not been afraid—often provoked from reporters. But it was the opposite of the characterization that both Rice and her father had given *George* in 2000 when, in response to a question about the 1963 bombings in Titusville, John Rice said his daughter shed "no tears" and felt "no terror . . . She grew up in the era and knew how to handle it. She had faith that we would protect her, and we would."[76]

In our interview, Rice also explained that her parents had not shielded her from segregation, but they had steeled her as much as possible against its effects. "You couldn't really even be protected from the racism [in Birmingham] . . . Our parents went to enormous lengths not to let it affect us . . . But we knew something was wrong that you couldn't go to a restaurant. We knew something was wrong that Cousin Cliff, on the Popeye Show . . . [an in-studio] TV show . . . let little black kids come once a week."[77]

"The parents were just determined that [growing up with segregation] wasn't going to become crippling; that you weren't going to feel that there weren't possibilities and that if you worked hard, you still weren't going to get very far."

Over time, then, and maybe by virtue of having to recount her history over and over to reporters, Rice has developed two narratives of segregated Birmingham: one for the time before 1963 and one for 1963 and the years after, a dichotomy that allows her to chronologically compartmentalize and separate the positive memories that dominate the private world of her childhood and the fear that pervaded the world outside the bubble her parents created for her.

Of course, Rice has still has not managed to reconcile all the contradictions of Birmingham, such as her recollection that class distinctions within the black community made no difference in her youth.[78] During an interview with Dale Russakoff of the *Washington Post*, Rice recounted a family visit to a white doctor after Angelena had contracted an infection.

> Dressed finely, as always, the trio arrived to find a well-appointed reception area, where white people were sitting. The receptionist sent them upstairs to the "colored waiting room," a cramped, dark space with peeling paint. But after the appointment, Rice recalls, the doctor walked them to his main reception area and said, "Reverend Rice, when you come back, why don't you come in after 5 o'clock on Saturday? You could come right in here."
>
> Rice says she never thought of the doctor's offer as a concession to her parents' class. "This was about race, not class," she says. What, then, of the blacks left behind in the colored waiting room? She pauses, as if revisiting a scene long fixed in her memory. "Well, it was about class, too," she says.[79]

It's not surprising that a child, even one as intelligent and aware as young Condo, would fail to grasp the full measure of the adult world around her. But even as an adult, Rice argues that class distinctions made no difference in Birmingham, though that was objectively untrue, particularly when it came to the civil rights movement: The middle class "actively resisted the Birmingham campaign" spearheaded by King and Shuttlesworth.[80] As Shuttlesworth said, "If we'd waited for the middle class to lead us, we'd still be waiting."[81] In fact, after one too many funerals of protesters, the normally politic Martin Luther King lost his cool and inveighed against not just the murderous segregationists, the silent moderates, and the "timidity" of the federal government but "the cowardice of every Negro . . . [who] stands on the sidelines in the struggle for justice."[82] Condoleezza Rice says she wondered as she watched her father and Fred Shuttlesworth sipping sweet tea on the front porch and talking for hours whether Shuttlesworth felt "disappointed" that John, like most ministers, wouldn't join his marches. "But they remained such good friends, and my dad did everything he could to help those ministers [who did march] and help the kids, especially."[83]

As human beings often do, Rice appears to have discarded the discrete memories that don't conform to the larger narrative she's constructed of Birmingham—memories like the middle class opposing the marches. To take a minor example, Condoleezza has said that not being allowed to go to Kiddieland didn't bother her as a child. "All of us knew Kiddieland was off limits . . . I never was one much for fairs or theme parks."

Only John Rice told a different story; he said he would drive five blocks out of the way to avoid the fairgrounds when the state fair came to Birmingham so Condoleezza wouldn't see the Ferris wheel, "which she longed to ride."[84] Either Rice didn't remember her sense of unfulfilled longing or she chose not to relate that feeling to her interviewer. Such a longing did not fit into Rice's narrative of Birmingham, which was that she was aware of the strictures of race but was not impacted by them.

Rice remembers her family's experience of racism the same way. She says they had "liberated" themselves long before King came to Birmingham. "I think that black Americans of my grandparents' ilk had liberated themselves . . . They had broken the code. They had figured out how to make an extraordinarily comfortable and fulfilling life despite the circumstances. They did not feel that they were captives."[85]

That understanding of her family's history may be the most important memory that Condoleezza took with her from Birmingham. For it would influence her worldview—and her understanding of obstacles, particularly in regard to race and racism—for the rest of her life.

And Condoleezza seems to have imposed it on every instance of her family history in Alabama—even those an outsider might say demonstrate the limits of their liberation. Take, for instance, the famous story of John Rice registering to vote: "The Democrats in Jim Crow Alabama of 1952 would not register him to vote. The Republicans did." When Condi told the Republican National Convention that story in 2000, she knew that the only way Rev. Rice had been able to exercise his fundamental right to vote had been on someone else's terms: The "Republican functionary" who secretly registered John required him to register as a Republican; Condoleezza conceded that had her father been given a choice, he likely would have registered as a Democrat.[86]

But Rice focuses not on the Faustian compromise her father had to make—his freedom to choose his political party in order to vote at all—but on the positive practical outcome. "I think he just wanted to vote, and he was just looking for a means to do it . . . I don't think it was a big psychological or philosophical—," Rice cuts herself off. "I think it was pretty instrumental, actually."[87]

Yet, each trip John Rice made to the ballot box illustrated the central contradiction of the lives of the Rices, the Rays, and the rest of the Negro middle class; namely, that however liberated they were in their own minds, they were still subject to the dictates of Jim Crow. It was a reality that conflicted with their strong sense of personal dignity and a conflict that Martin Luther King Jr. felt personally. King biographer Taylor Branch said the contradiction between that external reality and his internal pride inspired King's own "sharp inner divisions": "a sturdy dignity at war with enraging exclusion."[88] No matter how resolutely the Rices, the Rays, and King refused to let racism oppress them mentally, the space in which they were truly free was limited.

Condoleezza Rice understands that, but it is not the part of the history that she focuses on. In her mind, her family was free. "My grandfather had to confront [racism] every single day, in every conceivable way," says Rice, "but by the time my father's generation came along, you didn't have to confront racism every day if you didn't want to, because we lived in a black community. You had to confront it if you went two miles outside of our black community, in downtown Birmingham."

In her own mind, Condoleezza has limited racism's power chronologically and geographically, as if it didn't affect her parents as long as they were in Titusville or when John Rice went into the voting booth. In essence, that her father was able to vote is the important thing; that he was not free to choose his party is not. Condi doesn't acknowledge that her relatives' mental liberation did not free them from "enraging exclusion," partly because Rice's parents never showed her rage or bitterness at their circumstances and partly because they never dwelled on the fact that they were excluded.

As a result, today Condoleezza interprets John's voter-registration compromise not as evidence of oppression but as proof that personal determination can overcome circumstances. In fact, Condoleezza often remembers instances where others would see evidence of her parents' powerlessness as examples of their powerfulness; for instance, the colored waiting room incident: Rice remembered it not for what it said about the limits of her parents' power—that they couldn't wait in the white waiting room—but for how they were individually empowered by being invited to come into the white waiting room. She didn't focus on the concession that it had to be after regular hours on Saturday.

Rice believes her family had triumphed over oppression, and her memories of Birmingham focus on those triumphs, not the oppression.

The ultimate moral of her childhood may be that her parents successfully conveyed a sense of future possibility even in the dark present of American apartheid. Condoleezza's parents—indeed, her whole community—convinced her that while racism was a fact of life, racism was not the important thing; the important thing was to not be bothered by it: "I can remember my parents and others and teachers, as a matter of fact, saying racism is their problem, not your problem."[89]

The conviction that there were Negroes like her family who had broken the code and emancipated their minds led Rice to argue often that "individual will" should not be written out of the civil rights story; to do so was a slight to the legacy of her ancestors and those like them: "The legal changes made a tremendous difference, but not in the absence of people who were already prepared to take advantage of them."[90]

So for decades, Rice concentrated in interviews not on the martyrs and the saints of the movement—the conventional heroes of African American mythology, King and the marchers—but on the middle-class men and women who achieved success in spite of segregation. And that insistence on paying attention to those who had largely not participated in the mass movement for freedom made Rice sound removed from the collective understanding that African Americans had of their history, though Rice also praised the iconic heroes of the movement in her speeches.

Rice's seemingly contrarian interpretation of the tribulations and triumphs of black America's past—as well as, many African Americans suspect, of their collective woes in the present—provide the core of anti-Rice feeling in the black community today. "It's as if Rice is still cosseted in her beloved Titusville," wrote Gene Robinson of the *Washington Post* while accompanying Condoleezza on a trip to Birmingham as secretary of state, "able to see the very different reality that other African Americans experience but not to reach out of the bubble—not able to touch [it], and thus not be able to really understand it."[91] But empathy had never been John and Angelena's goal for their daughter; achievement had been. And her understanding that her family was already free helped Condoleezza believe there were no limits to her own possibilities.

Her unconventional worldview leads some African Americans to misunderstand Rice, arguing in essence that she is not "black enough," which is ironic because Condoleezza Rice is quintessentially African American.

The hard resolve, the discipline, the faith in one's own abilities and beliefs, no matter what the larger world attempts to present as reality, the masking in public of all but appropriate—and strategic—emotions: All were survival skills that John and Angelena and the rest of the Negro middle class had cultivated under segregation, along with their emphasis on proper speech and manners. They dressed better, behaved better, and worked harder at everything they did than white people of equivalent class, and they passed those values on to their children.

In fact, Birmingham's most lasting impact on Rice may be the skills and perspectives life there led her parents to arm Condoleezza with. Birmingham likely also inspired the determination with which John and Ann carried out that task. Each talent they cultivated in Condo was meant to increase her ability to compete and win, no matter the circumstances, as a black woman.

"Our parents knew black people faced a presumption of inarticulateness," says Rice's second cousin Connie Rice. "They programmed us to know: These [white] folks have a disability; they think they're better than you."[92] As a result, consciously or not, Condoleezza Rice's very posture is a consequence of growing up Negro in Birmingham: the way she holds her head erect, her shoulders square, her chin raised at almost all times. It was meant to project dignity and breeding.[93] And to this day, Rice's speech is much less clipped and "proper" in private than in her public appearances.

But her bearing was the least of the tools young Condoleezza took from Birmingham. As a Rice and a Ray, and a member of the Negro middle class, she had learned how to survive as a member of an elite, a minority within a minority. Discipline, discretion, and loyalty were second nature to her. There was never talking out of turn or out of school. She never rebelled. Along with those traits, she also took, of course, her intellect and her talents and the particular gifts of her parents: grace, elegance, and restraint from Angelena; a gregarious love of life—and football—from John. She was confident in herself and her opinions.[94]

And all those characteristics became hallmarks of her later life and her careers in academia and public service.

They would shield her from the harsh criticism she would sometimes receive as provost of Stanford University and national security adviser and then secretary of state to the second President Bush. But they would also make her less receptive to opposing opinions and perspectives, give her more faith in what she believed than in what others said, and render her less willing to show weakness or acknowledge error.

PART II
HIGHER LEARNING

CHAPTER FOUR

FALL

I don't know if in my recollection I whitewashed it, so to speak. All I remember is focusing on the fact that I was going to wear a uniform for the first time. I was probably so excited to get to Denver where I could skate year-round.[1]

CONDOLEEZZA RICE
Vogue
October 2001

T he move was supposed to be temporary. The Rices had been going to Colorado most summers since 1960 so John and Ann could take classes at the University of Denver and John could earn his master's degree in education. But John had finally decided he was never going to complete his degree by studying part-time; so in 1968, he took a year off from his job as dean of students at Stillman College to attend DU full-time.

While her parents were in class at the university, Condoleezza went to skating camp. The lessons had started as a kind of expensive day-care that first summer in 1960 when Condo was just five years old, but since then, skating had become one of her passions—along with the piano, of course. And by the summer of 1968, she was skating "every day, three hours a day."[2]

It was while waiting in the parking lot for Condoleezza to finish practice that John struck up a friendship with another dad whose daughter skated: Maurice "Mitch" Mitchell. Mitch happened to be the University of Denver's new chancellor. Mitch and John hit it off, and the chancellor asked John if after he completed his degree he'd be willing to come work for him at the university. It would be a

63

chance to make history, Mitch said; John would be the university's first senior black administrator.

When John mentioned to his boss at Stillman that he was considering Chancellor Mitchell's offer, Stillman's high-handed president, Dr. Harold N. Stinson, reportedly told Rice, "Well, if you're going, go now!"[3] And suddenly, what was supposed to be a temporary move became a life-changing opportunity.

The Rices were moving up in the world. In the space of three years, John had gone from high school guidance counselor in Birmingham to administrator at a major university. For the first time, the Rices would live, work, and study in an integrated world—and soon life in Colorado would provoke the greatest change of Condoleezza's young life, but all Condo cared about as the family relocated permanently to the West was that she'd get to skate year-round.

John thought the Denver public schools were inferior to the segregated schools Condoleezza had attended in Alabama, which was saying something, so he enrolled Condo in St. Mary's Academy, a Catholic all-girls prep school that taught the daughters of Denver's elite. SMA looked like a postcard; its modern buildings sprawled across twenty-four acres with the snowcapped Rockies in the distance. Its curriculum was rigorous: Latin, two foreign languages, and three years of high school science required. Because she had already skipped two grades, Condoleezza entered St. Mary's as a thirteen-year-old tenth grader, two years younger than most of her classmates. SMA's collegelike atmosphere would have intimidated the typical veteran of Alabama's Negro schools, but Condoleezza wasn't typical; and as one of only three black girls in her class, she would finally get to see if she really was twice as good as her white peers.

The early signs weren't promising; in Condo's first year at St. Mary's, a teacher told her her scores on the Preliminary Scholastic Aptitude Test indicated that she might not be "college material." She suggested Condoleezza consider junior college.[4] The teacher's view, which wasn't supported by Rice's "solid" test scores,[5] illustrated the downside of living and working with whites; now bias could reach parts of the Rices' lives, such as Condoleezza's school career, where segregation ironically had prevented it from entering.

John and Angelena told Condo to ignore the teacher's assessment, and she did. "She was well grounded [thanks to] her family," said Louise Turnbull, who taught Rice tenth-grade speech.[6] (In her senior year, Condoleezza would be assigned to be Turnbull's daughter Laura's Big Sister: "I wondered a little bit if Condi had been assigned to her because as a teacher, [the school] knew I wouldn't complain. In those days, there was still quite a lot of prejudice.")

As John Rice was discovering. The obvious Southern constraints of race didn't exist in Denver—there was less chance of a well-dressed mother and daughter stumbling into racism on a Saturday shopping trip, and Angelena could teach white children now at integrated schools. But still, Denver belied the notion that prejudice was a Southern affliction. Its public schools were just as segregated as Birmingham's—indeed, in 1973, Denver would be the first major city outside the South to be ordered to desegregate by a federal court. And as blacks were moving into formerly all-white neighborhoods, Denver's racial tensions were rising. In the well-to-do Park Hill area,[7] for instance, real estate brokers warned whites that the neighborhood's complexion was changing and encouraged them to move,[8] often buying their homes and then reselling them at a handsome profit to the blacks moving in.[9]

In this cauldron of racial change, John Rice was receiving an education of his own. Working for the first time in an integrated environment, John was learning that he had to calibrate how—and how quickly—he pushed for change at DU. Chancellor Mitchell had brought Rice in to increase the number of black students—in 1968, there were only about thirty-five blacks among DU's more than six thousand students.[10] John suggested the university should set a goal for minority admissions and work toward it, and budget funds for specifically for minority financial aid. But barely a year after his arrival, one of the vice chancellors, Wilbur C. Miller, wrote Rice:

> As you know, I do appreciate the problem you have been facing regarding minority scholarships, and I realize some of the frustrations you have met . . . I wish we could give you more positive information regarding monies that might be available but, frankly, I see the problem growing even more difficult as budgets begin to tighten. I also appreciate the fact that you would like to be able to talk about a certain percentage of minority enrollment at the University and, consequently, a certain percentage of scholarship funds that would be allocated to minority students. I can't help but say, however, that the

quoting of percentages is not only inappropriate but rather dangerous
for us. I am sure that with increased effort we can bring a larger number of minority students to our campus without quoting and using
definite percentage figures.[11]

While some of his colleagues thought Rice was demanding too much too
soon—and sometimes too arrogantly[12]—some of the leftist faculty thought he
wasn't pushing hard enough for change. One professor, Alan Gilbert, said Rice
had to be "the Uncle Tom dean." Gilbert was particularly disappointed when
John refused to step into a controversy over the firing of a black electrician the
university had discovered was unlicensed: "[Rice] went around telling black
people not to get involved in the debate."[13] John discovered that as a black leader,
he couldn't please all sides in newly integrated America. Invariably, some people
were going to think you should be more radical, while others were going to think
that you were already too radical. Rice ignored the criticism and went about
doing what he needed to do—some of it through channels in his official capacity
as assistant dean; a lot of it sub rosa.

While John was working inside the administration to bring more blacks to
DU, he set up an outside channel in the community. It would be a lesson in how
to operate—showing one face publicly and another privately within the black
community—that Condoleezza would remember when she became a college
administrator thirty years later. Given the political sensitivities of the times, John
knew DU would have to respond to pressure from Denver's black community,
and he ensured that there was always pressure. Sitting at his kitchen table, one
of Rice's allies, Dr. Fred Holmes, the first African American to run for mayor of
Denver, recalled, "We used to get together here and plan strategy to move the
university: number one, to recruit more black students; and number two, to treat
those there with respect and not like they were strangers."[14]

Rice, Holmes, and other black leaders choreographed each meeting the community leaders had with Chancellor Mitchell. One man would be assigned the role
of "pacifier," the responsible Negro who sympathized for the university's professed
constraints; another would play the angry black man, demanding immediate
reform; a third would vacillate between the two. "I think the chancellor used to
break into a cold sweat whenever he had to meet with us!" laughed Holmes. "Dr.
Rice was the one we would always feed information and get information

from . . . We would meet with him before and after." It's unclear whether Mitchell ever learned of Rice's role.[15] "John was too knowledgeable, too experienced, coming out of Alabama, to put everything out there with white people," said Holmes.

"He had a sly side to him," acknowledged Dr. Albert Fay Hill, the white Presbyterian minister who would recruit Rice to diversify the pulpit at Denver's tony Montview Presbyterian Church. Hill recalled a dinner with John and Ann Rice and Chancellor Mitchell where Mitch was holding forth on his many opinions on varied subjects. "Dr. Rice just had a twinkle in his eye. He knew what was going on. He did not ass kiss," said Rev. Hill.[16]

Outside his job at the university, John worked within the black community to recruit mentors for DU's black students so they wouldn't feel so isolated in Denver. In the summers, the Rices hosted barbecues where the black students could get to know the city's black leaders and one another. Like Westminster flop nights, there were hot dogs and hamburgers. "Ultimately, those few isolated black students came to form a very cohesive group," said Holmes. "Dean," as blacks universally called Rice, "taught black kids to never feel inferior," said Rogers McCallister, a fellow black Presbyterian. "He said that was half the battle."

But Rice wanted to do more than just help black students. Living in an integrated world for the first time, he realized just how little whites knew about blacks. To educate Denver's white student body, Rice created the Black Experience in America, the first course of its kind at DU. John considered the course "an attitude change class" explains Condoleezza Rice. "[He] was very aware that the University of Denver was a very privileged, very white university. . . . He had a sense that the black experience in America was shifting and changing. We'd come through the civil rights movement. We were now in the black power movement, and he wanted them to understand it."[17]

To that end, Dean Rice brought in black speakers—some of whom would be considered radical even today—hosting Lee Evans and John Carlos, the black Olympians who had raised their fists in a Black Power salute at the 1968 Mexico City Olympics. Two weeks later, he scheduled Nation of Islam leader Louis Farrakhan to speak on "black religion." He recruited Quincy Jones and civil rights crusaders Dick Gregory, Julian Bond, and Fannie Lou Hamer,[18] the sixth-grade-educated Mississippi sharecropper who had stood against the Dixiecrats at the 1964 Democratic National Convention and insisted to be seated as part of an alternate racially mixed Mississippi delegation.

Condoleezza attended many of the Black Experience lectures, including one by student radical and Black Power leader Stokely Carmichael. "One of the people I got to know very well was Stokely Carmichael," says Rice. "He was a good family friend. And you know, he was actually wonderful to be around."[19]

The Black Experience became so popular that the university expanded it to include a public lecture series. As a DU pamphlet put it, "This black-oriented seminar series is a continuation of the successful program instituted by the University of Denver and designed to bring the real story of the American Negro to the Denver community." Fittingly, the lectures took place in a classroom building on Race Street.[20]

Reflecting on the lessons he learned from Dean Rice, white left-wing political analyst Chip Berlet would write more than thirty years later, "He taught me about working for progressive social change and opposing institutional racism. He taught me that White people like me enjoyed privileges routinely denied to Blacks. He taught me that the proportion of Blacks serving in Vietnam was tied to economic and social policies at home. And he pointed out that along with this knowledge came an absolute moral imperative to act."[21]

John became a vocal critic of the Vietnam War. In 1970, when DU students organized the Woodstock West protest to observe the one-year anniversary of the Kent State and Jackson State massacres, Rice challenged the students, according to Berlet, "When tomorrow comes, will you be the perpetuators of war or of peace? Are you the generation to bring to America a lasting peace? Or did your brothers and sisters at Kent and Jackson State die in vain?"[22] A picture of Rice—solemn, impassioned, and imposing—reading the names of the DU community members killed in Vietnam sits in his folder in the university archives.

In Denver, Condoleezza watched as her father became an ever larger and more respected public figure, but that wasn't the focus of her attention. Her attention was concentrated on her rigorous workout schedule. She was up at 4:30 every morning for skating practice. "I was a noncompetitive competitive athlete. I was training, I was just terrible at it, but I was working really, really hard," remembers Rice.[23] She spent her mornings skating, then went to school, then usually straight home to practice the piano until bedtime. "It was nothing to hear her playing Beethoven and Bach until twelve, one, two, three o'clock in the morning," her father once told a reporter.[24]

As a result, Condoleezza was making few friends at St. Mary's. She accompanied the glee club and was on the debate club for a brief time, until she had to drop out because of her skating demands. "Between [skating] and piano, there wasn't much time for [anything else]," says Rice.

But there was time to excel in class. Despite the teacher's evaluation after reviewing Condoleezza's PSAT that she wasn't college material, she was proving herself to be better than most of her white peers. She became a state champion in Greek history, won a regional piano competition for young artists—which allowed her to perform with the Denver Symphony—and won a skating championship bronze medal in ice dancing.[25] "She was very self-assured," said Phyllis Bryant, a member of the Montview Boulevard Presbyterian Church, where Rice sang in the choir. "She appeared much older."[26]

In the midst of John trying to reshape the university and Condoleezza being an overscheduled child before the overscheduled child was an American archetype, Ann was teaching and tending to her family. John was right; the Denver public schools had their problems, but Ann persevered, teaching seventh-grade science to classrooms that were far more unruly than most of the segregated classes she had taught back in Alabama. Mrs. Rice was not a screamer, and she didn't seem to relish the role of disciplinarian; in fact, even in class, Angelena was reserved and refined, a Southern lady who would compliment even the boisterous students when they deserved it. Her most common reward was to say in her melodic, slightly high-pitched Southern accent: "You recite so beautifully." Her students would remember Ann most for that phrase—and because she taught "life science"—her lilting pronunciation of "SPY-ruh-GY-ruh."[27]

Outside her career, Angelena's major activity was keeping an immaculate home for Condoleezza and John. Ann had few friends, her intensely private life a sharp contrast to her husband and her daughter's outside activities. But her quiet existence was disrupted in 1970. When Condoleezza was fifteen years old, Angelena was diagnosed with breast cancer. "It's still an awful disease, but in those days, the treatment options weren't very good, and it was pretty awful," remembers Condoleezza.[28]

The entire Ray clan traveled to Denver for Angelena's surgery and her initial treatment. But Ann was determined to keep her daughter's life as normal as possible. So a day or two after her surgery, she sent her sisters and brother home; and the next day Ann, John, and Condoleezza went to a hockey game, as if their lives had not changed at all.[29] One again, thanks to her parents' commitment to making her feel protected and secure, for Condoleezza, it really hadn't. She would remember her mother's cancer as another lesson in how to be strong in the face of adversity: "She was tough as nails, and she not just survived it, I mean she completely overcame it."[30] After treatment, Ann appeared to be free of the cancer.

And yet, it must have been hard for her to send her siblings away so early in her recovery, not because she needed them to help her, but because she missed them so much. John was an adventurer, but it had been wrenching for Ann to leave the Rays behind in Alabama. Outside the family circle, she never had many friends—in Denver as in Alabama.[31] Indeed, during the Rices' two years in Tuscaloosa, three times a week, they had made the sixty-mile drive to Birmingham, John speeding up the Old Birmingham Highway, mostly to spend time with the Rays.[32] As their Tuscaloosa neighbor Geneva Williams put it, "They slept here, but they still *lived* in Birmingham."[33]

The outgoing Williams lived just two doors down on the Stillman campus from the small white clapboard house at 3 Geneva Lane where the Rices lived, but Ann never came to call. Instead Williams would call on Mrs. Rice, but after a few minutes of visiting, Ann would invariably call Condoleezza from her bedroom. "Play such and such number for Miss Williams. And I'd have to sit through a concert," said Geneva Williams laughing.[34] "Condoleezza and her mother lived a very closed life."

One of the trips to Birmingham each week was to take Condoleezza to her ninety-minute piano lessons at the Birmingham Southern Conservatory of Music. In 1964, she had been the first Negro student admitted. Rice remembers her father commenting as they left her audition, "Oh, she'll get in because they're probably just really glad that she didn't dance on the piano or something." At the time, Condoleezza didn't understand what her father was talking about: Why would anyone expect her to dance on the piano?[35]

In some ways, the Rices' most intimate world contracted in Denver even as their opportunities in the world outside greatly expanded. The Ray family had always been the biggest part of their social life, and the Rays weren't there. The other pole had been Westminster Presbyterian; their church in Denver, Montview Boulevard, was never the extended family that Westminster was. For one thing, there were at most ten black parishioners in a congregation of 3,600.[36]

Life under integration lacked the communal bonds that segregation had inadvertently created. Blacks and whites of Ann and John's generation didn't often form the kinds of interracial friendships that would become more common in Condoleezza's generation. As a result, the Rices' relationships with other blacks, who mostly lived far away from their home near the DU campus, were more distant than the tight-knit community they had known in Titusville. And their connections at Montview were cordial but bloodless, even though Condoleezza sang in the church choir—and even after Montview's pastor, Dr. Hill, asked John to join the pulpit in 1971 as a part-time associate pastor, the first black minister in the church's nearly seventy-year history.[37]

Housed in a regal Gothic cathedral in Park Hill, Montview Boulevard was one of the most prosperous churches in Colorado.[38] Dr. Hill, who had arrived in 1968, was not a timid man. A parachute demolitionist in World War II, a graduate of the liberal Union Theological Seminary in New York, and a former West Point chaplain,[39] he had come to Montview after being chased from New Rochelle, New York, by the mob. Hill had led a group of churchwomen in an effort to take down the local mafia and, with the help of the FBI, had largely succeeded. With a contract on his head (Hill carried a gun for a year), his wife implored him to take the offer that came from Montview.[40] Under Hill's liberal leadership, the congregation was swept up in the late-sixties zeitgeist and decided to diversify.

But John Rice wasn't Hill's first choice to integrate Montview's pulpit; he had interviewed two black ministers from Princeton and one from Union Seminary. The first two had higher offers elsewhere, and the third was too radical, Hill thought. "We were looking for someone who'd be . . . cool." And the diplomatic John Rice, who was socially conscious but not so radical he scared white folks, fit the bill.[41]

As an associate pastor, John assisted with the liturgy once a month and delivered the sermon once or twice a year.[42] But his most active role was in the extracurricular 49ers Contemporary Forum, a forty-nine-minute block between the 8 a.m. and 11 a.m. services when discussions or performances took place. More than once, Rice organized sessions examining the black experience in America, and Condoleezza played classical piano at one. "Holy moly!" said Hill. "She stood out as a child—like a bright light."[43]

Churches being reflective of their communities, Montview was not immune to the racial tensions of the times. The fight to desegregate the schools was roiling the city. "Some of my dear friends were 100 percent American [bigots]," said Hill. After a court order mandating busing was handed down in 1973, public school enrollment dropped by twenty-five percent as whites pulled their children out. Black students who went to formerly white George Washington High had to wait on their buses till the bell rang for classes to begin; authorities feared there'd be violence if the blacks waited outside for school to start.[44]

So it wasn't surprising that Hill took flak from some of his parishioners for inviting Rice to the Montview pulpit. And when he asked Allen Murayama, a Japanese-American, to become associate pastor in 1972, the meeting of the church's governing body grew heated.[45] "One man stood up and said, 'While we're at it, let's get rid of that black guy,' only he didn't say 'black guy,'" recalled Hill. Rice wasn't at the meeting, but he was aware of the tensions. "John handled it with aplomb. He was a man who could let it roll off his back. His life here in Denver was not always . . . " Hill's voice trailed off. "The big questions [about civil rights] had been answered, but the battles were still going on."[46]

Although Rev. Rice was happy to put himself on the front lines of integration, he was not going to let his family be either the targets of prejudice or integration's poster children. After services, the Rices didn't hang around to socialize. "John was very protective of his family," said Murayama. "He didn't want anyone to feel that because he was the assistant [sic] pastor, the family could be interrogated. They didn't have many friends in the church."[47]

What social life the Rices did have in Denver revolved around John's efforts in the black community: the barbecues for DU students and his attempts to recruit mentors for them. Though Condoleezza debuted at the Owl Club Annual Ball, the black social event of the season,[48] the Rices were mostly homebodies.[49] In fact, their social network was so limited that Condoleezza went to her high school junior prom at St. Mary's with her father's secretary's little brother.[50]

The Rices didn't even buy a home and plant roots; instead they lived in a succession of rented condominiums. John's Denver friends among the city's black leaders speculated that Rice needed his money to invest in Condoleezza. "They sacrificed everything for her," said Dr. Holmes.[51] A notion John's third wife, Clara, confirmed: "John said he turned his check over to Ann; everything was for Condoleezza."[52]

As a result, Condi—as she was increasingly known, having eschewed her father's nickname in favor of this one—lived a life of privilege rare for a middle-class girl. For example, three years after coming to Denver, her parents took out a loan to buy her a piano of her own, a $13,000[53] Chickering baby grand, when John was only making $16,500 a year.[54] In addition, the Rices were paying for private school, skating, and tennis lessons. The investment was paying off. As John was raising his game in the more complicated world of the University of Denver, Condoleezza was raising hers, too.

By the end of her junior year at St. Mary's, she had completed enough classes to graduate. Her parents wanted her to skip her senior year altogether, sparking one of the rare disagreements between John and Ann and their dutiful daughter. "I was adamant that I was going to finish high school," says Rice.[55] She was already two years ahead of everyone else, and she had a sense that senior year was a rite of passage.[56] So instead of leaving high school early, Condoleezza compromised. She enrolled at DU as a freshmen and completed her senior year in high school at the same time. Just fifteen years old, she went to her early morning skating practice, then to her college classes at DU; in the afternoon, she attended her classes at St. Mary's.[57]

"But frankly, by the time we got to senior prom, my life was in college," says Rice. "I'd joined a sorority, my friends were all in college, and I dragged this poor college boy to [my] high school senior prom. We stayed all of forty-five minutes. It was bad. I think he felt pretty out of place."[58]

In June 1971, Condi graduated fourth in her class from St. Mary's. Her yearbook picture presents a jarring contrast: While the other girls are fully physically mature, many wearing eyeliner, Condoleezza looks like a little girl, delicately holding a plastic branch of leaves, a ribbon across the top of her head, her embroidered collar floppy below her skinny neck.[59]

Nonetheless, Condi felt more at home in college than she had in high school. Even though she would suffer the first setback of her young life—at least most people would consider it a setback—young Rice took it surprisingly well, reflecting both her resilience and her detachment.

It happened the summer after her sophomore year at DU. Condi was attending music school at the Aspen Music Festival when she had a startling revelation about her abilities as a musician: "I wasn't even in the important part of Aspen. I wasn't even in the conservatory school. I was just in the piano school part, and these kids were unbelievable. They could play from sight things that had taken me all year to learn. I thought, *What are you doing? I think I'm going to end up teaching thirteen-year-olds to murder Beethoven or playing in a piano bar some place.* So, that's when I decided to change."[60] By change, she meant change the only long-term goal she had had in her young life: to be a concert pianist.

Condi's epiphany didn't surprise her piano teacher at DU's Lamont School of Music, Theodor Lichtmann. Years earlier, Angelena had called Lichtmann before Condoleezza started taking classes at Denver. "She said, 'I have this daughter who is very talented, and I want her to study with the very best,'" remembered Lichtmann. "I didn't tell her flattery gets you nowhere. [But] the opinion her mother had of her playing was much higher than it really was."[61]

Lichtmann said in his opinion, Rice was technically competent, but she was too detached emotionally to be a great pianist.[62] "To be a musician, you have to make someone else's thoughts and emotions your own. This is the same in music as in acting or dancing. I don't think she has that interest or inclination; particularly, taking someone's emotions, experiencing them, tearing them down, and building them back up. You have to be willing to be misunderstood, to be ignored."[63]

When it came to music, hard work and an iron will were not enough. In fact, to some degree, the qualities that had led generations of Rices and Rays to succeed even in the face of segregation were disadvantages; to play great music you had to *feel* it, and not just edifying or appropriate emotions, but the whole gamut of human sensation—despair and triumph, exhilaration and debilitation, fear and doubt, as well as confidence. And that was not how Condoleezza was raised. It was also not her personality. To be a great musician required not only discipline but disciplined abandon. And, as Lichtmann saw it, Condi couldn't let herself go.

That's why Professor Lichtmann wasn't surprised when Rice returned from Aspen and told him that she had seen children younger than her who were far more talented than she was. He already knew that. "Aspen, particularly then, was an extension of Juilliard," said Lichtmann. "The students were the top of the top."[64]

Lichtmann said Rice asked him, "Should I pursue this?"

"And I asked her, 'Do you have other interests?'"

Immediately, Condoleezza set about answering that question. In fact, finding a new major seemed to be her only reaction to the death of her dream of becoming a concert pianist. "I just remember feeling like, well, if I'm not going to do that, what is it that I'm going to do?" says Rice.[65]

Despite a life devoted to piano—from the age of three to seventeen—Condoleezza reacted with no visible emotion. Lichtmann said, regarding her career's abrupt end: "Some [students] are realistic; they decide, I don't have to walk on my elbows across corpses to do this."[66] Rice would later explain her dispassionate reaction by saying, "I don't do life crises. I really don't. Life's too short. Get over it. Move on to the next thing."[67]

It would become one of Condoleezza Rice's mantras, and she would restate it in one of our interviews. "Yeah, I don't do life crises . . . What's the point? You don't have that much of a life—life's not that long to spend a lot of time being obsessed with things that have gone wrong . . . I had to find a major—I knew what I had to do."

Few things better sum up both the strength and the detachment that the Rices and Rays had bred in Condoleezza. Music had not been a hobby for Rice; it had been her vocation. She had worked intensely on her skills as a pianist for most of her young years; endless practice was the one constant in her life other than her parents. And suddenly it was gone; and Rice's reaction, as a seventeen-year-old, was to soldier on. She had an emotional distance that allowed her to walk away from it without looking back. It was a rare dichotomy—to be both so intensely dedicated to something and yet sufficiently removed to abandon it without regret.

The root of Condoleezza's resilience was likely the unshakable confidence her parents had planted in her. So, even when she failed, she did not experience the failure as a personal reflection; she saw it merely as a fact of life. In fact, a few years earlier, Condoleezza had taken a similar moral from her short but intensely driven skating career: "What I learned is that you can have failures and keep going."[68] Later in life, she would also credit her faith in God and her belief that he has a plan for each of our lives as the reason that she accepted whatever happened in her life as his will.

"I've found I've done okay," says Rice, "You know, sort of trying to see what comes next and doing that well and thinking, *Oh, there are some things in life I'd love to do and, if they come along, that would be fine.* I'd love to do sports management at some point. I really am serious about that. I'd love to."[69]

Rice says the only effect her piano career imploding had on her was that when she became a professor, she would tell incoming students and their parents that they should not hew too closely to a preconceived academic or professional goal; it was okay to discover and rediscover oneself in college—just as she had done at Denver.

But another effect, whether merely coincidental or subconscious, seems to be that Condoleezza, over the course of the next thirty-five years, never again set a long-term goal for herself. That too would become a hallmark of Rice's career. In an interview, she said she'd never thought about whether her aborted piano career had anything to do with her aversion to long-term planning as an adult. "I don't plan very well. You're right. I tend to give in to serendipity an awful lot and take pathways that are before me. So maybe, maybe it had some effect, but that's that kind of deep psychological issue," she chuckles, "that I don't spend a lot of time thinking about—how it affected me that way."[70]

The same summer that Condoleezza had her epiphany about piano, John Rice was reaching new heights in his dream career: education. On July 1, 1972, Rice was promoted to associate dean of the College of Arts and Sciences."[71] It would not be the last time John and Condoleezza's careers in academia moved simultaneously in opposite directions. John was on a roll. After his first year at DU, his Black Experience in America course had been so highly regarded that the university had added "instructor, department of history" to his list of titles. Then in 1973, he was promoted to the new position of assistant vice chancellor for student affairs, "in order to assist in DU's Student Personnel Program and to coordinate counseling, financial aid, and work opportunity programs for disadvantaged and minority students throughout the university."[72] Henceforth, the black community would call him Vice Rice.

Both DU and the black community regarded him as a man who got things done, the crucial link between the two.[73] It had been a long climb from little Stillman College and even farther from Fairfield Industrial High School, but Rice was living his dream, turning his education-brings-opportunity sermons to the children of Titusville into action. In the process, he was transforming the university[74] and with it, potentially, the lives of generations of African Americans. It would be the pinnacle of his career.

He still had personal battles with the university: over salary,[75] expenses, and vacation pay[76] and especially over his academic title. DU eventually accorded Rice an adjunct professorship for teaching his popular course,[77] but the title carried neither the possibility of tenure nor professorial benefits.

Still, John kept working to improve the college experience of DU's black student body and the racial awareness of the entire university. At the university, he took up the concerns of black students, advocating for an ethnic studies major and university investment to create "the finest minorities library in the Midwest" to sustain it.[78] And beyond DU, he acted as a liaison between black parents concerned about the treatment of their children at Denver's newly desegregated public schools and Chancellor Mitchell, who sat on the board charged with implementing the court-ordered desegregation plan. Rice's efforts brought results; Mitchell wrote him in late 1974 to describe how he had taken the community's concerns about black students being harassed and tracked into low-level courses at formerly all-white schools to the board, and the board was changing their monitoring activities to address both problems.[79]

In addition, by 1975, John and Ann had essentially adopted the African American rookies of the Denver Broncos. He "became like our papa," former Bronco Rick Upchurch told the *Washington Post* in 2005. "He and Condi's mom would say, 'Come on over here, and we'll cook for you.' John told us how to carry ourselves as professionals, what we needed to do to be successful. He'd say, 'You're pros. The cameras will be on you. Don't get caught up in bad things and ruin your career. Get that education.'"[80]

In mentoring the NFL players, Rice was indulging two of his passions: guiding young people, which had brought him to Denver in the first place, and football.

After she dropped her piano performance major, Condoleezza did something she had never done before: She searched. She searched for a major and, after fifteen years grinding away at the piano, she searched for a direction. She tried English literature the first quarter of her junior year and "[hated] it." The second quarter, she tried government. "My project was to interview the water manager of the City of Denver. This was the most boring person [I'd] ever met in my entire life, and I thought, *Okay, this isn't it.*"[81] Then, in the spring quarter, Rice happened upon a class that changed the course of her life and, possibly, the course of history.

CHAPTER FIVE

REBIRTH

If I could wish one thing and do it over, the thing that I would do, in spite of all the
expectations of me and in spite of all the duties and responsibilities, would be to take a
little bit more time enjoying fulfilling them.[1]

CONDOLEEZZA RICE
Class Day Speech
Stanford University
June 1985

S
he was an eighteen-year-old black girl from Birmingham. He was a
sixty-four-year-old Czech immigrant who, after fleeing fascism and then
communism, had decided to hide his family's Jewish heritage even from
his children. But Condoleezza Rice and Professor Josef Korbel shared some surprisingly similar traits. Both had learned French and the social graces at an early
age. As children, their intelligence, ambition, and resolve had set both apart from
their peers, and as teenagers, both had been "quick-witted and opinionated."[2]
Most crucially, Rice and Korbel were products of families determined to dis-
prove majority cultures that believed them to be, at best, inferior and, at worst,
less than human. Josef's parents and grandparents had triumphed over anti-
Semitism the same way the Rices and Rays had gained education in spite of
slavery and Jim Crow: through an intense work ethic and a strong sense of self
and family.

Josef was born in 1909 in Galicia in modern-day Poland[3] and raised mostly
in what would become Czechoslovakia. His original last name was Körbel (pro-

nounced KER-bul). In September 1938, he was press attaché at the Czech embassy in Belgrade, Yugoslavia, when Britain, France, and Italy signed the Munich Agreement allowing Adolf Hitler to annex Czechoslovakia's Sudetenland region. The Czechs wanted to fight; but to avoid futile bloodshed, their president, who had only taken office the year before, acquiesced to the Europeans' betrayal.[4] Two weeks later, a letter arrived at the foreign ministry from the Czech Ministry of Defense: "Dr. Körbel and his wife are Jews."[5] Josef was fired.

Within six months, the Nazis had occupied the Czech capital, Prague. Körbel's name was on a list of Jews to be rounded up. For ten days, Josef and his wife spent their waking hours in cafés and restaurants and slept at a different friend's house each night—the Gestapo came at night—while their daughter stayed with relatives in the country. Two Yugoslav newspapers said that Körbel was their foreign correspondent, a lie that allowed the family to receive Gestapo permission to leave the country.[6] Just as the Nazi noose tightened, Josef, his wife, and his infant daughter escaped.

The threesome spent World War II in England, where they were baptized Roman Catholic and changed their name to the less Jewish-sounding Korbel (Kor-BELL). After the war, the Korbels returned to Czechoslovakia, and Josef was named ambassador to Yugoslavia at just thirty-six years old. But when the Communists in Prague toppled the elected president, the Korbels had to flee again. An Iron Curtain descended across Europe. With the help of friends in England and later the U.S. State Department, the Korbels found refuge in America, eventually landing in Denver.

Korbel's daughter Madlenka, whose name had been Anglicized in England to "Madeleine," would become the first female secretary of state. Madeleine Albright only learned of her Jewish heritage in 1997 when, sitting in the same office that Condoleezza Rice would one day occupy, a *Washington Post* reporter told her that more than two dozen of her relatives had been murdered in concentration camps, including her three grandparents who had been living when the Germans invaded Czechoslovakia.[7]

"Munich," as the agreement to cede Czechoslovakia's Sudetenland region to Hitler would come to be known, became an object lesson for generations of Europeans and Americans; by attempting to appease the German führer, London, Paris, and Rome had only whetted his appetite for conquest and postponed a war that would be far bloodier. As Winston Churchill noted, "The malice of the wicked [had been] reinforced by the weakness of the virtuous." And as a result, Josef Korbel's worldview had been personally tempered in the fires of the twentieth century.

By the time Condoleezza Rice walked into his class, Introduction to International Politics, in the spring quarter of her junior year at DU, Korbel—intense and cerebral—was the pipe-smoking embodiment of Old World refinement. Rice was immediately enthralled. She was particularly riveted by a lecture Korbel gave on the rise of Josef Stalin.

At the death of Vladimir Lenin, founder of the Soviet Union, in 1924, a battle had erupted between a fractious assortment of Communists battling for leadership of the party and the country. Initially, Stalin joined two other right-wing leaders to form a troika to prevent Lenin's number two, Leon Trotsky, from assuming Lenin's mantle. Over the ensuing years of political instability, with rare genius, Stalin engineered Trotsky's downfall. Then he swung left and eliminated the right-wing opposition, his former allies. In the end, Stalin emerged as the Soviets' supreme leader, though Lenin on his deathbed had said if Stalin ever rose to power, the Communist Revolution would be doomed.

For Rice, still searching for a major, it was "love at first sight."[8] "There was a deftness to Stalin's political maneuvering that was just kind of breathtaking," said Rice's longtime friend and fellow Soviet specialist Coit "Chip" Blacker.[9] "It's always been that combination of power and morality that I've found particularly interesting," Rice once told a reporter.[10]

Josef Korbel would play a critical role in Condoleezza's life; she called him her second father.[11] Despite being an unabashed liberal,[12] Korbel had initially refused to admit women students or hire female professors when he founded DU's Graduate School of International Studies. He believed they wouldn't get work in the academy or in government, so educating them at the graduate level was a waste of resources.[13] But by the time Rice met him, he was a fierce promoter of women, just as he had been of blacks and other minorities. And he would not be the last man so impressed by Condoleezza that in spite of deceptively dissimilar biographies, he took her under his wing.

Before Korbel's class, Condoleezza had only glimpsed the world of international power and intrigue while sitting with her father watching the nightly news, worrying over Castro's missiles. Now she was bathed in it: the history, the stakes, the leaders who determined the destiny of the world. She had discovered a passion to replace piano, one that she could delve into with the same discipline required to play a Brahms concerto. She changed her major to political science.

John and Ann had absorbed the disappointment of Condoleezza abandoning her musical career relatively well; they respected her decisions and knew that even at eighteen years old there was no point in arguing with her. Still, the Soviet studies gambit came as a shocker. "Condi is the kind of person who is very sure of herself and makes excellent decisions," said John later. "But political science? Here's the time for fainting. Blacks don't do political science."[14]

Of course, Condoleezza did lots of things that blacks didn't do—from figure skating to music camp. And John and Ann had largely been responsible; they wanted her to be extraordinary; and, as she became a woman, Condoleezza was no less committed to that goal.

More unusual than her new major was the area she chose as her concentration: the Soviet Union. The few blacks who studied political science generally concentrated on Africa, which in 1973 was in the process of emerging from four hundred years of slavery and colonialism to become a continent of independent nations. Rice explored instead the Soviet military: its relationship to its civilian masters; its links to the satellite countries of Eastern Europe like Czechoslovakia that the Soviets had forced, usually at gunpoint, to join their Warsaw Pact alliance. Condoleezza's obsession became the Soviet general staff and—the ultimate reason for studying the Soviet Union—the rivalry between the Superpowers.

The conflict between Washington and Moscow was the central drama of the post–World War II world, pitting totalitarianism against liberal democracy, communism against capitalism. The heart of the matter was power: who had more of it and what they would do with it. Power was also the central theme of the school of political thought that Rice quickly came to identify with: realism.

The father of realism, Hans Morgenthau, had reinvented the study of international relations with his 1948 book *Politics Among Nations*. Before Morgenthau, political scientists examined the past through diplomatic history and the present through international law. The former was a dismal analysis of esoteric facts and figures about diplomacy and war—"politics by other means";[15] the latter, a dry dissection of international treaties. Morgenthau went beyond history and law—which were limited in both what they could tell us about the present state of relations between nations and in their ability to predict the future. He distilled international relations to its elemental nature: "International politics, like all politics, is a struggle for power."[16]

Breaking with the idealistic notion most Americans held of their nation's place in the world, Morgenthau wrote, "All nations are tempted . . . to clothe their own particular aspirations and actions in the moral purposes of the universe. . . . There is a world of difference between the belief that all nations stand under the judgment of God, inscrutable to the human mind, and the blasphemous conviction that God is always on one's side."[17] An idealistic foreign policy that purported to know God's will was not only arrogant, according to Morgenthau, it was potentially disastrous, especially if it was morally right but politically a failure: "There can be no political morality without prudence; that is, without consideration of the political consequences of seemingly moral action."[18]

Morgenthau made international relations an immensely practical field: If you studied power and interests (what a state wanted), you could predict when states were likely to cooperate and when they were likely to compete; when they would ally and when they would war. Morgenthau's ideas gained such prominence in the postwar period that for Condi Rice's generation, he was not just one of many competing political theorists; he was alpha and omega.[19]

Rice's initial fascination with international politics was partly about people: Korbel and the stories he told[20] in thickly accented English at school and at home, where Condi was a frequent guest, made human the tragedy of Eastern Europe, where the actions of individual leaders had determined who would be free and who would be subjugated. But it was about power, too. Condi may have been a Southern lady by breeding and a classical pianist by training, but power had been a secondary theme running through her life—even her one truly leisurely pursuit, football, the game she loved from the age of four, was about breaking through enemy lines and gaining territory: "war without death."[21]

And, more important, Condoleezza had seen might battle right in the streets of Birmingham. She had seen with eight-year-old eyes white authorities corralling young Negroes into chicken-wire pens at the fairgrounds and Bull Connors's "irregulars" being trucked in with their sawed-off shotguns.[22] Martin Luther King was an idealist. He led Negroes into the streets of the Magic City to show the power of the supposedly powerless—not might but resistance. But by 1973, on Condi's trips back home to see her family in Alabama, it was clear what

King's hard-won victory had purchased in Birmingham: an unsatisfactory peace with uneven signs of black progress.

The Rices and the Rays were realists. They believed in real power, not moral suasion—particularly in individual power—whether Ann's repeated demonstrations of the power of her purse or Condoleezza's potential to become president of the United States.

Fate had landed them in an essentially amoral universe, where white police could kill Negroes with impunity and where Klansmen could bomb homes and churches without fear of justice. An idealist would have railed against the corrupt system or acted to topple it despite the long odds against success—as King and his followers did. But the realist maps out a plan to reach her goals in existing circumstances. And that's what both branches of Condoleezza Rice's family did; in the case of Granddaddy Rice, even changing his denomination from Methodist to Presbyterian in order to continue his education. Their realism empowered Condoleezza Rice's grandparents to overcome, at least within a restricted racist realm—just as a strategic sense of Realpolitik would allow John Rice to work from within the DU establishment to change it, with an accommodating mien to his white colleagues but a constant sense of purpose.

Both camps in Birmingham—the Rices and Rays on one side; King and Shuttlesworth on the other—believed the Negro should break the shackles of ignorance and despair. Both sides were fundamentally optimistic, faithful that one day, America would live up to her creed of liberty for all. But King, the idealist, believed the federal government and the white majority would grant Negroes their American birthright once the depths of injustice were exposed to the nation. For the Rices and Rays, the goal of understanding the white majority and the government was not to change them but to ascertain how within the context of societal realities to advance.

So, for example, her parents consciously prepared Condoleezza to take on the world however she found it. "My parents were very strategic," she told a reporter in 2001. "I was going to be so well prepared, and I was going to do all of these things that were revered in white society so well, that I would be armored somehow from racism."[23]

King sought to change the context in which all Negroes lived, to change reality itself. For the realist, reality simply was. The individual was primary, not the "community"; either the community would be uplifted in the process of thousands, millions, of individuals achieving their personal best, or it would be left behind. To realists that was not the focus of concern.

Of course, on this point, the Rices and the Rays differed. The Rays sought largely the advancement of themselves and their family, while the Rices sought more consciously the advancement of the race as well. The Rays, inspired by Daddy Ray, believed that in the end, you could only trust family.[24] They were a standoffish lot who saw themselves as distinct from—and in some ways, better than—the mass of their peers. "You're a Ray," Daddy Ray would say. The Rices were no more humble; they saw themselves as exceptional, too, but as educational evangelists, they saw their mission as the "upliftment" of the race—from Granddaddy Rice's founding church schools to John's work with young people to his sister, Dr. Theresa Love Rice's, missions to Africa. Their realism was tempered by idealism.

Take John Rice. It was not Rice's professions that demonstrated his idealism but his works. For instance, being a teacher or a preacher in John's age did not make a Negro an idealist; those just happened to be the professions most open to coloreds. Presumably, more educated blacks would have become CPAs or white-collar managers or joined other professions had they had the option—as they would a generation later. Rather, it was how John used his power that showed his idealism: to inspire young people to succeed—and to educate white America about the black experience, an endeavor worthwhile only to an idealist who believed he could change white attitudes.

Rice saw individual action as the route to collective empowerment for blacks: Realpolitik for the race. He viewed, according to his daughter, being able to register to vote the same way. He did what he had to do, without focusing on being forced to register as a Republican. An idealist might have felt humiliated or enraged at having to compromise his freedom to choose his party, but Rice made a pragmatic calculation: Some power was better than none. And what mattered was that he would get to vote.

In the ensuing decades after John moved to Colorado and then California, he never changed his party affiliation, though Angelena and the Rays were all Democrats. Rice had come to value his membership in the party, but not out of idealism or ideology. According to his widow, Clara, John cajoled Condoleezza to become a Republican long before she did because he believed "Republicans look out for each other and take care of each other. He was looking at it from the point of view of what was good for him and his daughter."[25] In other words, however it began, Rice's party affiliation became another practical calculation: Republicans took care of their own, so it was in his interest—and his daughter's—to be one.

Condoleezza would take John's lessons in personal and racial Realpolitik to heart and apply them throughout her life and career. She would tell the graduates of the University of Alabama in 1994, "As an educated person, you have tools to change your own circumstances for the better whenever you find them stifling and along the way to change the lives of others, too. But you have to believe— like many who had less reason to have faith in tomorrow but nonetheless did— that the locomotive of human progress is individual will. And then you have only to act on it, confident that you will succeed."[26]

Rice was sounding an idealistic note: "You have to believe." (Generally with realism, all you have to believe is that power matters: It's good to have it and bad not to.) But the quote's idealism is not of the King variety but her father's. The basic difference in the worldview of King and of Condoleezza Rice is that King believed if called, America almost miraculously would live up to the best in herself. Rice puts the power with the individual: "Individual will" is "the locomotive of human progress." It all came down to will, then power.

This is one of the few points about which Condoleezza Rice is an ideologue. She believes in the power of the individual to change his circumstances, whatever those circumstances may be—not to change the world, but to change his place in it. That belief would inspire Rice's views on discrimination, race, and gender. Along with her foreign policy views, it would also lead her to become a Republican—but a Republican who had a definite bent toward the libertarian side of the party rather than social conservatism.

So, Rice is "mildly pro-choice,"[27] emphasizing a woman's freedom to choose individually whether to have an abortion, though Rice personally has moral misgivings about the practice. Similarly, she supports affirmative action because she believes it leads to individual opportunity for individual blacks and other minorities to apply their individual will and succeed.

Rice does call herself a second-amendment absolutist. She believes that had there been a registry of gun owners, Bull Connor would have confiscated her father's arms, and John and his neighbors would have been powerless to defend their families against the night riders. The emphasis here is on both the right of the individual to bear arms and the importance of power. In Condoleezza's view, the only way to fight power is with power—and in some cases, firepower.

Decades after Denver, that concentration on power would become the dominant strain in Rice's public image, growing to such dimensions that it would eventually overshadow most everything else. Her private life would present a starkly different picture, but America and the world would never get to see that side of Condi. What they would see is what an African American colleague at Stanford would note about Rice in 2006. Initially, he observed in an interview that unlike many black conservatives on campus, Condoleezza Rice was not an ideologue. Then he paused and corrected himself: "No, she does have an ideology. An ideology of power."[28]

Back in her overachieving stride, Condoleezza earned her bachelor's degree from the University of Denver in 1974 at just nineteen years old. Though she still looked like a chubby-cheeked adolescent[29]—she had gained almost thirty pounds in her senior year after she stopped skating[30]—she was the most decorated member of her class. She had only become a political science major her junior year, but she received the Political Science Award, graduating cum laude and Phi Beta Kappa. In her college career, she had been a writer for the newspaper, a justice of the student government, a member of the Mortar Board honor society for women, and a sister of Alpha Chi Omega. At commencement, she was named Outstanding Senior Woman, and both Condoleezza and John received Pioneer Awards, presented by students to ten of their peers and two faculty members who had performed outstanding service to the community.

Just before winter quarter exams, Rice had played piano at a reception for members of the U.S. Civil Rights Commission. The Reverend Theodore M. Hesburgh, CSC, president of the University of Notre Dame, was one of the guests. Two years earlier, Hesburgh had presided over the admission of women for the first time in Notre Dame's 132-year history. The same year, President Richard Nixon replaced him as chairman of the U.S. Civil Rights Commission because of Hesburgh's criticism of the administration's civil rights record.[31] By 1974, Father Hesburgh was a force in higher education and an array of leftist causes. That year he published *The Humane Imperative: A Challenge for the Year 2000.*

Condoleezza impressed Hesburgh, a testament to her talent and presence; she would never become a world-class pianist, but she was a world-class performer, and Father Hesburgh joined a growing list of admirers. "I sat next to Governor Vanderhoof, who was greatly impressed and asked about you," wrote Chancellor Mitchell in a March 7 letter to "Miss Condoleezza Rice." "Since I'm *always* impressed, I wasn't surprised! Fr. Hesburgh phoned the other day and spoke with much admiration of your achievements. He said you visited at Notre Dame recently."[32]

A few months before her twentieth birthday, Condoleezza left her parents for the first time to attend the University of Notre Dame.

Rice was baking chocolate chip cookies in the kitchen of Lewis Hall, a former convent that had been converted to a dorm for graduate women, when Jane Robinett, a PhD student in American literature, walked in. Inspecting Rice's hockey pucks, Robinett asked, "What are you doing?" Condoleezza was baking the cookies as a thank-you for the guy who had helped her move in. Based on their mutual love of music—Jane played the violin—their protective parents, debate, and football, Robinett and Rice struck up a friendship that would still be strong more than thirty years later.[33]

Like many kids away from home for the first time, Condoleezza went wild— wild for a good Southern girl, anyway. She and Jane stayed out dancing till all hours and became football groupies. They debated whether to dress for breakfast based on whom they might meet in the dining hall. Condi learned to walk in platform shoes across Indiana ice. And on Friday afternoons, they drove Boris (Rice always named her cars) to go shopping downtown.[34]

It turned out Rice and Robinett shared a penchant for hunky football players. The men of the gridiron had qualities Condoleezza liked in a man. As Division I athletes—especially at football-crazed Notre Dame—they were highly disciplined; you didn't get to play for coach Ara Parseghian's Fighting Irish if you weren't. They practiced long hours and stayed physically fit. They were fun to be around, and they were strong. And football was a game of strategy, and Rice loved to talk strategy. Finally, gushed Robinett, "They're cute! They're beautiful physical beings."[35]

Wayne Bullock, the Notre Dame fullback who had helped Rice move her boxes into Lewis Hall, dated Condi for most of her first year at Notre Dame.

They'd go dancing or to dinner at the restaurants along the river or to basketball games. They'd rarely go to bars; although Rice drank, she wasn't really a drinker. Of course, Condi and Jane went to all the Notre Dame football games and met up with the boys afterward to go out. They even followed their men to the Orange Bowl in Miami, where Notre Dame was playing Rice's Crimson Tide of Alabama. After settling into the room they shared with three other women, all football-player girlfriends, they went hunting for the team. They found them, lying out by a hotel pool. "It was a like a Roman bath!" said Robinett. Since the teams were supposed to be sequestered before a game, and this was a *bowl* game, the girls beat a quick retreat after checking out the men.[36]

In the spring, Wayne, who was an undergraduate and still two years older than Condi, was about to graduate. As Robinett told the story, Bullock wanted to take his relationship with Condi to a more serious level. But Rice, only twenty, wasn't interested in a relationship that might lead to marriage. During a walk on campus, when Condi was supposed to let Wayne down gently, Rice's platform shoe broke, and she twisted her ankle. Bullock had to carry her back to Lewis, and the breakup didn't happen. "Poor Wayne Bullock really liked her a lot," said Jane.

But that wasn't the way it happened. It was Rice who wanted to get more serious. Only the part about spraining her ankle was true. The two eventually broke up, and Bullock was drafted by the San Francisco 49ers that summer.

Condi and Jane usually ate together in the dining hall—their football-player boyfriends didn't eat with civilians—but when Condi was alone, she ate at the black table; then like now, black students often self-segregated in the cafeteria. Sometimes Rice and Robinett integrated the black table together. Once when there was only one place left and Jane turned to walk away, defensive end Gene "Q.T." Smith made her "honorary Negro" and told her to sit down.[37] Condi had no problem "hanging black," and she wouldn't later in life either. But she had her standards, those she had inherited from her parents.

Angelena treated all the friends Condi brought home to Denver like honored guests. But it was clear she preferred some, like doctoral student Robinett, to others.[38] Always well turned out herself, Ann also kept a spotless home; it was her domain, and she was queen. She had impeccable manners and expected her guests to as well, even if they were three-hundred-pound linemen.

Condoleezza took that attentiveness to manners with her to South Bend, literally. On one trip back to school after Christmas break, according to another

Robinett story, Rice's traveling companion, another black Notre Dame student named Michelle, became deeply agitated about something or other and grew loud and animated. As other passengers started to turn to look, Rice reportedly told Michelle, "Don't act niggerish." Back on campus one night while Michelle, Condi, and Jane were hanging out with some black women undergrads, Michelle threw the incident back at Condoleezza.

Rice vigorously denies that she used the N-word or any variant of it. "I consider [the adjective] as insulting as the noun. So I would never use such a word. I would have probably told her—I don't remember the incident, but . . . I can imagine telling her don't act like an idiot."[39] The term "niggerish," while inarguably offensive, to Rice's parents' generation, particularly in the South, may have been an acceptable (if self-deriding) description of uncouth, unmannered conduct, especially in public. But Michelle, not surprisingly, according to Robinett, didn't appreciate it.

When Condi returned to Notre Dame for the second year of her master's program, she dated another football player: John "Dubie" Dubenetzky, a strapping blond running back. Unlike Wayne, Dubie was always willing to mix it up with Condi; she liked the give and take of argument.[40] She was also discovering that she liked bad boys, not sweet, sensitive guys, but men who were men. "She doesn't want to be adored," said Robinett. "She likes wit. And she likes a man who won't just say yes to her."

Of course, Condoleezza worked, too. She completed a two-year program in a year and half, earning her master's degree in international relations and economics in December 1975.[41]

After her year and a half of living dangerously, Rice returned to Denver. Once again, despite having "fallen in love" with political science, she was at loose ends. She had landed a job as an executive assistant at Honeywell, but before she could start as the girl Friday to one of the company's vice presidents, the company restructured, and her position was eliminated. She had lost her first job before she even started.[42]

So Rice did what generations of overeducated Americans have done: She applied to law school. In the meantime, she picked up her life where she had left off before moving to South Bend. She sang in the Montview choir, taught piano, and watched lots of football. Living back at home, she shared her parents' hospitality with the young black players of the Denver Broncos. And she started seeing Rick Upchurch, a fourth-round draft pick wide receiver who was just two years older than Condi. Upchurch, number eighty, was in his first season in the big leagues and becoming a fan favorite for his punt return game.[43] In his rookie season, he rushed for ninety-seven yards and made another 436 yards receiving.[44] The other NFL players named him 1975's Rookie of the Year. In his second season, he set an NFL record for punt-return touchdowns and went to the Pro Bowl.

Condoleezza was impressed. She had already wowed all the ball players who clung to John and Angelena's orbit by recapping their good and bad plays better than some of the men remembered them. She had never missed a Super Bowl since she watched the very first one with her father when she was thirteen. Condi was many guys' dream woman: attractive, charming, and a lover of football. But she was also John Rice's daughter. Most of the guys kept their distance, but apparently not Upchurch. (Robinett speculated that since Rice loved to flirt— "she flirted with Dubenetzky *all* the time"—that she and Rickie Upchurch probably kindled their relationship that way. With very few exceptions, Rice wouldn't comment on her personal life in our interviews.) Condi and Rickie started seeing each other, and soon things got serious.

Upchurch had had a much less idyllic childhood than Condoleezza. The second of eight children, he was born in Toledo, Ohio, and raised by his grandparents. When he was in the sixth grade, his grandmother died. Five years later, cancer took his grandfather, his "rock," leaving Upchurch to fend for himself.[45] With the help of two families, one black and one white, he made it to junior college and then to the University of Minnesota, where he majored in communications and became a football star.

He asked Condi to marry him, and she said yes. They never got as far as a ring and dress,[46] though Rice's Birmingham friend Deborah Carson swore they did.[47] Upchurch has never confirmed there were wedding plans. The relationship ended, Robinett said, because Rice had an epiphany—actually, one epiphany that led to a second. Condi and Rickie, according to Jane, passed in front of a church or synagogue, and Condi made a comment about religion. "It just went right over his head," said Jane, "and she knew [the relationship] wasn't going to work on an intellectual level."[48]

Jane and Condi agreed that though they were attracted to football players for their masculinity as well as their discipline and inner strength, a football player needed a cheerleader for a wife. And neither of them was a cheerleader.

It was the closest Rice would ever come to marriage. (Upchurch would later marry and have four children.)[49] But Upchurch wouldn't be the last pro football player Rice dated. Perhaps as she got older and took on ever more powerful positions, Rice—like many professional black women—found herself in a world with fewer and fewer black men. In 1976, black women were ten percent more likely than black men to attend college. (Thirty years later, black women would be earning degrees at twice the rate of black men;[50] and there would be nearly twice as many black women in Rice's age cohort, between forty and fifty-nine, with advanced or professional degrees as black men.)[51] And though Rice sometimes dated interracially, she preferred black men, according to her friends and family. And the NFL's ranks had plenty.

While Rice was on her unplanned sabbatical after Notre Dame, her old mentor Josef Korbel suggested she take some classes at DU's Graduate School of International Studies. When Korbel learned she planned to go to law school, he intervened in the only way the gentle, yet high-handed former diplomat knew how. He took Rice aside and said, "You are very talented; you have to become a professor."[52] For Korbel, it was that simple. "He was nothing but supportive and insistent, even pushy, about me going into this field," she later said of Korbel.[53] Rice had spent most of the past decade on college campuses because of her father's work, but she had never seriously considered an academic career. Nonetheless, Rice ditched law school—acceptances in hand from DU, the University of Colorado, the University of Michigan, and Notre Dame—and became a political scientist.[54]

She may not have been called to a career in international relations, but now that her course was set, Rice plied it with the same tenacity she had brought as a four-year-old to subduing "What a Friend We Have in Jesus" on the piano. In class, she was engaged and engaging. "I knew she would do very well . . . [though] it was unclear how far she'd take this," said professor Alan Gilbert, who later became a harsh critic of the George W. Bush administration.[55] Gilbert taught Rice Comparative Communism with Korbel; among the topics they covered in examining the historical development of different Communist regimes was the Molotov-Ribbentrop Pact. Korbel defended the agreement between Hitler and Stalin, which effectively allowed Hitler to invade Poland after he had captured Czechoslovakia without worrying about fighting a two-front war: one to the west with the European powers and one to the east with Stalin. Korbel defended the pact as another example of Stalin's strategic genius and his success in building the Soviet state. Though a staunch anti-Communist, Korbel pointed out that Stalin was the only leader who had pledged to defend Czechoslovakia against the Nazis at Munich and that the Communists had paid the greatest price in defeating Hitler in World War II.

Gilbert criticized the Molotov-Ribbentrop Pact from the left, arguing that it led to the surprise German attack on Russia in 1941 and that Stalin's strategy, aligning with fascists to protect Mother Russia from war, represented an abandonment of socialist ideals. "And here was Condi taking in this discussion," said Gilbert, "a spectrum of opinion among two professors that I doubt was ever duplicated in any English-speaking university [because it was so radical: one teacher defending Stalin and the other defending socialism]. Condi became quite sympathetic to how the Soviets played the leading role in World War II."

A passionate leftist, Gilbert taught Rice and her peers that they had to challenge authority and question conventional interpretations of history. In addition to history, he taught her political theory and Plato: "the Bloom translation, the Straussian neocon translation, which I made fun of," Gilbert emphasized.

For a year as a doctoral student, Rice followed "the Korbel plan," a year of independent study conducted closely with a faculty member that resulted in a long paper. Marrying her first love and her newfound passion, Rice chose music and the Soviet Union. Rice and Gilbert were very close, according to the professor; he said he would have been her thesis adviser if he hadn't taken a year off. Amazingly, Gilbert believed Condi was a kindred spirit: "I thought she was a radical, at least in sympathy. [Her interest] wasn't really Great Power realism. If I had to put her in a category, I'd say she was closer to Marxist."[56]

Gilbert's observation is jarring. It is possible that Rice did agree with some elements of the Marxist school of international relations, which held that economic interests determined events on the global stage, or that she thought the Marxist school held some useful tools for analyzing world politics. Or perhaps she merely cultivated the impression in her professor that she agreed with him in order to enhance their relationship. Or perhaps Gilbert was simply wrong.

The most important aspect of Gilbert's reflection is not whether Rice agreed with him but that he believed she did—because it is a surprisingly common refrain in Rice's career. Many of her former bosses or mentors (Gilbert, Brent Scowcroft, former Stanford University president Gerhard Casper) were convinced when Rice worked for them that she held the same worldview they did. And each, after she left his employ, was left scratching his head as he saw Rice make a 180-degree turn away from the core beliefs he thought they shared. Many of them would question whether she had actually identified with them when she worked for them or had opportunistically conformed to their opinions to advance her career or impress them. Or whether she had genuinely undergone some dramatic transformation that led her to alter her former opinions. "She did this with me and Korbel. She's doing it with Bush now," speculated Gilbert. "I don't think she doesn't believe [what she espouses]. But she believes what is in her interest and what advances her."

Another reason Gilbert may have thought that Rice was at least a sympathizer with radical political causes was that her years as an undergrad and a doctoral student were the peak of what might be called Rice's black consciousness, at least in a conventional sense. It was also the peak of the country's awareness of black issues. The King assassination, the subsequent urban unrest, the rise of Black Power, and an unselfconscious black nationalism had led to the greatest awareness of black identity and demands for equality perhaps in modern American history.

It was a full decade after the Civil Rights and Voting Rights acts, and America was moving beyond simply ensuring blacks' ability to vote. More years than not in the 1970s, the Supreme Court handed down rulings that supported busing, affirmative action, and color-blind housing practices. Popular media were filled with depictions of the Negro condition and the fight for opportunity. And affirmative action, which aimed to uproot the institutional racism that had barred blacks from most jobs, was in vogue. From the rarefied world of private schools and universities to corporate boardrooms, previously lily-white institutions were tripping over themselves to open wide the gates of opportunity. And outside the mainstream, blacks were demonstrating their newfound race pride, declaring "Black is beautiful!" and demanding ever-greater progress ever faster. The zeitgeist didn't escape Condoleezza. "When you're black and female, you have to work twice as hard," she had said in a DU recruiting brochure.[57]

She was speaking from experience. In her freshman year, Rice had sat in a lecture hall when out of the blue came an attack on blacks. The professor was explaining the theories of William Shockley, a Nobel Prize–winning physicist who considered his most important work to be his study of "dysgenics," the negative effect on the population of supposedly less intelligent races, particularly blacks, reproducing faster than whites. Shockley's theories were widely criticized for being unscientific, and they forever tarnished his reputation—as a path-breaking physicist, he had brought the silicon to Silicon Valley, founding what became the $130 billion semiconductor industry. (After winning the Nobel Prize, he accepted an appointment at Stanford in 1963.)[58]

But Condoleezza's professor supported Shockley's racial theories, prompting Rice to rise to her feet. "I'm the one who speaks French," she argued. "I'm the one who plays Beethoven. I'm better at your culture than you are. This can be taught!"[59] In other words, she was proof that Shockley was wrong; if blacks could be taught all the aspects of "white" culture, then there was nothing inherently superior in white genetics.

But Rice's black consciousness was also notable for what it was not. It was not a global, tribal identification with black people. Her defense was an intellectual argument rooted in particularity; through expressing her individual excellence, she was a testament to the race's abilities. It was not based on the Black Condition, à la W.E.B. DuBois, or grand pronouncements that blacks were equal to whites, but on an objective provable fact: Blacks could perform as well as whites. True to her "home training," Condoleezza saw herself as an individual. But her race was not separate from that individuality; in fact, her uniqueness was a service to her race.

And her race was also a service to Condoleezza. There were few African American women getting PhDs in the late seventies/early eighties and hardly any earning them in the study of the Soviet Union. That gave Rice an advantage in the race for predoctoral fellowships ("pre-docs") to study outside DU. In 1980, she won such a fellowship from the Ford Foundation[60] that made her free labor for any school that would take her. Rice wrote to the best arms control programs in the country, including Stanford and Harvard. Harvard didn't write back.[61]

Perhaps Rice's letter, written on pale blue stationery embossed with CONDOLEEZZA RICE in gold letters across the top, didn't impress Harvard. Or perhaps the old-world grace of a handwritten letter—in 1980—was lost on the dons along the Charles River. But Chip Blacker, the assistant director of Stanford's Center for International Security and Arms Control, was intrigued from the moment he opened the envelope. Few graduate students had their own personalized stationery, and unlike the letters from most, which ached of desperate flattery, Rice's was well argued and unsentimental. More than the candidate's race or her gender, noteworthy though they were, Blacker was struck by her age. "It was pretty clear she was on some type of a fast track because she was significantly younger than she should have been . . . There was a quality bar that she cleared long before anyone thought through . . . 'she's female, and she's black,'" he said. "That came like an afterthought."

Blacker called a friend on the Ford Foundation's selection committee. He was unequivocal; Stanford should snap Rice up. Even before that endorsement, Rice had made a friend in court. She was a master networker. She didn't have a five-year plan she was working toward; instead she believed, largely thanks to the faith in predestination that Presbyterianism preached and the unshakable faith in herself that Ann and John Rice had nurtured, that there was no point in setting long-term goals—her aborted career as a pianist showed her the futility in that—and she handled setbacks that would have crushed others by learning her lesson and moving on. She tackled the task at hand and subdued it; she believed she would end up wherever God wanted her to be.[62]

In this case, he may have had a little help from her fans. Alexander George, who was influential on the Stanford faculty, had met Rice at the International Political Science Association's first meeting in Moscow in the summer of 1979. George told Blacker that Rice was phenomenal. Rice's old professor Alan Gilbert telephoned Nannerl Keohane, a professor of political theory at Stanford he had befriended; Gilbert gave Rice a ringing endorsement. Korbel, who had died three years earlier, may have helped his protégé as well; he had likely mentioned her to his friend Jan Triska. Triska, who fled Czechoslovakia the same year as Korbel after the Communist coup, was a member of the political science department, too; and Rice certainly mentioned Korbel's impact on her career when she went for her interviews at Stanford.

Rice liked Stanford as much as Stanford liked her, so she signed on for a year as a pre-doc while she ground out her dissertation on the relationship between the Soviet and Czech militaries. Then, at the end of the 1980–81 school year, she made a move that, as former Stanford president Donald Kennedy put it, "in academic circles was unusual enough to be extraordinary." Rice was hired to be an assistant professor at Stanford starting in the fall of 1981 as a freshly minted

PhD. It was a joint assignment to the arms control center. "Very few people go from a doctorate at the University of Denver to a first-class research university," said Kennedy. "It was a product of [Condi's] set of extraordinary talents."

It was also a function of her race and gender. Stanford didn't need another Soviet specialist; they had three of the most renowned in the world. When he offered her the job, political science department chairman Heinz Eulau told Rice she was an affirmative action hire. If she survived the three-year probationary period and eventually came up for tenure, Eulau said in his stern German accent, "only thirty percent [of assistant professors] get tenure. And it will not matter to us one bit how you came here or what color you are or what gender you are; you'll have to win it on your own."[63]

"Fair, absolutely fair," said Rice.

But on her merits alone, Condi hadn't made the cut. No one doubted that she was smart enough to be a junior faculty member, but if she had been twice as good, race and gender would not have had to enter into the decision. Instead, those "after-thoughts" had tipped the scales in her favor. Was the contradiction between her supreme self-confidence and being hired as an affirmative action case unsettling?

Not for Rice. "I didn't understand what was really going on," she would say twenty-five years later. "[I] vaguely probably understood that they didn't usually find their faculty at the University of Denver and vaguely understood that there was something unusual about this process. But I was also twenty-six years old and taking the job offer at face value—and I knew I'd given a terrific job talk."[64] Rice had given her job talk—part colloquium, part interview, part thesis defense, and part lecture explaining her academic research—before the entire political science department. "I knew it was really good."

There was no room for a sense of inferiority or doubt in Rice's conscience, even at the moment that she was judged less than perfect. "I've always said I can't go back and re-create myself as a white male . . . As long as I'm not ever asked to do anything that I'm not capable of doing or competent to do, I'm not going to worry about other people's motivations for [offering me opportunities]."[65] And for many proponents of affirmative action, including Rice, her case embodied exactly how such programs should work: providing qualified minorities the opportunity to prove themselves.

When Alexander Dallin, one of the political science department's Great Men of Eastern European Studies, hosted a reception the next fall, newly arrived

Condoleezza Rice stood out. "A lot of assistant professors are geeky and a little bit unworldly, and she wasn't," said history professor David Kennedy, who had just become associate dean in the School of Humanities and Science[66] and responsible for overseeing political science. "To meet a twenty-six-year-old assistant professor who had that much poise and self-possession was pretty unusual . . . She had a very self-confident manner without being overbearing or arrogant."[67] Rice's intelligence and energy—she was rarely seen without her trademark smile—came through so strongly that the chairman of the department asked her to teach a class with him, a way of socializing a rookie professor but also a high compliment.

In the space of just nine years, Rice had successfully remade herself from an aspiring pianist dedicated to a life on the concert stage—until her father convinced her otherwise, she had been planning to apply only to Juilliard for college—to a counter of nuclear missiles. She had risen from the student-daughter of an administrator at a regional university to the ranks of one of the most prestigious faculties in the world. And she had done it all without a hiccup of doubt or trepidation. She was the incarnation of the American dream, but also of the distinctly American act of reinvention.

John and Angelena deserved a lot of the credit, but her upbringing alone couldn't entirely explain Condoleezza's rise. "Lots of us are raised with empowering parents," said Blacker, who would become Rice's closest friend. "Through some mechanism that I don't think any of us, including Condi, fully understands, she managed to grow to adulthood without any real sense of limitation, cognitive or otherwise, so that when [opportunities] presented themselves—appointment to the faculty when she was twenty-five, Brent Scowcroft offering her the job at the NSC when she would have been all of thirty-four, being provost at thirty-eight, or national security adviser [at forty-six]—those doubts that most of us have [weren't there]. With Condi, it's almost never a question of, should I do this or do I have the ability? It's, do I *want* to do this?"[68]

David Kennedy witnessed that unbridled self-confidence again and again in Rice's early years at Stanford. The deans met regularly to discuss issues surrounding junior faculty: who was having problems; who was a rising star that the university had to make sure it didn't lose to the competition. "Every year, the question would come up, 'What about Condi Rice? She's doing so much: She's speaking off campus, she's on this committee and that committee' . . . We tried to protect the assistant professors and keep them out of [nonacademic commitments] so they could build their core professional credentials," meaning academic research and publishing, said Kennedy.[69]

Each year, Kennedy dutifully mentioned the deans' concern to Rice, telling her that while everyone was very proud of her, many senior faculty were concerned she was spreading herself too thin. Her response, put as graciously as possible, according to Kennedy, was, "Look, I'm single, I don't have a family. I don't envision having a family in the near future. My career is my life. I can manage it, thank you very much."[70]

At one of the deans' meetings, a colleague sharply challenged Kennedy, pointing out that Rice wasn't making adequate progress in her academic career; she was taking longer to publish her first major book than she should. (She would publish *Uncertain Allegiance: The Soviet Union and the Czechoslovak Army*, based on her dissertation, in 1984.) Kennedy's equally pointed response: "Whatever the pace or mix of things she's doing, this woman has success just stamped all over her. You can't be with her and not know this. And maybe it won't be a conventional success, but the fact is she has got her life under control." This proved to be the case.[71]

While Condoleezza's career in academia was just taking off, John Rice's was crashing. By the early eighties, his supporters at the University of Denver had left. The atmosphere surrounding racial issues and the plight of African Americans was also changing—with the exception mostly of elite schools like Stanford and Fortune 500 companies that saw affirmative action as a business imperative in an increasingly diverse nation. The election of Ronald Reagan in 1980 had been a watershed. Reagan ran on an anti–affirmative action platform and preached against "welfare queens" whose poverty was not the result of discrimination past or present but of their own indolence and greed. Soon affirmative action would be under full-scale assault. The national mood had shifted, from seeking to root out oppression to asking why blacks couldn't take care of themselves; less than twenty years after King had gone to Birmingham, the "post–Civil Rights era" was at hand.

In light of changing priorities and tightening budgets, John Rice was demoted after his benefactor, Maurice "Mitch" Mitchell, left the chancellorship to become head of the Center for the Study of Democratic Institutions. It was perhaps fitting that Rice's own end was tied to Mitchell's. Mitchell had personally recruited him in 1968. All that seemed very long ago by the time Mitchell left in 1978 to head the center. Controversial from its inception as a liberal think tank to combat McCarthyism and congressional laxity in the face of its abuses, the center became an anchor of the New Left, dedicated to safeguarding democracy against official excess. Later, it took on the causes of peace, poverty, inequality, and the environment. Shortly after Mitch agreed to lead the center, its inability to raise funds led to the center being absorbed by the University of California at Santa Barbara.[72]

Rice, one of Mitchell's great DU legacies, would soon be gone, too. In April 1978, then vice chancellor Rice had been granted an appointment for the next school year at an annual salary of $28,760;[73] $23,364 came from the university resources budget and $5,396 from the arts and sciences budget for Rice's Black Experience seminar.[74] Less than a year later, Rice had been downgraded to a "senior consultant" for student development.[75]

The '78–'79 school year had heaped insult upon indignity. Under the new regime of chancellor Ross Pritchard, Rice's every action was scrutinized. Outside his job, the university scolded him for not paying his and Angelena's delinquent student loans.[76] At work, they insisted that every expense he submitted for his course had to be signed by a superior.[77] By the end of the academic year, university officials had even cut his paltry pay for teaching the course from $5,396 to just $3,000. When Rice complained, dean Ken Purcell wrote back that an investigation "not tied to any specific individual" determined that three thousand dollars was appropriate compensation for part-time teaching.[78]

Condoleezza watched—first as a doctoral student at DU and then from Stanford—as John endured his fights with the new administration. "His disagreement with the chancellor was because he actually challenged the chancellor," says Rice. She can't remember what the particular issue was. "[My father] just thought that the guy was flaky . . . He, very early on, didn't think this chancellor was going to work out, and my father was not one to keep his mouth shut." And in Condi's view, that led to John's troubles.[79]

John had always wanted tenure, but even under Chancellor Mitchell, the departments wouldn't grant it to him. Now he was paying the price. By the following school year, he was back to using his Reverend title in his official university correspondence, back to where he had begun his professional life thirty years before. He was DU's director of religious services. (Some memos from the administration referred to John as Dr. Rice;[80] he had received an honorary doctorate from Chicago State University in 1976.)[81]

Then, in the spring of 1982, the usual reappointment letter never arrived. Instead, on May 20, dean of student life Robert Burrell called Rice into his office. The religious services program was being "phased out." By the end of the '82–'83 school year, the University of Denver would no longer require John Rice's services.

The next day, Burrell sent Rice a letter that was marked "Personal and Confidential." It presented the former vice chancellor of the University of Denver an ultimatum.[82]

> Option 1: Continue as Director of Religious Services for the full 1982 fiscal year on a half-time basis at an annual rate of $14,500. On June 30, 1983, the position would be terminated.
>
> Option 2: Continue as Director of Religious Services on a full-time basis for six months from July 1, 1982, until December 31, 1982, at an annual rate of $29,000 ($14,500 gross for six months). On December 31, 1982, the position would be terminated.

After a decade and a half of service and only four years short of his regular retirement, the university did not even extend the courtesy of time. "As you know, I will be leaving the campus on May 28, 1982," wrote Burrell. "I would like for you to indicate to me before that date which of the two options you prefer. I want to have this completed prior to my departure." Rice was fifty-eight years old. Ann was teaching science at Gove Junior High School.[83]

The usual legal wrangling ensued, with Condoleezza advising her father each step of the way how to protect himself. John's lawyer John Birkeland's opening bid included a request for three years salary as severance; an arrangement to "continue Dr. Rice on the rolls of the university staff in some nominal capacity until his normal retirement age of sixty-two; use of an office and telephone at DU until he could find other employment; continued health and life insurance benefits; and continued use of the university library."[84] In the end, Rice received $14,500 in exchange for leaving the university at the start of the 1982–83 academic year. The university agreed to pay him $9,500, roughly a third of his annual salary, for the next three years.

On September 30, 1982, vice chancellor Tom Goodale wrote Chancellor Pritchard: "I am pleased with the settlement we have made, and I believe this represents the best of all possible solutions."[85]

It certainly did seem that way to Rev. Rice.

Condoleezza said her father, in the end, did "all right. I mean, they were not unhappy to have him leave in a way that was not going to have him sue the university and expose it. So he did all right. But it was really sad. And for a while, he was pretty bitter about it because . . . this [new chancellor] had come out of nowhere, and [my father] had really been loyal to the university. But he couldn't have stayed there; there was just no way. He had no respect for the chancellor.[86]

"Unfortunately for my father, he left . . . and then the chancellor, I think, left two years later, with the university pretty much in ruins," said Rice.

In the coming decades, Condoleezza would do her best to make sure her father's legacy at DU was honored; when the alumni association awarded her its highest honor, she said she would accept only if, when her picture was posted with the other Evans Award recipients, John's was, too.

Her father's summary termination may have reaffirmed the lessons Birmingham had already taught Condoleezza. Righteousness in the absence of real power was practically meaningless. Rice would advise her future protégés never to rely on institutions, even one on whose behalf you have mightily labored.[87] As Hans Morgenthau had written, power was everything.

CHAPTER SIX

STAR

I believe (and this is a hunch and I guess if we did this that I would spend
a lot of time in church praying that I was right) that the Soviets would not
even threaten the Germans. Within six months, if events continue as they are going,
no one would believe them anyway.[1]

CONDOLEEZZA RICE
National Security Council Memo
January 12, 1990

S tanford's search for its next president had been conducted with more
secrecy than a National Security Council meeting. The candidates could
be counted on two hands; they were mostly well-known professors who
held a wealth of administrative experience, high-fliers likely on their way to top
positions at their current schools. As a result, the selection committee members
were forbidden to tell even their spouses where they were traveling, lest word
escape that a member was going to a certain city, which would lead the searching
minds of academia to deduce who they were going to see. Since cell phones were
not yet ubiquitous, committee members were presented with sealed envelopes to
give their families—to be opened only in an emergency—containing the number
where they could be reached.

In February 1992, four members of the search committee flew to interview
University of Chicago provost Gerhard Casper. Meeting at a restaurant was out of
the question, not to mention Casper's office on campus. Instead, history professor
James Sheehan, trustee George Hume, assistant dean of students and director of

Stanford's American Indian program Jim Larimore, and Condoleezza Rice went to Casper's Hyde Park home. The stated purpose of the visit was to gather information, not conduct a job interview: What did Casper think were the most important issues facing higher education, what were the crucial issues facing Stanford, and who did he think were the best candidates to assume Stanford's presidency?

Almost immediately, Casper turned the tables on his guests, peppering them with questions about the dismal state of their school. The federal government had accused the university of essentially stealing. The issue was so-called indirect costs, the funds that accompanied research grants to pay for professors' incidental research expenses, like lab space and electricity. Washington alleged that Stanford was misrepresenting the extent of its indirect costs in order to pay unrelated bills. The scandal had forced the resignation of president Donald Kennedy, sullied the university's reputation, and threatened to undermine its credibility with funders.

And that wasn't the only crisis. A 1989 earthquake had caused damage that would take ten years and $250 million to repair.[2] The *Wall Street Journal* editorial page had been on a virtual jihad against Stanford's humanities core curriculum. The course, required of all freshmen, had been called Western Culture until student activists in the eighties, arguing it privileged the study of "dead white men" to the exclusion of women and people of color, forced a change to a more inclusive course called Cultures, Ideas, and Values (CIV). The *Journal*, following the lead of University of Chicago intellectual Allan Bloom, whose 1987 jeremiad *The Closing of the American Mind* had been a best seller, repeatedly portrayed Stanford as the center of the "political correctness" movement debasing American higher education and threatening honest inquiry. The debate had gained Stanford national notoriety, but not of the sort universities coveted.

To save Stanford, the board of trustees had given fifteen members of the university community—trustees, faculty, staff, and students—the supreme responsibility of finding the next president.

Casper's inquisition was made all the more fun because he had no intention of going to Stanford. But he was struck by the frankness of the search committee; no one had any illusions about the seriousness of the problems Stanford faced or how hard the next president would have to work to fix them. One committee member was particularly impressive in accessing Stanford's liabilities and assets: Condoleezza Rice. When Casper finally accepted the job, after months of more meetings, he said Rice had played a major part in turning him around. "I was very impressed by not only how quick Condi was on the uptake, how quickly she understood if something bothered me or what seemed to be behind a certain question [I asked], but also how straightforward she was in dealing with the issues."[3]

That Rice had been asked to join the search committee was a measure of the respect she had won in a decade at Stanford. She had been granted tenure in 1987 in a relatively smooth review,[4] despite the concern of some members of the committee that her résumé was longer on university committee work than academic writing. She had gained a reputation as an excellent teacher, receiving superlative reviews from students and winning two teaching awards.[5] And the university had encouraged the political science department to move along her tenure case because Harvard had come to its senses and was wooing her,[6] as were Yale and Columbia and MIT.

By the time Casper met Rice, she was almost universally liked and admired on campus. But the most remarkable thing about her was that she had helped end the Cold War.

Condi had assimilated to Stanford like sugar dissolving into hot tea. The university's blend of Western individualism, academic excellence, and emphasis on cultivation of the whole person—intellectual, physical, and social—was ideally suited to a pianist–figure skater–football fan turned Sovietologist. (With more Olympic athletes than any other top-rated university, the well-rounded scholar-athlete was a cliché at Stanford.) If Titusville's black middle class had planted the seeds of her success (a superior sense of self, a redoubtable ability to see the world as she needed to see it rather than as it was) and Denver had given her a new passion, it was at Stanford, among the foothills and the sandstone arches, that Rice grew into a leader.

The eighties had been an enchanted time for Rice. Normally a "baby professor" concentrated on getting tenure, focusing on research and publishing. But unlike most junior faculty, Rice seemed free of self-doubt or worries about what she *should* be doing; she took opportunities as they presented themselves. She did long fellowships at the Council on Foreign Relations and the Hoover Institution. She joined university committees on admissions and athletics. She was always moving forward as if, like a shark, she would die if she stopped. Only she seemed to be aiming for no specific goal. She was ambitious with no particular ambition. And yet instead of appearing restless, she exuded a calm confidence.

As a teacher, she entranced her students. As a colleague, she delighted her peers. The university administration was so captivated by the young professor that President Don Kennedy frequently dropped by her office to say hello[7]—not a normal occurrence in the life of a twentysomething assistant professor.

Her social life was equally full. At the end of her second year at Stanford, Rice first met Randy Bean at a reception for junior faculty and journalism fellows. Bean had been a reporter with Bill Moyers in New York. But it wasn't until she returned to Stanford the following year as a freelance contractor for the arms control center that Rice and Bean bonded. They were neighbors in the warren of offices in Galvez House, and Rice and Blacker were the only people close to Bean's age. Condi and Randy's first bond was a love of sports. But they quickly discovered an even deeper link: their closeness to their fathers, both of whom were preachers, Rice's Presbyterian and Bean's Episcopalian. "Our fathers were our primary parent," said Bean. "[Condi] loved her mom, too . . . but our dads were it! We would throw ourselves in front of a train for them."[8]

They swapped tales of going to their first football games and stories about meeting their favorite players. In the fall of 1982, they bought season tickets to Stanford Cardinal football and basketball, and in the ensuing twenty-three years never relinquished them. "And damned if she's not making me pay for them the whole time she's gone!" laughed Bean. (In the summer of 2006, as Stanford renovated its stadium, eliminating a quarter of the eighty thousand seats, Bean, for the first time, would invoke Rice's name to keep choice spots. "Someday the secretary of state is going to be back. You don't want her sitting in the end zone, do you?")

When Condi was on campus, she and Randy went to every home football game and most home basketball games. They traveled to NCAA championships when Stanford qualified and followed Cardinal football to away games up and down the western United States, as well as all Stanford bowl appearances. (They were so football crazy that Bean once had a boyfriend who called himself a football widower.) And every summer, the twosome would troop off to New York for U.S. Open tennis. Intensely competitive, between the annual tourneys, they played vicious tennis of their own.

But for all that united Bean and Rice, as much divided them—especially their politics. Randy was a true-blue Democrat who had stumped for John F. Kennedy as an eleven-year-old. Rice was a newly minted Republican with the passion of the converted. Condi had voted for Carter in 1976 in her first presidential election. But she was disgusted by his naïveté toward the Soviet Union.

The Cold War had endured for more than a generation. If the United States waged the twilight struggle successfully, it would contain the Soviets within their rotting military dystopia; if America looked weak, the Russians' expansionist ideology would lead them to encircle the world's democracies. The worst-case scenario was that Russian adventurism in the Third World or opportunism in Eastern Europe or Germany—or a simple miscommunication between Washington and Moscow—would result in World War III. After the U.S. loss in Vietnam while Rice was in college, demonstrating American resolve was more important than ever.

Yet when the Soviets invaded Afghanistan in 1979, Carter had said he was "shocked" Moscow had not kept its word. Rice, just twenty-nine years old, was flabbergasted. As a realist, she knew that strength mattered, not promises. And as a student of the Soviet Union, she knew that Moscow was deceitful, duplicitous, and deadly calculating.

On his vow to confront the Soviets and restore American military preeminence, Rice voted for Ronald Reagan in 1980. Two years later, she changed her party affiliation to Republican. "I was attracted to Ronald Reagan's strength," Rice told a reporter in 2000. "Then my political views developed in favor of smaller government. It was the constitution and foreign policy, not social issues, that drew me to the Republican Party."[9]

But what she viewed as the Democrats' condescending attitude toward minorities confirmed her decision. Watching the Democratic convention in 1984, she was repelled by their appeals to blacks on the grounds, she argued, that they were hapless victims. It was the perception of blacks—and especially of herself—she loathed most.[10] Weakness to Condi was unacceptable. Yet speaker after speaker at the convention nominating Walter Mondale talked about "women, minorities, and the poor, which basically means helpless people and the poor," Rice told the *Washington Post*'s Dale Russakoff seventeen years later—"still fuming," as Russakoff put it—"I decided I'd rather be ignored than patronized."[11]

The ultraliberal Bean saw that exasperation as precisely Rice's problem: She couldn't empathize with those less fortunate than she was. "Somebody would be bellyaching about being black and victimized, and she would just get crankin'," said Bean. "I'd say, 'You overcame. You did it. But not everybody did. And you can't judge those who didn't, who either didn't have the parents, didn't have the head start, didn't have the love, didn't have the church . . . or got hurt somehow, got left behind. Not everybody's you!'"

The irony was obvious. Bean, who had grown up white and upper middle class in Montclair, New Jersey, trying to educate Rice, a black daughter of Jim Crow Alabama, to the limits that impeded millions of Americans from fulfilling their ambitions. "It used to bum me out," said Bean. "I'd say, 'This is something you should just *know*.'"

But what some would come to judge as Rice's distance from the plight of many African Americans flowed from the same source as her accomplishments: her upbringing in Titusville and her parents' training. John and Ann had instilled in Condoleezza first the belief that she was a superlative individual, and second a faith that race would not limit her horizons. Rice had extrapolated and applied those rules to all black people. She didn't ignore the continuing difficulties many faced, like poverty, but fundamentally believed obstacles existed to be overcome. And she couldn't countenance using them as an excuse for failure. As she often said in her own life, "Move on. Get over it."

Her stepmother, Clara Rice, said it wasn't Condi's fault. "I think they put her on such a high pedestal that she couldn't see down far enough. She can't tolerate [unsuccessful blacks]. She feels they are trifling, so they don't need to be looked after. Sometimes I look at Condoleezza, and I feel a little bit sorry," said Clara, "because I think that she missed out on some of the real core lessons: just love for your race. I *love* black folks . . . I kind of get disgusted with them when they act up and mess up, but they're my people . . . And I just think she would rather just remove herself and not even associate [with certain types of blacks]."

Over the course of a dozen football seasons, Bean probed Rice about what it was like growing up under segregation. "I would ask her things like 'Did you internalize the rejection? How did it make you feel?' . . . She didn't feel dinged by it, because she felt so protected." Then Bean paused. "I think she did [feel the pain], but I think it was hard to admit to. Admitting to any of that vulnerability was losing the battle, and she just wasn't going to let that happen."

In Stanford's liberal but accepting atmosphere, political sameness was not a requisite for friendship. Rice, Bean, Blacker, and his partner, Louie, became an inseparable foursome. They borrowed John Rice's Lincoln town car and went road-tripping. Louie drove, Randy sat in the passenger's seat, and Condi and Chip made trouble in the back. Blacker and Bean would become Rice's best friends from her Stanford days. Chip would attend her swearing-in as secretary of state; Randy would arrange the California contingent for her surprise fiftieth birthday party in Washington.

Long before that, Bean and Blacker became like family to the Rices and Rays. When John and Ann visited Condoleezza at Thanksgiving or Easter, they took Randy to dinner, too. When Rice won the Gores Prize for Excellence in Teaching, Bean sat with her parents at the 1984 commencement. The Rices were beaming. Here was Condoleezza, not yet thirty, in her academic regalia, being honored by one of the best universities in the world. "They were the people who taught me what parental love was," said Bean.

When Condi went home the next Easter, John said he was worried about Ann; she seemed forgetful. A few months passed, and she started falling. Just before the Fourth of July, she was diagnosed with a brain tumor, likely metastasized cancer. Rice telephoned Blacker after midnight on August 18, 1985. Her mother was gone. Condi was supposed to fly home to see her the next day. "I was not there when she died. I've always regretted that," said Rice. "I wish I'd gotten on a plane a day earlier, but that's the way it is. And I'm grateful that I'd been home three weeks before that."[12]

Condi asked Chip to come over. They stayed up until the wee hours, and he held her. It was the first time he had ever seen her lose her composure. "I did what I could," Blacker recalled. But even more memorable than Condi's trembling anguish was her state when they woke up at 7 a.m. after a few hours sleep. She had completely regained her usual poise, at least on the outside; she was steady and strong.

Blacker drove her to the airport, and she flew home to Denver to do what had to be done. She comforted her father. She oversaw the funeral arrangements. And when the mourners returned sullen from the service, Condoleezza surprised them all by suggesting they play some of Angelena's favorite hymns: "The Lord Knows How Much You Can Bear," which Ann had played a lot during her illness, and "What a Friend We Have in Jesus." Condoleezza sat at the piano and led them.

Rice's stoicism became legend. In circumstances where others would have succumbed to grief, she seemed to grow more steely.

Randy was sleeping on a mattress in the office of Condi's two-bedroom house, her first, purchased for just $125,000 before the Silicon Valley real estate boom. (Bean had found herself without a place to stay.) "That fall cemented something [between us]," said Bean, though Condi rarely took Randy's invitation to share her pain. "Later, Condi told me that it saved her life, having me there. Who knew? . . . Ultimately, I think there's where we became sisters. She was devastated, but it was really important for her not to have anyone know that . . . She is *so* private emotionally that you could meet her a month [after Angelena died] and never know what she was going through. She's very good at compartmentalizing and being able to say, 'Okay, this is this. And this is that. And this is what needs my attention now.'"

In that sense, Condoleezza was every inch Angelena's daughter. Strength was the Ray family legacy. Weakness in the face of Jim Crow was unacceptable. It was the strength of the black community, both individually and collectively, that had allowed them to defeat the system's assaults on their personhood. But it also made it more difficult to show vulnerability, even to your friends. To the Rays, that's what family was for: your first and last support, as Daddy Ray always said. "[Her friends] have no clue what went on behind her closed doors," said Rice's cousin Yvonne German. "It's not to say you can't trust your friends. [But] we don't call her the cousin. We're the siblings. Because that's what we are in every way that matters."[13]

As a tonic to Condi's grief and Randy's homelessness, the women decided to splurge on a trip—to Cincinnati. Rice's Bengals were playing Bean's Giants. Randy's godparents were friends of the Bengals' co-owners and scored excellent tickets: first row, upper deck, at the fifty-yard line. They arrived on the Friday before the game and ferreted out where the Giants were staying. Bean stalked Harry Carson and Phil Simms until Rice pulled her away. On game day, they ate breakfast at Bob Evans—biscuits with sausage gravy—and were in the parking lot by 9:30 for the 1 p.m. kickoff.

The Giants lost and Randy sulked, but Condi insisted they go hang out by the Bengals' locker room. A regular NFL groupie, girlishly attractive at thirty-one, Rice was ecstatic when her team emerged. This time, it was Randy's turn to pull Condi away from the players, an indiscretion for which she would never be forgiven. That Monday, Rice and Bean flew back to Palo Alto, where Condi was spending the year working as a Hoover Institution National Fellow and editing a book on the Gorbachev era in the Soviet Union.[14]

Hard on the heels of Ann's passing, John moved to Palo Alto, ostensibly to be closer to his daughter. But devastated by Ann's death, he sank into a profound depression.[15] Condoleezza tried to find her father something to restore his sense of purpose. Stanford threw its resources behind the Rices. "Everybody wanted to help Condi," said Kennedy. "There was a sense [that] 'this is somebody we need to make happy.'"

John started working with Stanford's school of education and the mostly minority, mostly poor East Palo Alto schools. But a job wasn't enough to rebuild his life. He let the small apartment Condoleezza had rented for him descend into chaos. He played his music at deafening levels "because he didn't want to think," he explained to Clara Bailey, a principal he met at one of his sessions with East Palo Alto administrators. "He told me after I got to know him that he actually came out here to die . . . He was going to drink and eat himself to death, he said."[16]

It was a wholly foreign image of the father she idolized, and Condi apparently took some time to see it plainly. Clara was struck by how destitute John seemed. His car was so decrepit that under the dash was a mass of wires that entangled passengers' feet. Stuffing hung from the bottom of the couch in his apartment. He owned a minimum of clothing: a few pairs of pants, one jacket. Clara charged him a living room suite on her Levitz card.

Clara found herself attracted to the oversized warmth of Rice—to her great dismay. Long divorced, she had been literally praying to God for a husband. "It looked like God was saying, 'This is who I'm sending you.' And I'm arguing with God, 'No, you're not! He's too old! He's sick! He don't have no money!'" she laughed. "I was telling God, 'No, Lord. You know I prayed and told you that I need somebody that can take care of *me*!' But it looked like the more [I fought, the more] John and I became soul mates. We became so close. So I gave in."

Clara and John started seeing each other in October 1988. By the following March, they had been married in a wedding chapel in Las Vegas. On May 1, they held a proper Christian ceremony at Clara's house, which became their home. Condoleezza, Clara's son Greg, and a clutch of relatives and close friends attended, including John's sister Theresa and the Ray aunts and uncles; John was like a brother to them.

Under the force of John's love, they became a family. Condoleezza picked up on Clara's example and learned how to care for the man who had always cared for her: opening an account at the local big and tall store and sending John and Clara on vacations. "She got good at it!" said Clara. "Condi is very family oriented . . . I think one reason [our] relationship has remained as strong as it has is because she really realizes how much I loved her dad and how much he loved me."

While her family was changing, her professional life was an uninterrupted string of triumphs. She had always been a dynamic speaker; it was one of the aspects of Rice that made her most memorable. David Kennedy, her former associate dean, would witness her power when they did dog-and-pony shows as part of Stanford's centennial celebrations. Rice, Kennedy, and the world-famous physicist Sidney Drell, one of Rice's early champions, led discussions with alumni and big donors examining the state of the Soviet Union and the future of the Cold War. "She stole the show," said Kennedy. "Up on that platform, she was in complete control of everything . . . She impressed me, several times over, at how adept she was—as the Italians say, *preparatissima*—she was superprepared. Nobody caught her out on anything—didn't matter where the question came from, she had a good answer. A good answer, not just a blowing-smoke answer."

Her gift for succinct analysis, arresting even by the standards of college professors, became a theme in Rice's career, impressing a succession of powerful men who saw her potential and propelled her ever upward. Such was the case when Brent Scowcroft visited Stanford in 1984.[17] Scowcroft was a venerated member of the Republican foreign policy establishment and vice chairman of Kissinger Associates, Inc. He had come to California to give a lecture at the Lawrence Livermore National Laboratory. Afterward, he and the director went to Stanford for dinner. Their guests were the leading minds in the arms control field, and Condi Rice. In the midst of the discussion, Rice rose to give her views. Looking back, Scowcroft said, it wasn't what she said but how she said it. "This is a pretty specialized field, and she was just outstanding in the face of these *really* outstanding academic experts," though she looked more like an undergraduate than a professor. "It was an outstanding performance by any measure . . . I thought, *I need to get to know her.*"[18]

Scowcroft (who had known Josef Korbel from his own days teaching at the Air Force Academy in Colorado) made it his business to give Rice's career a push. He invited her to conferences and introduced her to the luminaries of national security. Rice was suddenly an A-lister. In addition to making sure the bright young professor was seen and heard, Scowcroft kept in touch personally. When his old friend George Bush won the presidential election in 1988, Bush asked Scowcroft to return to government as national security adviser. After accepting the job, Scowcroft's second call (after his would-be deputy Robert Gates) was to Rice. She had already been offered jobs at State and Defense in the new administration,[19] but Scowcroft told her, "There's nothing like working for the president."[20] The NSC was the president's staff.

After the Reagan years, Bush wanted a less ideological administration. His litmus test would be competence. He chose Scowcroft, a cautious retired general with a PhD who had also been Ford's national security adviser, as his NSA, and James Baker as secretary of state—a tough-minded pragmatist who was also close to Bush (Bush was godfather to Baker's daughter). The Bush men sought to build a Soviet policy that was free of Reagan's cataclysmic rhetoric about the Evil Empire and firmly rooted in realism. (Reagan himself had started to make the shift over the course of his two terms.)[21] Rice fit the bill. "One of the problems in dealing with the Soviet Union was that people tended to be emotional: The Soviet Union was evil incarnate or was this kind of romantic idealistic notion of mankind gone astray," said Scowcroft. "I didn't find her in either extreme."

The decision to accept the White House job was not a "slam dunk" for Rice.[22] Unlike a lot of the men and women drawn to Washington, she didn't crave the air of power inside the Beltway. After a lot of consulting with friends and her father, she took it, but not before seeing to her top priority—her students.

Jendayi Frazer, an army brat who had grown up in the U.S. and Germany, was so enthralled with Professor Rice as an undergraduate that she would take the last spot in the long line of students snaking from her office door. That way, she could stay as long as she wanted, discussing the fundamentals of political science without worrying about being pushed out by another student. Rice had convinced Frazer, who was also an African American woman, to get her PhD. Now a third-year doctoral student, Frazer was starting her dissertation. Just when she needed Rice most, her mentor was leaving for Washington.

Rice set up a fund for Frazer to call her in D.C. Despite the crushing work-load of the NSC jobs, Rice made time for Frazer when she came to Washington; she would put huge red Xs through whole pages of her dissertation drafts. When Frazer was running low on cash, Rice lent her money. And before she left, she introduced her protégé to the most passionate educator she knew—John Rice—so when she needed it, she would have a shoulder closer to home. (Rice would later bring Frazer with her to the George W. Bush NSC, then get her appointed U.S. ambassador to South Africa, and later assistant secretary of state for African affairs.)

Condi arrived in Washington on February 1, 1989,[23] for her first real job in government:[24] NSC director for Soviet and East European affairs. (She'd be promoted to senior director and special assistant to the president the following year.) It was an extraordinary time to be working on the Soviet Union, perhaps the headiest since the days when she had worried about Soviet missiles in Cuba streaking toward Alabama. Soviet premier Mikhail Gorbachev had launched a series of reforms since coming to power in 1985, promoting greater transparency in government and looser control of society by the Communist Party. (When a reporter asked Gorbachev what the difference was between his reforms and the Prague Spring, the Soviet leader replied, "Nineteen years.")[25]

To the West, Gorbachev seemed to be marshalling the forces of history. Weeks before the 1988 New Hampshire primary, *Time* magazine dubbed him "Man of the Year."[26] Then, a month before Bush assumed the presidency, Gorbachev addressed the United Nations General Assembly, declaring the Soviets' Eastern European allies no longer had to fear tanks sent from Moscow rolling through their capitals; they were free to pursue their own political course domestically.[27] In fact, Gorbachev encouraged the Soviet satellites to experiment with socialist reform as the Soviet Union was.[28]

In contrast, when the Bush administration took over, its leaders orchestrated a top-down review of every significant foreign policy the previous administration had pursued. The impression spread—not just in the United States but in Western Europe and the Soviet Union—that the Americans were being left in the dust by Gorbachev.[29] And there was another problem. After eight years of Reagan's inspiring rhetoric, the patrician Bush was a national anticlimax. Even when he was excited, he sounded flat, his speeches bloodless. Frustrated, the president asked his staff to step up the pace. He wanted to be able to announce something,

something big, that would show that the administration was getting ahead of developments, that it had what Bush would often refer to as "the vision thing."

Unimpressed by the review (National Security Review-3) of policy toward the Soviet Union—it was "mainly a 'big picture' document, short on detail and substance"[30]—and with the boss demanding action, in March, Scowcroft asked Rice to write him "a U.S.–Soviet policy."[31] She did, in a few days.[32] Thirty-four-year-old Rice's strategy would become the centerpiece of American policy toward the Soviet Union. Picking up on Gorbachev's own rhetoric—by accident, not by design[33]—the document argued that containment of the Russian threat had worked and that the time had come for the United States to move "beyond containment to the integration of the Soviet Union into the international system."[34]

Rice's phrase suggested a U.S. policy that didn't view Russia as an implacable enemy that had to be destroyed and, true to realist dictates, reflected the changing chessboard. Gorbachev's predecessors had believed socialism had to be built in isolation from an international system dominated by capitalism until the day it was strong enough to defeat it. But by Gorbachev's day, it was clear socialism was an economic failure. His reforms were meant to save it by finding a third way, closer to the democratic socialism practiced to varying degrees in Western Europe.

The president used the phrase "beyond containment" in his first commencement speech at Texas A&M on May 17, and two weeks later in a speech in Germany following a summit of the North Atlantic Treaty Organization, the military arm of the American-European alliance.[35] The president liked it. The Soviets liked it. Even the press liked it, a rarity for Bush.

Just three months into the job, Rice was already making a difference. For those who knew her work ethic, it wasn't surprising. As her Stanford colleague David Kennedy said, Rice was *preparatissima*. She was so driven to know more about her topic than anyone else, lest she be found wanting, that she seemed to have a near obsession with mastering every detail, every fact. That's why she could pump out a U.S. policy toward Moscow in forty-eight hours. To her colleagues in Washington, it was admirable but weird, like she had a chip on her shoulder, something to prove.

When the administration sought to exploit the opening Gorbachev had given to the "captive nations" of Eastern Europe, Scowcroft tasked Rice with running "enterprise groups" to determine how to best help the different Soviet satellites work themselves free of Moscow's orbit. When there was no money for the democracy-encouragement projects—it was the summer in Washington, three-quarters through the fiscal year, and funds for new programs were scarce—Rice scoured the budget and found the cash. Now Scowcroft was regularly taking Rice into his Oval Office meetings with the president. "[President Bush] became very enamored."[36]

The lowest level position on the National Security Council is director, the one Rice held. (She was the key person on the Soviet Union because her immediate supervisor, Robert Blackwill, the NSC's senior director for Europe and the Soviet Union was a Europeanist, not an expert on the U.S.S.R.) "In Washington, it's not about the title, it's about how much face time you get," said Ivo Daalder, an expert on the National Security Council at the Brookings Institution. "Even as a low-level staffer, she had high-level influence."[37] In addition to being competent, creative, and tireless, Rice was a pleasure to be around. Few in Washington combined those traits.

Then, in the summer of 1989, the world changed. At first, no one noticed. Not the White House, not the State Department, not even the CIA. In the middle of the languorous European vacation season, East Germans started arriving at West German embassies all over Eastern Europe. First it was Hungary. By mid-August, 150 East Germans had arrived at the West German embassy in Budapest, with hundreds more coming each week, demanding to be taken to West Germany.[38] Then it was Czechoslovakia. As Rice and Philip Zelikow wrote in their 1995 book *Germany Unified and Europe Transformed*, "thousands of East Germans were scaling the walls into the West German embassy [in Prague] . . . by late September over five thousand people had crowded into the muddy grounds of the embassy."[39]

West German chancellor Helmut Kohl, in a sharp break with years of West German accommodation to Cold War realities, did the unthinkable. He called for German unification. East Germany, economically weak at home and faced with its Soviet patrons taking a hands-off attitude abroad, was in no position to resist. When demonstrators who had been filling the streets in increasing numbers through the early fall marched in Leipzig on October 9, onlookers expected the worst. Instead, the East German secret police, eight thousand strong,[40] did nothing. Exactly one month later, through what Zelikow and Rice describe as a bureaucratic mistake,[41] the East German government repealed the exit visa requirements that it used to keep its own citizens prisoners in their own country. In jubilation, thousands of East Berliners descended on the border crossings into West Berlin. The stunned border guards were overwhelmed. Without prompting, the crowd seized the Berlin Wall. Young people danced atop the symbol of Europe's division into East and West, the same wall that Reagan had used as a backdrop for his challenge to Gorbachev that if he were a real reformer, then "tear down this wall!"[42]

The momentous news was greeted like most news in Bush's ordered, rational White House: with caution.[43] The president had been pondering his own explicit call for German unification even before Kohl's, but many of his advisers worried that a mad dash to overturn Communist regimes across Eastern Europe could lead to chaos, starting in East Berlin. As much as the Bushies craved an end to the Cold War, they knew that managing that end was equally important.

Two of the biggest obstacles to midwifing the orderly birth of the "new world order" were Washington's allies France and Britain, especially Britain. Prime Minister Margaret Thatcher reminded anyone who would listen that in the space of just forty years, a united Germany had twice plunged Europe into war. Now it would be an economic colossus at the center of the continent. French president François Mitterrand was less concerned, with the caveat that the new Germany be firmly wedded to the European Community, a way to keep in check any troublesome impulses that might still lurk in the German soul.

Bush, for all his self-deprecating (and ultimately politically self-destructive) assertions that he didn't do "the vision thing," had already supplied the Atlantic Alliance with a blueprint for the future: "Europe whole and free," including a united Germany and a globally integrated Soviet Union. Condoleezza Rice had been a principal architect of that vision, and now she would play a central role in building its real-world foundations.

For the next year, Rice worked with Blackwill and Scowcroft at the NSC and with Ross and Baker at the State Department, devising a formula for negotiating German reunification that would mollify the Western allies and the Soviets, who, after all, had lost more than 12 million citizens on World War II's Eastern front in what Hitler called "the war of annihilation" against the Slavic peoples— and more than 350,000 men just in the battle for Berlin. Moscow would not surrender the fruits of the Great Patriotic War so dearly purchased in Soviet blood without delicate persuasion.

That started with the preparations for Bush's first summit with Gorbachev, in Malta the month after Kohl's call for unification. The president needed to know how the Russians were taking the rapid developments in Germany and Eastern Europe (Hungary and Poland were considering holding free elections). Rice provided the president's presummit analysis. The four-point memo, dated November 28, 1989, detailed these points.

1. "The Soviets had lost control of their policy toward Eastern Europe. They had not anticipated current developments."
2. The Soviets opposed German reunification and their "worst nightmare was a reunified Germany aligned with NATO."
3. They were scrambling to find ways to continue the division of Germany.
4. Presently, "there was still no panic in Moscow over the German issue," but if Soviet influence began to wane, they would call for some "pan-European collective security" or a formal peace treaty with Germany. (In 1989, Germany was still technically an occupied nation subject to the rule of Britain, France, the U.S.S.R., and the U.S. To relinquish their rights to the defeated nation, the Russians could insist upon a formal treaty.)[44]

Rice was right on all counts. But by the time the Russians would be worried enough to propose a pan-European security arrangement for a united Germany that would marginalize the U.S., as one Russian official told another, "that train [had] left the station." Kohl had ignited the Germans' passions. And what everyone, including the German chancellor, had first envisioned as a piecemeal process of first monetary union, then political confederation, and then finally—maybe three or four years hence—full federation was clearly not going to happen so gradually. The East German state was coming apart at the seams economically and politically. It wouldn't survive a gradual unification. The West Germans and the Americans decided that German unity had to happen fast. The question was, what would the Soviets do? They still had massive quantities of men and weapons stationed in East Germany.

Again, it fell to Rice to tell the most powerful man in the world how the game would play out. Her memo to Blackwill, dated January 23, 1990, stated that "creeping unification—because everyone is afraid to talk about [the terms of unification]—is probably not very smart." She said the U.S. had to seize the opportunity while Moscow was confused about what it wanted to achieve in Germany, while the Soviets' own domestic problems made Western assistance to Russia indispensable, and while Washington and Bonn had momentum on their side. If the Four Powers that had defeated Germany in World War II and the two German states negotiated, the Americans and Kohl could *probably* make unification a fait accompli before the Russians knew what hit them. Then she wrote the most important words she had ever written: "I believe (and this is a hunch, and I guess if we did this that I would spend a lot of time in church praying that I was right) that the Soviets would not even threaten the Germans. Within six months, if events continue as they are going, no one would believe them anyway."[45] It was just like Hans Morgenthau had said: Power mattered. The West had it. The Russians didn't.

Washington plunged ahead, with Rice and her bosses at the NSC hoping that they could slow the progress of Big Power negotiations over Germany's future long enough to allow the two Germanys to do much of the work of unification, so that when the Four Powers actually came to the table, Moscow (and London and Paris) would have little opportunity to gum up the works. Scowcroft feared giving the Soviets the opportunity to slow or even derail the move to union by exploiting Britain and France's misgivings. He also worried about putting the two Germanys—one an elected democratic government, the other a longtime Soviet stooge—on equal footing.[46]

Over at the State Department, the officials in charge of European policy wanted to give the Soviets at least the semblance of a real voice, in the belief that that would be the only way to keep them inside the tent. To resolve Scowcroft's fears, they came up with what would be called Two Plus Four.[47] The two Germanys would take the lead (which meant the West Germans since East Germany was unraveling faster each day), and the Four Powers would come second. But everyone would sit together, ostensibly deciding the future in harmony if not in unison. The Germans would not be treated like the vanquished, and the Four Powers would not feel robbed of their say.

Baker called Bush from a conference in Canada, where he was meeting with foreign ministers from around the world. Baker had gotten approval for Two Plus Four from all the players. Now Bush was resistant; he asked if Baker was sure Chancellor Kohl would buy a process where the Four Powers were so prominent. "There was obviously some pushback," said Baker.[48] The pushback was from the

NSC. Scowcroft didn't realize the idea was so far advanced and still wasn't convinced it wouldn't allow Russia to stall unification. Rice agreed with her boss.[49] It was, as Baker put it, "the only time that her part of the NSC was singing off tune with us at State." It would take Baker's insistence to the president and a couple of calls between Bush and Kohl to seal the deal. But the way it had happened led to the administration's most serious tensions over German unification.[50]

Before the Canadian conference, Rice had traveled with Baker to Moscow, where he had floated the Two Plus Four trial balloon to Gorbachev. She had helped conceive the incentives to convince Moscow that a NATO-aligned Germany was safer for the Soviet Union than a neutral one that could build its own nuclear weapons. When the Two Plus Four talks started in March 1990, Rice was one of only three Americans present. She was the only delegate from any of the six nations who wasn't white and male. More important, she was the only American not from the State Department.[51] From an inside-the-Beltway perspective, it was perhaps the most crucial rule.[52] She ensured that non State Department views would be represented, that the other parts of the U.S. government would stay on board throughout the sensitive negotiations, and that interagency rivalries wouldn't scuttle the talks or muddle the president's vision, as so often happened in Washington.

After the first March meeting, Rice reported back to the White House that the Soviets seemed unprepared but that Britain and France were not totally on board with the American agenda and that the West German delegation was not fighting hard enough to get what Bonn and Washington had agreed to.[53]

As important as the German question was, Rice was working simultaneously on the not unrelated issue of how to modernize U.S. nuclear missiles in Europe, as well as developing strategies on conventional forces, including the number of soldiers that the U.S. and the U.S.S.R. should be able to keep on the continent. Summer would bring no respite: Soon she would be formulating the president's talking points for three diplomatic main events in as many months: the Superpower summit with Gorbachev in May, a NATO summit in London in July, and a G7 economic summit the same month.

At the May summit, Bush unexpectedly got Gorbachev to agree that any sovereign nation, including a united Germany, had the right to decide its own alliances. Rice passed a draft to the Russian ambassador of the statement Bush planned to deliver at the joint press conference at the summit's end.[54] It would relay Russia's acquiescence to Germans deciding what alliance they would join.

The Russians had no objections. But by agreeing that a united Germany was free to join NATO, the statement would communicate something much larger, something Mikhail Gorbachev had already come to terms with: The world had spun out of Moscow's control. The crown jewel of Soviet foreign power, East Germany, would be lost. The Soviet Empire was dead. And Condoleezza Rice had had the honor of delivering the death certificate.

On September 12, 1990, the six foreign ministers of the four victorious allies of World War II and the divided Germanys sat at a long table in Moscow and signed the Treaty on the Final Settlement with Respect to Germany. On October 3, at the moment of German union, the Four Powers relinquished all rights and responsibilities over the country. By the end of 1991, the Soviet Union itself would be no more.

By then, Rice would be gone from Washington. Weeks before German reunification, Saddam Hussein had invaded Kuwait. The administration turned its attention from Europe to the Middle East. On the day Iraq invaded in August 1990, rather than watch her colleague Richard Haass hunt and peck on the computer, Rice typed the president's talking points for his first public message.[55] Bush marshaled an unprecedented coalition to push Hussein back to Baghdad, and in short order, it did. American military might had brought victory on the battlefield, and American diplomacy had ensured that other nations paid the bill for the war. It was a triumph for any president. An election loomed, and with the primaries just nine months away, Bush enjoyed an approval rating of eighty-nine percent.[56]

Rice had committed to two years in the White House. She had participated in events she couldn't have imagined. Now she knew all that drama, all that policy and strategy, all that attention to what really mattered in the world would give way to politics. It was a measure of her value that the president of the United States himself asked her to please stay. It was a measure of her strength that she told him, "No, Mr. President."[57]

Rice had had a hand in the greatest redrawing of the world map in a half century. Not surprisingly, the experience had left its imprint on her. She had witnessed what principled American leadership could accomplish. In the face of the European allies' timidity and cynicism (Margaret Thatcher had initially proposed Soviet troops remain in a united Germany "indefinitely," a kind of insurance policy for Europe),[58] George Bush had led. That leadership had brought forth a new and safer world.

The American-led coalition's determination to dislodge Saddam Hussein from Kuwait provided an instructive corollary: When Washington had the courage to take the initiative, it could create an international consensus to enhance global security and protect the peace. It was Bush's meticulous concentration on America's relationship with the Great Powers, allies as well as rivals, that allowed him to unite virtually every nation—including the U.S.S.R., though Iraq had been its closest ally in the Middle East—to confront and then reverse Hussein's aggression.

And Rice drew another lesson from German unification. Even inside the administration, there had been concerns about the instability that a breakaway Eastern Europe and a weakened Soviet Union could bring, concerns that multiplied when the U.S.S.R. imploded: the nuclear weapons that were stationed in the outlying Soviet republics, the proliferation of the crumbling power's nuclear components, the spread of nationalist revolutions. The new world might prove even more dangerous to America than the old one. Though no one could see around those corners, Bush's dedication to the ultimate goal, the reunification of Europe and the end of the Cold War—both right and righteous—would prove to have been the correct course. When Rice returned to Washington to serve under another President Bush, that lesson as much as any other would influence her actions, especially in the Middle East after September 11 and particularly in Iraq.

Bureaucratically, she had seen how a disciplined national security process could implement a president's vision, overcoming the often contradictory perspectives of the different government departments. The linchpin had been Scowcroft.[59] Because he had the trust of the secretaries of state and defense, he could play the national security adviser's role of honest broker. The secretaries knew that the general both spoke for the president and accurately conveyed their opinions to the Oval Office. And it wasn't just these men, the "principals," who gave Bush perhaps the most disciplined foreign policy team America had known. It was also their deputies, who understood the premium their bosses placed on cooperation, not competition.[60]

Personally, the inexperienced Rice had learned how to use her own power in the service of her goals. Working inside the bureaucracy, she saw when to charm and when to strong-arm, when to rely on her formidable ability to persuade those who disagreed and when to go around them. She had demonstrated a knack for high-stakes office politics. Through her obsessive focus of being pre-pared, she had inspired the confidence of the most powerful men in the world.

Soon, she also learned a brutal lesson about U.S. politics—not during her service in the White House but in the defeat of President Bush by Arkansas gov-ernor Bill Clinton in the 1992 election. As she and Zelikow would assert, "In trying to discharge [global] responsibilities, George Bush collided with America's festering ambivalence about its role in the world. The country found little joy in the West's Cold War victory, only questions about what the forty-five-year com-mitment had done to America at home."[61] Rice believed that Bush lost because Americans were weary of the battle they had won. Bush had paid a price for his global leadership, as well as his perceived lack of sensitivity to "the concerns of his own country."

In Bush's son, Rice would find the same leadership qualities but also the political savvy the father had seemingly lacked—the perfect package for a world in dire need of American guidance and an electorate that nonetheless demanded its president's attention.

When she returned in April 1991,[62] Stanford seemed much smaller. Rice had only been tenured for a year and a half when she left campus. She returned a victorious Cold Warrior. Advising the leader of the Free World had reinforced her already impressive confidence. (When Bush introduced Rice to Gorbachev at the beginning of the 1989 Malta Summit, the president told the Soviet leader, "She tells me everything I know about the Soviet Union."[63]) Political science col-league Daniel Okimoto had witnessed the same growth spurt after Rice returned in 1987 from her fellowship at the Joint Chiefs of Staff. "[Each time] she came back a different person: more confident, more able to deal with outside demands and criticisms, more ambitious," said Okimoto. "There were these stepwise func-tions related to her exposure in Washington." Jendayi Frazer, Rice's PhD pro-tégé, noticed the change, too. "When she came back, she was focused in a different way," said Frazer, "a little harder. There was a stiffer spine."[64]

Her friends noticed another change in Rice, too. She returned to Stanford "more Republican." "This is what happens. Whatever you are going in, because of what's required of you in those jobs, you internalize the politics and policy preferences of the administration," said Chip Blacker, who in the Clinton administration would work in the same position Rice held under Bush (and who'd turn to his Republican friend for advice on how to work the bureaucracy). Stanford also contributed to hardening Rice's Republicanism; in what Blacker termed a "hostile environment," she had to develop the capacity to defend herself as a Republican, which further sharpened her arguments and her positions.

As Rice would tell the Republican National Convention in 2000, the first Republican she had known was her father, John Rice.[65] Condoleezza said her father was a Republican because the bigoted 1950s' Democrats wouldn't register him to vote. Blacker said John remained a Republican, in part, because he relished the shock value; it upended assumptions about race and party affiliation. But Rice's widow, Clara, said John told her he was a Republican because he felt "Republicans look out for each other . . . He was looking at, how can I get ahead? How can my daughter get ahead?" said Clara. "I'm sure she had been listening to him saying, 'Honey, *that*'s where you need to be, to get into the Republican [party]. They'll do this for you and that.' And he was right."

Condoleezza often took her father's advice, though not usually at the time it was offered. The delayed response had led to the demise of Boris, Rice's Notre Dame, car after John and Clara begged Condi to trade him in for a Mercedes. And most momentously (according to some African American women), when Clara suggested when Condi became secretary of state that she get rid of the flip in her hair.

Perhaps it was John's pragmatic Republicanism that led Condoleezza when she returned to Stanford to seek out the most prominent Republican on campus. George Shultz, Reagan's secretary of state, was working at the Hoover Institution and led a "highly discriminatory" three-person lunch group.[66] The members all agreed that Rice should be invited to join. "She is so funny, lively, and bright," said Shultz. "So you see, we're discriminating, but not in the way you think: We only want bright and fun people. Then we added Gerhard Casper, but only after he stopped being president. We didn't want that kind of brass around spoiling the fun!

"I remember her strength," said Shultz. "She has things to say and a point of view. You may disagree with her, but you had better keep your powder dry because she has good arguments to back up what she believes."[67]

Rice told Shultz she wanted to gain corporate business experience. Chevron had just lost board member Carla Hills to the administration. Shultz asked Rice, "How would you like a big, bad oil company?"

"That's about as interesting a business as there is," Condi replied. Shultz set up a lunch for Rice with Chevron chairman Ken Derr. About ten minutes into the meeting, Derr invited Rice to join the board.[68]

Soon, she added a long list of others: Transamerica, Hewlett-Packard, and Charles Schwab,[69] as well as the J. P. Morgan International Advisory Council.[70] To each, she brought her Russian and European expertise, her civilian-military background, and her Washington connections. "I told her, 'Condi, go slow. Pick what's really interesting to you. Don't take every offer,'" said Shultz. Instead, she added a bunch of nonprofit boards, including RAND Corporation, the William and Flora Hewlett Foundation, the San Francisco Symphony, and the University of Notre Dame.

Just as she had parlayed her academic credentials into a policy role, she now turned her policy experience into corporate bona fides—and eventually dollars. By the time she would leave Stanford, Rice would have $250,000 in Chevron stock and an annual income of $60,000 from her board work.[71] Now Rice was the complete package; high-level business experience had been just about the only credential her résumé lacked.

She gained facility in a new arena both more lavish and more hard-nosed than academia or government. She maintained her links to the policy world by serving as a consultant to the NSC. She worked as a Hoover Institution fellow and a senior fellow at the International Institute at Stanford, which Shultz had founded. She launched a career as a paid consultant (a talking head) on Soviet affairs for ABC News,[72] giving millions of Americans their first sight of the brainy woman who knew the Russians. Rice was juggling commitments—board work, teaching, writing, helping Stanford select its next university president— that would have overwhelmed most people. "She is at her best when she's keeping all these issues in her mind at once," said Shultz.[73]

Despite her new higher profile, Rice was at a loss when Gerhard Casper called her to his office. Condi stopped to see Blacker on her way to Building 10. "Why do you think he's calling?"[74]

"I think he's going to ask you to be dean of the School of Humanities and Sciences," suggested Chip.

Rice was skeptical. She hadn't even been a department chair; a promotion to lead vast H&S would be unprecedented. But Blacker figured Rice had impressed Casper during the presidential search. "He wants to send a signal that this is a new time," said Blacker. "And I think he thinks that you would be great at it."

"Hmm," was all Rice said.

When she returned after a long meeting with Casper, she was shaking. "He didn't ask me to become the dean of the School of Humanities and Sciences," Rice started, then paused. As Blacker waited, his head slightly forward, Rice said, "He, he asked me to be provost."

"You're shitting me," said Chip.

"No, I'm not."

"You're shitting me."

"No, I'm *not*." (She had been, literally, speechless for thirty seconds when Casper asked her to take the job.)

Casper had found Stanford singularly bureaucratic, even for an institution of higher learning. The cloud of the indirect cost scandal, the earthquake, and the vilification in the *Journal* had taxed the university's finances as well as morale. To recover, Casper decided he needed a change agent. Condi Rice was it. "I had had a little longer than a year in which I had every reason to be impressed by her intellectual acuity, her persuasiveness, her understanding of Stanford and universities more generally, and I had also come to discover that she and I shared some characteristics: the notion that a university should be about teaching, learning, and research. A university did not have a political mission as such.[75]

"The other aspect in which we had similar values," Casper added with a boyish chuckle, "was I was just completely impatient with all of these processes at Stanford. There was a committee, two committees, three committees, thrown at *everything*. . . . I had the impression that Condi shared my impatience. Indeed, if anything, she was perhaps even more impatient."

Though she had no significant management experience, Casper figured if Rice could deal with generals and cabinet secretaries, she could deal with tenured professors. "Secondly, that she was a woman and black certainly did not harm her in my eyes. I believed very strongly that we needed to do more for these groups in university leadership." Still, had Rice not impressed Casper during the presidential search, it was highly unlikely he would have offered her the job. As it had been with Scowcroft, it had been Rice's flawless performance that brought a rare opportunity.

Casper's decision split the campus. The provost selection committee had short-listed Rice's name, but in the early balloting, she was never one of the top vote getters. In the end, she was included to present a wide variety of candidates in terms of experience and pedigree. Because Rice was a comer, she made the cut, but there were finalists on the list with far more management experience and service to the university: former deans, nationally recognized scholars.[76] Rice wasn't even a full professor; the political science department had to fast-track her promotion so the provost wouldn't be an associate professor.[77] Since the move from associate with tenure to full professor was usually a formality—and since Blackwill from Rice's days at the NSC was trying to lure her to Harvard—that part of the equation was less controversial.

The university's old guard shared the selection committee's consternation; Rice hadn't paid her dues. The younger generation, as well as most women and minorities, were elated. Condi would be the first African American or female to occupy the provost office and the first provost under sixty. Veteran black administrator Ewart Thomas, bursting with pride, declared to the stately Casper, "You've got balls!"[78]

"It was funny," said Randy Bean. "There was a period of about five years when . . . she wasn't expecting stuff, and it kept falling in her lap . . . And I said, 'Well, God, you gotta do this, too . . . We'll get great tickets to stuff.'"[79]

Most professors would have been reticent to take on the top managerial job, especially with a résumé as devoid of experience as Condi's, but self-doubt was not an affliction she suffered.

It was a company tradition at Chevron to name an oil tanker after each board member. In September, they were christening the M/T *Condoleezza Rice* in Rio de Janeiro. Chevron asked Rice whom she'd like to invite to Brazil for the occasion. She listed her immediate family: John, Clara, her stepbrother Greg. Astonished at her economy, Chevron said Shultz had brought twenty-eight people. Rice invited her aunts and uncle from Birmingham and Chip and Randy. (Blacker dubbed them "the little white caboose.")[80] Condi decided to make the trip a last blowout before buckling down to the provost job.

Chevron flew them all business class from San Francisco to Miami, then on to Rio. They stayed at one of the best beach hotels. Each of the teams that had contributed to the M/T *Condoleezza Rice* threw a dinner: the Brazilians who had built her, the Japanese who had financed her, and the Americans who owned her. (The crew was Norwegian and Italian.) By day, Alto and Connie Ray and Clara and John shopped and went sightseeing. By night, Condi, Randy, and Chip drank caipirinhas and danced till the wee hours with whoever happened to be standing next to them. For five days, they partied like Rio was the whole world, a world without responsibility.

At the official christening ceremony, the back of the hulking tanker was draped in cloth. Along the dock below stood the sailors, the crew, and the local shipbuilders in their work clothes. After the speeches, Rice—who had learned some Portuguese on the plane ride down—cut a string, and a bottle of champagne flew up and crashed against the hull.

The setting was more exotic and the partying more intense, but her friends and family were the staples of Condi's life, what she missed most in Washington. She could be a grind on the job—rising before dawn to work out, in the office by 8:30, there till 7, taking work home most nights and weekends.[11] But when she was with family, she was home. And her definition of family was broad and deep.

After her return from Washington, Rice had lived with John and Clara. To them, family was a set of concentric circles: first relatives—the assortment of aunts, uncles, brothers, in-laws, and cousins who came from Birmingham and Virginia for the holidays when Rice would make her famous turkey. Next was church family from Clara's New Jerusalem Baptist. Then Condi's friends, a multiracial stream of young people at parties, dances, and barbecues.

That was what her blackness meant to Rice: her inner circle "and the capacity to relate to one another in that intensely familiar way," said Blacker, "this deep, deep interlaced, interwired, deeply connected group of people who are in one another's faces all the time to [an] extent that is unusual in white families in this country because [whites] don't have to. It's a protective wall. That's what she thinks of when she thinks of being black."

The idea of blackness as an abstraction, a link that bonded all people of the same color, didn't figure into Rice's view of the world or herself. Outside her circle of intimacy lay the world of strangers, black as well as white, against whom the protective wall of family and friends was united. "[Her] disposition is to believe she has more in common with another African American than with a random white person," said Blacker. "But it's this experientially based thing; it's not commonality of interest."[82]

Rice experienced blackness culturally, not politically. It was central to her self-conception; she believed it was contained in every fiber of her being—from the way she was raised to her values to the way she saw the world. That was why Rice found the charge that her critics would often level at her—that she was somehow inauthentic—nonsensical. "I have been black all my life," she would reply.

The charges of inauthenticity stemmed largely from her limited view of black solidarity. She didn't believe that race determined one's political party. She didn't "code shift," speaking differently when talking to black people than to whites. In fact, she rarely gave public signals that she was racially self-aware—unlike Colin Powell. For example, when Powell and Time Warner CEO Richard Parsons, also black, spoke at an event at the Council on Foreign Relations, the crowd was overwhelming white. But the first question came from a young African American professional. Since council rules prohibit reporting what the then secretary of state said to the man, suffice it say Powell and Parsons slipped effortlessly into a fraternal, familiar—almost familial—patois, "talking black" (perhaps a first in the halls of the CFR). Powell did the same thing in the corridors of the State Department, code shifting with the black security guards. To them, it said he was a "brotha."[83]

Rice never did. "She's not putting on something or taking off something," said Frazer. "She is who she is." Those who knew her best never questioned the role race played in her psyche; to them, it was clear. "There's a sense of 'the community,'" said Frazer, "and she is very much a part of the black community, as a cultural factor and phenomenon."[84]

Her internalization of her racial identity led Rice to act as a mentor to a number of African American women at Stanford. But she didn't see a brother or a sister in the face of every African American.

Her racial consciousness also influenced her dating life. Rice preferred black men. And like many professional black women,[85] she complained and commiserated about the lack of eligible ones. "It was bad for any single woman here in suburbia," said Bean, "but it was even worse for her."[86]

The professional African American men she could find were dreadfully boring. And one thing that Rice could not abide was boring people. "She had this parade, I swear, of about seven or eight of these unbelievably highly accomplished black men—gorgeous! PhDs, lawyers, doctors, vice presidents, presidents, owned their own companies, money, all the demographics were [good]," said Bean. "But she'd get back [from her dates], and I'd say, 'How'd it go?' There'd be this pause. And I'd say, 'Not another one!' And she'd start laughing—because they were *so dull* . . . We decided somebody needed to do a PhD on the dearth of personality in the accomplished black male. It was like something had got spent on the way up the ladder.

"She said, 'You know what? The fun guys are all bad boys. And these guys are kind of the Goody Two-shoes.'" It wasn't a question of Rice's standards being too high, said Bean. "I met a couple of them, and she wasn't wrong."[87] Rice's closest friends confirmed, as did her stepmother: "Condoleezza likes bad boys."

She was an alpha female. And she was unwilling or unable to turn it off, even in service to the polite conventions of courtship. It seemed she wanted a man who was strong enough to handle a woman as strong as she was, not one who required a woman who was needy or submissive. While many men liked to think of themselves as chivalrous and commanding—and many women let them—Rice didn't. "Sometime John and I would go to dinner when she was dating," said Clara. "The guy would want to drive, and she'd say, 'No, I'll drive my car.' And then when we'd get there, he'd say, 'I'll go park it.' [She'd say,] 'No, you get out, I'll go park it.' Even if *John* would try to open the door [for her, she'd say], 'Oh, Daddy move, move, move!' I told John, 'She's going to really have it hard, especially if a man wants to be a man. But she's very independent—not just about that, but about anything.'"

By all accounts, vanity wasn't one of her problems. She wasn't self-centered or materialistic, her near-obsession with shoes notwithstanding. Like many black women, she had her "hair issues." From the time she was a little girl, it was thick and hard to manage. "It's very coarse," said Clara. "She really has to have someone to work with it." John and Clara marveled one day when Condoleezza went to a stylist who made her hair supple and shakable. "All day long she was [flipping her head around]. John and I would poke each other: 'Look, look, look.' And she would be throwing that hair like she was a white girl!"[88] Clara laughed.

But the fact was, Condi was never very focused on starting a family. "She'll pick up little kids, but she's through with them after that," as her stepmother put it. "She doesn't care much for children." Not that any of her relationships ever got that far. Outside her liaison with former Bronco Rick Upchurch, Rice's most serious relationship, according to friends and family, was with Gene Washington. After graduating from Stanford in 1969, Washington became the San Francisco 49ers' first-round draft pick.[89] After a decade playing in the NFL, he became a TV sports reporter,[90] an assistant athletic director at Stanford,[91] and then an executive with the NFL. He met and dated Condi in the 1980s. If she was ever going to get married, Rice's friends said Washington had been the most likely candidate. Instead, he became a kind of permanent escort. Most of Rice's friends said the romantic part of the relationship ended long ago, and both Rice and Washington publicly insisted they were just friends.

Because few people at Stanford knew the details of her personal life, some believed Condi was dating Chip. And more than one associate—from the Ivy League to Washington—said they knew someone who knew that Rice was gay. But none of those stories ever led to anyone claiming to be a former girlfriend. Once Rice was famous, her sex life would become the fodder of gossip and the *Boondocks* cartoon. A lesbian performer would write a tribute song to her, as would a male country singer. Even the *New York Times* would publish a tongue-in-cheek story about a speculated affair with Canada's attractive foreign minister.

By 2007, many of Rice's friends doubted she would ever marry. Rice often said, "I always thought you get married because you want to get married *to* someone." And she had simply never met that person. "[Condi's] life is so full, so wall-to-wall," said Bean, "I would never call her lonely. I think the spiritual part of [her] keeps her from feeling that ache in the soul kind of stuff. . . . I think she's okay with [being single for now] because she doesn't have time not to be."[92]

CHAPTER SEVEN

PRELUDE

I don't do committees.[1]

CONDOLEEZZA RICE
First meeting of the Twenty-Sixth Senate of the Academic Council
Stanford University
September 30, 1993

W eeks of protests had failed to get the university's attention.[2] At day break on Wednesday, May 4, forty Chicano students made camp outside Building 10, condemning the administration's "open hostility toward minorities."[3] The protestors declared they would live in tents outside Casper's and Rice's offices until the president and provost agreed to their demands: the extension of a formal apology to Cecilia Burciaga, the university's highest-ranking Hispanic dean, who had been fired over spring break as part of $5 million in budget cuts; the creation of a Chicano studies major; the founding of a community center for largely Hispanic East Palo Alto; and the imposition of a university-wide ban on grapes in solidarity with the United Farm Workers union.[4]

Three of the students went on a hunger strike. When a friend asked Provost Rice if she was bothered by young people starving themselves over her policies, Condi responded, "I'm not hungry. I'm not the one who's not eating."[5] She told Jendayi Frazer, now a junior professor at DU, "If they decide they want to go on a hunger strike, that's their decision."[6]

But the fasts finally sparked negotiations. At 11:30 on Friday night, the university and student leaders reached an agreement on what steps Stanford was willing to take toward meeting their demands. The next morning, Casper and Rice went to the tent city on the quad to carry out the ceremonial reconciliation. The previous night, student leaders had demanded that the president and provost sign the list of university commitments. When Casper and Rice refused, the students dropped the issue. But now they insisted again. "We were regarded with intense hostility," recalled Casper.[7] Irritated that the students were going back on their agreement, Casper signed nevertheless.

But not Rice. During the earlier talks she had yelled at one point, "That's it! I'm tired of negotiating," said former dean of students Michael Jackson. "Gerhard told her, 'Calm down; this is not Shevardnadze or some Politburo member.'"[8] Now, as her fellow administrators prayed that she would just sign the paper so it would all be over and they could go home, Rice stood on principle. Casper pointed out that the statement committed the university to nothing it had not already agreed to do. Condi relented and added her signature to his.

It was one of Rice's softer moments. Nearing the end of her first year as provost, Condi had developed a reputation as a take-no-prisoners administrator, to put it mildly. She had wowed faculty and her fellow managers with her grasp of complex issues and her powers of persuasion. At her first meeting of the Faculty Senate, the elected representatives of Stanford's professorate, for example, she had announced that the university had to cut $18 million to $20 million from its $1.5 billion budget over the next three years, on top of $40 million dollars in already instituted cuts.[9] By calling on the faculty's love of the university, she won them over. At a staff meeting in November, she had preached, "I understand that people are tired and they're weary. I'm going to ask you if you will be willing to roll up your sleeves and commit to thinking that almost no task is really impossible . . . Have faith in your own resilience and your own strength."[10]

And Faculty Senate members enthusiastically described her first budget presentation as "the best budget speech" they'd ever heard. "Condi didn't know diddly-squat about budgets, but she had internalized this stuff," marveled a colleague. "It was astonishing."[11]

But Rice had also developed a reputation as an autocrat. In one meeting, when she was unmoved by a manager's argument, he told her, "You don't understand" and restated his case. "That was it," recalled an administrator who was present. "The next week we laid [his unit] off."[12] When Marsh McCall, an emeritus classics professor, publicly criticized a university ad campaign, Rice called him to her office. She told him, "Either you're a member of the team, or you're not a member of the team," McCall would later tell a reporter.[13]

Rice didn't tolerate opposition or mistakes. Her wrath didn't erupt with trembling fury. Instead she grew almost immobile. Her eyes narrowed and her spine stiffened. Then she launched a verbal vivisection of whoever had challenged her. "I observed a coldhearted, merciless way of dealing with people," said a former employee who had been shocked to learn Rice's father was a minister. "There was so little compassion, so little humanity. . . . It was a major mistake to disagree with her. People who were not aware of that danger generally paid a price."[14]

Drama professor Harry Elam, a friend of Rice's, remembered a session of the Faculty Senate steering committee at which the Women's Caucus was scheduled to present a report. "[Condi] kept them waiting outside just to wait."[15]

A participant at another Rice meeting with senior faculty women who voiced concern over a loss of morale among female junior professors said talking to Rice "was like talking to a brick wall. You'd try to say something, and she would say [banging on the table], 'No, no, no!' All I could think of was Khrushchev banging the shoe at the UN . . . She was a Sovietologist; she learned her lesson well from her subjects."[16]

Rice refused to even meet with graduate students who were considering unionizing, said one of their representatives. "[Her attitude] was 'I'm intelligent, I'm right, so just sit down and shut up' . . . She was really quite nasty to me. As a result, I withdrew from campus politics."[17]

Ewart Thomas, the black veteran administrator, actually pulled Rice aside. "Condi, you don't have to eviscerate people," he told her. "Leave them with their dignity."[18] A decade later, it was still a common refrain among faculty, administrators, and much of Rice's staff: She had robbed those who confronted her of their dignity.

Shock at the new Condi was amplified by the contrast with the Rice everyone thought they knew. As a colleague, she could be distant, but she was unfailingly polite and respectful. "The public person was so poised, so charming, [that] these impressions were met with disbelief among alumni, even students," said a former administrator.[19]

It marked an abrupt change in the life of the university. Many faculty, staff, and former administrators believed that under President Donald Kennedy, Stanford had developed a bureaucracy that overrelied on consensus. "It took a ridiculous amount of time," said history professor David Kennedy, "but it was Politics 101, and Condi wasn't willing to do it." Because Rice as provost was the chief operating officer and the internal face of university leadership (Casper being the face of the university to the world), most critics blamed her.

Nowhere was Rice's intransigence more vividly—and more publicly—displayed than in a handful of Faculty Senate meetings in 1998. Casper and Rice had begun their collaboration in 1993 with a series of high-profile actions that demonstrated their commitment to affirmative action. They refocused the Office of Multicultural Development on staff affirmative action and reinstated a vice provost position overseeing faculty diversity. At her inaugural Faculty Senate meeting, Rice declared, "Affirmative action needs attention, as well as women's issues and the issue of junior faculty."[20] Taking a page from her father's playbook as a dean at DU, Rice formed a committee to study how to increase the number of minority graduate students.[21] But after a succession of high-profile denials of tenure to highly qualified women—and the provost's seeming unwillingness to use her power of review to overturn them—some women faculty questioned the administration's commitment to gender diversity.

In November 1993, the Provost's Committee on the Recruitment and Retention of Women Faculty, established by Rice's predecessor, issued a report painting a dismal picture.

> According to data compiled by the American Association of University Professors (AAUP) for 1992–93, when compared to the University of Chicago, Cal Tech, MIT, and universities in the Ivy League and the Pac Ten, Stanford's ranking with respect to the percentage of women faculty is *third from the bottom for all faculty and fifth from the bottom for full professors*. [emphasis in the original]
>
> Only at two technical schools, Cal Tech and MIT, is the percentage of women faculty lower than ours. Ironically, Stanford, which has been coeducational since its founding, has a lower representation of women on its faculty than do Yale, Princeton and Dartmouth, institutions that have had all male student bodies until recently.[22]

Commonly known as the Strober report, after committee chair and education professor Myra Strober, the document made sixteen recommendations for improving the status of women at Stanford. As Strober told the university news service, the way to judge whether the committee had been successful would be to interview junior female faculty three or four years later and "hear them say they find this is a most supportive place in which to do their work."[23]

But in May 1998, the Faculty Senate Women's Caucus concluded that the situation had grown worse. In presenting its report on the post-Strober years, the caucus said it felt "an increasing sense of unease . . . about a potential decline of the university's effective commitment to gender equity," and "a decline in vigilance will slow Stanford's gradual progress toward gender equity."[24] The presenters acknowledged what they called small increases in the percentage of women faculty and tenured female professors, but they said those gains were offset by demoralization among junior women. Since 1980, they said, seven men had been hired for every three women, and they claimed there was a "slight indication" that tenure rates for women were declining.

"Given the weight placed on evaluations in hiring and promotion," said history professor Estelle Freedman, "and given research that suggests that women are disadvantaged in these evaluative processes, we feel we must take special caution to control for unintentional gender bias." Noting that affirmative action was no longer used in making tenure decisions, the caucus suggested that that policy be reconsidered, as well as departmental timetables and goals for diversity hiring. Many of the proposals in the report, Freedman said, emphasized the need for leadership by the provost, deans, and department chairs.[25]

Provost Rice rose to present her own report, based on a separate study the university had undertaken. "I'm the provost and the chief academic officer, so I'm the one responsible for this area," said Rice. "I'd like it to be very clear that I simply do not believe that there has been a turning back . . . The numbers will show that in fact we continue to make slow and steady progress on the hiring and tenuring of women at Stanford." Rice's transparencies depicted an increase in women faculty from 14.7 percent in 1992 to 18.1 percent in 1997 and increases in each of the university's schools. Moreover, Rice said, the 1993 Strober report had been wrong: Stanford's large engineering school, overwhelmingly male, had pushed the university to the bottom along with the Massachusetts Institute of Technology and California Technical University. She displayed charts comparing

Stanford to five unnamed elite universities at the school level—humanities and sciences, law, engineering, business, etc. "Stanford and these other universities look pretty much alike," she said.[26]

Rice acknowledged some "red flags" in a handful of departments and in the number of senior-level faculty women but emphasized that "tenure rates are not differential by men and women, and we simply have to say that." Junior-faculty low morale was due to misperceptions created by a few high-profile cases of tenure denial, Rice contended; there was no structural problem at Stanford. Rice said the university should correct its limited shortcomings through better hiring and mentoring of all junior faculty. She noted that she had appointed two vice provosts to deal largely with diversity and reminded the faculty of Stanford's "incentive funds" to pay for billets for minorities and women in disciplines where they were underrepresented.

She was most emphatic about affirmative action: "I am completely opposed to the introduction of affirmative action criteria at the time of tenure . . . I myself am a beneficiary of a Stanford strategy that took affirmative action seriously, that took a risk on a young PhD from the University of Denver, where Stanford doesn't normally get its faculty." She said she had also benefited from Casper's "thinking outside the box" and naming as provost a 38-year-old black woman who had never chaired a department.[27]

The members of the Women's Caucus and their constituents, lining the walls of the most heavily attended Senate meeting of the year, were unimpressed. Rice was making the same argument she had for years: There was no bias. It was exactly that attitude that incensed the women; all you had to do was *look* and *listen* to know there was a problem at Stanford, they thought.

Though she didn't say it as explicitly in the meeting, Rice believed, as she had told the university-run *Stanford Report* days before, "It's just that this is a very competitive and tough place."[28] To her, the caucus's report was exactly the kind of excuse making she loathed—looking for barriers instead of conquering them.

Rice's statistics-laden argument won over many if not most of the largely male Senate, but Susan Okin, a respected political scientist and a Women's Caucus member, challenged the provost's assessment. Okin said that the School of Humanities and Sciences (H&S), the university's largest, had used "a form of affirmative action . . . not only in hiring, but also at the time of tenure and promotion from at least 1983 to 1993." (Rice was tenured in 1987.) "I would like to know when exactly that policy changed, who changed it, and whom they consulted about the change, and also why it was changed, especially during a period when Stanford is supposedly trying to increase the diversity of the university."[29]

Then Okin read a letter from the grievance officer Rice had appointed to look into the most controversial of the recent tenure denials, that of history professor Karen Sawislak. The history department had voted unanimously—except for one abstention—to grant the labor historian tenure, but the department's approval was reversed when the case reached the dean of H&S. Sawislak appealed the denial, first to the dean and then to the provost. The grievance officer Rice appointed determined, "The decision of the dean to deny tenure was one which a person in the position of decision maker might reasonably have made, albeit by placing the most negative possible construction on the candidate's record." Okin asked how the provost could contend that Stanford was still committed to diversity if the university had moved from using affirmative action in tenure to considering it "reasonable" to read a female scholar's application in "the most negative possible" light.[30]

Sawislak's case—which had generated protests and petitions—along with a handful of other tenure denials and the suicide of a Chicana associate professor that fall led many professors to conclude there was a crisis among junior women faculty, whatever its dimensions and whatever its causes.

When Okin quoted the grievance officer's appraisal at the Faculty Senate meeting, Rice snapped, "Those are not my words!" according to a Rice supporter.[31]

Okin would tell a reporter years later, "Nobody stood up for me. That's Condi's power. She was completely commanding. People behaved as though they were helpless. That shook me."[32]

Whatever affirmative action policies previous administrations had pursued, Rice said, "I'm the chief academic officer now, and I am telling you that, in principle, I do not believe in, and in fact will not apply, affirmative action criteria at time of tenure.[33]

In the end the Senate voted, as the caucus recommended, that the provost report annually on the university's efforts to recruit and retain women faculty.[34] But the battle had been joined.

In the weeks ahead, Rice would make an argument she hadn't made to the Senate. She declared that there had never been a policy at Stanford to take gender and race into account when making tenure decisions. And she produced a document that explicitly barred a different standard for women and minorities.[35]

Only Rice knew it was not that simple. Ewart Thomas, dean of H&S from 1989 to 1993 and a friend of Rice's (he would throw the black community's going-away party for her when she left Stanford for the Bush campaign), had sent a letter to Rice's office confirming that during his deanship and that of his predecessor, Norman Wessells (from 1983 to 1989), there had indeed been a policy of applying affirmative action in borderline tenure cases—not a different or lesser standard.[36]

Former president Donald Kennedy told the *San Jose Mercury News* the same thing. "President Casper called me and read me the riot act," said Kennedy. "I said, 'Wait a minute, I'm reporting history here' . . . Essentially his position was, 'you shouldn't have told a reporter; it made a problem for my provost and my administration.'"[37]

Kennedy was surprised by the "forcefulness" with which Rice espoused what he too considered a change in Stanford's affirmative action policy. "Condi would [not] have been criticized at all, because she was both African American and a woman, for saying that in the case of equal qualification, some marginal preference should be allocated to minorities or women."

Rice was technically correct; affirmative action in tenure decisions was against written policy. "But [Wessells] said it on several occasions. He encouraged departments in that direction," said Kennedy. If a department was considering two "equally distinguished" candidates, one a white male and one a black female, and the department preferred to hire the white male based on, say, his area of expertise and the fact that the black woman's expertise was in an area that was already represented in the department, then Wessells would give an additional billet to the department so it could hire both candidates—though, based purely on the department's needs, the black woman would not have won tenure. "We did that," said Kennedy. In 1999, Wessells, then at another school, told *Stanford* magazine in the 1980s, "There was an understanding that you could take factors like gender and race into consideration at the time of tenure."[38]

The creative ambiguity existed for legal reasons; to state unequivocally that in cases where there was a "tie" Stanford would hire a woman or a minority over an equally qualified white male would have invited legal action. But because tenure deliberations were confidential and the decisions usually boiled down to judgment calls, there was no way to know whether individual professors, who made the initial tenure decision, had applied Wessells's rule. Rice argued, "I cannot—and the university cannot—elevate to the level of policy, statements of belief."[39]

Rice's refusal to acknowledge the situation was not black-and-white, and her disregard for what respected community members would have sworn under oath was true, offended even those who agreed that affirmative action had no place in tenure decisions—and most of the faculty, eighty percent white and seventy-two percent male, did agree. Many of her African American friends believed Rice was spinning the data in service of her views and the administration's objectives, ignoring structural realities that adversely affected women and minorities, such as nonacademic demands on their time, like mentoring students of their race or gender, and the greater likelihood that minorities and women studied nontraditional areas of inquiry, making it harder to impress tenured establishment peers.

Moreover, since some minority candidates clearly had benefited from a system that decided borderline cases in their favor during the time Rice came up for tenure, many of her colleagues suspected Rice so ardently denied what Thomas and Kennedy said because she felt personally implicated—that either she had benefited from affirmative action in her own tenure case or that she feared her peers would suspect she had.

At least two political science professors who sat on Rice's tenure review committee said affirmative action had not been a factor. Though her academic output was limited, she was not considered a borderline candidate. But her friend Chip Blacker put it slightly differently. "Generally in the social sciences you need a second book and a handful of articles at the best journals" to get tenure, he said. "Condi had a single authored book, but she had one very important journal article . . . in *World Politics*, which borrowed heavily from organizational theory, so it was interdisciplinary. It was really good. I think she was tenured on that piece."[40]

So did Rice. But tenure committee members said that wasn't the case. In addition, Lieutenant General William E. Odom, one of the leading experts on Soviet civilian-military relations, Rice's area of concentration and the area on which she was being judged for tenure, said her piece "The Party, the Military, and Decision Authority in the Soviet Union"[41] was "very clearly written" but unimpressive.[42]

In the early seventies, Odom had argued that there was no inherent tension between the political ideology of Soviet leaders—party before self—and the ethos of the military—mission before self. Another scholar, Roman Kolkowitz, had posited that military professionalism and Communist ideology were incompatible. At issue was what kind of control—and therefore how much control—the Soviet political leadership had over the military, as well as who was really in charge. Rice's journal article sought a nuanced middle ground, arguing that there was a "loose coupling" between political and military elites. "I couldn't even figure out what that meant," said Odom. "[As a scholar] she just wasn't significant. It would be very hard for me to figure out why Stanford gave her tenure on [the basis of] her publications."

A foreign affairs expert very close to Rice added, "She's a conventional mind. Except for the book she did with Zelikow on Germany, the stuff she [wrote] by herself is mediocre."[43]

"Would she have gotten tenure as a white male? Maybe. Maybe not, but maybe," said a knowledgeable Stanford source. Of the one book she had published at that point, a work about the Czech army, based on her thesis, he said, "It wasn't something that would set political science on fire . . . But she had a good publications record, she had visibility, she was an excellent teacher, and she had . . . service [to the university] and presence. People get tenure on that basis—but not necessarily and not often."[44]

Ironically, what made Rice a standout in political science was not her scholarship but the power of her character; she was dynamic and engaging, qualities that most of her colleagues lacked. "I think [Condi's getting tenure] had to do with her perceived trajectory," Blacker conceded. "People were betting on her as someone who was going to be a very lively presence. And sometimes you take risks."[45]

Given her confidence, Rice never doubted that she deserved tenure, but she did believe that using affirmative action would call into question the credentials of almost every minority or female faculty member. "She said she wouldn't want, and she would expect I would feel the same way," said Harry Elam, "our tenure diminished by saying there was a different standard."[46]

Former *Stanford Daily* columnist Ngai Croal would have a similar complaint about Rice. In 2001 Rice told *Newsweek*, "Professors [pulled] punches with black students about low-quality work, even though these were kids who had gone to Exeter."[47] As Croal saw it, Rice was devaluing the credentials of every African American who had attended Stanford, just as she didn't want her own diminished. "If she witnessed this, then the logical question is, what action did she take?" he said. "And if she didn't take action, then I would be very suspicious of the remarks. And they're apocryphal; she [now] works for a man who has benefited from the soft bigotry of low expectations, yet she chooses to shit on black students, *her* students."[48]

Rice rarely shared the stresses of the job with her family or friends; she just worked out harder. (Though she did apparently have a thing for Kentucky Fried Chicken in some times of strain.)[49] She plunged into her music; she had restarted piano lessons in the summer of 1995 and was playing in a chamber music group. And she visited the after-school program she had help found in East Palo Alto for poor but motivated kids of color.

At first, Rice's lessons with the music department's director of keyboard studies, George Barth, were not very intense. They began with a Chopin nocturne and most of a Beethoven sonata. Then Rice told Barth she wanted to work much harder; she planned to perform a Brahms quintet with the renowned Muir String Quartet. It was a challenging piece, and Rice worked as many as ten hours a week with Barth, impressing him with her dedication, given her responsibilities. She wanted all the criticism he could give, softly repeating his every instruction as if committing it to memory.

Rice liked the German composers, especially Johannes Brahms, in whose work she said there was "unresolved tension." Some of that tension grew from Brahms's often-contradictory style. There was also tension in his harmonies; in one of his late pieces, written in falling thirds, he constantly gave the listener a musical reference point and then introduced a note that didn't seem to belong. There was a sense of striving in the music—sometimes strained, sometimes heavy with baggage—that never reached closure. That Condoleezza Rice, so self-contained, would most enjoy the music of unfulfilled striving suggested an inner life more complex than her perpetually composed exterior indicated.

She later told a music reporter that she thought of Brahms as being "passionate without being sentimental. You have to be pretty disciplined . . . I'm one of those people that if you put [a piece of music] in front of me, I can read it. But if you ask me to play it by ear or with improvisation, I have a much harder time, so I guess I'm tidy and disciplined even when I'm playing the piano."[50] As her undergraduate music professor Theodor Lichtmann said, she didn't do abandon.

Paul Brest, dean of the law school and an amateur violist, had brought the piano part for Robert Schumann's piano quartet to his first meeting with the new provost and told her it was time for her to return to playing. Brest, Rice, and a group of friends played chamber music regularly at his house, working through most of the piano quintet repertoire. At a faculty amateur music evening, the quartet performed two movements of the Schumann piano quintet, and Rice played "two pianos," Brahms's Variation on a Theme by Joseph Haydn, with Barth. In her chamber music group, as in her classes with Barth, Rice demonstrated extraordinary "give and take," said Brest, "more give and take than I see in some other parts of her life."[51]

Rice escaped into the silliness of Hollywood blockbusters with Brest's Summer Movie Group, pointing out the errors in 1997's *Air Force One* with Harrison Ford. Her other extracurricular passion, in addition to her corporate board service, was her work with the Center for a New Generation (CNG).

Clara and John had recruited Condoleezza to speak at a graduation ceremony for eighth graders in East Palo Alto. Impressed by the poise of the brightest kids, Condi asked Clara over dinner what programs the Ravenswood City School District, which covered the largely poor cities of East Menlo Park and East Palo Alto, had for the gifted. Clara said it was difficult enough getting resources for the underperforming kids; there was little left for the strongest students.[52] The median family income in 2000 in East Palo Alto was $14,000, compared with $56,000 in Palo Alto and $112,000 in nearby Atherton. Only ten percent of Ravenswood seventh graders would score at the "proficient" level in English on statewide exams, and only nine percent would be rated proficient in math, compared with eighty-two and seventy percent, respectively, for Palo Alto.[53]

With the help of a well-heeled friend, Condi founded the CNG, an afterschool program where motivated students could receive instruction in math, language arts, science and technology, and, of course, music. Rice made sure the kids had art, ballet, a choir, and a band. She raised money for uniforms and brought Colin Powell in to speak.

The goal of CNG was to beat the odds, to equip students with the same tools—self-esteem, a capacity for hard work, and a belief in the future—that John

Rice had instilled in the children of Titusville. The ninety students, ranging from the fourth to the eighth grade, were being prepared for high-school college-prep classes. The graduating eighth graders attended private schools or joined national preparatory programs like Upward Bound and College Track. When a student voiced to Rice her skepticism that there was any point to all the extra work because fifty percent of Ravenswood kids never even graduate from high school, Rice replied, "What makes you think you have to be one of those fifty percent?"

That was Rice's philosophy at Stanford, too, particularly when it came to black women. Long before she became provost, she had mentored Jendayi Frazer. But Frazer had sought Rice out. Sharon Holland had not.

Holland, an assistant professor in English—and a liberal, activist, African American lesbian—had been suspicious when Rice approached her on the quad. A PhD from Michigan, Holland had been fighting the power since her undergrad days at Princeton: sitting in at the dean's office, pushing for (and winning) changes to university policy around the issue of sexual assault. So as soon as she entered Rice's office, she announced, "If this is an attempt to co-opt me, I'm more savvy than that."[54]

Rice told Holland she had heard a lot about her and just wanted to get to know her, to keep track of what and how she was doing. "Maybe because I was a black woman, doing the work I was doing, she knew how lonely I'd be," said Holland.

The associate professor and the provost became close—somewhat incongruously, since Holland was one of those demoralized junior faculty members the Women's Caucus was always talking about. Holland's time in the provost's office would be among her most pleasant memories of Stanford. The benefits of her relationship with Rice were tangible. When Holland was in the process of purchasing a house during the dot-com boom, Rice stepped in with monies from a discretionary fund to help stave off the disastrous effects of multiple bidding.

When Holland told Rice the English department was treating women and people of color unfairly (lesser qualified white men were being mentored and given more time to publish before a tenure decision was made), Rice told her that if she had problems with the department, she should just come to her. And then she gave Holland her usual stoic advice: "'If you get tenure, great; you have a nice house. If you don't, then you sell [and go somewhere else].' She was trying to tell me, 'It's about you, not the institution,'" said Holland. "Without Condoleezza Rice's help, I don't think I would have survived."

Finally a white professor in the department told Holland, "These people are just racist. You need to move on."[55] When Holland received a last-minute offer from the State University of New York at Albany, she took it.

She would leave behind skeletons, including the suicide of Lora Romero. Like Rice, Romero had been a Ford Foundation fellow. When she killed herself on October 10, 1997, she was just thirty-seven years old.[56] While participating in the Aztlan University teach-in three years earlier, Romero had told the Chicano hunger strikers, "There's a tendency in U.S. culture as a whole and on campuses to interpret political action as being juvenile, coming out of emotion rather than intellect, and as being extraneous to the university. What you are doing is an intellectual act, and don't let anybody tell you otherwise."[57]

In her suicide note to Holland, Lora told Sharon to pick up her dog, Scully, at the kennel. When she received the letter, the first person Holland called was Rice, whose secretary pulled her out of a meeting with trustees. For a week after Lora's suicide, an unmarked police car kept vigil outside Sharon's house. Holland figured Condi was looking after her.

Holland wasn't alone. When Dean Michael Jackson was being courted by another university, Rice acted swiftly to keep him.[58] When Lucius Barker, chair of the political science department, wanted to recruit an assistant professor, Rice made sure H&S had the billet to do it.[59] Like her father had at DU, Rice often operated discreetly. When an effort to recruit a black professor over the resistance of a department was exposed by an impolitic African American colleague, Rice had to deny that she had given an ironclad guarantee.[60]

"She was really good to black faculty in general [and] to the black community," said Harry Elam. "It was the opposite feeling with women and the Latino faculty."[61]

Tellingly, Elam and Rice never overtly discussed race or her efforts: "I spent enough time with her that we could have, and we didn't." As had been the case growing up in Titusville, for Rice race wasn't something you discussed much; you just did what you had to do, and the community took care of its own.

As much as Rice protected the black faculty, they protected her. Ewart Thomas decreed that no one would speak ill of Condi publicly. The black solidarity was particularly vexing to Holland's fellow progressive feminists because, though Holland agreed with the Women's Caucus, she refused to criticize Rice.

Condi's place in the bosom of the black faculty did not translate into identification with blacks in general, however. When Rice was just another professor, it was a sometimes-discomforting irony, such as when Rice's observations about the shortcomings of poor African Americans spoiled a lovely dinner with Thomas.[62] Then, Rice's limited sense of racial solidarity had been a nonissue, especially because she rarely discussed race.

But her critics charged that as provost, Rice's apoliticism had political consequences. For one white feminist, the effect was as clear as the difference between Rice as provost and Thomas as dean of H&S. "A lot of people he brought in were at the point of promotion and tenure when Condi became provost, and it was a night-and-day kind of thing . . . When John Hennessy replaced Condi, it was night and day again. . . . [Hennessy] acknowledged there was a problem here and that to deny the problem [was] to make it worse."[63]

While black faculty made allowances for one of their own—allowances many of them said they would not have made for a white provost—and white liberals were often conflicted about criticizing a woman of color, black students had none of those concerns. When the administration proposed consolidating all the minority student organizations under one budget and one roof, black students rebelled. "Once these organizations were put under the same roof, it would be easier to make cuts to all of them," said former *Daily* columnist Croal. At a forum to discuss the issue in the winter of 1994, he challenged the decision. Rice replied, "I have been black all my life."[64]

"It was racial jujitsu," said Croal a decade later. "It was calculated . . . My question was about her policy." To many liberal African American students, Rice's race was secondary.

Rice sounded a similar note in her final speech as provost, her Class Day address to the class of 1999: "Do you hold to the notion that you must find role models only in people who look like you, or that you can be a role model only for your own?" she asked. "Identity and history are double-edged swords. On the one hand . . . one is who is not grounded in his own culture is most assuredly lost. Identity and cultural connection are as important to your humanness as individual development.

"But when that history becomes tinged with victimization, the dangers are many. Today, everyone is angry about something that has been done to them, something they have been denied. Every group, every nation, every ethnic group seems caught up in 'Why me?'—holding on to the old wounds to find the moral high ground of victimization and suffering. To the degree that I have suffered more than you have, my demands and my interests take precedence over yours.

"This is a dangerous business."[65]

The previous winter, Condoleezza had announced she would step down at the end of the academic year.[66] Wanting to return to what she called her first love, international politics, she planned to work for an investment bank dealing with "private financial capital and economic growth" abroad.[67] In the meantime she would help Texas governor George W. Bush with his run for the White House, but not full-time. "[I'll] do what I can for him on the side," Rice told *Stanford* magazine.[68]

Rice was leaving Stanford stronger than she found it. She had balanced the budget ahead of schedule and would leave her successor a small surplus, even after increasing the incentive funds for hiring minorities and boosting the financial aid budget. Academically, she and Casper had remade the undergraduate experience, introducing courses that ensured freshmen and sophomores would have the opportunity to be taught by Nobel laureates in intimate intellectual contact.[69] And there were myriad smaller accomplishments, like endowing teaching chairs for performance in the music department.

Most significantly, Rice had shaken up Stanford's "we've always done it this way" complacency, right down to how the university ordered its paper clips.[70] Beginning in her second year as provost, other universities constantly approached her to ask if she'd consider their presidencies. Even as secretary of state, Rice would say of the position, "In some ways, it's still the best job I ever had."[71]

She acknowledged that she had been too brutal—in the beginning. "I was really young, and I didn't really know how to be a boss . . . I kind of like being verbally combative," said Rice. "I didn't really think, *What does it mean to be in a meeting with fifteen people and the provost says your presentation was really junk?* I mean, how does that affect that person who's given that presentation? And I had to learn to get better at that."

But Rice's critics said the problem persisted for more than her first few years. In November 1998, dozens of female professors and researchers filed a grievance with the Department of Labor. The women alleged they had been the victims of "widespread" gender discrimination. The *San Jose Mercury* quoted a Labor Department attorney who claimed the law required affirmative action be applied in promotions, not just in hiring, by any organization receiving federal money.[72] (Stanford received more than $500 million a year.)[73]

Casper called the investigation political, claiming Rice was singled out by the Clinton administration because she was a black Republican. Similarly, the other side later claimed the case languished because the incoming Bush administration sat on it. The investigation would resume without explanation in 2005[74] and is still under way.

Years after Rice's departure, Stanford would smart from what some still called her "reign of terror." "Even now I really fear the lengths she would go to," said one person who was both critical and laudatory of Rice, his dread audible. "A lot of her decisions weren't bad; it was the way she approached leadership, which was despotic."[75]

Toward the end of her tenure, Rice invited the women who had done battle with her to her office. "We had one fence-mending lunch where I felt," said one woman as tears suddenly came to her eyes, "she was so gracious and so did not hear a word [we said]—so formally nice and . . . and practically useless."[76]

Rice dismissed the harshest criticism. "I was having to do difficult things," she said. "People [were] out defending their narrow interests. Why would I feel hurt about that? That's what I expect people to do."[77]

More surprising were the additional explanations Rice reportedly gave at the time. She told more than one confidant that the clashes with Chicanos were really "about the black/brown thing," meaning the competition between African Americans and Latinos for power.[78] She saw the tensions with some African American students the same way. "All this stuff I didn't have access to until I learned it from Condi . . . skin tone issues," said Blacker. "I had never heard the expression 'high yella' . . . I said, 'What the hell does that mean?' And she said, 'Some of it is, I look a particular way to other African Americans' . . . So there was some of that."[79]

Black faculty felt much of the opposition toward Rice stemmed from white resentment. "She was a black woman telling [whites] how to run something they created," said Holland. "I think her style could have used some polishing, but if she had been a white man, she would have been seen as just another seriously difficult and frustrating conservative, people wouldn't have [considered] her the devil incarnate."[80]

Friends said that early on, some of the greatest resistance to Rice's leadership had come from the white male establishment, the deans who headed schools and felt Rice had jumped the line because of her color and her sex. In one of her first meetings, a dean had treated Rice dismissively, said Randy Bean. "It was, like, 'Okay, babe, now that you've gotten where you're going . . . this is what I want.' She backed him off at the other end of the tank. He was floored that anybody would stand up to him. She got a lot of shit. And I think part of her [behavior] was 'Hey, I am here. Deal with it. And this is what needs to be done.'"[81]

Said Blacker, "I think she was right to be apprehensive that unless she demonstrated that she could take the heat, people would try to undermine her. And no one really ever tried to undermine her because they knew at that level, in university terms, she was ruthless.

"She also made many members of the dominant culture uncomfortable because she shattered myths," he said. "But it's not as threatening to the majority culture because it is the majority culture. So the majority culture reaches out and tries to assimilate you . . . Look what happened in her case: The doors of power were thrown open. Corporate boards, foundation boards. . . . that's the way majorities stay majorities—ultimately, they keep pulling people in. And she was perfectly happy to do that."

But whatever part race and gender played in generating opposition to Rice was likely secondary to the role played by her inexperience as a manager and its varied manifestations: her inability or unwillingness to "manage down," her impatience with consensus building, her inflexibility.

"Condi, to that point in her life at least, would sometimes read a challenge in debate as an ad hominem attack," explained Blacker.[82] But Rice was also practicing workplace Realpolitik. As she advised protégé Kiron Skinner, "People may oppose you, but when they realize you can hurt them, they'll join your side."[83] And that she would not grow out of.

"She doesn't care for criticism," said Rice's stepmother, Clara plainly. "If she says something, even though it's proven wrong, [to change her mind] is like admitting that she has made a mistake. She wants to be perfect . . . Growing up, everyone treated her and acted like she was [perfect]: finishing college so early and accomplishing what she did, she just has a superhigh standard of herself. [I'm] not saying that's all bad, but then it can cause other personality flaws, [like] being stubborn."[84]

Even a source who worked closely with Rice and strongly praised her said, "She [has] a great quality: she can make up her mind under adverse circumstances, but once she makes up her mind, it is very hard to get her off a particular line."[85] Said Paul Brest, "Could somebody else have been in that position and not created quite so much resistance? Sure . . . Condi's intuitions are not [to] compromise." Watching Rice after she returned to Washington, Brest added, "You see some very strong common strains."[86]

In the end, Rice (and Casper) may have been exactly what Stanford needed. "After the indirect costs scandal . . . the system needed to be shocked," said former dean Jackson. "Wherever I go, from Singapore to Budapest," said Casper, "they hold me responsible for American foreign policy, and I will say to anyone who will listen, 'She was an outstanding provost.'" Added Blacker simply, "She did what had to be done—sometimes with too much zeal."[87]

CHAPTER EIGHT

TRANSITION

People that work hard and make the right decisions in life can achieve anything they want in America.[1]

PRESIDENT-ELECT GEORGE W. BUSH,
in naming Condoleezza Rice Assistant to the President for National Security Affairs
Governor's Mansion
Austin, Texas
December 18, 2000

C ondoleezza was trying to explain to her father exactly what she would be doing. The national media had made the logical connection between Rice leaving her post at Stanford in the summer of 1999 and the approaching presidential campaign. But Rice insisted she was only helping Texas governor George Bush's presidential bid. Should he win, she said, she would not follow her candidate to the White House; she was planning on working in the private sector for a while. It wasn't a ruse. Condi had told friends and family the same thing.

And John Rice had reacted with dismay even to that news. He didn't want his daughter to leave Stanford.[2] She had broken a barrier in the arena the Rices valued most, education, climbing higher than John had ever gone.

"You're going into *politics*?" John Rice demanded.

"No, Daddy," said Condoleezza. "I'm just going to help on the campaign."[3]

But George W. Bush had a way of winning people over. He had done it in Texas, defeating the charismatic Ann Richards in 1994 to claim his first political office. He won reelection four years later with sixty-nine percent of the vote, including twenty-one percent of the black vote, an impressive showing for a Republican and proof of his bipartisan appeal.[4]

Rice had first met Bush at an event at the White House when she was working for his father.[5] "The first time I *met him* met him," she said, was in 1995. Rice had telephoned "President Forty-One" to tell him she was coming to Houston for a Chevron board meeting and would love to come say hello.[6]

But the president was planning to be in Austin for George W.'s first legislative session as governor. He invited Rice to come along. Condi arrived early and sat in the governor's office for an hour, talking life, politics, and baseball;[7] Angelena had taught the great Willie Mays[8] at Fairfield Industrial High School.

By the time they sat down in George Shultz's living room at Stanford in April 1998[9] over coffee and cookies[10] with a handful of Republican intellectuals Shultz had gathered to "chat" with Bush,[11] the chemistry between Rice and W. was palpable. "He and Condi really clicked, you could see it—on a human level," said Shultz. The chat turned in a four-hour seminar on economic and foreign policy. "None of us knew whether he'd be a candidate yet. He didn't know."[12] Bush told Shultz the group should meet for more of these sessions down in Austin.

In July, Shultz convened the first meeting at the Governor's Mansion of what would come to be known as the Vulcans, named for the Roman god of forge and fire who built the armor, weapons, and thrones of the gods—and stood, cast in Alabama iron, atop Red Mountain in Birmingham. In addition to Rice, the invitees included Bush's father's secretary of defense, Dick Cheney, and Cheney's former Pentagon aide, Paul Wolfowitz. Colin Powell, another former Bush lieutenant, who wouldn't be invited to join the Vulcans, was out of the country, on a Mediterranean cruise with the former president and his family, including W.'s wife and daughters.[13]

In August[14] the governor and the provost met without the others. Since President Bush had left the White House, Condi had made a habit of visiting the Bush family compound in Maine once every summer.[15] In the early years, she helped Bush write his presidential memoir, *A World Transformed*. Stealing away to Kennebunkport became a favorite escape for Rice, along with weekends playing tennis at the Fairmont Mission Inn in Sonoma and summer master classes with the Muir in Utah and Montana. "It really was like a family relation with them," said a Stanford colleague.[16]

In 1998 President Bush asked Rice to come to Maine on some very specific dates. "George is going to be here," he told her, "and I want you to spend some time with him."[17] Bush was in the final throes of deciding whether to run. The conspicuous hole in his résumé was his lack of foreign policy experience. He knew little of the world, and he wanted Condi to explain it to him. From their times together he knew she could and, as important, he knew he'd like it. She was an uncommon academic: funny, fun, and optimistic, like Bush. "I like to be around her. I like lighthearted people, not people who take themselves so seriously," he would later tell a reporter. And "she's really smart!"[18]

For two and a half days, "we spent a lot of time out on the boat and in different places, talking about what you would face in foreign policy if you were president,"[19] remembered Rice. While fishing,[20] playing tennis, and working out side by side (she ran on a treadmill while he rowed and biked),[21] Condi and W. bonded.

"In a political sense, I think he kind of courted her," said Rice's Birmingham girlfriend Deborah Carson. "He really went after her.

"When she first started going down to Texas . . . I'd say, 'Are you going to work on the campaign?' and she said, 'Oh, no, no, I'm just going to go hang out and talk and I'm going to help him with some of his ideas.'

"I said, 'Condi, you're going to be on that campaign!'

'No. Uh-uh!'

"'Yes, you are.' And over time she got sucked in. He's *very* charming."[22]

Rice was drawn to Bush.[23]

"First of all, I thought he was wonderful to be around," she volunteered with a smile from the couch in her expansive State Department office when asked for her first impressions. "He was warm and funny and easy to be around," she repeated.[24]

"I thought he had just an incredibly inquisitive mind . . . you could barely finish an explanation before he was digging into it. And he was the first to say he didn't have much experience in foreign policy, but then we would start talking, and he would talk about dealing with this Mexican governor or that Mexican governor. And he'd been on these various trips [overseas], and I thought, 'Hmm, [he's] got a little bit of foreign policy background here,'" she nodded. "I thought he was somebody who was really sharp and asked really good questions and was also fun to be around."[25]

The attraction was platonic, Rice's friends and family insisted—despite speculation to the contrary that would take place in the coming years in black beauty salons and supermarket tabloids. Nevertheless, Brenda Hamberry-Green, Rice's own stylist, who had spent years commiserating with Condi over the challenges successful black women faced in finding a good man, noticed those ruminations ceased when Rice started working for Bush. "He fills that need" for a male presence, Brenda decided. "Bush is her feed."[26]

There was no denying Bush was a bad boy—literally, for most of his adult life. "He was an immature rich-kid brat," a friend would tell a reporter in 2000.[27] The year Condi had been an overachieving junior at DU, for instance, from 1972 to 1973, W. had served a less than regimented tour of duty in her native Alabama as a Texas National Guardsman.[28] While the well-mannered and disciplined Rice was discovering her love of political science and Hans Morgenthau's realism, the hard-drinking Bush was excessively enjoying what his friends would come to call, according to *Rolling Stone,* Bush's "missing year."[29] Condi was eighteen. George was twenty-six.

In fact, if any pair illustrated the reality of a black woman having to be twice as good to get half as far, it might have been Condi and W. Condoleezza was the product of two lines of African American strivers who saw themselves as "aristocratic"[30] but decidedly were not.[31] Her alma maters, with the underwhelming exception of St. Mary's Academy, were segregated schools and the middle-class bastions of DU and Notre Dame, but from the age of three she had been a study in discipline.

Bush—the grandson of a U.S. senator and the scion of a Connecticut Yankee family who came of age in West Texas, Houston, and Andover, Yale, and Harvard Business School, the elite Northeastern private schools of the establishment—had been a gadabout[32] until his fortieth birthday when, after a famous night of partying at the luxurious Broadmoor resort in Colorado, he decided it was time to stop drinking.[33] As Rice's mentor Brent Scowcroft figured it, Bush hadn't known who he was until he was forty-five.[34] He had done a dismal turn as an oil executive and had five better years as co-owner of the Texas Rangers baseball franchise,[35] his "first serious job,"[36] before becoming governor.

By the time Rice met him, Bush had became a Christian teetotaler and a devoted family man. They shared a strong religious faith, a belief in American power, similar senses of humor, and a conviction that sports was a metaphor for life. He admired her brains. She valued his instincts as a leader. Politically, she liked his "compassionate conservatism," the philosophy that those who wanted to lift themselves from poverty and ignorance should be given the opportunity. That had been the leitmotif of the Rice family for four generations. Most important, they were both iconoclasts. They saw themselves as outsiders on the inside: Rice as a function of her race and gender, Bush because he had never fit in as a Texas boy with the Northeastern elitists he came to disdain as snobs.[37]

"There was this connective stuff—that was really fully under way by the summer of 1999," said Rice's friend Blacker, "that made her open to what she always characterizes as [his] intuitive intelligence and, because he trusted her, made him open to the more structured way that she provides information . . . But what made it possible was this preexisting, almost structurally determined closeness because of the number of contact points.[38]

"There's a funny kind of transfer of energy and ideas that's almost—not random, but unstructured. It's as though they're Siamese twins joined at the frontal lobe. He's *extremely* comfortable with her. And she's extremely comfortable with him."

Even as a governor and a presidential candidate Bush remained a maverick, even a bit of a revolutionary.[39] It was just who he was. Rice recalled the debate within the campaign about Bush's May 2000 speech on America's nuclear posture. The candidate was going to propose what amounted to unilateral reductions in American's nuclear arsenal, tied to the development of an antiballistic missile shield that had become known under Reagan as "Star Wars." "[It was] pretty risky for the governor of Texas, [especially when] nobody really trusted his foreign policy credentials," said Rice.[40]

So risky that the Vulcans thought it might be best if Bush just "played defense" on the issue of nukes and missile defense. But the governor said, "No. Because I *intend* to do this, I have to go to the American people and tell them what I'm going to do' . . . and I thought, *Well, that's a novel concept.* It was that kind of boldness that I think came through."

By the summer of 1999, Rice was leading the Vulcans and doing for Bush what she had done for nearly a generation of Stanford students: reducing a complex and chaotic world to understandable facts. There were still flubs on the campaign trail, like when Bush flunked a Boston TV reporter's surprise quiz on world leaders[41] or when he couldn't tell a reporter for *Glamour* who the Taliban were (after she gave him a clue—"repression of women in Afghanistan"—he said, "Oh. I thought you said some band. The Taliban in Afghanistan! Absolutely. Repressive.")[42]

And even Condi had her gaffes. Retelling Bush's *Glamour* moment, Elaine Sciolino of the *New York Times* reported:

> Of course, Afghanistan is also not Ms. Rice's primary area of expertise. Asked in an interview to support her assertion in her recent article in *Foreign Affairs* that Iran is trying to spread "fundamentalist Islam" beyond its borders, she replied, "Iran has been the state hub for technology and money and lots of other goodies to radical fundamentalist groups, some will say as far-reaching as the Taliban."
>
> When reminded that Iran was a bitter enemy of the Taliban and that the two countries had almost gone to war in late 1998, she replied, "They were sending stuff to the region that fell into the hands of bad players in Afghanistan and Pakistan." She did not identify "the bad players." (In a subsequent conversation, she said that of course she knew that Iran and the Taliban were enemies.)
>
> On Iraq, she believes that President Saddam Hussein is an evil man, but declined to say what a George W. Bush administration would do to get rid of him.
>
> Despite her deliberate vagueness in areas with which she is unfamiliar, she has a reputation for being a quick study.[43]

Earlier in the piece, Sciolino had written, "A series of interviews indicate that Ms. Rice is much less sure-footed when the terrain is unfamiliar. Her silky voice becomes choppy, her crisp sentences vague."[44]

But such assessments were rare. Rice was impressive and commanding. It was the vision that she and Bush conveyed of America's role in the international arena—walk softly and carry a big stick, in essence—that drew the attention of the foreign policy establishment. Rice detailed the philosophy in a piece for *Foreign Affairs*, the premier foreign policy journal, taking aim at Chip Blacker's old boss with a sharpness rarely seen in the staid realm of international affairs.

The Clinton administration has assiduously avoided implementing [a disciplined and consistent foreign policy] . . . Instead, every issue has been taken on its own terms—crisis by crisis, day by day . . . The Bush administration had been able to reduce defense spending somewhat at the end of the Cold War in 1991. But the Clinton administration witlessly accelerated and deepened these cuts . . . The increased difficulty in recruiting people to the armed forces or retaining them is hardly surprising.

Moreover, the administration began deploying American forces abroad at a furious pace . . . The other major concern is a loss of focus on the mission of the armed forces . . . The president must remember that the military is a special instrument. It is lethal, and it is meant to be. It is not a civilian police force. It is not a political referee. And it is most certainly not designed to build a civilian society. Military force is best used to support clear political goals, whether limited, such as expelling Saddam from Kuwait, or comprehensive, such as demanding the unconditional surrender of Japan and Germany during World War II. It is one thing to have a limited political goal and to fight decisively for it; it is quite another to apply military force incrementally, hoping to find a political solution somewhere along the way. A president entering these situations must ask whether decisive force is possible and is likely to be effective and must know how and when to get out.[45]

The piece was a realist manifesto. Parts could have been penned by Hans Morgenthau himself.

Power matters, both the exercise of power by the United States and the ability of others to exercise it . . . To be sure, there is nothing wrong with doing something that benefits all humanity, but that is, in a sense, a second-order effect. America's pursuit of the national interest will create conditions that promote freedom, markets, and peace . . . America can exercise power without arrogance and pursue its interests without hectoring and bluster.[46]

It was a rhetorical direct hit. Clinton's people—and Josef Korbel's daughter, Madeline Albright, in particular—were outraged. They felt the attack was unfair on most of its points and presumed the existence of a world far simpler than the one in which we live. But other than Clinton Democrats, just about the only foreign policy experts who didn't agree with Rice's piece were the "neoconservatives." They found the would-be Bush doctrine imprecise and, like Clintonian foreign policy, unwilling to prioritize. They disliked its realist dogma and a nod Rice made to the United Nations, even as she criticized Clinton's overreliance on international consensus.

Rice did an admirable job of managing the Vulcan neocons—Wolfowitz, Richard Perle, and Dov Zakheim, the latter two of whom had worked at Reagan's Pentagon—deftly defusing their conflicts with the rest of the team: Richard Armitage, a Colin Powell confidant who, like Powell, had worked for Reagan's defense secretary, Casper Weinberger; Bob Zoellick, whom Rice had worked with during the first Bush presidency; Stephen Hadley, who had been Wolfowitz's aide at the Pentagon; and Bob Blackwill, who had been Rice's boss at the National Security Council. It was Blackwill whom Chip Blacker credited with teaching Condi the fine art of bureaucratic infighting before she became provost: "As she has been known to say, 'Sometimes you have to shoot a few up front in order to get people's attention.'"[47]

But the neocons didn't trust her, especially Perle, who had fallings-out with Rice throughout the campaign because of his hard ideological edge and lax message discipline, the trademark of the Bush campaign.[48] Neocons believed Rice was too close to George H. W. Bush personally and politically. And it was the errors of the first President Bush, the consequences of his lack of vision and his cautious timidity, that the neocons hoped to correct during the presidency of the second.

At home, still greater tests awaited. In February 2000, John Rice suffered what appeared to be a massive heart attack. Ann Reilly Dowd, a reporter from *George* magazine, had come to Palo Alto to profile the Republican front-runner's brainy black foreign policy guru (the media always called Rice "brainy"). In the middle of an interview, as John described carrying his wife and eight-year-old daughter to Ann's mother's house to avoid the stench of the gas bomb that had exploded next door, his eyes rolled to the back of his head and his head slumped to his chest. Dowd called 9-1-1 and then Condoleezza.[49]

When Rice arrived, John was splayed out on the floor receiving "shock treatments." Dowd reported that Rice's first move was to comfort her: "Almost serene, Condi said, 'God works in strange ways. Thank God you were here.'"[50]

After asking if anyone had called Clara, Rice went to her father. "Daddy, it's Condoleezza. I'm here. We're going to the hospital. We're going to take good care of you." Only after she calmly drove Dowd to the emergency room and John was admitted did Rice allow the first tears to stream down her face. "There's nothing more we can do but pray," she said.[51]

Not unlike his daughter, John Rice had a formidable stubbornness. He suffered from heart disease. A previous attack and complications from his diet and his weight—he weighed about 350 pounds—had already landed him in a wheelchair.[52] But John ignored his doctor's orders to stop eating pork, said Clara. "Any parts of a pig, he wanted. And he ate it." The doctor had told him the only thing keeping him alive were the dozen pills he took every morning and each night. But his sister Theresa Love had fallen ill and come to California to be hospitalized, and Theresa begged John to come see her several times a day. As a result, he had forgotten to refill his prescriptions. Clara didn't realize he wasn't taking his medication.[53]

At the hospital, doctors told Clara and Condi that John had suffered "a serious arrhythmic episode"—an irregular heartbeat. Before medics revived it, his heart had stopped, depriving his brain of oxygen. A respirator was breathing for him. The doctors wanted to "pull the plug. They thought he was brain-dead," said Clara. "The brain scan was all scrambled. I said, 'I know my husband and he would want to live!' He used to tell me, 'If I'm in an airplane and it falls I'm gonna find a way to live!'"[54]

"I said, 'My husband wants to *live*. Give him a chance!'"

Without Clara's consent to withdraw life support, the hospital put Rev. Rice in a room. After two or three days, Clara brought him a portable radio and tape player, along with his favorite jazz recordings. On the fourth or fifth day, his eyes suddenly fluttered and his fingers moved. The doctors took him off the respirator, and he breathed on his own. When Clara and Condi started singing "In the Garden," his favorite hymn, and forgot the words to the second verse, John picked it up. That's when Clara knew he'd be all right.

They moved him to a convalescence facility. The lack of oxygen had left him partially paralyzed and unable to speak normally. He struggled through intensive therapy. Chip's partner Louie and Condi's Aunt G stayed on top of the medical staff. As soon as he was well enough, John demanded to go home. Initially Condoleezza balked—how would Clara give him the round-the-clock care he needed? Finally Rice hired three gargantuan Pacific Islanders to tend to his needs at home. She paid one so much that he left the facility.

"[John] never had a bedsore," Clara boasted. "They'd start with that Keri lotion, from his head to his feet. I said, 'If I ever get in this position, I want to be cared for just like John.'"

In the thick of the campaign, Rice traveled more than she had anticipated would be necessary. She called home from the road, and the phone was put to John's ear. With America at peace and standing alone atop the world military, economically, and even culturally, Rice had thought foreign policy would be a secondary issue in the campaign. She had failed to realize that the greatest asset she brought to candidate Bush was herself. The press loved her. The political reporters tended to focus on the political advisers like Karl Rove, but Rice received more ink than all the other policy advisers combined. She ended up jetting around the country. She spoke at the first annual Texas Conference for Women, wowing twenty-five hundred women with a wide-ranging keynote address delivered without notes;[55] in Illinois, she courted black and women voters;[56] across the country, she costarred with Bush's mother and wife in the "W Stands for Women" tour.[57]

Rice was often front and center on strategic issues. When Bush unveiled his bold nuclear policy initiative, for instance, it was not the gray-haired wisemen who stood behind him conferring legitimacy (Kissinger, Scowcroft, Shultz, Powell) and answered questions about specifics, but Rice.[58]

On the dais of the Republican National Convention in Philadelphia, having been accorded a coveted speaking slot during prime time, she showed even more dramatically why she was a rare asset to the Republicans. She eviscerated the Democrats for their bigoted past—the racist "tests" that had prevented her now-ailing father from registering to vote in 1952 Alabama—and their condescending victim-based appeal to blacks today.

It was partisan red meat, giving little sign of Rice's politically ecumenical private life. In the middle of one of her arguments with Blacker, when Chip seemed to sound a lot like a Republican (as a hard-core realist, he often did), Condi asked him, frustrated, "Why *are* you a Democrat?"[59]

"Because I'm much more comfortable with our Jesse than I could ever be with your Jesse," said Blacker, referring to ultraliberal Jesse Jackson and Jesse Helms, the ultraconservative Republican chairman of the Senate Foreign Relations Committee.

Rice laughed and replied, "I'd have to think about that."

That Condoleezza hadn't thought about the Jesse question was another testament to her politics. Helms, by virtue of his Senate seniority, played a central role in the world of American foreign policy, but Rice didn't concern herself with his controversial views on social policy, race, sexuality, or AIDS. She was more focused on American power in the world than intramural scrimmages at home. Besides, she believed that the Republican Party being a "big tent" was a good thing. She didn't seemed bothered by Pat Buchanan, who had immediately succeeded her at the podium at the 1992 Republican National Convention—her first convention appearance—and declared,

> Friends, this election is about more than who gets what, it is about who we are. It is about what we believe. And what we stand for as Americans. There *is* a religious war going on in this country. It is a culture war as critical to the kind of nation we shall be as the Cold War itself. For this war is for the soul of America. And in that struggle for the soul of America, Clinton and Clinton are on the *other* side and George Bush is on our side.[60]

Conventional political wisdom held that Buchanan's ad hominem attack on gays, feminists, and liberals that night helped drive moderates to Clinton.

Rice didn't see Buchanan or the conservative wing of the party's battle against affirmative action and other domestic issues as centrally important—any more so than their opposition to gay or abortion rights, though she personally supported both. Blacker believed it was generational. "I came of age politically during Barry Goldwater's convention in 1964," he said. "I saw the swing away from East Coast liberal Republicanism to this other thing—it was built around not-so-subtle appeals to race. Counterposed to that was the civil rights struggle. You had to choose sides. And the right side was obvious to me.

"She's just that much younger," he continued. "She remembers the Birming-ham bombings, but she was only nine . . . I was thirteen. It makes a big differ-ence." Blacker believed, "You basically have to be ahistorical in order to be a Republican if you're a member of any minority group. She has chosen to be that way because she is forward-looking. And she likes the notion of being a positive agent for change."

In contrast to Buchanan's appeal to social conservatives, George W. Bush's convention was a politically diverse, multihued variety show, prominently show-casing Rice and Powell. Candidate Bush pleaded to the National Association for the Advancement of Colored People (NAACP), "Give me a chance to tell you what's on my heart" and acknowledged, "There is no escaping the reality that the party of Lincoln has not always carried the mantle of Lincoln."[61] Still, Rice knew African Americans were not enamored with her party or her candidate. Somewhat apprehensively, she asked Deborah Carson, "Do you think black folks are really going to go out and vote?"[62]

"Uh-huh," answered Democrat Carson. "Most definitely."

And they did—in unprecedented numbers. The only presidential candidate to ever garner a smaller share of African American votes than Bush was Gold-water.[63] But shortly after the polls opened in Florida, reports began filtering out of widespread confusion. Even the most educated voters in Palm Beach County said they weren't sure whom they had voted for. The new "butterfly ballot," designed by the Democratic county supervisor of elections Theresa LePore and printed in letters large enough for senior citizens to see without their reading glasses, ran to multiple pages, and it wasn't clear where you should punch to vote for a particular candidate.

As the votes were counted on election night, some television networks called the election for Gore, then recanted. The vice president called the governor to concede defeat. Then, on his way to the hall, presumably to give his public con-cession, his motorcade inexplicably turned around. He called Bush and, in surely one of the most extraordinary conversations in American political history, with-drew his concession. Lawyers descended on Florida. As a recount began, brawls broke out at counting stations. The campaigns battled on the airwaves for public opinion. International observers didn't know whether to be amused or appalled—the self-proclaimed greatest democracy couldn't hold a proper election.

Watching the fiasco unfold from California, Rice never lost her trademark confidence.[64] She talked to her friend Deborah Carson two or three times during the weeks of the Florida recount. Civil rights activists were charging that African Americans had been disenfranchised by the confusing ballot in heavily black Palm Beach County, and by the allegedly willful inclusion of blacks who had never been to prison on lists of ex-convicts to be excluded from voting under Florida law.

Rice dismissed the allegations. She told Carson, who said that she could have sworn she heard nervousness in Condi's voice, "That's nothing. That's nothing."[65]

"And I said a couple of times, 'Well, will they protect the votes?'" recalled Carson. Condi just repeated, "'Oh, that's nothing. That's nothing,'" Carson said.

Then, Deborah made "the mistake" of confessing, "Condi, I hope to God . . . I want you to be national security adviser. I really, really do. But I do *not* want George Bush to be president. I'm sorry."

Rice replied, annoyed, "Well, he's a *good man*!"

"All right, okay, I'm not going to say anything else to you about it," said Carson. And for the next six years, she wouldn't.

Though he lost the popular vote, Bush won the election after the Supreme Court ruled five to four, at 10 p.m. on December 12 in *Bush v. Gore*, that the Florida recounts must stop, effectively giving Bush, ahead by 537 votes, Florida's twenty-five electoral votes and the presidency.[66]

Bush announced Rice's appointment as national security adviser the Sunday before Christmas, live from the Governor's Mansion in Austin. By that time it was hardly news.[67] Condi called Clara to give her a heads-up. John's nurses raised the head of his bed so he would see the television. Rice was only the second member of the Bush team to be unveiled. The first, true to custom, had been the secretary of state, Colin Powell. Bush said that naming two African Americans as his first appointees was indeed intended to send the message[68] that the president-elect was sincere about widening the Republicans' big tent, that it had not been empty campaign rhetoric. On the same day that he announced Rice's appointment, Bush appointed two other high-level advisers, a woman and a Hispanic. In explaining each of his choices, he used the word *trust*.[69]

There was galloping speculation about whom Bush would name to complete the national security "troika" and become secretary of defense. The early favorite was Dan Coats, a former Indiana congressman, a compromise candidate. As one Bush adviser told the *New York Times*, "Cheney didn't want Powell's guy; Powell didn't want Cheney's guy."[70] Powell reportedly wanted Tom Ridge, the governor of Pennsylvania; vice president–elect Dick Cheney was said to back the neocon Paul Wolfowitz.

In introducing Rice, Bush called her "not only a brilliant person [but] an experienced person . . . She is a good manager. I trust her judgment. America will find that she is a wise person."[71] As far away as Germany, where they remembered Condi's role in smoothing the path to reunification, diplomats cheered the choice.[72] "I will be seeing her on a daily basis," Bush said.[73]

Unlike Powell, who the day before had given a lengthy discourse on the incoming administration's foreign policy, Rice said few words. "It's a wonderful time for the United States in foreign policy because it's a time when markets and democracy are spreading, when our values are being affirmed around the world, and yet it's a time of great challenge . . . [President Bush] will conduct a foreign policy that combines humility with strength." Then she retold the story of her upbringing in segregated Birmingham, adding, "You will see in the presidency of George W. Bush recognition of how important it is that we continue the last thirty-plus years of progress toward one America."[74]

Back in Palo Alto, Clara wasn't sure how John took his daughter's historic ascent (his "little star" would be the first female national security adviser). John wasn't having one of his good days. His eyes showed no acknowledgment of Condi's appointment. "Oh, it looked like it made him so upset," said Clara. "He was loo-o-o-king. We wanted him to smile. 'Look at your baby!' But I don't know, maybe he didn't even realize what was going on. We don't know what was going on in his head . . . he made no comment."[75]

Knowing how her husband relished the holidays, Clara had trimmed the back room that housed his hospital bed with a small Christmas tree and decorations. On December 22, as she was climbing into the bed they once shared, she heard a deep gasp from John's room. Since he never made any vocal complaint, she was terrified.

"I started screaming," she said. She and Condoleezza had decided that if John's heart stopped again, they wouldn't restart it. It had taken him so long to partially recover from the last attack.[76]

At his mother's shriek, Greg ran from his room. Clara hollered, "It's John! It's John!" Then she fell on her knees next to her bed, crying, "Lord, please, *not* John!" Greg was pleading to John's motionless body, "Hold on, John, hold on." As he called the paramedics, he asked Clara to go into the room and talk to John. Clara couldn't get off her knees.

When the paramedics arrived, she failed to tell them not to revive him. Condoleezza arrived and they went to Stanford Hospital. "They had him in an emergency place, all strapped to the table," said Clara. "And they said, 'He's gone. We took a brain [scan]. Nothing is going but his heart.'"[77]

Condi asked softly, "Clara, are you going to let him go this time?"

"I guess so," said Clara.

Teary-eyed, Condoleezza whispered to her father, "Daddy, say hello to Mother for me."

"And his blood pressure started going back up," Clara said, clapping her hands. "I said, 'Unstrap him. He needs to go in a room!' They had pushed him back in a little [alcove] to die."

For more than two days John Rice hung on. Condi's friends and her Aunt G, who had flown out on the twenty-third, took shifts sitting with John, Clara, and Condi. Randy Bean left only to go home to change clothes. At about nine o'clock on Christmas Eve morning, Clara took Greg's advice and finally went home to take a shower.

As Clara walked in the house, the phone rang. John was gone. "He waited for me to leave," she said. "They say that's the way they do."[78]

It was about 9:30 on Christmas Eve. John had been on morphine, but no feeding tube or life support. At his side were Condi, G, Chip, and Louie. "We were with him when he drew his last breath," recalled Blacker. "That was one of the only other times I saw [Condi] lose her composure."[79]

"[Life] was—is—very different for her," said Chip. "Losing one parent is hard enough, but when you lose the second, it doesn't matter what age you are, you're instantly an orphan. But, again, she pulled it together and did what Condi does under such circumstances, which is be a model for how one is supposed to conduct oneself . . . She had precious little time. She was in Washington within a week of his death. She had to find a temporary place to live, at least, and she had to be there for the transition."

At Rev. Rice's funeral, his "eating buddies" told stories of their culinary exploits at the restaurants of Palo Alto. Rice had demanded grits at more than one, and when the restaurateurs had told him they didn't know how to cook grits, he had said, "You just buy 'em and I'll show you."[80] And he had.

Clara had told Condoleezza that someone should sing "his song." Condi said Clara should do it; she'd accompany her on the piano. Clara said she couldn't. With Ray steeliness, Condi said, "Yes, you can."

"If we sing it, we're going to have to be standing together," Clara finally conceded. "I need your support."

Condi sang soprano and Clara sang alto while a musician played "In the Garden."

I come to the garden alone,
While the dew is still on the roses;
And the voice I hear, falling on my ear,
The Son of God discloses.

And He walks with me,
And He talks with me,
And He tells me I am His own;
And the joy we share as we tarry there,
None other has ever known.

"[We] even had the nerve to do the second verse," said Clara Rice.

The homegoing service, as Baptists call their funerals (Condi let Clara hold the service at her church instead of Menlo Park Presbyterian), was so packed, the crowd flowed up into the choir loft and out of the building. A band played "When the Saints Go Marching In."[81]

When Bush had asked Rice to join his staff, she had told him she wasn't sure she could do it. "I said I didn't go through forty-whatever at that time years it was of my life with this close relationship with my father to be on the other side of the country when he was in this condition. I was going to, believe it or not, try to commute to deal with it because I told [Governor Bush] I won't be absent from his life."[82] Condoleezza had also suggested to Clara that the three of them move to Washington; Rice said she could get her stepmother a job at the State Department.[83]

Now John's passing made all those considerations moot. Condi would go to Washington alone.

PART III
PATH TO POWER

CHAPTER NINE

TRANSFORMATION

She went through a political metamorphosis . . . she went from being a George Herbert
Walker Bush Republican to being a George W. Bush Republican.[1]

COIT BLACKER
Stanford University
August 4, 2006

A s Rices and Rays have always done, Condoleezza steeled herself to the loss of the most important person in her life and got on with the pressing business at hand; she had work to do. She loved her life in northern California, but her sense of duty to George W. Bush drew her back to Washington—that and the chance to complete and build on the revolutions she had helped to unleash during Bush's father's term. In Rice's view, the ad hoc foreign policy of the Clinton administration had failed to capitalize on those gains, but now the second Bush presidency would strategically reshape the world to America's interests. "They were going to seize control of this beast and drive things forward," remembered Chip Blacker.[2] Apparently, Condi believed, Washington was the next step in God's plan for her.[3]

And yet she had no illusions that her second tour of duty in the White House would compare to the first: The Cold War was over and America's attention was focused inward, plus that was where George W. Bush's most passionately felt priorities lay. The expectation, as former House Speaker Newt Gingrich put it, was that "[Bush] would go from education to Social Security . . . and have a really bright national security adviser and a world-respected secretary of state and a vice president who knew virtually everybody on the planet. And those three would really do foreign policy."[4]

As national security adviser, Rice's first task was to put together her National Security Council staff. Reflecting Bush's priorities and what she felt were the mistakes of the Clinton years, when the NSC grew in size and stature to become its own center of gravity in U.S. foreign policy, Condi cut the staff by a third, eliminating the sections that dealt with international environmental and health issues, as well as the communications and legislative offices. Her model for how to run the NSC—a staff of advisers on foreign policy to the presidents—was her old boss Brent Scowcroft. Like Scowcroft, Rice believed the NSC should leave formulating and implementing policy to the Departments of State, Defense, and so on. "She sees her task as making sure Bush is briefed and staffed to play his role in foreign and security matters, advancing his strategic agenda while thinking through big issues such as guidelines for foreign intervention, and serving as an honest broker of differences among the major policy players," reported the *Washington Post* in February 2001. "[Rice] expects to be seen and heard far less than her predecessor, Samuel 'Sandy' Berger."[5]

To staff the NSC, Rice predictably turned to many of her colleagues from the first Bush administration—the last time the Republicans had held the reins of executive power—including some of her former bosses. That they would work for Condi now was a testament to how far Rice had risen. One of them, Bob Blackwill, had noticed the changes in Rice when she was leading the Vulcans during the campaign: "She was much more confident. She was no longer the midlevel staffer that I had supervised. Second, she had flowered beyond the Soviet perspective; she did not see the world so much through the Moscow optic. The third thing I noticed was that those innate skills of managing people were much more developed. She managed the Vulcans quite exquisitely, all these egos . . . me, Wolfowitz, Zoellick, Armitage. Try to think of more contentious, ego-driven [people]."[6]

When he came to work for Rice at the NSC after a stint as ambassador to India, Blackwill was even more impressed. "If you had said to me on the day I left the [first Bush] White House, 'Is she going to grow to a point in a decade where [she's] a plausible national security adviser?' I would have said probably not—and that's as someone who greatly admired her . . . [but] Condi obviously had this enormous capacity to grow."[7]

That was apparent when the Bush administration sat down to its first NSC meeting on January 30. These highest-level gatherings of the NSC—bringing together the president, the vice president, the national security adviser, the cabinet secretaries responsible for national security (State, Defense, and Treasury), and the chairman of the Joint Chiefs of Staff—were called the Principals Committee. Vice President Dick Cheney had argued that when the president was absent, he should lead the principals.[8] But Bush had rejected Cheney's proposal in favor of historical precedent; Condi would chair principals meetings when the president was absent.

It was also obvious in that first NSC meeting that Secretary of State Colin Powell was the odd man out. The only item on the agenda was the Middle East. Powell argued that the most urgent problem in the region was the Israeli–Palestinian conflict. But Bush was reluctant to plunge into the quagmire that had cost Bill Clinton valuable time and energy at the end of his presidency and left him with nothing to show for his efforts except a new Palestinian uprising.[9]

The conversation moved to Iraq, and, according to Karen DeYoung in her authorized biography of Colin Powell, *Soldier*, Rice said, "We have a regime change policy that isn't really regime change."[10] Since 1998, when Clinton had signed the Iraq Liberation Act, working for the overthrow of Iraqi dictator Saddam Hussein had been official U.S. policy. But the effort so far consisted mainly of funding anti-Hussein Iraqi exile groups and patrolling "no-fly zones" in the country's north and the south. And the U.N. sanctions intended to prevent Hussein from building or acquiring dangerous weapons had grown increasingly porous, while the privations of the Iraqi people were being reported regularly in the international media.

Before international support for sanctions collapsed altogether, the Bush team decided it needed a more aggressive strategy. Secretary of Defense Donald Rumsfeld believed the sanctions were already worthless. "I [worry] about arms, weapons of mass destruction," Rumsfeld said, meaning chemical, biological, and nuclear arms that could inflict far greater casualties far more efficiently than conventional arms.[11]

At the second NSC meeting on February 5, Powell outlined proposals for tougher sanctions. The White House had already decided to increase the amount of funds the United States sent to anti-Saddam exile groups. And Rumsfeld won

Bush's approval to take bolder action the next time Baghdad shot at American and British jets patrolling the no-fly zones.[12]

But Bush, Powell, and Rice were still caught off guard[13] when they received word during the president's first foreign trip, to Mexico, that the United States Air Force was bombing Baghdad. After CNN aired footage of the damage, the president spoke to the assembled journalists and concealed his surprise that—operating under the new rules of engagement—U.S. forces had bombed command and control centers near Baghdad. Bush claimed it was a "routine mission." In her remarks to journalists, Condi Rice repeatedly made the same point.

Though Rumsfeld had been responsible for what could have been the first foreign policy embarrassment of the administration, it was Powell who usually found himself on the wrong side of the White House. On March 6, for example, Secretary Powell told the *Washington Post* that the administration would continue Clinton's strategy of negotiating with North Korea to convince it to end its quest for nuclear weapons. But the White House had decided no such thing; on the contrary, it had an aversion to all things Clintonian.

Condi Rice called Powell before his 8:30 staff meeting the next morning. "We've got a problem," she said. "Have you read your newspaper yet?"[14] The *Post* had run Powell's comments in that day's edition. Within hours, Powell retracted his previous comments, and Bush declared there would be no talks with North Korea until the administration was certain Pyongyang had abandoned its nuclear weapons program.

In the space of three months, Powell would be vindicated and Washington would indeed sit down with Pyongyang, without the North Koreans having abandoned their nuclear program,[15] but it was already clear to anyone paying attention that Powell was the black sheep of the administration.[16] And whenever he broke from the flock, it fell to Condi Rice to bring him back. Indeed, the national security adviser's gentle but firm corrections of the secretary of state became a set piece in Bush's first term.[17] If the role bothered her, Rice never let on.[18]

The administration's first foreign policy crisis not of its own making exploded over the South China Sea on Sunday, April 1. An EP-3E Aries II turboprop surveillance plane, one of the navy's most sophisticated—able to monitor ships, submarines, and ground communications—collided with a Chinese F-8 fighter jet, apparently killing the Chinese pilot. The twenty-four American crew members set down safely on the island of Hainan, home to a Chinese naval base.

The midair collision and the crew's detention by Chinese authorities pro-voked the most serious confrontation between Washington and Beijing in more than three decades. Condi's focus during the campaign on great-power relations seemed prescient.

Rice tried fruitlessly to raise her counterpart, Qian Qichen—chief foreign policy aide to Chinese premier Jiang Zemin—who was traveling with his boss in Latin America.[19] After eleven days of heated rhetoric and calls on talk radio for Washington to retaliate economically against China unless the American crew was released, Powell negotiated an end to the crisis, with Rice running interfer-ence with her Chinese counterpart. By issuing a public apology, Bush even made good on his pledge that despite its enormous might, America would tread hum-bly in the world.

But administration critics saw Powell and Rice's deft diplomacy as the excep-tion to the Bush rule. As a story in the *New York Times* summed up at the end of July, "In his first six months in office, President Bush has abandoned a treaty on fighting global warming, rejected protocols enforcing a ban on germ warfare, demanded amendments to an accord on illegal sales of small arms, threatened to skip an international conference on racism, and vowed to withdraw from a land-mark pact limiting ballistic missile defenses."[20]

Instead of respecting allies, as they had promised to do during the campaign, the administration appeared determined to offend them. For Western Europe especially, the administration's rejection of the Kyoto Protocol, the global com-pact intended to reduce emissions of greenhouse gases, became the emblem of the Bush doctrine. Knowing it faced insurmountable opposition in the Senate, Clinton had chosen not to send the Kyoto treaty to the Hill for ratification. But Bush wanted to be more transparent. Powell had argued for a nuanced message: Washington would not support Kyoto but was determined to work with its allies to find other ways to reduce greenhouse gases.[21] Instead, Bush had sent a letter to the Senate in March saying there would be no mandatory emissions cuts. For good measure, at a lunch with European Union ambassadors, Rice pronounced[22] Kyoto "dead on arrival."[23]

In the United States, the decision to abandon Kyoto was not nearly as con-troversial as it was in Europe; many observers agreed Washington should not sign on to the treaty, but few understood why the administration had trumpeted its opposition with such indelicate flourish. It was bad politics. Editorial writers, scholars, and diplomats argued that Bush's single-minded unilateralism was damaging America's standing abroad.[24]

Rice said they were wrong. On the eve of the president's first overseas trip in June, she told reporters, "These are friendly, respectful, outgoing relationships, and [President Bush] is going to have a chance to renew them. The notion somehow that we have tremendous tensions with our European allies, I think, is frankly just not right."[25]

Condi was not the only administration official assiduously spinning the press. Even Powell, whose dissents over Bush policies were so public now that they were the fodder of Washington dinner parties, insisted there was "solid cooperation" between America and her allies.[26] But it was Condi who was emerging as the administration's defender-in-chief.

She had become a mini-celebrity during the presidential race, in part because she had the most compelling personal story of anyone involved in either campaign—the childhood in segregated Alabama, the rise to the heights of power—and in part because she was mediagenic—attractive, looking even younger than her forty-five years, and female and black in a world where sources and talking heads were overwhelmingly white and male. It wasn't diversity that TV producers and magazine editors sought so much as variety to hold the attention of their readers and viewers.

But most of all, Rice had been a master rhetorician. She could spin just about anything. She was always good for a sharp quote, especially on the kind of tension-filled issues that campaign coverage ran on, and no argument or question stumped her. For journalists she had been the complete package. Adoring headlines like "Condi Rice Can't Lose"[27] had graced magazines and newspapers. The editorial page editor of the *Dallas Morning News* even cheered, "The girl's got game."[28]

The same talent for debate and persuasion that Mrs. Turnbull had recognized in the St. Mary's sophomore and that had drawn the attention of Brent Scowcroft now made Rice indispensable to the Bush administration. She was its most articulate spokesperson by far. Over the next four years, Bush would come to rely on Condi in that role, and Rice in turn would become the most recognizable national security adviser since Henry Kissinger.

But Condi's growing profile didn't assuage the foreign policy establishment, which was increasingly skeptical of what many viewed as Bush's unreasoned unilateralism.[29] To some extent that wasn't surprising: the establishment tended to favor diplomacy and multilateralism, and Bush was cut from different cloth. Rice had even made a point of noting during the campaign, "Governor Bush has not spent the last ten years of his life at Council on Foreign Relations meetings."[30] (The CFR was known as the clubhouse of the foreign policy establishment.)[31]

During the campaign there had been widespread speculation among the establishment that there would be tension between the moderates on Bush's foreign policy team who favored multilateralism, like Powell, and the neoconservatives, like Rumsfeld's aides at the Pentagon, Paul Wolfowitz and Douglas Feith, who were more disposed to the unilateral exercise of American power. Clearly, many in the foreign policy establishment thought, the neocons were winning.

It was true that with the rare aberration of Bush's apology to China after the EP-3E crisis—a transgression that neocons said had caused "profound national humiliation" to the United States[32]—the neocons enthusiastically backed Bush's muscular unilateralism.[33] But Bush's foreign policy was, in part, merely the outcome of a higher Bush priority: the reinvigoration of the strong executive branch. Bush and Cheney both believed that in the wake of Watergate, the presidency had been hamstrung by an excess of oversight,[34] and they intended to remedy that problem. Their belief that the president was the decider—not the Republican Congress, not the Democratic opposition, and not the courts—naturally led to unilateralism abroad, just as it led to unilateralism in the administration's dealings with Congress at home. But the effect internationally was, as Rice would say, a "second-order effect."

Bush had not come to Washington to be a foreign policy president. He had come to change America domestically, and on that front he knew exactly what he wanted to do: Cut taxes, create and enforce educational standards in schools, reform the financially doomed Social Security system, and open up the Arctic National Wildlife Refuge to oil drilling. Such precision did not exist in the international realm. (In fact, James Baker III, Bush's father's secretary of state and the man who had led Bush's side in the Florida recount, once described W.'s core principles as "God and exercise.")[35]

Now that he was in office, Bush's foreign policy consisted mostly of the broad goals Rice had built by marrying his instincts to her realism: Be strong and resolute, focus on the national interests, nurture and control great-power relations, and use the military for fighting wars, not building nations. Generally, they would think boldly and strategically, not swat at flies as Clinton had, but other than missile defense, the administration had few distinct international goals. And when it came to Kyoto and other treaties, like the antiballistic missile treaty that precluded Bush's missile defense system, the path was clear, based on their broad goals—U.S. interests and sovereignty demanded a unilateral course.[36]

With Rice, who was well known within the foreign policy establishment, and so many of Bush's father's men on his team, the establishment had hoped Bush's foreign policy would resemble his father's. Rice's piece in *Foreign Affairs*, largely a realist treatise, had suggested that it would. Only W. was not his father. He was bolder. He was also less experienced; whatever his advisers' pedigrees, he lacked Bush Sr.'s decades in government. W. had been governor of Texas for a term and a half before becoming president; George Herbert Walker Bush had been ambassador to the United Nations, director of the CIA, and vice president. But the most important difference would be one of philosophy. Bush the elder was both less ideological and more multilateral than his son, not just in policy, but in personal temperament, too.

The fact that Condoleezza Rice moved effortlessly from being a true believer under one Bush to being the best articulator of the vision and values of the other was "a substantial migration," as her friend Chip Blacker put it. Gary Hart, both the first and the last Democrat Rice worked for,[37] found the distance from Bush I to Bush II greater than Rice's move from Hart Democrat to Bush I Republican, at least as far as foreign policy was concerned. "It's a stretch from Scowcroft to Wolfowitz," said Hart, referring to Rumsfeld's neocon deputy.[38]

The question from those in the establishment who knew Rice, then, was, what had changed? Had Rice's balance-of-power multilateralist instincts changed? Or had she made some Machiavellian calculation that in this administration the center of gravity was with the hawks and shifted her views accordingly? Or was she just supporting the views of her boss? Some suspected Rice was simply outgunned by the neocons.

Indeed, pundits and Washington hands had speculated before the Bush administration took office that the "titans" with whom she'd have to work on national security would dwarf Condoleezza. Each of the other players had decades of experience as high-level officials in government; they knew how to get their way. Powell had been Reagan's national security adviser and chairman of the Joint Chiefs of Staff and was a bona fide star; Cheney had been the youngest

White House chief of staff ever before serving as secretary of defense for Bush I; Rumsfeld had been President Ford's chief of staff and the youngest secretary of defense ever and was now on a second tour as the oldest. Thirty years before, President Nixon had already decided Rumsfeld was "a ruthless little bastard."[39] Collectively, the conventional wisdom ran, these men might present an unscalable Mount Rushmore to Condoleezza Rice, whose only previous White House experience had been as a senior staffer on the NSC.

But as national security adviser, it seemed Rice was holding her own. True to the image Stanford colleagues had had of her as a young professor, she was forceful without being insulting, confident without appearing arrogant. When differences of opinion threatened to explode in principals meetings, she moved the titans toward consensus. If consensus couldn't be reached, she emphasized the points of agreement, then guided them to the next item on the agenda.[40] By most accounts she was phenomenally well organized;[41] under her stewardship, NSC meetings ran with lightning efficiency.[42]

One thing she couldn't manage, though, was the increasing hostility between Powell and Rumsfeld. By summer, all of Washington knew the State Department and the Pentagon were at war. It was a pitched battle over policy and approach, pitting Rumsfeld's neocon unilateralists against Powell's realist internationalists.[43] Between the two camps stood Rice—but no one knew exactly where because she didn't play the Washington game of leaks and recriminations. She kept out of the public fray; a study in discretion and discipline all her life, she kept her own counsel and kept her counsel to the president to herself. As she promised in an early interview with the *Washington Post* when she started the job, her role was to staff the president.

But Rice didn't always protect her boss; she couldn't. No amount of tutoring could replace real-world experience. An early example had come on April 25, when Bush told ABC News that the United States would come to Taiwan's defense if China ever attacked the island. The statement sounded like a straightforward if audacious declaration of support for an ally, but it was bolder than the president realized. It suggested an end to what diplomats and analysts called the "strategic ambiguity" that had undergirded U.S.–China relations for thirty years. Neither Beijing nor Taipei knew for certain what Washington would do if Taiwan formally declared its independence from the Chinese mainland—in fact, Washington didn't really know—and that kept Taiwan from making a rash decision that would provoke a war with China and perhaps drag in the United States to defend Taiwan. Now the president of the United States had said America would go to war with China. The administration sent Scowcroft on a secret mission to Jiang Zemin to smooth over Bush's gaffe.[44]

Meanwhile, Condi had her own limitations. No one doubted that she was intelligent and capable—she was. But she had never been known as a great original thinker who expanded the boundaries of knowledge or understanding.[45] As Scowcroft said of their fateful first meeting, when he decided to shepherd her career, it was not "what she said"—she proffered no extraordinary insights or revolutionary paradigms—"but how she said it."[46] She was a brilliant synthesizer and debater, not an innovator.[47] As a Rice friend and university professor said, "She [didn't] jump out as an intellectual star."[48]

Of course, the president didn't need a Nobel laureate; he needed someone to translate his instincts into policy and, because Condi knew Bush's mind as well as anyone—what range of policies he was likely to accept and what he would reject—she expertly fulfilled the role of adviser to the president. She managed his "paper flow," deciding what documents and reports coming out of the vast national security bureaucracy he needed to see and which he didn't, and she presented him with options for action that were within his comfort zone.

And as the Bush administration hit its stride, there was no doubt that Rice was emerging as a foreign policy leader.[49] There was also no question where she stood on its top priority: on missile defense, she sided with the hardliners at the Department of Defense and, more important, with the president. Building a system of interceptors to destroy incoming ballistic missiles before they reached the United States would effectively gut the 1972 Anti-Ballistic Missile (ABM) treaty between the United States and Russia. Moscow opposed the missile shield and, since the Americans lacked the technology to make it work anyway, the State Department believed that there was no need to force the question. But Bush disagreed, and he told Rice to take the lead.

In July, Condi flew to Moscow to meet with Russian president Vladimir Putin to negotiate an agreement that would get Bush his shield and convince the Russians to go along. As usual, Rice portrayed the overture—an offer to massively reduce strategic nuclear weapons in exchange for Moscow's acquiescence on missile defense—as the president's, but White House aides said the strategy was all hers. Carrying the offer at all was a diplomatic coup: Rice had threaded the space between State and Defense to find a compromise both could live with. And if Moscow would concede to modifying the treaty thanks to the American incentives, it would be a high-profile demonstration that America was not determined to go it alone on every foreign policy issue.[50]

That Rice went to Russia instead of the Secretary of State—the first top foreign policy official in the administration to do so—was lost on neither the press nor foreign leaders.[51] Earlier in July, Condi had been constantly at Bush's side during the G8 summit in Italy and throughout his European tour. Behind the scenes, she had been instrumental in getting Bush to restart talks with North Korea and to continue the multibillion-dollar *Plan Colombia*, a military assistance program initiated under Clinton that was designed to eradicate coca.[52]

In the end, the administration couldn't change Putin's mind, and in December President Bush would announce plans to withdraw unilaterally from the ABM treaty. (In June 2002, the treaty expired.) But Washington and Moscow did agree to cut their nuclear arsenals by two-thirds.

As Rice's power in Washington grew, so did her celebrity. In September she was featured in a five-thousand-word profile in *Vogue*. The lead photo, splashed across two glossy pages, showed Rice inside her immaculate all-white condo at the Watergate, seated at a Chickering grand piano in a black strapless evening gown. It was the piano John and Angelena had given her for her fifteenth birthday. The cover line read:

White House Wonder: The Amazing Life of Condoleezza Rice.[53]

Rice was standing at her desk in her West Wing office when her executive assistant came in to deliver the news.[54] It had been only a week since Annie Leibovitz had shot Rice for *Vogue*.[55] "What a strange accident," Rice thought as she called the president to tell him some sort of plane had hit the World Trade Center in New York. On a trip to Florida to highlight his education plan, Bush had the same thought as Condi: "What a weird accident."[56]

After Rice hung up, she went down to her regular nine o'clock staff meeting. As usual, she went around the table asking her staffers for overnight updates from around the world. About three people in, her assistant burst in again. The note she handed Condi said a second plane had hit the other tower. *My God*, Rice thought, *this is a terrorist attack.*[57]

She broke up the meeting and headed for the Situation Room to gather the principals. Colin Powell was on a mission to Latin America—Rice worried if he was all right; if this was an all-out attack, the Secretary of State could be a target. As the principals or their deputies gathered in specially designed studios at their headquarters, their images beamed onto screens in the White House Secure Video Conferencing Center, news came of an explosion at the Pentagon. Then word came (which would later prove wrong) that the State Department had been attacked with a car bomb.[58]

The administration's counterterrorism chief, a bulldog of a man named Richard Clarke, a holdover from the Clinton administration, was certain the attack had come from al-Qaeda. The terrorist group had a fondness for simultaneous attacks, "spectaculars" in the parlance of terror watchers. In 1998, they had simultaneously blown up the U.S. embassies in Kenya and Tanzania in East Africa. This might not be over.

Rice told Cheney and Clarke that the Secret Service wanted them all in the bomb shelter, and Clarke suggested everyone not needed to coordinate the emergency response to the attack evacuate the White House.[59] As the Secret Service hustled the vice president to the hardened bunker beneath the East Wing, in the Situation Room Rice directed Clarke to lead the videoconference with the agency heads; Clarke was the expert, and in times of crisis, it seemed, Rice knew how to lead even when it meant following.[60]

The Air Force was hopscotching the president around the Southeast. From Barksdale Air Force Base in Louisiana, Bush pledged to the nation in a taped address, "The United States will hunt down and punish those responsible for these cowardly acts."[61] By that time the world had already watched as the twin towers came crashing down. In the heat of the maelstrom, the president looked small[62] and his strong words rang hollow; his wavering voice and creased brow gave the impression of a shaken man.

By Friday the fourteenth, all that had changed. Visiting what had instantly become known as Ground Zero, Bush stood amid the rubble, seized a bullhorn, and, placing one hand on a fireman's shoulder, said, "I can hear *you*. The rest of the world hears you. And the people who knocked these buildings down will hear all of us soon!"[63] And to those watching on television, George W. Bush seemed to grow six inches. His shoulders were straight and his eyes steely. It was a look the world would come to know well. Bush had been transformed, and with him the mission of his administration. American foreign policy had a direction for the first time since the end of the Cold War—a war on terror—and Bush's foreign policy had a focus.

The attack sparked a readjustment of the world's posture toward the Bush administration, or at least toward the United States: Overnight, condemnation turned to solidarity. In a signed editorial in the left-leaning French daily *Le Monde*, editor-in-chief Jean-Marie Colombani wrote, "In this tragic moment when words seem powerless to convey the shock, the first thing that comes to mind is this: We are all Americans! We are all New Yorkers, just as surely as John Kennedy proclaimed himself in 1963 Berlin to be a Berliner. How else could we feel, but as in the darkest moments of our history, profoundly bound to this people and to this nation, the United States, to whom we are so tied and to whom we owe our freedom, and therefore our solidarity."[64]

Before the attacks, Condi had been planning to fly home to Birmingham at the end of the week. After years of turning down their invitations,[65] she had finally agreed to keynote the Birmingham Civil Rights Institute's annual commemoration of the 1964 bombing of the Sixteenth Street Baptist Church, an act of homegrown terrorism that had taken the lives of four little girls, including Rice's kindergarten classmate Denise McNair. Condi's aunts and uncle were planning "a big time" for Birmingham's most famous daughter's homecoming.[66]

Instead Condi called her Uncle Alto and Aunt Connie to say that she was fine and not to worry. Like a message sent by telegraph, the word spread from relative to relative.[67]

Only she wasn't fine. As Rices and Rays had always done in times of great loss, she projected an air of stoic unflappability. And just as John had done throughout his illness, no matter how poorly he felt, she hid her anguish. But the trauma of the attacks was keeping her up at night, and nothing ever kept her up at night. No matter how great the upheaval or stresses around her, Rice had always slept soundly, the product of her unshakable self-confidence and her Presbyterian faith that everything that happened in our lives was a part of God's plan. But after 9/11, she spent two fitful nights, the image of the collapsing towers haunting her. Then she came home after ten on the night of September 13 and

turned on the television news to see the band of the Queen's Guard at Bucking-
ham Palace playing "The Star-Spangled Banner." Only then did she cry, and that
night she returned to her normal pattern of wakeless slumber.[68]

It took Deborah Carson two weeks to reach Condoleezza; Carson kept getting her voice mail. Finally she settled for letting her son Joseph, whom Condi
called her godchild, though he really wasn't, leave a message on Rice's home
phone, singing his three-year-old's rendition of "The Star-Spangled Banner."

When they finally connected, Rice told Carson of her heartrending trip to
Ground Zero with the president on the fourteenth. The stirring images of Bush
atop the rubble hadn't extended to include the glassy-eyed New Yorkers who had
approached the president's entourage in the eerily quiet caverns of Lower Man-
hattan, begging, "Please protect us."

"She said it was awful," remembered Carson. "She said she never, ever
wanted to face something like that again."[69]

And Condoleezza meant it. The attacks of September 11 had as profound an
impact on Rice as anything in her life, save her parents. The attacks invested
Condi, like everyone else in the administration, with a new sense of purpose, but
they also led her to reevaluate the way she saw the world, especially what was
possible—and necessary—to achieve through American foreign policy. "The
kind of focus she put on freedom . . . changed after 9/11," said a Washington
colleague and longtime friend.[70]

The first casualty of Rice's old way of looking at the world was realism. Even
before 9/11, George Bush—with his emphasis on values over interests—had
already tapped into something in Rice. "There was [always] with her a tension
between realism, which is very secular and value free, and her religious side,"
said Chip Blacker."[But] his influence on her is huge. She went through a political metamorphosis, where she went from being a George Herbert Walker Bush
Republican to being a George W. Bush Republican."[71]

And now the terrorist attacks had made realism's analytical flaws as plain as
its moral failings. First, realism was predicated on the assumption that the primary actor on the world stage was the nation-state. But this enemy was not a
state. Second, they had no interests, at least not in the rational sense that realism
understood interests; they had not attacked the United States to gain territory or
resources. Finally, realism didn't take into account ideology; it assumed universal
constants, like the thirst for earthly domination, but these adversaries claimed

divine inspiration. As a result, there was literally nothing on earth that could deter them.

They had to be defeated. That required finding, stopping, and killing the terrorists, wherever they were, who were already plotting to murder more Americans, and removing the conditions that had bred a generation of potential recruits in the Muslim Middle East. The source of much of the alienation of young Arab Muslims, Rice believed, was a "freedom deficit" at home—a sense of powerlessness to determine their own and their societies' destinies and a lack of nonviolent channels to express their resulting frustration. The attacks had demonstrated that, thanks to technology, disillusionment in one country could explode on the shores of another, wreaking more devastation than ever before possible.

The United States couldn't prevent zealots from perverting Islam to deadly purposes, but it might be able to induce change in the oppressive societies that allowed no other outlet for popular dissatisfaction than fundamentalist religion that extremists exploited to preach that America, the ultimate symbol of Western dominance, was the cause of Arab frustration. Rice's conclusion, like Bush's, was that the Middle East had to be transformed. Until its alienated people, especially its young men, could find nonviolent channels of self-expression at home, Americans would never be safe. In the twenty-first century, America had to save the world to save itself.

Rice's motivation was not the same as the neocons'. They believed that the superiority of American values and military might meant the United States had a moral duty to transform the world. But in Rice's view, an idealist foreign policy was more a means to a realist end. Doing good in the world was still a "second-order effect," as she had written in her *Foreign Affairs* piece. The first-order aim was to protect the United States—but now that demanded, in Condi's view, a "transformational" foreign policy aimed at changing the internal politics of other countries.

The administration's response to the September 11 attacks took shape almost immediately. For the time being, eschewing Rumsfeld's deputy Paul Wolfowitz's calls to consider attacking Iraq, President Bush ordered the destruction of al-Qaeda's training bases in Afghanistan and the removal of Afghanistan's Taliban regime, which was harboring Osama bin Laden.

On October 7, the U.S. and U.K. air forces began hitting Taliban targets. When Operation Enduring Freedom "dragged on" for three weeks, pundits and politicians began to warn of a quagmire,[72] but by December 7, Taliban resistance had dissolved, and the administration enjoyed its first victory in the war on terror. In the process, as U.S. officials frequently said, America had liberated a Muslim nation.

In his January State of the Union address, President Bush expanded the war on terror to include rogue states that could potentially provide terrorists with weapons of mass destruction. He described them as "an axis of evil": Iraq, Iran, and North Korea. Bush also declared that Washington would support peoples and nations that sought to breathe free. Bush and Rice began speaking publicly about the need for change throughout the Arab world, including democratization in countries that had long been allied with Washington, such as Egypt and Saudi Arabia. In February, Bush told a conservative think tank that it was "insulting to suggest that a whole region of the world or the one-fifth of humanity that is Muslim is somehow untouched by the most basic aspirations of life."[73]

It was a bold break with business as usual.[74] Previous administrations, playing by the rules of Realpolitik, had often turned a blind eye to internal oppression as long as countries supported Washington in the global war against communism. The new message was clear: When it came to American relations in the Middle East, Realpolitik was dead.

By the spring of 2002, six months into the post-9/11 era, the administration was talking seriously about taking the next step in transforming the Middle East. Rice believed that it was impossible to contemplate changing the realities of the region as long as Saddam Hussein, "the ultimate spoiler," sat in power in Baghdad.[75] By summer the deliberations about removing Saddam Hussein had moved farther along than even many administration officials knew.

In early July, Richard Haass, the State Department's director of policy planning and a friend who had worked with Rice in Bush I, went to see Condi in her West Wing office for their regular meeting. Haass held a yellow legal pad with a list of agenda items. When he came to the subject of Iraq—when he planned to make the State Department's definitive case on the difficulties and downsides of an attack on Saddam Hussein—Rice stopped him cold. "Don't waste your breath," Haass remembered her saying. "The president has already made the decision."[76]

Haass was stunned. After the meeting, he returned to the State Department and reported the news to his boss: The United States is going to war with Iraq. Powell told him he was wrong. When Haass insisted, Powell made some calls and found that Haass was right. There had been no formal decision-making process. "We always thought it was going to be like a more traditional National Security Council process," said Haass, "where you were going to have more formal discussions and ultimately more formal decisions. So the idea that the president in his own mind had already reached the decision that Saddam pretty much had to go . . . I was surprised that things had reached that point that early. I got the sense of finality."

But the decision wasn't quite final. Though the administration had been considering secret war plans for months, Bush hadn't yet signed off on one. Powell called Condi to request private time with the president. On August 5, Bush had Powell to the White House residence for dinner. Condi was there, too, as she usually was when Powell met with the president. For two hours, Powell laid out all the complexities of invading and occupying Iraq, telling Bush, "You are going to be the proud owner of twenty-five million people . . . all their hopes, aspirations, and problems . . . It's going to suck the oxygen out of everything . . . *This will become the first term.*" [77]

Powell suggested Bush take his case to the United Nations so, one, the United States could go in with as many allies as possible if it went to war, and two, the president would have the political cover of having tried diplomacy first. The next day Rice reportedly told Powell, "That was terrific . . . and we need to do more of those."[78] As usual, Condi was playing the conciliator, walking the line between the hawks and Powell.

But soon the line became impossible to walk. Three weeks after Powell and Rice's dinner with the president, Vice President Cheney declared before a meeting of the Veterans of Foreign Wars, "There is no doubt that Saddam Hussein now has weapons of mass destruction . . . There is no doubt that he is amassing them to use against our friends, our allies, and against us."[79] Cheney's speech went beyond anything the president or the CIA had ever said about the urgency of Saddam's WMD threat. Cheney's goal was to keep Powell and a host of Republican realists who were coming out against the possible war from slowing what he saw as the need to take out Saddam.

Leading the Bush I wisemen in a chorus of nos was Rice's mentor Scowcroft,[80] who had recently written an op-ed for the *Wall Street Journal* titled

"Don't Attack Saddam." Then Scowcroft went on CBS's *Face the Nation* and repeated the dangers of a war with Iraq: There were too many risks to toppling Hussein—from biochemical attacks on U.S. soldiers to the possibility of regional upheaval—which was why Bush's father hadn't carried the first Gulf War to Baghdad. And besides, the United States hadn't caught al-Qaeda leader Osama bin Laden yet.[81]

The administration's retribution was swift: Rice took Scowcroft to task for not warning her about his op-ed,[82] and though Scowcroft headed Bush's Foreign Intelligence Advisory Board, his access to the White House was greatly reduced.[83]

But the administration was also causing its own bumps along the way to what was increasingly clearly a march to war. On September 6, for instance, White House chief of staff Andy Card told the *New York Times* that the administration had always planned to "roll out" the campaign to sell Congress and the public on the need to go after Saddam in September. It was simple timing, Card said. "From a marketing point of view, you don't introduce new products in August."[84]

As usual, it fell to Rice to make the case more persuasively. The day after Card's ill-chosen words ran in the *Times*, Rice appeared on a special "pre-9/11 anniversary" episode of CNN's *Late Edition with Wolf Blitzer* news talk show. Blitzer pressed her on the case against Saddam, particularly in light of Cheney's speech. Rice skirted Cheney's dramatic declaration, instead replying, "There is no doubt that Saddam Hussein's regime is a danger to the United States and to its allies . . . It is also a danger that is gathering momentum, and it simply makes no sense to wait any longer to do something about [it]."[85]

Blitzer played a tape of former UN weapons inspector Scott Ritter addressing the Iraqi National Assembly and making the opposite case.

[Begin videotape]

SCOTT RITTER, FORMER UN WEAPONS INSPECTOR: My country seems to be on the verge of making an historical mistake, one that will forever change the political dynamic which has governed the world since the end of the Second World War; namely, the foundation of international law as set forth in [the] United Nations charter, which calls for the peaceful resolution of problems between nations.

[End videotape]

BLITZER: I wonder if you want to respond to what Scott Ritter directly said, there are no serious threats to the United States from Iraq's weapons of mass destruction program?

RICE: Well, I'd [be] very interested to know how one can dismiss a weapons of mass destruction program that was well documented . . . in 1991; that was being documented until 1998 when the inspectors left; that continues to gather momentum.

It's not just the United States that's making this case. This case is being made by independent analysts, as well . . . This is a man who has attacked his neighbors twice, who represses his own people, who's tried to assassinate a former American president, who pays $25,000 to Hamas bombers—by the way, some of whom blew up Hebrew University and, with it, five Americans. He has a long history.

. . . It is under the UN charter that the resolutions were put together that are supposed to constrain Saddam Hussein and to disarm him so that he is not a threat to peace and security

He is the one who is responsible here. He is the one who has to answer. The burden of proof is on him to show that he has disarmed—not on the United States, not on Great Britain, not on the members of the international community.

BLITZER: Based on what you know right now, how close is Saddam Hussein's government . . . to developing a nuclear capability?

RICE: You will get different estimates about precisely how close he is. We do know that he is actively pursuing a nuclear weapon. We know that there have been shipments going into . . . Iraq, for instance, of aluminum tubes that really are only suited . . . for nuclear weapons programs, centrifuge programs.

We know that he has the infrastructure [and] nuclear scientists to make a nuclear weapon. And we know that when the inspectors assessed this after the [first] Gulf War, he was far, far closer to a crude nuclear device than anybody thought, maybe six months from a crude nuclear device.[86]

Cheney had been the secretary of defense during the first Gulf war, and Paul Wolfowitz had been one of his chief aides. They had been stunned by how close Saddam had come. That shock, coupled with their resulting doubt in the capabilities of American intelligence to detect Hussein's progress, no doubt fed their fears that once again Saddam could be further along than anyone knew.

"The problem here," said Condi, "is that there will always be some uncertainty about how quickly he can acquire nuclear weapons. But we don't want the smoking gun to be a mushroom cloud."[87]

The phrase would become the most famous one Condoleezza Rice had ever uttered. Her principal point in the interview, to which she returned nineteen times, was that America could no longer wait for gathering threats to become actual attacks. That, she said, was the lesson of 9/11.

> The single most important lesson that I've learned [in the last year] is that, unfortunately, you will always be surprised about the magnitude of events; that you will be surprised, particularly in this world, with terrorism and weapons of mass destruction, at how much damage can be done by a few people; and that you should not wait to be surprised by evil people who may wish you real harm with weapons of mass destruction that would make September 11 look small in comparison . . . We're in a new world. We're in a world in which the possibility of terrorism, married up with technology, could make us very, very sorry that we didn't act.

It was a powerful message, especially coming just days before the first anniversary of 9/11, and it would prove to be, in the end, the administration's strongest argument for invading Iraq, drawing a majority of the American public and much of the opinion-making elite to its side. In essence, the argument was that after 9/11, it was better to be safe than sorry.

The next week the argument was repeated in the National Security Strategy of the United States of America (NSS), the strategic plan of U.S. foreign and security policy, the first one issued since the September 11 attacks. As NSA, Rice had been the strategy's driving force. In fact, she had decided that the State Department's Richard Haass's original draft hadn't gone far enough and had had the strategy rewritten by Philip Zelikow, a University of Virginia professor and coauthor of Rice's second book.[88]

Tellingly, the final version of the strategy used realist language to convey a new transformationalist foreign policy: "[The United States seeks] to create a balance of power that favors human freedom: conditions in which all nations and all societies can choose for themselves the rewards and challenges of political and economic liberty."[89] Rice had used the same phrase in a speech in April to describe America's role after World War II, "when American leadership expanded the number of free and democratic states . . . to create a new balance of power that favored freedom."[90]

True to the spirit of the Bush White House, the strategy was bold, declaring that the United States would be willing to act preemptively to defeat perceived threats before they fully materialized "as a matter of common sense and self-defense." And parts of the document read like an intellectual justification of the transformation of Condoleezza Rice from Cold War realist to post-9/11 transformationalist.

- In the Cold War, especially following the Cuban missile crisis, we faced a generally status quo, risk-averse adversary. Deterrence was an effective defense. But deterrence based only upon the threat of retaliation is less likely to work against leaders of rogue states more willing to take risks, gambling with the lives of their people, and the wealth of their nations.

- In the Cold War, weapons of mass destruction were considered weapons of last resort whose use risked the destruction of those who used them. Today, our enemies see weapons of mass destruction as weapons of choice. For rogue states these weapons are tools of intimidation and military aggression against their neighbors. These weapons may also allow these states to attempt to blackmail the United States and our allies to prevent us from deterring or repelling the aggressive behavior of rogue states. Such states also see these weapons as their best means of overcoming the conventional superiority of the United States.

- Traditional concepts of deterrence will not work against a terrorist enemy whose avowed tactics are wanton destruction and the targeting of innocents; whose so-called soldiers seek martyrdom in death and whose most potent protection is statelessness. The overlap between states that sponsor terror and those that pursue WMD compels us to action.[91]

But it was exactly the opposite of what Rice had written in her *Foreign Affairs* article during the 2000 campaign: "The United States must approac regimes like North Korea resolutely and decisively . . . These regimes are living on borrowed time, *so there need be no sense of panic about them* [emphasis added]. Rather, the first line of defense should be a clear and classical statement of deterrence—if they do acquire WMD, their weapons will be unusable because any attempt to use them will bring national obliteration."

Precisely for the reasons that Rice had cited in 2000, the NSS's arguments were not wholly persuasive. While nonstate actors like al-Qaeda had no territory or treasure to protect and were therefore immune to the implicit blackmail of "classical deterrence"; that was not true of North Korea or Iran. If they were discovered to have transferred WMD to terrorists, they would still expose themselves to "national obliteration." And there was no indication that Pyongyang or Teheran were "more willing to take risks, gambling with the lives of their people, and the wealth of their nations" than the Soviet Union had been. That reality had not changed between 2000 and 2002. What had changed was 9/11; the attacks had created the "sense of panic" in America's leaders that Rice had abhorred two years earlier.

The strategy might not hold water as a blueprint for American foreign policy. In fact, it could be counterproductive in that, following the administration's logic, if any rogue state acquired nuclear weapons, the United States would have to act to end the regime or remove the weapons. But it provided ample justification for overthrowing Hussein. Iraq's regime was in the "overlap between states that sponsor terror and those that pursue WMD." Hussein had already proven, in his war with Iran, that he was "willing to take risks, gambling with the lives of [his] people, and the wealth of [his] nation." Saddam had used "weapons of mass destruction as weapons of choice" and as "tools of intimidation and military aggression against [his] neighbors."

Of course, Saddam had never used WMD to threaten America. But no one could say he wouldn't, given his history—a history neither North Korea nor Iran shared.

To further complicate matters, while Powell was building support at the UN for a new resolution against Hussein, the dictator declared he would allow UN inspectors back into Iraq for the first time in four years. Even more bothersome, North Korea announced to U.S. diplomat James Kelley that it was enriching uranium, a precursor to producing nuclear weapons. The Bush administration argued that North Korea was different from Iraq. With the United States making war plans for Iraq, it couldn't do otherwise. But no one knew the exact state of

Iraq's nuclear program or whether it even had one; North Korea had just admitted it did.[92]

On October 10, Congress voted overwhelmingly to authorize the president to use military force in Iraq, less than a month before the 2002 midterm elections. In a break with historical precedent, the Republicans, the party in the White House, picked up seats.

On November 8, the administration received its UN resolution, but in a compromise it had to drop the "all means necessary" language that would have triggered an automatic military response if Hussein again hampered the work of weapons inspectors.

By January, as U.S. forces streamed into the Persian Gulf, the French realized the Americans were serious about war, and that no French, Russian, or Chinese judgment about the necessity for a second UN resolution authorizing the use of force was going to stop them. President Jacques Chirac sent an envoy to Condi Rice to make the case against war—it could destabilize the already volatile Middle East and it would increase al-Qaeda recruitment, diplomat Maurice Gourdault-Montagne told Rice. Condi replied that leaving Saddam in power posed bigger risks.[93]

At about the same time, Rice and Chip Blacker sat together over dinner at Galileo, a swank Italian restaurant in Washington. Chip told Condi that Hussein was "guilty of attempted genocide, a serial violator of UN Security Council resolutions, a despicable human being, and he leads a despicable regime and has weapons of mass destruction. And I have no objection to using force to remove him. I'm just not sure we can walk and chew gum at the same time: do Afghanistan and the struggle against al-Qaeda and its affiliates *and* take on this job."[94]

"That's basically been the excuse all along," said Condi, "that there are other, higher priorities than taking this guy out. If not now, then when?"

Blacker said after the war in Afghanistan was a little further along.

"I'm sorry, I don't agree," said Rice. "I think that's an excuse for inaction."

Blacker's argument, like that of Scowcroft and many of the Republican realists, was that Iraq was not central to the war on al-Qaeda and that the United States should finish that work before starting another major military project. But Condi, like Bush, saw the end of Hussein as the prerequisite for changing the Middle East.

The administration sent Colin Powell back to the UN on February 5 to make its case to the world. Powell detailed Iraq's suspected WMD program, from the mobile biological and chemical weapons labs, to centrifuges whose "only purpose," he said, was to enrich uranium to produce nuclear weapons, to Saddam's suspected links to al-Qaeda.

Powell's evidence was compelling, at least to the American public,[95] seventy percent of whom believed Powell had proved that Saddam had WMD.[96] Powell even managed to convince a prominent segment of the media elite—what Bill Keller of the *New York Times* called the "I-Can't-Believe-I'm-a-Hawk Club." By Keller's estimate, the club included columnists from the *Times*, the *Post*, *Time*, and *Newsweek*, and the editors of the *New Yorker*, the *New Republic*, and *Slate*. "We reluctant hawks may disagree among ourselves about the most compelling logic for war—protecting America, relieving oppressed Iraqis, or reforming the Middle East—but we generally agree that the logic for standing pat does not hold. Much as we might wish the administration had orchestrated events so the inspectors had a year instead of three months, much as we deplore the arrogance and binary moralism, much as we worry about all the things that could go wrong, we are hard-pressed to see an alternative that is not built on wishful thinking. Thanks to all these grudging allies, Mr. Bush will be able to claim, with justification, that the coming war is a far cry from the rash, unilateral adventure some of his advisers would have settled for."[97]

Over cheese and crackers in the dining room off the Oval Office, the president, Condi, her deputy, Stephen Hadley, and White House press secretary Ari Fleischer watched most of Powell's ninety-minute speech to the UN live. Afterward, Bush called Powell to congratulate him.[98]

The next day the president appeared in the Roosevelt Room, Powell by his side, to demand the UN accept its responsibilities and pass a second resolution authorizing the use of force unless Hussein disarmed immediately. "The UN must not back down," Bush told the television cameras. "All the world can rise to this moment . . . The game is over."[99]

But there would be no second resolution and, arguing that toppling Saddam Hussein was the next battle in the war on terror, Bush took the boldest step yet of his presidency. On March 19, he launched the invasion of Iraq with a bombing campaign meant to shock and awe.

CHAPTER TEN

SCHOOLED

Acknowledge that you have an obligation to search for the truth.[1]

CONDOLEEZZA RICE
Stanford Commencement Speech
June 16, 2002

ondoleezza Rice stood in her West Wing office and asked herself, "Where *are* the oil workers?"[2] U.S. troops had seized Baghdad on April 9, less than three weeks after the start of the military campaign.[3] On May 1, President Bush landed on the deck of the aircraft carrier *Abraham Lincoln* in a Viking fighter jet. Beneath his window, where the pilot's call sign was normally stenciled, letters spelled out "George W. Bush, Commander in Chief."[4] Bush declared "major combat operations in Iraq" over, and a banner[5] behind him proclaimed, "Mission Accomplished." Fewer Americans, 138, had died in six weeks of Operation Iraqi Freedom than had in four days of Operation Desert Storm, Bush's father's war to drive Hussein from Kuwait.[6]

But Iraq's civilian workforce had disappeared; schools, factories, water treatment plants, oil production facilities—all had ground to a halt. As a result, many Iraqis had less electricity after the invasion than they had under Hussein.[7] "It turns out we had one erroneous assumption," said Rice four years later, "that you could decapitate these ministries and that you'd have a civil service underneath that would actually take up the day-to-day running [of the country] . . . You can have all the planning you want, if you've got that wrong assumption, then [it's] going to fall apart.[8]

And after the initial triumphant images of Iraqis welcoming American soldiers, Iraq looked like it was falling apart. The breakdown in services and infrastructure wasn't the only problem; there was a security vacuum, too. On May 27, for the first time in weeks, Saddam loyalists killed American soldiers—the first signs that an insurgency was developing. Then, locals who worked for the Coalition Provisional Authority (CPA), the organization charged with securing and rebuilding the country, started turning up dead. The letters found on their bodies warned Iraqis who cooperated with the Americans, "We will chop off your rotten head and put it on the tanks of your American cousins and feed your body to the dogs."[9]

Though Rice, as usual, projected confidence publicly, the White House was in fact shocked by the widespread mayhem.[10] To figure out how to get the country running again, Rice asked her NSC lieutenant for military affairs, Frank Miller, to reconstitute the Executive Steering Group. The ESG had been in charge of coordinating the postwar plans of the various U.S. government departments that would supervise Iraq after Hussein was deposed. Now it was clear that restarting Iraq's infrastructure would require all those departments' expertise, in everything from energy production to currency. Ostensibly the Department of Defense (DoD) was in charge, but despite the hundreds of millions of dollars Congress had given the administration, there was little evidence of rebuilding. "For the first couple of months, we believed that [DoD] had a plan to handle what was going to happen after the statue [of Saddam] came down," said Miller. "When it became clear that they didn't, Condi said, 'Start the ESG back up.'"[11]

But was it too late? Three weeks after President Bush's "mission accomplished" speech, Richard Lugar, the Republican chair of the Senate Foreign Relations Committee, said bluntly, "Victory is at risk."[12]

To make matters worse, three months after the invasion, a special military unit working under experienced arms inspectors still couldn't find Hussein's alleged weapons of mass destruction. Hans Blix, who had been the UN's chief weapons inspector in Iraq until just before the invasion, told a British paper that "lower level" members of the administration had "leaned" on him when he couldn't find WMD and then launched a smear campaign against him.[13] Critics began to charge that the U.S. and U.K. governments had manipulated intelligence to exaggerate the urgency of the threat Saddam posed. They called into question the allegations of stockpiles of WMD and Saddam's supposed efforts to buy yellowcake in Africa, which had been highlighted in the president's State of the

Union speech in January, as well as much of Powell's UN presentation. The bulk of the administration's case for urgently going to war was coming under fire.

And so was Condi Rice. Until the summer of 2003, all but the most partisan Democrats regarded Rice as the media usually portrayed her: the brilliant and attractive woman who had risen from segregation to advise a president. She had been the ubiquitous and usually flawless spokesperson for the administration's policies. Now the administration's inability to find WMD, the growing chaos in Baghdad, and the perceived lack of postwar planning raised questions about both the administration's veracity in building its case for war and its competence in planning for the postwar conditions. And those questions inevitably reflected on Rice.

First, the postwar coordination between the government agencies had been run by the NSC. Why hadn't the administration considered the possibility that services would break down after the invasion leading to chaos? Second, there was the question of whether Washington had sent enough troops not only to win the war but to secure the peace. While military planning was the responsibility of DoD, it was the national security adviser's job to make sure the president and the principals had considered what could go wrong. Finally, there was the war between the Departments of State and Defense.[14] The national security adviser was supposed to oversee the interagency process to make sure that the president's priorities were being carried out, and there was no higher priority than stabilizing Iraq, but clearly State and Defense were not cooperating. If interagency coordination wasn't functioning, it stood to reason, critics said, that Rice wasn't doing her job.[15]

In response to the rash of stories about why Rice wouldn't—or couldn't—make secretaries Powell and Rumsfeld play nice together, NSC spokesman Sean McCormack told the press that Rice didn't think refereeing intramural squabbles was her job. "Our primary job, as Condi has identified it, is to staff the president and coordinate among the agencies," McCormack said.[16] That answer satisfied few in Washington. How could Rice coordinate the agencies if she couldn't control the men who ran the two most important departments? The suspicion grew that Rice was out of her league. In the early months of the Iraq war, it was true that she had a hard time even getting information out of the CPA to advise the president. But as she had with 9/11, Rice would learn from Iraq. And as was often the case for her, the lesson would be about power. Only this time, it wouldn't be about the power of so-called non-state actors; it would be about her own.

The criticism of Rice finally boiled over at the feet of the president in July. The tipping point was her role in Bush's claim that Saddam Hussein had sought to buy uranium for his nuclear program from Niger. The media had dubbed the accusation "the sixteen words": "The British government has learned that Saddam Hussein recently sought significant quantities of uranium from Africa," said Bush in his State of the Union.[17]

But the CIA didn't believe the intelligence was reliable and had told the White House that. In fact, the preceding October, the CIA had made the White House remove the accusation from a speech Bush was to give on the rationale for war. When vetting the State of the Union address months later, the agency failed to note that the charge had been revived. When the press learned that the CIA didn't believe the claim—just as the WMD hunt in Iraq was turning up empty— administration critics demanded to know how an intelligence claim that the CIA had disputed had made it into the president's speech.

Pressed for an answer, Rice explained to reporters that when the CIA vetted Bush's speech, they didn't object to the "sixteen words." Moreover, she said, the agency had never told her deputy Steve Hadley, who was in charge of vetting the speech,[18] why the claim had to be taken out of the October speech.

After Rice gave journalists her explanation for the error, CIA director George Tenet publicly took responsibility for the mistake, but privately he was miffed. Later the agency released two memos they had sent to the White House detailing exactly why the phrase had to be stricken from the October speech: The intelligence behind it was questionable. At that point, Hadley came out and offered his own mea culpa for not remembering the assertion was suspect and for not removing it from the State of the Union. But Condi Rice did not.

So when the president addressed a July 30 news conference before leaving for his August vacation, a White House reporter asked, "Mr. President, you often speak about the need for accountability in many areas. I wonder then, why is Dr. Condoleezza Rice not being held accountable for the statement that your own White House has acknowledged was a mistake in your State of the Union regarding Iraq's attempts to purchase uranium [from Niger]? And also, do you take personal responsibility for that inaccuracy?"[19]

First the president gave a long defense of taking the country to war, then a much shorter but emphatic defense of Rice.

I take personal responsibility for everything I say, of course. Absolutely. I also take responsibility for making decisions on war and peace. And I analyzed a thorough body of intelligence—good, solid, sound intelligence—that led me to come to the conclusion that it was necessary to remove Saddam Hussein from power.

We gave the world a chance to do it . . . I don't want to get repetitive here, but it's important to remind everybody that there was twelve resolutions that came out of the United Nations because others recognized the threat of Saddam Hussein. Twelve times the United Nations Security Council passed resolutions in recognition of the threat that he posed. And the difference was, is that some were not willing to act on those resolutions. We were—along with a lot of other countries—because he posed a threat.

Dr. Condoleezza Rice is an honest, fabulous person. And America is lucky to have her service. *Period*.[20]

For added emphasis, the president banged on the lectern eight times in the course of his seventeen-word defense of Rice, with the final thump coming as he said, *"Period."* It was the most impassioned statement he made during the hour-long news conference—and he had spoken about North Korea's nuclear program, Iraq, Mideast peace, the possibility of an impending al-Qaeda attack that summer, and 9/11.

Hours later Rice appeared on PBS's *NewsHour with Jim Lehrer* and offered her mea culpa. "The president of the United States has every right to believe that what he is saying in his speeches is of the highest confidence of his staff," said Rice. "That's why we go through a clearance process. That's why the process is so rigorous. In this one case, the process did not work. We did have a clearance from the agency, but frankly, looking back, perhaps we should have remembered that it was taken out of the Cincinnati speech [in October]. We simply didn't.[21]

"But what I feel, really, most responsible for is that this has detracted from the very strong case that the president has been making [for taking action against Iraq]. There are people who want to say that somehow the president's case was not strong, the intelligence case was not strong. I've read a lot of intelligence cases over my almost twenty years now in this field, and this was a very strong case."[22]

But what about Rice's mushroom cloud comment, asked *NewsHour* senior correspondent Gwen Ifill: "What you said, going into the war, using very stark language . . . looking for a smoking gun which could become a mushroom cloud . . . You also said that there were aluminum tube purchases, which indicated that the reconstitution of the nuclear program might be under way. You also said there were satellite photos that showed that buildings were being rebuilt in places where there had been a nuclear program before. Taken together, this was all to make the point that Saddam Hussein was possibly on the verge of reconstituting a nuclear weapons program. Is that, in retrospect, supportable?"

> **RICE:** It's absolutely supportable, and listen to the list that you just gave. What this was, was a description of his procurement network. We knew that he had, as Colin Powell talked about in his presentation at the United Nations, an active procurement network to procure items, many of which, by the way, were on the prohibited list of the nuclear suppliers [*sic*] group . . . magnets, balancing machines, yes, aluminum tubes, about which the consensus view was that they were suitable for use in centrifuges to spin material for nuclear weapons.
>
> **GWEN IFILL:** That's something that the International Atomic Energy Agency did not agree with.
>
> **RICE:** Well, the DCI, the director of central intelligence, the consensus view of the American intelligence agency, was that given the specifications, given that this had been Saddam Hussein's kind of personal network, given the expense that they had gone to get these tubes, that they were most likely for this use, but there were other elements as well—facilities that were being rebuilt.
>
> It was a case that said he is trying to reconstitute. He's trying to acquire nuclear weapons. Nobody ever said that it was going to be the next year, but the question was that if it was possible that he might have one by the end of the decade, and if it was possible, as the National Intelligence Estimate said, that if he acquired fissile material, it might be far sooner than that. Was that a threat that you could allow to sit unanswered? . . .
>
> And when you look at that picture, and you look at this picture in the Middle East, this incredibly volatile region, and you look at his ambitions, Saddam Hussein's ambitions for power in the Middle East that were demonstrated in what he did in Iran and what he would later do in Kuwait,

this was a threat that had been out there too long. And as the president said today, we wanted the international community to deal with it . . . It sat there and sat there. It was time to deal with it.

Rice sounded more defensive than Bush had that morning; the president had appeared ornery but strong, in good humor and complete control. He had handled the Washington press corps like so many curious children, alternately telling jokes and soberly restating his case for invasion. But Bush's terse defense of Rice took a totally different tone from the rest of his remarks, particularly because it was so impassioned; it seemed hard to imagine Kennedy calling his national security adviser McGeorge Bundy "fabulous" or Nixon saying that of Kissinger or Reagan of Powell. But Bush considered Condi like "a sister"[23]—and the Bushes defended family.

On August 19, the last day of Rice's vacation, she received news that promised to further slow rebuilding efforts in Iraq. She was on the tennis court at the Greenbrier Resort in West Virginia—a favorite retreat in summer and winter from her Washington duties—when an aide ran up and told her a truck bomb had obliterated the United Nations headquarters in Baghdad.[24] As her convoy sped back to Washington, Rice called into the Situation Room for an update. Sergio Vieira de Mello, the handsome and charismatic Latin American diplomat whom Rice herself had urged to take the job of leading the UN's Iraq mission, was dead.[25] In the end, twenty-one other UN workers and international observers would also die from wounds suffered in the attack, and the UN and most international nongovernmental organizations would withdraw from Iraq, most never to return in significant numbers. To Rice the situation was clearly becoming untenable. She acted to change the dynamic in Iraq.

When she had gone to see Bush in Crawford weeks before the attack on the UN, she had discussed bringing Iraq's reconstruction back into the purview of the NSC. Absolute trust had been the basis of Rice and Bush's relationship, and they had only grown closer while Bush was in the White House; Rice spent more time with the president than anyone, most of it in the West Wing, but also at Camp David and in Crawford. At the White House she saw the president seven or eight times in a typical day and regularly joined the Bush family for Sunday dinner.[26]

Now Rice argued that she needed greater "connectivity" to the CPA and its administrator, L. Paul "Jerry" Bremer. Bush agreed. Rice would soon bring back her old NSC boss, Bob Blackwill, an experienced bureaucratic infighter, to get a handle on what was happening in Baghdad.

Because she didn't know. "The truth of the matter is nobody was getting much information out of the [CPA]. Jerry had alligators all around him, and he was trying to run the place," says Rice. "And there was a missing link. For most things it didn't matter. . . . You don't really need Washington making every decision when you've got a Coalition Provisional Authority out there. Let them make the decisions."

But Rice's aides said the Department of Defense was the bigger problem. While Powell's tensions with Rumsfeld were widely known inside the Beltway, Rice's battles with the secretary of defense were largely private. In fact, her discretion had led the press to call her "sphinx-like."[27] But her former staffers say she struggled mightily against Rumsfeld's Machiavellian mix of confidence and bureaucratic ruthlessness.[28] In one tactic, according to an NSC source, Rumsfeld would arrange to see the president without briefing Rice or Powell on his agenda. "In Clinton, [Bush I], and Reagan the NSC actually managed cabinet [members'] meetings with the president. But he . . . would go in to the president, hit him with six different [items], claim that everybody was in support of them, the allies loved it—we're good to go, basically—and then go back and tell his people at DoD, 'The president said okay. You don't need to clear this with State or NSC.' And start implementing it."[29]

And Rumsfeld's lieutenants followed his lead. They willfully stalled discussions in deputies committee meetings, chaired by Rice's number two, Hadley, or left early. The deputies meetings were where policy options, including the postwar plans, were supposed to be hammered out before being presented to the principals for final discussion, but Frank Miller, Rice's NSC director for military issues, said the undersecretary of defense for policy, Douglas Feith, refused to share information. "'It's *my* job.' That's the way Feith played it," Miller said.[30]

In principals meetings, Rumsfeld played the same bureaucratic hardball. Years later NSC staffers still complain about writing memos laying out policy options, only to have Rumsfeld claim that he hadn't read them and therefore couldn't discuss the issue. Said one staffer, "We'd spend multiple, multiple man-hours generating this up for Rice to say, 'Okay, we are gathered here to decide what we're going to do about this and here is how I frame it.' Rumsfeld again and again would say, 'I didn't have time to read it' or 'I just got it, so, I'm not prepared to talk.' Which was usually not the case . . . because his staff would be telling us that he felt very strongly about column A or page two or paragraph one."[31]

The secretary of defense managed to pull off his bully tactics, said a former White House staffer, because "Rumsfeld shows zero weakness, zero . . . You didn't realize that a Powell, an Armitage, or even a Rice were just a little bit intimidated, just a little bit unsure, somewhere . . . until you saw Rumsfeld talk. All of them at some level, even the president, had little chinks here and there in their armor: Sometimes [they said] things to be careful about not hurting that person or [this person's feelings]. There was an empathy—what you expect in normal human interactions . . . You never saw it in Rumsfeld.[32]

"Rumsfeld was just a nasty, better bureaucratic player, and he always had Cheney. He could get Cheney to go into the Oval [Office], which allowed him to outflank Rice."

In the summer of 2003, as Iraq was exploding, Powell's deputy, Richard Armitage, went to Rice and told her that the NSC was "dysfunctional" under her leadership. According to Powell's biographer Karen DeYoung, Armitage said, "'You don't resolve things." Rice thanked him for his comments and, according to Armitage, said, 'I don't want to read about this in the press."[33]

Rice denies that the interagency process was dysfunctional. "People generally think something is dysfunctional when they didn't get their way," she says. "It was *difficult*, because we were doing really, really difficult issues." She also rejects the now widely held belief in Washington that the postwar difficulties in Iraq had anything to do with interagency rivalries. "There were plenty of tensions between State and Defense . . . There were a lot of frictions because you had a structure by necessity where Defense had the lead, but increasingly, State had equities. [But] that wasn't going to be solved by an interagency process."[34]

Finally, Rice disputes Powell's claim that he had held less sway with the president than Rumsfeld. "I don't understand that because Colin Powell had as much access [to the president] as anybody. Colin used to come have dinner with the president. I don't think Don ever did that . . . I'd like to know what [Colin] means. I'd like to know what three examples, four examples, five examples there are."

But even Rice's supporters in the administration say the process was dysfunctional. Rumsfeld wasn't the only complicating factor—perhaps he wasn't even the greatest. In the Bush administration, the vice president wielded unprecedented power in foreign policy formulation. In the estimation of at least one former State Department official, Cheney's national security staff within the Office of the Vice President amounted to another NSC.[35] "The vice president has certainly usurped many of the prerogatives that have traditionally accrued to the national security advisers," wrote analyst David Rothkopf in his history of the NSC."[36]

And while the vice president's role was stronger than usual, the secretary of state's was weaker. So the usual bureaucratic perspectives of the State Department—diplomacy, negotiation, multilateralism—were less prevalent in the administration's foreign policy. As Rice's friend Chip Blacker, a former Clinton NSC staffer, put it, "[Condi] always had a good relationship with Powell. But in the end it couldn't overcome the fact that George Bush was not going to bring him into the inner circle."[37]

It wasn't that the president disliked his secretary of state. The two just never clicked. Perhaps the tension grew from Bush's feeling that Powell was neither sufficiently loyal nor deferential. He was a favorite background source for Washington journalists and freely admitted his differences with the administration. Or maybe it was simply politics; Powell was of a different ideological stripe than the rest of the Bush team, more multilateral, more in line with Bush Sr.'s NSC.

The president had brought together strong-willed men with a wealth of experience but discordant views, but then, according to several White House staffers, for whatever reason, he didn't want to manage the discord. Bush was uninterested in having Rice haul his senior advisers into the Oval Office to adjudicate their disputes.[38] "His close friends agree that Bush likes comfort and serenity; he does not like dissonance," *Newsweek* would report in 2005.[39]

Unmanaged, the personal and political differences between the president's advisers—in contrast to the sober collegiality of his father's NSC—led to the rampant personalization of policy. So, Defense ignored State's voluminous Future of Iraq Project before the war and vetoed allowing Bremer's predecessor, Jay Garner, to take two State Department Arabists with him to Iraq.[40]

Caught between the principals and their conflicting ideologies, Condoleezza Rice faced an unenviable task. A former White House staffer described her tenure as NSA as "a little bit like the Battle of the Marne for her."[41]

"She had to make a decision every day, many of them: Which of the many issues that I might disagree with this principal or that principal or they disagree with one another about do I magnify and take to the president? . . . You only have so many cartridges in your belt. You cannot go in to the president every day: 'I got another one for you . . . ' So she had to constantly try to manage [Cheney, Powell, and Rumsfeld]."

Rice's closeness to the president, in both geographic and personal terms, meant she knew how he wanted to run his bureaucracy. So in the principals meetings, she sought consensus where she could, took conflicting issues to the president once they were sufficiently clarified, and if they never were, kicked the ball down the field.

But that was the problem. Critics, both inside and outside the administration, describe policies that the NSC was too slow to handle, too muddled in its handling of, or never handled at all, from planning for the occupation of Iraq, to the administration's belated intervention in Mideast peace negotiations, to the slow formulation of a policy on North Korea.

Sometimes Rice's style worked—as in the case of North Korea, eventually. She played a key role in the idea of "six party talks" that brought South Korea, China, Japan, and Russia into talks with North Korea and the United States, splitting the difference between the Pentagon's and Cheney's wanting to avoid "rewarding" North Korea for continuing its nuclear programs and the State Department's desire to hold bilateral talks. In 2007, the talks would produce a deal with Pyongyang.

But at least as often her approach didn't work. The question was how much of the "dysfunction" in the Bush NSC was Rice's fault and how much was the president's.

An adage of NSC watchers holds that every president ultimately gets the process he wants. "Whether it's the process he needs or not is a different issue," said a former administration official. "I don't know . . . whether Condi Rice or anyone else pushed back and said, 'Mr. President, this may be the process you want, but let me explain the potential downsides or shortfalls of this kind of a process. Let me make the case for something else.'"[42]

Scowcroft was more blunt: "It's the president's [fault] making [the process] work or doing something about it . . . in the end, it's the president."[43]

True to her Rice and Ray family roots, Rice eventually went around the obstacle—in this case, Rumsfeld. When Frank Miller couldn't get information from the secretary of defense's lieutenants, Rice told him to call his old contacts at the Pentagon, where he had worked for twenty years before coming to the NSC. "Over time they knew we were obtaining information [from within DoD], and they didn't know how we were stealing it. That caused some resentment," said Miller.[44]

By the beginning of October, Rice's more prominent role in the postwar process became public when an internal memo went to the principals confirming that the Iraq Stabilization Group, an NSC ad hoc committee that included Blackwill and Miller, would now oversee reconstruction efforts in Iraq as well as Afghanistan. At a NATO conference in Colorado Springs—in the same hotel where Bush had decided to give up drinking seventeen years earlier—when European journalists asked Rumsfeld why U.S. reconstruction efforts were being placed under the NSC, he told them, "I think you have to ask Condi that question."[45] When a German broadcaster followed up, pressing for Rumsfeld's opinion, the secretary railed, "I said I don't know. Isn't that clear? You don't understand English?"[46] Administration officials said the reorganization didn't amount to a change in responsibilities; Bremer would still report to Rumsfeld. But to assuage Congress—which was concerned about how wisely the administration would spend its recent $87 billion funding request—the White House said putting Rice in charge would bring budget and oversight responsibility "right into the White House."[47]

Even to her NSC staff, Rice minimized the significance of the change. "She told us all, 'No, I'm not in charge," remembered a senior staffer. "[Then she said], 'Okay, here's what we're doing . . .' and she was *clearly* in charge."[48]

Still, in one of our interviews, Rice downplayed the bureaucratic infighting in the administration, saying her increased "connectivity" to Bremer and the CPA was merely a recognition that as the postwar focus turned to questions of Iraq's political future—questions the administration had not answered in their planning for the postwar period[49]—the White House needed to have a greater hand in directing what happened in Baghdad: "When were you going to have elections? Were the elections going to precede the [creation of a new] constitution? . . . What issues really have to be decided back in Washington and which ones don't? We weren't getting enough information from the Coalition Provisional Authority prior to their making decisions to make that call."[50]

But Bremer's lack of connectivity was part of a larger problem that Rice left unstated; as one former Defense Department official said, "Rumsfeld [had] demanded responsibility for all of postwar Iraq and then did nothing with it."[51] According to Bob Woodward, Rice told Blackwill she was less urgently concerned about the situation on the ground in Iraq than she was worried about the "dysfunctional U.S. government."[52]

The question was, what difference would Rice's greater responsibility make? In Iraq, where the U.S. troops were now facing a full-blown insurgency, the dismal military equation would remain unchanged as Bremer and American commanders continued to react too slowly to the insurgency's evolving tactics. Predictably, the deteriorating security situation would hamper renewed reconstruction efforts; each time contractors rebuilt an oil pipeline, insurgents blew it up. But under Rice's direction, the political transition toward a return to Iraqi sovereignty did take on new speed and deliberateness.

In Washington, Rumsfeld would chafe under the reorganization, telling Rice Bremer worked for her now,[53] which wasn't technically true. But Rice was taking on more and more responsibility. For instance, when Bremer told Rice during a call in November that he had a plan for the transition to Iraqi sovereignty, Rice replied, "Don't you think you should come back here and talk about this . . . This is really a kind of presidential-level decision."[54]

When Rice told Bush she had asked Bremer to come to Washington, Bush asked, "Why'd you do that?"

"Because I think we'd better have this discussion here."

It was not the first time Rice had nudged the president toward what she thought was the right direction. That summer the administration had debated whether to send U.S. Marines into Liberia to quell a violent uprising by armed thugs who had chased humanitarian relief organizations out of the war-ravaged nation. In that case, Rice had sided with Powell and the State Department against DoD, which opposed sending in U.S. forces.[55] "Powell had done his brief, Rumsfeld had done his brief, it had gone back and forth, back and forth," recalled Jendayi Frazer, Rice's deputy for Africa. "[Then] the national security adviser said, 'Okay, now. I think Marines may need to go in' . . . and the decision was made that we were going in."[56]

Such instances of direct and semipublic intervention by Rice into policy formulation had been rare. In fact, she was famous for listening and letting the principals debate during NSC meetings, seldom interjecting her opinion. But having broken Rumsfeld's monopoly on Iraq policy, Rice now took firm hold of the reins. Directing Bremer back to Washington to meet with the president was just one example where she began forcefully pushing policy to correct the administration's course.

Another came before Christmas. Rice had recruited Larry Diamond, a Stanford colleague and a specialist in democracy in developing countries, to go to Iraq. Diamond returned with news that the UN was willing to go back in for the first time since the deadly attack on its Baghdad headquarters. The United States needed the international body's help in orchestrating the political transition: The leading Shiite cleric, the Grand Ayatollah Ali al-Sistani, was objecting to the transition plan Bremer and the White House had worked out in November, known as the November 15 Agreement.

"[Rice] made it happen; she got the UN back in there," said Diamond. "It saved our butts, frankly. We would not have been able to maintain the November 15 plan without the . . . adaptations and agreements [the UN] negotiated, and gotten to the interim government or even gotten to the difficult state we're at [today]."[57]

"As a result of her assuming overall charge, we made a number of adjustments and moved toward a much more pragmatic, less ideological position that made the pursuit of stabilization in Iraq at least somewhat more possible," including building a strategy to bring disaffected Sunnis into the political process and reversing much of Bremer's de-Baathification policy, which had fired most of the country's civil-service managers, said Diamond, who would nonetheless write a book taking Rice to task for reacting too slowly to problems in Iraq.

But the end of 2003 marked a turning point for Rice. She took a newly prominent role across the board, flexing her muscles on the issues Bush cared about most—from Iraq to North Korea. Just as Washington had decided she had been run over by "the titans," the star pupil was learning to play the game in a very different NSC from the one she had come of age in. "[Initially] her attitude had been that she was going to be like Scowcroft," said a former staffer. "She was going to let State and DoD take the lead in their policy areas . . . [Now] she took charge of a lot of sensitive policy areas and ran them."[58] It was a palpable change, and one the president had signed off on because, as Rice's friend Chip

Blacker said, "She did what the president wanted her to do . . . And you can only reach that far and no farther."[59] Now, as a former senior White House official put it, "she was the man."

Rice's new assertiveness didn't erase the mistakes of the first nine months of war. One of the chief duties of the national security adviser was to protect the president from making major mistakes, and she hadn't. For example, Rice modeled her NSC on Brent Scowcroft's, but Scowcroft had said, "My approach to almost every question is to view it with informed skepticism . . . if it doesn't work, what happens?"

It was not a critique that Scowcroft fashioned in 2003 as the administration's mistakes in Iraq were becoming increasingly clear; it was a point he made in 1987 as a member of the Tower Commission investigating the NSC's role in Iran Contra. "The heart of good policy formation," he said, "is not just coming up with ideas. It is testing the ideas against the things that can happen in the real world and usually do."[60]

"Informed skepticism" had been the basis of Rice's academic scholarship, and as an exceptional debater, she regularly employed it in her arguments against her opponents. But where had Rice's informed skepticism been in the run-up to the Iraq war? Many of the fateful decisions taken (and not taken) before the administration went to war were not within Rice's power to control, from Bush's management style, to the personalities of his cabinet, to the fact that the president had created an alternate and more powerful pole for national security advice in the person and office of the vice president. But some factors were within Rice's power to influence and indeed, in some cases, were likely exacerbated by her own traits and actions, which tended to enable the president's missteps rather than check them.

Most important, perhaps, the dynamic that characterized Rice's relationship to the president was born of the campaign, when she had concentrated on translating Bush's ideals and vision into substantive policy options. In the White House, too, Rice and Bush saw her as his facilitator, not his skeptic. "He thinks in big terms," said Chip Blacker. "She would not want to frustrate his tendency to think about what it would take to really transform the Middle East," for instance.[61] So rather than concentrating on the potential downsides of invading

Iraq, Rice focused on how to make it happen. In fact, said Richard Armitage, Powell's deputy, Rice and her deputy, Steve Hadley, made other officials feel like they "were not on the team" if they introduced doubt into the discussions. "Condi, in my view, [felt that] anytime someone wasn't ready to do immediately exactly what the president wants, it was almost disloyal."

Another problem was that in the classic Scowcroft model of the NSC, Rice respected the administration's initial division of labor too much and for too long. On March 5, 2003, for instance, two weeks before the shooting started, Jay Garner, head of the first civilian administration in Iraq, met with Rice in her West Wing office and detailed the problems with planning for the postwar, from the lack of funds at his disposal to rebuild Iraq to what many in the military believed was the insufficient complement of troops to secure the country after the war.[62] Rice and Hadley had also received a confidential briefing from their own NSC military aides, entitled "Force Security in Seven Recent Stability Operations," that suggested that postwar Iraq would require far more troops than the Pentagon planned for.[63]

But at the time—as Rice would later say of both domestic security before 9/11 and disaster assistance after Katrina—deciding troop levels and reconstruction budgets were not her "accounts"; they belonged to the Department of Defense. And, as she said in one of our interviews, "We didn't want to try to run it out of the White House. You need an agency that's going to take it and do it. Defense had the contracting authority, [and] the Coalition Provisional Authority reported to the Defense Department in order to provide unity of command."[64]

But it was Rice's responsibility to ensure that once U.S. troops were engaged, there was ongoing "review" of the administration's policies. Her own envoy to the region, Bob Blackwill, would return from Iraq in 2003 and say that he couldn't discern what America was trying to do there militarily or politically. He asked Rice and Hadley to do a review of the current military plans, but it never happened.[65] And her Stanford colleague Larry Diamond would write to her in April 2004, "I did not meet a single military officer who felt, privately, we had enough troops." His "blunt" memo ended, "We are in serious and mounting danger of failing in Iraq." Diamond never received a reply.[66]

Nonetheless, those entreaties eventually led Rice to understand that the Scowcroft model wasn't working in this administration and that she had to accrue more responsibility and more power to herself and the NSC.

Many administration officials believe Rice was slow to realize that she needed to become more involved operationally sooner because she emphasized her role as adviser to the president rather than as the manager of the process.[67] The neocons, in particular, once they broke with the administration over Iraq, argued that one of the Bush administration's principal flaws was that Rice was too close to Bush.[68] Michael Ledeen, a fellow at the American Enterprise Institute, said that the most powerful people in the White House were "women who are in love with the president: Laura [Bush], Condi, Harriet Miers, and Karen Hughes."[69] He cited Rice's Freudian slip at a dinner party in 2004, where she reportedly had said, "As I was telling my husb—" before abruptly correcting herself and finishing, "As I was telling President Bush."[70]

The dinner party in question was an off-the-record gathering at the home of *New York Times* Washington bureau chief Philip Taubman. Rice told me she didn't recall ever making the now famous comment. "I swear I don't remember any such slip of the tongue," she said. "I was stunned when I read that the next day. I don't think it happened. I really don't."[71] Not everyone at the dinner party does remember it. In fact, some of the attendees are certain that she didn't say it, though other guests swore she did.

More to the point, even Rice's supporters say she put her advisory role before managing the process, but, again, that may have been more a function of the president's needs than of Rice's preference. As James Baker put it, "[George H. W. Bush] didn't need staffing; he could have been his own national security adviser . . . That left Brent time to manage the process."[72] Having tutored George W. Bush before he became president, Rice knew that this president did need staffing.

But friends and family speculate that Rice's personal relationship with Bush skewed her view of him, blinding her to his failings. "She thought he could do no wrong," said one of Rice's friends, an assessment shared by many of her friends and family.[73]

Kenneth Adelman, a neocon who had once predicted in the editorial pages of the *Wall Street Journal* that Iraq would be a "cakewalk," later offered, "Not only did each of [the members of Bush's national security team], individually, have enormous flaws, but together they were deadly, dysfunctional."[74] And Rice did share characteristics with the other Bush principals that were mutually reinforcing, often negatively. Most crucial was the absence of self-doubt.

Rice's Titusville neighbors had first noticed Condoleezza's supreme self-confidence as a little girl, and it had grown with her. As her friend Blacker said, "I doubt she's ever lost a night's sleep as national security adviser or secretary."[75] Bush was so confident of his own views that, unlike other presidents—his father, Clinton, and Reagan, among them—he didn't feel the need to seek the advice of his political opponents or even his own party's leaders on Capitol Hill.[76] Similarly, Vice President Cheney believed so strongly that Iraq posed an unacceptable threat in the post-9/11 world, and that the CIA was an inept organization, that, whether willfully or not, he accepted only the intelligence that validated his opinions.[77] Rice's supreme belief in herself was the same confidence that convinced her as an nine-year-old who couldn't eat a hamburger at a Southern lunch counter that she could one day be president of the United States. And it was so great that when Powell came to Bush before the war to say that there was a problem with the postwar command structure—that both the civilian and the military chiefs on the ground would report to Rumsfeld—Rice reportedly told him, "That's not right. That's not right." (Powell was right.) Powell noted that when the civilian administrator and the military commander disagreed, the resolution would come from the Pentagon, not from the White House or the NSC, but neither Rice nor Bush thought it was a problem.[78]

Rice's overconfidence may also have led her to miss the fact that the administration had no single war plan—if anything, it had too many—from the Department of State, the Department of Defense, and the NSC—and these were never married into a single document. Once the war started, Garner and then Bremer were steering on their own, developing tactical plans as best they could. Had the administration had a unitary document shared and debated in the principals committee, perhaps it would have noticed that many questions remained undecided even after the war began, including who would lead the new Iraq after Saddam and what political process the Americans would use to find that person.[79]

The principals' hubris, coupled with the administration's interagency dysfunction ("State's bureaucracy produced policy [and] DoD, just because it was State, would kill it and we would get nowhere," said a former NSC staffer),[80] led to many of the prewar mistakes, from the faulty analysis of intelligence to the unrealistic assessment of the difficulty of occupying and remaking Iraq. That overconfidence went unchecked because the institutions that usually urged caution about military action—the State Department, the CIA, and the uniformed military—were weakened in the Bush administration.[81]

But Rice's own experience also prejudiced her toward action in Iraq. Her time working for Scowcroft in the first Bush administration had taught her firsthand that principled American leadership could bring dramatic change in the world. Despite his reputation for deliberateness, George H. W. Bush had pushed for rapid German unification before any of his advisers. "The president wanted us to go fast," said Baker.[82] Scowcroft had advised caution, and Scowcroft had been wrong and the president had been right, Rice may have recalled.

And both Rice's conversion to transformationalism and her understanding of Morgenthau's imperative of power led her to believe that invading Iraq was the right decision. The war was going to be a rapid demonstration of American power (realism) that would transform the Middle East (idealism) and be over by Christmas. But none of those inside the loop—the president, the vice president, Rumsfeld, or Rice—had developed contingency plans in case their fundamental assumptions turned out to be flawed, such as Iraq that would function normally once Saddam's regime was "decapitated." "This [was] our blunder," said one former administration official. "You could say, 'We took the lid off the Balkans and look what happened,' but we didn't analogize."[83]

Finally, Rice was living in a bubble of her own. Even though she religiously kept to her regular Sunday calls, her connection back to what she called her normal life, her loved ones never raised what was happening in the world in their talks with Condi. They didn't discuss the changing national mood from unconditional support of the president post-9/11 to skepticism or the rising tide of criticism that the administration's actions—and its most eloquent spokeswoman—were facing. They also didn't share their own doubts with Rice. "She never wants to hear anything negative about President Bush," said Deborah Carson.[84] "She never learns from me anything that anybody is saying negative," said Rice's stepmother, Clara. "When I talk to her, it's 'You're doing a great job' . . . I have to be that to her. Because I know that's what John would be and would want me to be."[85]

A former Stanford colleague contrasted Rice's job as a university administrator to her position as national security adviser: "In a university, you cannot escape criticism. . . . The problem with the White House is they can stop reading papers, they can stop talking to people who disagree with them. *They* can become an ivory tower."

Just as it had been Rice's responsibility to ensure that the administration's prewar assumptions were subjected to reasoned skepticism, it was also her job to ensure that the president heard the mountain of negative assessments from inside the government once the occupation had begun. But Bob Woodward describes "an atmosphere [that] too often resembled a royal court, with Cheney and Rice in attendance, some upbeat stories, exaggerated good news, and a good time had by all. . . . In [those] moments where Bush had someone from the field there in the chair beside him, he did not . . . ask what the visitor had seen and thought."[86]

Here too Rice may have been a prisoner of her own unique history. The administration's modus operandi would have been familiar and comfortable to her because aspects of both could be found in the communities that bred her. Birmingham's sequestered black middle class had valued discretion, and the extraordinarily close-knit Ray family had taught Rice the importance of looking after one's own, as well as the need to be strong and resolute. One of the morals of her own biography had been that what mattered was what you and your self-defined society believed, because the world beyond was often wrong in its most critical judgments, as it had been in segregated Birmingham about the worth of a little black girl. And that history had instilled in Rice a conviction in the veracity of her own judgments and of those closest to her, even when—perhaps especially when—those judgments conflicted with the "objective" reality of outsiders.

Rice also shared Bush's, Cheney's, and Rumsfeld's distrust of bureaucracy and time-consuming consensus building. It had been apparent in the way she approached her job as provost: You decided what needed to be done, and then you did it. "I think [Rice and Bush] tended to reinforce each other along those lines," conceded Blacker.[87]

Since Rice also had a preternatural aversion to whining, she would have seen the administration's bureaucratic battles simply as survival of the fittest—or, as her protégée Jendayi Frazer put it, the department with the best brief won.[88] It was bureaucratic Realpolitik. And Rice saw complaint as weakness, action in the face of impediments as strength. John and Ann had taught her to go through, around, or over hurdles. So, rather than complain about being outmaneuvered by Rumsfeld, she dealt with it, telling her deputies to do what they had to do to get the information they needed, and she sent her own people to Iraq. Like any realist, she adapted to the world as it was, and she ultimately grew more powerful than Rumsfeld.

But until then, her Titusville rules were ineffective in the rough-and-tumble game Rumsfeld was playing. Ironically, had Rice for once concentrated on the problem itself rather than "getting over it," she might have realized that much sooner how dysfunctional her interagency process had become. She might have suggested to the president that much earlier that Iraq reconstruction needed to be brought into the White House or, if that was politically problematic—as more than one of her former aides insisted—she might have moved sooner to compensate for the overly rosy scenarios coming out of Rumsfeld's Department of Defense.

Rice's ultimately successful adaptation may have also been impeded by her trouble, according to friends and family, with acknowledging error. Though as secretary of state she would eventually concede, figuratively, that the administration had made "thousands" of "tactical errors,"[89] when the occupation of Iraq seemed to be going off the rails, Condi's—and her colleagues'—inability to admit error compounded the delay in making a course correction. From the president down, with the notable exception of Powell, who seemed to admit errors almost as soon as he realized them, the principals insisted that the plan was working in the face of unrest that solidified into an insurgency and eventually provoked a quasi–civil war. "Condi has an incredible gift to speak quickly and articulately in front of television cameras and to come up with memorable formulations, but that gift is also a curse because she then falls victim to her own convictions—be it the 'mushroom cloud' or the 'birth pangs of democracy,'" said a Rice colleague.[90]

Added a longtime friend, "She's blazingly smart and knowledgeable . . . compared to the president, but [they both believe] you make a decision and you never look back. They and some of the other senior White House administrators [don't] counterbalance each other. On the other hand, if you're right, sticking to your guns can be a very good thing."

Some of her defenders, particularly her family, go so far as to suggest that Rice's heart wasn't in much of what she did as national security adviser—she was simply doing her duty, as Rays and Rices have always done.

When I see "some of the things that she agrees to go along with, I say, 'That just couldn't be Condi's thinking,'" said Clara Rice, though she couldn't recall what issues or statements she found discordant with her sense of Condoleezza's own beliefs. "But she's going to do what the president asks her to do, or tells her to do—to her own detriment . . . I have been looking and listening and saying, 'You're being *too* loyal, girl.' Whereas Colin Powell wasn't going to let anybody compromise him: If it's wrong, it's wrong, I don't care who said it or who you are."[91]

But those who loved her failed to see that Rice was always in the inner circle. She genuinely believed—and would continue to believe—in the mission in Iraq.[92]

On January 28, 2004, David Kay, who had just resigned as chief weapons inspector for the Bush administration, testified before the Senate Armed Services Committee. "We were almost all wrong," said Kay.[93] He told a reporter that he didn't think there had ever been WMD stockpiles in Iraq, despite what Western intelligence services had believed.

Five days later, during a session with editors and reporters at the *Washington Post*, Colin Powell was asked whether he would have recommended an invasion if he had known Saddam didn't have WMD. "I don't know, because it was the stockpile that presented the final little piece that made it more of a real and present danger," Powell responded. "[The] absence of a stockpile changes the political calculus; it changes the answer you get."[94]

Once again, the secretary of state received a call from Condi.[95] The next day Powell told reporters (as he had done in the *Post* interview, in fact) that the decision to go to war had been the right one.[96]

To the American public, though, Kay's assessment was mind-boggling. Polls showed that most Americans thought WMD was the casus belli. Many also thought we had gone to war in Iraq because Saddam Hussein had either launched the attacks on New York and Washington or supported those who had. The administration had encouraged that view, sometimes explicitly and sometimes subtly. After Kay's testimony, for the first time a majority of Americans, fifty-four percent, said the administration had "misinterpreted or misanalyzed" intelligence on WMD. And a significant number, forty-one percent, said the Bush team had "purposely misled the public" in an attempt to build its case for war.[97] The early signs of a credibility gap were emerging.

Rice called Kay at home the morning after his Senate testimony. The former inspector came in to meet Bush, Cheney, Card, and Rice. The president wanted to know how the CIA could have been so wrong. Rice didn't say much during the meeting, but the next day she asked Kay back to the White House for a one-on-one discussion. In one of Woodward's most telling scenes, he describes Rice telling Kay, "I should have been smart enough."[98]

Rice meant she should have considered the possibility that the "evidence" of Saddam's WMD programs—the orders for expensive specialized aluminum tubes, the additions to buildings known to have housed WMD facilities—were the elaborate subterfuge of a corroding dictatorship; collapsing regimes often feigned strength to appear more menacing than they were. Rice said the same thing had happened in East Germany before the communists fell.

Rice wasn't the self-reflective kind, but if she had been, she might have also wondered how she could have gotten Iraq so wrong. Only Rice didn't think she had—at least not in what mattered most. Overthrowing the dictator had been the right thing to do. As for planning for the postwar period, she would tell me three years later, "War is war. We made a lot of mistakes, I'm sure of it. But there are a lot of mistakes we didn't make, too."[99]

A collective gasp echoed through Room 216 of the Hart Senate Office Building. Former Watergate prosecutor Richard Ben-Veniste had asked national security adviser Condoleezza Rice if she recalled the title of the Presidential Daily Briefing that was delivered to President Bush on August 6, 2001. Rice had answered, "I believe the title was, 'Bin Laden Determined to Attack Inside the United States,'"[100] astounding those attending the April 8, 2004, hearing of the 9/11 commission, officially known as the National Commission on Terrorist Attacks Upon the United States.

The administration had initially refused to let Rice testify, on the grounds of executive privilege. One reason they had finally consented was Richard Clarke: In March the former White House counterterrorism chief and Rice's former staffer had published *Against All Enemies: Inside America's War on Terror* and since then had been making the rounds of the news shows, charging that the administration had been slow to respond to the al-Qaeda threat before September 11.

"I blame the entire Bush leadership for continuing to work on Cold War issues when they [came] back in power in 2001," Clarke had told *60 Minutes*'s Leslie Stahl. "It was as though they were preserved in amber from when they left office eight years earlier . . . Iraq, Star Wars. Not new issues, the new threats that had developed over the preceding eight years."[101] And Clarke had singled out Rice. "There's a lot of blame to go around, and I probably deserve some of the blame, too. But on January 24, 2001, I wrote a memo to Condoleezza Rice asking for, urgently—underline urgently—a cabinet-level meeting to deal with the impending al-Qaeda threat. And that urgent memo—wasn't acted on."

For weeks Rice had done as good a job as could be expected—better, in fact—in attempting to refute Clarke's charges. Pundits praised her "combination of academic high-mindedness and . . . bulletproof poise" on the news shows.[102] Rice had already testified for hours before the commission, but neither those appearances nor her television interviews had quieted the growing chorus that she testify publicly.

Once she took her seat before the ten commissioners, Rice was, as usual, impressive: In answer to the charge that the administration had ignored warnings in the months before 9/11—especially the August 6 Presidential Daily Briefing, or PDB, that Commissioner Ben-Veniste referred to—Rice said, "Let me read you some of the actual chatter that we picked up that spring and summer: 'Unbelievable news in coming weeks'; 'Big event . . . there will be a very, very, very, very big uproar'; 'There will be attacks in the near future.'"

Given the seriousness of the issue before them, the commissioners' questions challenged Rice as she had never before been publicly challenged. But she was a quick study, and the more she talked about 9/11 and the administration's preattack record, the more persuasive she became. The week before, for instance, Ed Bradley in a *60 Minutes* interview had listed the administration officials who had said that al-Qaeda had not been considered an urgent priority: "The former chairman of the Joint Chiefs of Staff at the time says [the administration had] pushed terrorism to the back burner; the former secretary of the treasury says it was not a priority; Mr. Clarke says it was not a priority. And Bob Woodward, who talked with the president, he is saying [in his new book] that for the president it wasn't urgent; he didn't have a sense of urgency about al-Qaeda. That's the perception."[103]

Rice had responded, "Ed, I don't know what a sense of urgency, any greater than the one we had, would have caused us to do differently. We weren't going to invade Afghanistan in the first months of the Bush administration. Dick Clarke himself said that if the strategy that we were pursuing, that we were developing, had been completed on January 27th, it would not have stopped 9/11. What we were trying to do was put together a strategy that might finally, over a period of time, actually eliminate al-Qaeda."[104]

Now the commission's cochairman, Democrat Lee Hamilton, asked virtually the same question: "The president told Bob Woodward that he did not feel that 'sense of urgency.' I think that's a quote . . . The deputy director for Central Intelligence, Mr. McLaughlin, told us that he was concerned about the pace of policymaking in the summer of 2001, given the urgency of the threat. The deputy secretary of State, Mr. Armitage, was here and expressed his concerns about the speed of the process. And if I recall his comment, it is 'We weren't going fast enough.'"[105]

But this time Rice replied, as if she were leading a seminar at Stanford, "Let me begin with the Woodward quote, because that has gotten a lot of press. And I actually think that the quote put in context gives a very different picture."

The question that the president was asked by Mr. Woodward was: Did you want to have bin Laden killed before September 11th? That was the question.

The president said: "Well, I hadn't seen a plan to do that. I knew that we needed to, I think the appropriate word is, bring it to—bring him to justice. And of course, this is something of a trick question" . . . I think you can see here a president struggling with whether he ought to be talking about pre-9/11 attempts to kill bin Laden. And so that is the context for this quote . . .

The president goes on, when Bob Woodward says, "Well, I don't mean it as a trick question, I'm just trying to get your state of mind," the president says: "Let me put it this way. I was not—there was a significant difference in my attitude after September 11th—I was not on point, but I knew he was a menace and I knew he was a problem. I knew he was responsible, we felt he was responsible for bombings that had killed Americans.

"And I was prepared to look at a plan that would be a thoughtful plan that would bring him to justice and would have given the order to do just that. I have no hesitancy about going after him. But I didn't feel that sense of urgency, and my blood was not nearly as boiling."

Whose blood was nearly as boiling prior to September 11th? And I think the context helps here.

It was something Rice often did in debate. She had done it at Stanford as provost.[106] Whenever she was not prepared for a challenger's question and answered it less then perfectly or, as in the case of the *60 Minutes* interview, avoided answering it, Condi did her homework and later refined her reply.

When Commissioner Ben-Veniste's turn to question Rice came, the exchanges grew heated. Ben-Veniste launched in: "I want to ask you some questions about the August 6, 2001, PDB. . . . The extraordinary high terrorist attack threat level in the summer of 2001 is well documented. And Richard Clarke's testimony about the possibility of an attack against the United States homeland was repeatedly discussed from May to August within the Intelligence Community, and that is well documented. You acknowledged to us in your [private] interview of February 7, 2004, that Richard Clarke told you that al-Qaeda cells were in the United States. Did you tell the president, at any time prior to August 6th, of the existence of al-Qaeda cells in the United States?"[107]

RICE: First, let me just make certain . . .

BEN-VENISTE: If you could just answer that question, because I only have a very limited . . .

RICE: I understand, Commissioner, but it's important . . .

BEN-VENISTE: Did you tell the president . . .

RICE: . . . that I also address . . .

[applause] It's also important that, Commissioner, that I address the other issues that you have raised. So I will do it quickly, but if you'll just give me a moment.

BEN-VENISTE: Well, my only question to you is whether you . . .

RICE: I understand, Commissioner, but I will . . .

BEN-VENISTE: . . . told the president.

RICE: If you'll just give me a moment, I will address fully the questions that you've asked. First of all, yes, the August 6th PDB was in response to questions of the president . . . It was not a particular threat report. And there was historical information in there about various aspects of al-Qaeda's operations. Dick Clarke had told me, I think in a memorandum—I remember it as being only a line or two—that there were al-Qaeda cells in the United States. Now, the question is, what did we need to do about that? And I also understood that that was what the FBI was doing, that the FBI was pursuing these al-Qaeda cells. I believe in the August 6th memorandum it says that there were 70 full field investigations under way of these cells. And so there was no recommendation that we do something about this; the FBI was pursuing it. I really don't remember, Commissioner, whether I discussed this with the president.

BEN-VENISTE: Thank you.

RICE: I remember very well that the president was aware that there were issues inside the United States. He talked to people about this. But I don't remember the al-Qaeda cells as being something that we were told we needed to do something about.

BEN-VENISTE: Isn't it a fact, Dr. Rice, that the August 6th PDB warned against possible attacks in this country? And I ask you whether you recall the title of that PDB?

RICE: I believe the title was, "Bin Laden Determined to Attack Inside the United States." Now, the . . .

Rice paused when the audience gasped, but she was not going to let her response end there.

BEN-VENISTE: Thank you.

RICE: No, Mr. Ben-Veniste . . .

BEN-VENISTE: I will get into the . . .

RICE: I would like to finish my point here.

BEN-VENISTE: I didn't know there was a point.

RICE: Given that—you asked me whether or not it warned of attacks.

BEN-VENISTE: I asked you what the title was.

RICE: You said, did it not warn of attacks. It did not warn of attacks inside the United States. It was historical information based on old reporting. There was no new threat information. And it did not, in fact, warn of any coming attacks inside the United States. ·

BEN-VENISTE: Now, you knew by August 2001 of al-Qaeda involvement in the first World Trade Center bombing, is that correct? You knew that in 1999 . . . we had thwarted an al-Qaeda attempt to blow up Los Angeles International Airport and thwarted cells operating in Brooklyn, New York, and Boston, Massachusetts. As of the August 6th briefing, you learned that al-Qaeda members have resided or traveled to the United States for years and maintained a support system in the United States. And you learned that FBI information since [1998]. . . . indicated a pattern of suspicious activity in the country up until August 6th consistent with preparation for hijackings. Isn't that so?

RICE: Do you have other questions that you want me to answer as a part of the sequence?

Rice's voice was clear and composed, her eyes penetrating. She was not going to let the commissioner have control.

BEN-VENISTE: Well, did you not—you have indicated here that this was some historical document. And I am asking you whether it is not the case that you learned in the PDB memo of August 6th that the FBI was saying that it had information suggesting that preparations—not historically, but ongoing, along with these numerous full field investigations against al-Qaeda cells—that preparations were being made consistent with hijackings within the United States?

RICE: What the August 6th PDB said, and perhaps I should read it to you . . .

BEN-VENISTE: We would be happy to have it declassified in full at this time, including its title.

[Applause.]

RICE: I believe, Mr. Ben-Veniste, that you've had access to this PDB. But let me just . . .

BEN-VENISTE: But we have not had it declassified so that it can be shown publicly, as you know.

RICE: I believe you've had access to this PDB—exceptional access. But let me address your question.

BEN-VENISTE: Nor could we, prior to today, reveal the title of that PDB.

RICE: May I address the question, sir? The fact is that this August 6th PDB was in response to the president's questions about whether or not something might happen or something might be planned by al-Qaeda inside the United States. He asked because all of the threat reporting or the threat reporting that was actionable was about the threats abroad, not about the United States. This particular PDB had a long section on what bin Laden had wanted to do—speculative, much of it—in '97, '98; that he had, in fact, liked the results of the 1993 [World Trade Center] bombing. It had a number of discussions of—it had a discussion of whether or not they might use hijacking to try and free a prisoner who was being held in the United States—Ressam. It reported that the FBI had full field investigations under way. And we checked on the issue of whether or not there was something going on with surveillance of buildings, and we were told, I believe, that the issue was the courthouse in which this might take place. Commissioner, this was not a warning. This was a historic memo—historical memo prepared by the [CIA] because the president was asking questions about what we knew about the [domestic threat].

BEN-VENISTE: Well, if you are willing . . .

RICE: Now, we had already taken . . .

BEN-VENISTE: If you are willing to declassify that document, then others can make up their minds about it. Let me ask you a general matter, beyond the fact that this memorandum provided information, not speculative, but based on intelligence information, that bin Laden had threatened to attack the United States and specifically Washington, D.C. There was nothing reassuring, was there, in that PDB?

RICE: Certainly not. There was nothing reassuring. But I can also tell you that there was nothing in this memo that suggested that an attack was coming on New York or Washington, D.C. There was nothing in this memo as to time, place, how, or where. This was not a threat report to the president or a threat report to me.

BEN-VENISTE: We agree that there were no specifics. Let me move on, if I may.

RICE: There were no specifics, and, in fact, the country had already taken steps through the FAA to warn of potential hijackings. The country had already taken steps through the FBI to task their fifty-six field offices to increase their activity. The country had taken the steps that it could, given that there was no threat reporting about what might happen inside the United States.

In three hours of grilling, Rice argued that a chief cause of American vulnerability was the division of labor between the FBI and the CIA and the fact that they didn't share information. The FBI, responsible for domestic security and located within the Department of Justice, was dedicated to law enforcement and crime fighting. The CIA, an independent agency that concentrated on international threats and intelligence, including terrorism, was not allowed to work in the United States. Americans didn't want a domestic spy agency, lest it become a source of government tyranny like the Gestapo or the KGB. Forty-two times during her testimony, Rice used some variation of the word *structural* to describe the problem. Five times she noted that the administration had only been in office "two hundred and thirty-three days."

The questions from former Nebraska Senator Bob Kerrey were just as pointed as Ben-Veniste's, though Rice and Kerrey managed to keep their exchange more affable, usually. Kerrey started off—why was not clear—by saying how impressed he was with Rice's personal story. "Indeed, I'd go so far as to say moved by . . . what's [*sic*] you've accomplished. It's quite extraordinary."

He tussled with Rice over her repeated use of the phrase "swatting at flies." The Bush administration had done nothing to retaliate for the bombing by al-Qaeda of the U.S. Navy ship *Cole* in the final weeks of Clinton's term. "How the hell could he be tired?" Kerrey asked of President Bush. Next, they sparred over the semantics of whether the administration had been given a "plan" or not for going after al-Qaeda by Dick Clarke when it came to office—Rice called it "a set of ideas" and "a paper." As Kerrey tried to move to his next question, Rice insisted on explaining why it was not a plan:

MR. KERREY: Well, let me move into another area, Doctor.

MS. RICE: So we were not presented—I just want to be very clear on this, because it's been a source of controversy. We were not presented with a plan.

MR. KERREY: Well, that's not true. It is not . . .

MS. RICE: We were not presented—we were presented with the . . .

MR. KERREY: I've heard you say that Dr. Clarke—if that 25 January 2001 memo was declassified, I don't believe . . .

MS. RICE: That January 25 memo . . .

MR. KERREY: I don't . . .

MS. RICE: That January 25 memo has a series of actionable items having to do with Uzbekistan, Northern Alliance . . .

MR. KERREY: Let me move to another area.

MS. RICE: May I finish answering your question, though? Because this is an important point.

MR. KERREY: No, I know it's important. Everything that's going on here is important, but we got—I get 10 minutes. So . . .

MS. RICE: But since we have a point of disagreement, I'd like to have a chance to address it.

MR. KERREY: Well, no, actually, there's going—we have many points of disagreement with Dr. Clarke that we'll have a chance to . . .

MS. RICE: I think . . .

MR. KERREY: . . . we'll have a chance to do in closed session. You can't— please don't filibuster me. It's not fair.

MS. RICE: Do you mean . . .

MR. KERREY: It is not fair. I have been polite, I have been courteous. It is not fair to me.

[Applause.]

MEMBER OF THE PUBLIC: [Boo.]

MR. KERREY: I understand that we have a disagreement.

MS. RICE: Commissioner, Commissioner, I'm here to answer questions. And you've asked me a question, and I'd like to have an opportunity to answer it.

MR. KERREY: No, it . . .

MS. RICE: The fact is that what we were presented on January the 25th was a set of ideas . . .

MR. KERREY: Okay.

MS. RICE: . . . and a paper, most of which was about what the Clinton administration had done, and something called the Delenda plan, which had been considered in 1998 and never adopted.

MR. KERREY: Okay.

MS. RICE: We decided to take a different track. We decided to put together a strategic approach to this that would get the regional powers—the problem wasn't that you didn't have a good counterterrorism person. The problem was you didn't have [an] approach against al-Qaeda because you didn't have an approach against Afghanistan, and you didn't have an approach against Afghanistan because you didn't have an approach against Pakistan. And until we could get that right, we didn't have a policy.

MR. KERREY: Thank you for answering my question.

MS. RICE: You're welcome.

Despite Kerrey's best efforts to use his limited time otherwise, Rice had given the answer she wanted to give, and, alluding to his mistake of calling her "Dr. Clarke," she told the former senator that she didn't think she looked like Dick Clarke.

Kerrey ended his ten minutes, it appeared, wanting to dispel the spin that Rice had put on the August 6 PDB: "This is what the August 6th memo said to the president, that 'the FBI indicates patterns of suspicious activity in the United States consistent with preparations for hijacking' . . . That's the language of the memo that was briefed to the president on the 6th of August."

Rice responded, "And that was checked out, and steps were taken through

FAA circulars to warn of hijackings . . . I can tell you that I think the best antidote to what happened in that regard would have been many years before to
think about what you could do, for instance, to harden cockpits. That would
have made a difference. We weren't going to harden cockpits in the three months
that we had a threat spike."

Then Rice launched into a soliloquy, the closest to an emotional appeal that
she came in the hearing:

> The really difficult thing for all of us—and I'm sure for those who
> came before us . . . is that the structural and systematic changes that
> needed to be made, not on July 5th or not on June 25th or not on
> January 1st, those structures and those changes needed to be made a
> long time ago so that the country was in fact hardened against the kind
> of threat that we faced on September 11th. The problem was that for a
> country that had not been attacked on its territory in a major way in
> almost 200 years, there were a lot of structural impediments to [fight-
> ing] those kinds of attacks . . .
>
> I fully agree with you that in hindsight, now looking back, there
> are many things structurally that were out of kilter. And one reason
> that we're here is to look at what was out of kilter structurally, to look
> at what needed to be done, to look at what we already have done, and
> to see what more we need to do.
>
> But I think it is really quite unfair to suggest that something that
> was a threat spike in June or July gave you the kind of opportunity to
> make the changes in air security that could have been—that needed to
> be made.

As usual, Rice would be the administration's best witness. Even critics who
said she had evaded more questions than she answered were impressed by her
ability to take the heat. The combination of absolute discipline—at no point did
she waver from the administration line—cool, strongly reasoned arguments and
(usually) polite steeliness was classic Rice. Her mother had the same toughness,
and John Rice had wielded a sharp tongue at his third wife Clara's school board
meetings, challenging anyone who challenged her, often to his wife's embarrassment. In that sense, Condi was carrying on a long tradition from what Kerrey
called her "moving" past.

As Rice later told her Palo Alto hairdresser, Brenda Hamberry-Green, "I can outtalk anybody. Nobody is going to beat me talking."[108] Hamberry-Green, who had been watching the hearing on television, told Condi she was proud Rice had hung tough under the barrage of questions. She wasn't the only African American who found herself cheering for President Bush's adviser despite opposing the president and most of his policies. Untold numbers of black folks found themselves, surprisingly to many, in the same position. Politics was politics, but here was a black woman, by turns icy and charming, and always sharp, parrying for hours with a panel of suited white men (and one white woman) and not giving an inch. The world had never seen anything like it.

It wasn't only African Americans who were impressed. In a *Time/CNN* poll, forty-eight percent of respondents said the administration had done all it could to prevent the attacks, a significant boost after Rice's testimony.[109] In a *Newsweek* poll, fifty-two percent of adults said the failure of the FBI and CIA to communicate information about terrorists in the United States contributed more to the September 11 attacks than administration inattention, and only a quarter believed the administration's lack of focus played a more important role than intelligence agency failures.[110] But Rice didn't succeed in refuting Clarke; the *Newsweek* poll found sixty percent of Americans believed the administration had underestimated the terrorist threat and focused too much attention on issues like Iraq and missile defense.[111]

On Saturday night, two days after Rice's testimony, the administration released the entire August 6 PDB.[112] Predictably, Bush's supporters said it vindicated the White House; most of the document dealt with bin Laden's historical desire to attack the United States. Bush's opponents said it was clearly a warning: Though it lacked specificity, it spoke of current "patterns of suspicious activity in this country consistent with preparations for hijackings or other types of attacks." That was present tense. In a news analysis for the *Los Angeles Times*, Ron Brownstein wrote, "Questions of credibility may become a growing challenge for Rice—and the president she serves."[113]

The following week, the *Washington Post* ran a piece describing Bush's behavior the day after he had received the August 6 PDB, a period when, Rice had testified, "The president of the United States had us at battle stations."[114] Reported the *Post*:

President Bush was in an expansive mood on Aug. 7, 2001, when he ran into reporters while playing golf at the Ridgewood Country Club in Waco, Tex. . . . Bush seemed carefree as he spoke about the books he was reading, the work he was doing on his nearby ranch, his love of hot-weather jogging, his golf game, and his 55th birthday.

"No mulligans, except on the first tee," he said to laughter. "That's just to loosen up. You see, most people get to hit practice balls, but as you know, I'm walking out here, I'm fixing to go hit. Tight back, older guy—I hit the speed limit on July 6th."

A White House spokesman defended the president. "The intelligence was nonspecific and pointed to attacks overseas," he said, repeating the administration mantra. "We directed embassies and bases abroad to button up and directed the domestic agencies to make sure they were buttoning up at home, as well . . . If we had had any information that could have prevented the attacks on New York and Washington, D.C., the president would have taken strong and decisive action to stop them."

The 9/11 commission issued its final report on July 22. During more than nineteen months of deliberations, the commission reviewed 2.5 million pages of documents and conducted 1,200 interviews.[115] Its sweeping recommendations called for the most dramatic remaking of government since World War II. The report recommended reorganizing the Pentagon, the CIA, the FBI, the State Department, the White House, Congress, and the private sector.[116] One of the few sources of frustration for the public was that the report assiduously avoided reaching any conclusion on whether the attacks might have been prevented.[117] But in an era the commission's senior staffer, Ernest R. May, a history professor at Harvard, called nearly as poisoned by partisanship as the 1790s or the 1850s, "composing a report that all commissioners could endorse carried costs."[118]

Individuals, especially the two presidents and their intimate advisers, received . . . indulgent treatment. The text does not describe Clinton's crippling handicaps as leader of his own national security community. Extraordinarily quick and intelligent, he, more than almost anyone else, had an imaginative grasp of the threat posed by al-Qaeda. But he had

almost no authority enabling him to get his government to address this
threat . . . Passages in the report dealing with the Bush administration
can be read as preoccupied with avoiding even implicit endorsement of
Clarke's public charge that the president and his aides "considered terrorism an important issue but not an urgent issue." I think myself that the
charge was manifestly true—for both administrations.[119]

And yet, in its diplomatic way, the report was still damning.

> We believe the 9/11 attacks revealed four kinds of failures: in
> imagination, policy, capabilities, and management . . .
>   Before 9/11, al-Qaeda and its affiliates had killed fewer than 50
> Americans . . . The U.S. government took the threat seriously, but not
> in the sense of mustering anything like the kind of effort that would be
> gathered to confront an enemy of the first, second, or even third rank.
> The modest national effort exerted to contain Serbia and its depreda-
> tions in the Balkans between 1995 and 1999, for example, was orders
> of magnitude larger than that devoted to al-Qaeda.
>   . . . Both Presidents Bill Clinton and George Bush and their top
> advisers told us they got the picture—they understood bin Ladin was
> a danger. But given the character and pace of their policy efforts, we
> do not believe they fully understood just how many people al-Qaeda
> might kill, and how soon it might do it.
>   . . . By 2001 the government still needed a decision at the highest
> level as to whether al-Qaeda was or was not "a first-order threat,"
> Richard Clarke wrote in his first memo to Condoleezza Rice on Janu-
> ary 25, 2001. In his blistering protest about foot-dragging in the Pen-
> tagon and at the CIA, sent to Rice just a week before 9/11, he repeated
> that the "real question" for the principals was "are we serious about
> dealing with the al Qida threat? . . . Is al Qida a big deal?"
>   . . . But no one forced the argument into the open by calling for a
> national estimate or a broader discussion of the threat . . .
>   We return to the issue of proportion—and imagination. Even
> Clarke's note challenging Rice to imagine the day after an attack posits
> a strike that kills "hundreds" of Americans. He did not write "thou-
> sands."[120]

The commission stuck to criticizing general structural problems in sharing information and coordination of government action: "No one was firmly in charge of managing the [missed opportunities] and able to draw relevant intelligence from anywhere in the government, assign responsibilities across the agencies (foreign or domestic), track progress, and quickly bring obstacles up to the level where they could be resolved. Responsibility and accountability were diffuse. . . . In our hearings we regularly asked witnesses: Who is the quarterback? The other players are in their positions, doing their jobs. But who is calling the play that assigns roles to help them execute as a team?"[121]

But a former 9/11 commission staffer was considerably less diplomatic. He singled out Condi Rice as one of the quarterbacks who was missing in action: "[Rice] and Hadley felt domestic agency oversight was not their job. If she was so concerned about the threat spike in the summer of '01, why wasn't she calling Tom Pickering, the acting FBI director, to ask what he's doing [to investigate domestic threats]? There's a concept of her job stopping at the water's edge."[122] Rice had said as much during her testimony.

> I didn't manage the domestic agencies; no national security adviser does. And not once during this period of time did my very experienced crisis manager say to me, 'You know, I don't think this is getting done in the agencies; I'd really like you to call them together or make a phone call.'
>
> In fact, after the fact, on September 15th, what Dick Clarke sent to me—and he was my crisis manager—what he sent me was a memorandum or an e-mail that said, after national unity begins to break down again [after the September 11 attack has receded]—I'm paraphrasing—people will ask, did we do all that we needed to do to arm the domestic agencies, to warn the domestic agencies, and to respond to the possibility of domestic threat? That, I think, was his view at the time. And I have to tell you, I think given the circumstances and given the context and given the structures that we had, we did.[123]

Commissioner Timothy Roemer, a former Democratic Congressman who had written the House legislation forming the commission,[124] pressed Rice on her domestic agency responsibilities, saying "So, Dr. Rice, let's say, then, the FBI is the key here. You say that the FBI was tasked with trying to find out what the domestic threat was. We have done thousands of interviews here at the 9/11 commission; we have gone through literally millions of pieces of paper. To date, we have found nobody—nobody at the FBI who knows anything about a tasking of field offices [to be on guard for a domestic threat]. We have talked to the director at the time of the FBI during this threat period, Mr. [Pickering]. He says he did not tell the field offices to do this. And we have talked to the special agents in charge [the heads of each FBI office]. They don't have any recollection of receiving a notice of threat . . . Isn't that some of the responsibility of the national security adviser?"

Rice responded, "The responsibility for the FBI to do what it was asked was the FBI's responsibility . . . If there was any reason to believe that I needed to do something . . . I would have been expected to be asked to do it. We were not asked to do it . . . Mr. Roemer, I was responding to the threat spike and to where the information was. The information was about what might happen in the Persian Gulf, what might happen in Israel, what might happen in North Africa. We responded to that, and we responded vigorously.[125]

But the former commission staffer, as well as a longtime Washington friend of Rice's who knows the NSC, believed she should have taken a more hands-on approach. "It was her job to get the agencies to work together," said the staffer. "Pre-9/11 she had something Bush didn't have, which is a staff member yelling at her . . . [CIA director George] Tenet is rushing around, genuinely freaked out, and Rice is saying, 'Don't worry, Dick Clarke is on top of it.'"[126]

It was true that everything about Clarke's first memo to Rice on January 25, 2001, requesting an immediate cabinet-level meeting had been urgent. "The memo is Clarke trying to grab her by the lapels and scream," said the former commission staffer. But Rice believed in structure and discipline. She wanted to take the time to get the underlying policies toward Afghanistan and Pakistan right.

Tenet would later tell Bob Woodward that he believed Rice "just didn't get it in time."[127] Tenet thought that if the FBI had run simple credit checks on the two 9/11 hijackers that its own field offices had detected were in the United States, Nawaf al-Hamzi and Khalid al-Mihdhar, "they would have found that the two men had bought ten tickets for early morning flights for groups of other Middle Eastern men for September 11, 2001. That was knowledge that might conceivably have stopped the attacks."[128]

Woodward's 2006 book, *State of Denial*, also described a meeting on July 10, 2001, where Tenet and the CIA's counterterrorism chief Cofer Black were so concerned with the intelligence "chatter" the agency was picking up on bin Laden that Tenet decided to go see Rice immediately. Tenet told Rice that though he lacked specifics, surveillance had intercepted more than thirty-four conversations from bin Laden associates alluding to "Zero Hour" and "something spectacular."[129] Black told Woodward, "The only thing we didn't do was pull the trigger to the gun we were holding to her head."[130]

When reporters asked Rice about the meeting related in Woodward's book, she responded, "I don't recall a so-called emergency meeting . . . What I can be quite certain of is that is that I would remember if I was told, as this account apparently says, that there was about to be an attack in the United States. The idea that I would have somehow ignored that, I find incomprehensible."[131]

But after trying to get Rice to translate the threat warnings into action, Woodward writes, Tenet's "initial angst about Rice turned to distress, and then disdain."[132] Why was clear: As the 9/11 commission's report said, "In the summer of 2001 . . . Tenet, the Counterterrorist Center, and the Counterterrorism Security Group did their utmost to sound a loud alarm."[133]

But the former executive director of the 9/11 commission, Phil Zelikow—who coauthored with Rice a book on German unification and would later serve as her counselor at the State Department—provided a far less critical appraisal of Rice.

Zelikow acknowledged that bridging the gap between the FBI and the CIA was the responsibility of the national security adviser "to some degree." But he added, "A lot of that becomes very operational and technical, and the national security adviser can't meddle very effectively in that. You try to make sure that people are at the table [and] they *were* at the table . . . and the Bush administration from the start was seeing this through the template of being a foreign scare.[134]

"The job [of the national security adviser] is to do what the president would need done and address issues more or less at the level that the president would engage in," said Zelikow. "And maybe on that score, the most fundamental question is if the president was tempted at more aggressive options against al-Qaeda, you might have then wanted to get a more active engagement by the Department of Defense in thinking about those options. And the national security adviser didn't get that for the president. But, in fairness to the national security adviser, the president didn't express that preference strong enough, so there was a clear requirement for her to do something with it."

The 9/11 commission's report provided an implicit counterexample where the dysfunctional national security system had worked, proving, as the report said, "good people can overcome bad structures." It was the millennium plot to blow up Los Angeles International Airport. The terrorists were thwarted on the eve of the 2000 New Year, when customs agents thought a man crossing into the United States from Canada was suspicious, searched his car, and found explosives.[135]

But Condoleezza Rice was not one to improvise; she had been concerned with restoring order and discipline to the NSC after eight years of the Clinton administration. That was why she had placed Clarke back in the hierarchy where he belonged. At the time Clarke complained to his deputy that the new arrangement would slow the principals' response time. But again, Rice may have been a prisoner of her own history. Observed the former commission staffer, "[Clarke's] Transnational Threat Directorate, as it was called then, was an office not in the Scowcroft model [of the NSC]. It was this growing empire which handled all these global threats like terrorism . . . It could go around the deputies committee and straight up to the principals." It was also a part of the NSC that was operational. Finally, Rice focused on nation-states, said the staffer: "You deal with Big Powers, our regional interests. [She thinks,] 'The grown-ups are back. We're going to do this seriously.' The report is clear on this."

And there was something else. "Let's just say Richard Clarke as a personality is not someone Condi would seek to cultivate," said Chip Blacker. "Clarke is a kind of take-no-prisoners kind of guy." Rice's predecessor called Clarke a "pile driver."[136]

In the final analysis, though, said Zelikow, "the things that kept us from stopping 9/11 were both more tactical at one level and more fundamental at another. More tactical in the sense that the operational things that we missed . . . weren't missed because of those policy [reviews Rice launched] . . . Yet, the really strategic things they would have needed to do . . . that took this problem more seriously, in our view, involved decisions and choices that no one was putting on their agenda . . . and to be effective would have to have been put on the agenda not on September 1, 2001, but sometime before that, and probably in the Clinton period." Acknowledging that he had known Rice for almost twenty years, Zelikow recused himself from writing anything about her in the final commission report and said he tried to analyze her actions as if she were a historical figure he had never met; he told me he believes his assessments "represent a durable [historical] judgment."

Like Rice's handling of Clarke, her testimony before the commission said as much about Condi as it did about the administration and 9/11. Rice's points were correct: It was not the national security adviser's job to run the FBI, and before 9/11 the government was not structured to deal with foreign threats that became domestic threats. The commission made those points in its final report.[137] But because she relied on the hierarchy and the structure as it existed, as she would until the difficulties in Iraq taught her otherwise, Rice wasn't going to follow up with the FBI; she believed she had been hypervigilant by passing the threat information on to the bureau.

Rice's testimony also showed her phenomenal skill at spinning—for instance, her claim to Kerrey that the January 25 memo was not a plan but "a series of actionable items having to do with Uzbekistan, Northern Alliance." As Kerrey noted, the first attachment to the memo was entitled "Strategy for Eliminating the Threat from the Jihadist Networks of al-Qida: Status and Prospects."[138] And despite Rice's—and Bush's—testimony, the commission's final report revealed that two CIA analysts involved in preparing the August 6 PDB "believed it represented an opportunity to communicate their view that the threat of a bin Laden attack in the United States remained both current and serious."[139] They didn't see the PDB as a historic at all.

In the final analysis, Rice's actions before 9/11 were reasonable: She restored what she saw as the appropriate—if outdated, as Clarke charged—hierarchy to the NSC; she worked to craft a regional strategy to deal with al-Qaeda rather than attacking it in isolation; and she logically expected the FBI to do its job. But those moves were not the actions of someone who understood the magnitude of the threat. And in that, Rice was not alone. As the commission concluded, few officials in either administration understood the threat. But Rice's best friend, Chip Blacker, disagreed with that finding. Though Blacker thought there was little the Bush administration could have done to prevent 9/11, he said, "The Clinton administration, in particular in the last two or three years was on this one . . . there was real consciousness about the centrality of this threat and that was because Clarke was close to [national security adviser Sandy] Berger, and Berger was close to Clinton . . . If Bill Clinton had been less constrained by the Lewinsky scandal, things might have played out very, very differently."[140]

In Rice's view, the Bush administration was at "battle stations" in the summer of 2001, at least in the context of the pre-9/11 world. But those charged with monitoring the threat—Clarke, Tenet, and the rest of the counterterrorism group—clearly didn't agree. And neither did Blacker. "They made some serious mistakes at the beginning by hewing so closely to the agenda they took into office with them." But he added, "In that respect, they're not so different from other administrations."[141]

Of course, Condi Rice conceded none of those points. And her strict discipline in sticking to her talking points had a downside; she sounded at times robotic, an image that took hold in the public consciousness, even though it was far from the Condi that those close to her knew. For instance, when Ed Bradley interviewed Rice on *60 Minutes*, he asked how she felt about Richard Clarke's apology to the families of the 9/11 victims during his commission testimony days before. Rice could only offer, over and over, that it was important to "stay focused" on who had perpetrated attacks. When Bradley repeated, "But my question is, how did it make you *feel*? Did you think he was grandstanding? Did you think it was sincere?" Rice replied, "Everybody understands the deep tragedy that has happened here." When Bradley asked twice whether she would apologize, Condi repeated that it was necessary to stay focused.[142] Her refusal to answer Bradley's question directly was understandable seven months before an election, but it sounded heartless and mechanical.

Beyond political considerations, it was also true that apology was not in Rice's personal lexicon; like George Bush, she met criticism with strength, not contrition. Humility does not come easily to the Rices, said Condi's cousin Connie Rice,[143] and it was anathema to Condoleezza. "She's not that flexible," said Clara Rice. "She strives for perfection. [And admitting a mistake] is like a sign of weakness."[144]

That Condi was so good at staying on message sometimes led interviewers to wonder whether she was deluding herself, being careful about how she framed her statements, or spinning the truth. When Wil S. Hylton of *GQ*, for instance, asked Rice about the discord between Powell and Rumsfeld in early 2004, Hylton reported:

Shortly after I interviewed Colin Powell, I met with Condoleezza Rice in her office at the White House, a bright and white and airy room that looked like a wedding cake turned inside out, where Rice sat prim and pretty beneath an Impressionist painting in a black business suit and bright red lipstick, smiling politely as she lied through her teeth about the war between the State Department and the Pentagon, as though no such conflict could possibly exist . . .

"There isn't some kind of little DoD cabal out there," she snapped . . .

"As a government . . . we use all of the elements together in order to effect policy. They're working always in concert."[145]

But Rice wasn't lying; she just chose to see the world differently. In the same vein, Woodward reported a conversation between Rice and Frank Miller. Miller was exasperated at Rumsfeld's machinations. "He's a bully," Miller said.

"Oh, no," replied Rice.

"Condi, come on. It's me."

"Don's Don . . ." was Rice's answer.[146]

Even with a trusted adviser, Condi wouldn't go off script. Perhaps she thought carping about Rumsfeld was a waste of time, and Rice concentrated on the practical: Do what you have to do.

Blacker insisted that she wouldn't lie. Referring to a remark she had made during a post-9/11 press conference, he said, "It was an overstatement for Condi to have said, 'Who could have imagined jetliners flying into buildings.' Well, that's exactly the problem; she didn't have to imagine it. But, again, the intel is not so [clear] that you would say, 'Tell the FAA and do all this stuff because they're going to fly airplanes into buildings.' And the previous attacks had been significant but not catastrophic. And it takes a certain capacity to imagine the worst. You don't do that on a day-to-day basis."[147]

Rice admitted to the government's failure of imagination in her testimony. But Blacker made another point she didn't. "To a degree that would probably surprise most people, senior officials live off of executive summaries. There literally is not time in the day for these folks to plow through even the essential materials."

And even Rice and Clarke agreed on the most crucial point—at least as far politics was concerned that summer of 2004: Nothing the government was considering in its national security policy would have prevented 9/11 from happening. Whether greater vigilance, on Rice's part or someone else's, would have overcome the structural problems of the CIA and FBI not communicating was unknowable. But for her part, Rice was certain, she had done all she could have.

Though the 9/11 commission's report led political analysts to conclude that the White House "[dodged] a bullet that allies were convinced was heading its way,"[148] the report did call into question two of the central themes of Bush's reelection campaign: that Iraq was linked to 9/11—a notion the president reinforced in June when he backed Vice President Cheney's assertion that Iraq had "long-established ties with al-Qaeda"[149]—and that the war had made Americans safer. On the contrary, the report, said, "[if] Iraq becomes a failed state, it will go to the top of the list of places that are breeding grounds for attacks against Americans at home."[150]

By the summer of 2004, there was reason to fear just that possibility; the insurgency had grown far beyond Saddam's Baathists to include foreign jihadists, some aligned with al-Qaeda, launching ever more daring attacks. Ordinary Americans seemed to react only to the "CNN effect"; public opinion moved up and down with what cable news was reporting. So when Saddam Hussein was captured on December 13, 2003, the president's approval rating broke fifty percent. Then when news emerged in April of alleged abuse of Iraqi prisoners by U.S. troops at Abu Ghraib prison, the president's approval rating fell to its lowest point since before the September 11 attacks.

Rice had been trying to get the administration to focus on formulating a detainee policy that would have likely had ripple effects to places like Abu Ghraib, but Rumsfeld was still in charge of detainee issues, and for months he wouldn't cooperate with Rice's policy review. And once Rice had moved the principals to finally engage the issue, Rumsfeld, with Bush's apparent acquiesce, waved off months of interagency coordination with the comment, "These are bad guys." And the policy had been left hanging.[151]

But Condi was increasingly able to beat Don. As the United States prepared in May 2004 to hand sovereignty of the country back to the Iraqis, for instance, and the civil war between State and Defense continued to rage, Powell argued that once Iraq was sovereign and the United States had an ambassador there, the State Department should take the lead on Iraq policy. According to Woodward, Rice decided "she was not going to have the question of who was in charge subject to Rumsfeld's whim." She went to the president. Bush ruled that after the turnover, State would take the lead.[152] It was a clear and increasingly common sign of the new reality in the Bush foreign policy team: Rice was "the man."

The dismal talk of a possible quagmire in Iraq faded when Bremer signed over sovereignty to Ayad Allawi, Iraq's interim prime minister, on June 30, 2004; despite the growing chaos, Rice was making progress on her political track. Bush was attending the opening session of a NATO summit in Istanbul when Rice slipped him a handwritten note that read: "Mr. President, Iraq is sovereign. Letter was passed from Bremer at 10.26 a.m. Iraq time   Condi" Bush scrawled on the note, "Let Freedom Reign!"[153] In Baghdad, Allawi promised, "a national unity and tolerance and brotherly behavior and spirit of peace and prosperity will prevail."[154] But it didn't. In August, insurgent attacks jumped to three thousand, one thousand more than in July. In the constant flow of bad news from Iraq, Rice reportedly told her staff she felt like "that little Road Runner character, hanging on to a branch and spinning my little feet with news stories coming along and chopping at the branch."[155] And spinning she was. In the heat of the presidential campaign and the party conventions, Rice remained Bush's most unflappable spokesperson, never publicly betraying a shadow of doubt, even when Republican senators started to say the administration might be going over a cliff in Iraq.[156]

So when the *New York Times* reported in early August that twenty months of Bush administration policy aimed at curtailing the nuclear ambitions of North Korea and Iran had failed—an assertion that went straight to the heart of the Bush campaign's major theme that Bush was a war president who, like him or not, kept America safe—it was Rice who went on *Meet the Press* to make the counterargument: "It was, in fact, the president who really put this on the agenda in his State of the Union address, the famous 'axis of evil' address. And our allies have really begun to respond."[157]

With America divided over the war, the campaign was even more bitter than the 2000 race. But Massachusetts senator John Kerry's critique of Bush's performance was blunted by his own problems: In a flub of a question on the campaign trail, Kerry had said he voted for a war appropriations bill before he voted against it. The quote, which fit neatly in the Bush campaign's portrayal of Kerry as a "flip-flopper," resonated with voters' misgivings that the Democratic candidate couldn't be counted on to stick to his convictions.

But lost in the Sturm und Drang of the campaign was former weapons inspector David Kay's impassioned rebuke in August of Rice's National Security Council before a Senate intelligence committee examining the intelligence failures that led to 9/11 and, later, the mistaken belief that Iraq had stockpiles of WMD. "Every president who has been successful, at least that I know of, in the history of this republic, has developed both informal and formal means of getting checks on whether people who tell him things are in fact telling him the whole truth," said Kay.[158]

> The recent history has been a reliance on the NSC system to do it. I quite frankly think that has not served this president very well . . . The dog that did not bark in the case of Iraq's WMD weapons program, quite frankly, in my view, is the National Security Council . . . Where was the National Security Council when, apparently, the president expressed his own doubt about the adequacy of the case concerning Iraq's WMD weapons that was made before him? Why was the secretary of state sent to the CIA to personally vet the data that he was to take to the [UN] Security Council in New York, and ultimately left to hang in the wind for data that was misleading and, in some cases, absolutely false and known by parts of the Intelligence Community to be false? Where was the NSC then?

The NSC had no comment.

Later Kay told Bob Woodward, "[Rice] was probably the worst national security adviser in modern times since the office was created."[159] It was an opinion that many Washington insiders, and at least one of Rice's aides, held; he felt Condi had allowed the decision-making process, and Rumsfeld in particular, to run her, rather than running the process.

When the polls opened on November 2, every major survey of public opinion put Bush and Kerry in a statistical tie.[160] Rice had been traveling with the president for the last four days of the campaign. As Air Force One touched down at Andrews Air Force Base back in Washington, Bush's political guru Karl Rove showed Rice the exit polls. She was amazed at the results; in her home state of Alabama, the most solid of the solid Republican South, Bush was leading Kerry by just one point. If the data were accurate, they suggested a Kerry blowout. Rice walked out of the president's cabin so she wouldn't have to see Bush's face when Rove gave him the news.[161]

Rice was clearly devastated at the prospect that a second President Bush, a second "good man," might go down in his bid for reelection. The Bushes were like a second family to Condi. "The Bushes are wonderful," she says, describing their relationship. "You must have people like this in your life you've known a long time, you would trust with your life, you would do anything for them."[162]

Rice didn't know that her old friend Randy Bean had served as a foot soldier for the Kerry campaign, working to inflict the loss President Bush for several hours feared he had suffered.[163]

In the end, Rice's worry was needless. The race came down to Ohio. A switch of just sixty-eight thousand votes from Bush to Kerry would have given Kerry Ohio's twenty electoral votes and with them the presidency,[164] but in the end Rove finally delivered his man a popular-vote majority, allowing the president to claim he had received a "mandate." In reality, the electorate remained astonishingly divided: While Bush had won more votes than any candidate in history, more than sixty million, Kerry also had received more votes than any candidate in a previous election, more than fifty-seven million.

With his second term in hand, three days after the election, the president and the first lady flew to Camp David, accompanied by Bush's chief of staff, Andy Card, his wife, and Condi. That afternoon Bush met with Rice. He asked her to take Colin Powell's place as his secretary of state. According to friends, Rice knew Bush might ask her to be secretary of state and had let it be known around the administration that she was planning to return home to California. "No way. I don't want that job!" she had told Deborah Carson.[165]

She was tired.[166] "Four years is a long time," says Rice, recalling her state of mind at the time. "Especially with terrorism and two wars, four years is a long time."[167]

She suggested to the president that he might want a new team after everything they had been through. Then she told him, "The question for me is not where I go [to Defense or State]. I'll go where you want me to go. The question is do I stay. And that's what I have to grapple with."[168]

After a weekend of reflection, Rice told Bush she would serve at State. Her friends and her stepmother said Condi decided to stay because "she just can't say no to that man."[169]

But sitting in her State Department office two years later, Rice offers another explanation. "Well, I thought there was more we could do. Over the first three years we'd basically broken down a lot of the old system; 9/11 had changed a lot of the strategic environment. Then we invaded Iraq. That changed the global strategic environment. We were handling the Middle East in a very different way. And," she sighed, "and I've been very cognizant of the need to put it back together in a different configuration, but one that lays a foundation. And so I thought, 'Well, I'll try to do that.'"

Rice was speaking with uncharacteristic pauses, and she said the last words gently, as if placing them on the polished coffee table before her. Crossing and uncrossing her legs, tugging at the bottom of her cherry red skirt, Rice looked weary for the first time during the interview, an image that belied the aura of Alabama steel that surrounded her public persona.

But once again, Rice followed God's plan. It certainly had not been hers. In the end, she thought she owed it to the president, to the country, and, "to a certain extent," to the world. "The United States is very powerful, and unless the United States acts to reconstruct on the ruins of the old system, then that reconstruction can take turns and directions that I think wouldn't be very good."[170]

CHAPTER ELEVEN

POWER

There hasn't been a time like this since the 1940s . . . We have a great opportunity to
spread freedom and democracy as an antidote to this ideology of terror.[1]

CONDOLEEZZA RICE
Secretary of State
This Week, ABC News
January 20, 2005

November 14 was Rice's fiftieth birthday. Her aunt G, Genoa McPhatter, came up from Virginia; Alto and Connie Ray flew in from Birmingham, Clara Rice and Randy Bean from Palo Alto, and Laurie
White from Los Angeles. G was Condoleezza's most frequent guest in Washington. Usually they hung out, ate, and shopped, or G went shopping for Rice and,
back at her Watergate condo, Condi chose what she wanted and sent the rest
back. But whatever they did, it usually involved shopping.

The celebration was going to be a weekend-long event. After a birthday dinner out the first night, they all went back to Condoleezza's. The second night
they were headed to another restaurant when Rice's car made a wrong turn.

"This is not the way to the restaurant," Condi protested.[2]

"I don't live in Washington," said G. "I don't know where I'm going."

As the car pulled into the driveway of the British ambassador's residence,
Rice protested, "I'm not going in there. Look at how I'm dressed." She was wearing pants and a suede jacket.[3]

"Condoleezza, just get out," said G. Inside, Rice was shocked to find 120 of her closest friends waiting.[4] "I think that's the only time that something's been put over on her," said McPhatter.[5]

They had been working for months to pull off the surprise. Bean had planned to fly in with a bunch of Rice's California friends for a birthday bash, but Rice staffer Sarah Lenti had suggested a surprise party. Rice was ushered upstairs, where a sleeveless red satin Oscar de la Renta gown awaited her, a gift[6] from one of her favorite designers. When she emerged at the top of the stairs, the guests applauded. Colin and Alma Powell were there, as was George Shultz. And the president and first lady came later. It was a who's who of Washington. (Don Rumsfeld had not been invited.)[7]

It was a glittering evening; but even on Condi's night, politics and the contradictions of life were close at hand. With Bush's reelection only fourteen days old, the president and Randy Bean eyed each other warily. "If looks could kill we'd both be dead,"[8] said the woman who calls Rice her sister of the man who calls Condi his sister.

Randy thought back to their first meeting in Austin, in the library of the Governor's Mansion on the eve of the Stanford–Texas game. Bush had been charming and warm, and they had bonded over politics and the media. It had been five short years—and millennia—ago. "[Bush and Laura] were so real in '99 and so phony in 2004," said Bean. "He was so evil. He was so mean . . . And I thought, *You know . . . you do wear this office. You put it on like an invisible cloak.* And they wore that office as something very phony. It was just unbelievable, the difference . . . it was Stepford Bush."

Two days after the party, President Bush announced Rice's nomination as secretary of state. "During the last four years I've relied on her counsel, benefited from her great experience, and appreciated her sound and steady judgment. And now I'm honored that she has agreed to serve in my Cabinet," said the president. "The Secretary of State is America's face to the world. And in Dr. Rice, the world will see the strength, the grace, and the decency of our country."[9]

Bush didn't mention that Rice would be the first woman of color to serve as secretary of state, but he did retell her biography: "Above all, Dr. Rice has a deep, abiding belief in the value and power of liberty, because she has seen freedom denied and freedom reborn. As a girl in the segregated South, Dr. Rice saw the promise of America violated by racial discrimination and by the violence that comes from hate. But she was taught by her mother, Angelina [*sic*], and her father, the Reverend John Rice, that human dignity is the gift of God, and that the ideals of America would overcome oppression. That early wisdom has guided her through life, and that truth has guided our nation to a better day." At the mention of the discrimination in Birmingham, Rice bit her lower lip, and when Bush mentioned her parents, her eyes welled.

After a warm kiss on the cheek, which would become the subject of much gossip and even a *Washington Post* story on public-official etiquette, Rice spoke briefly. "Mr. President, it has been an honor and a privilege to work for you these past four years, in times of crisis, decision, and opportunity for our nation. Under your leadership, America is fighting and winning the war on terror. You have marshaled great coalitions that have liberated millions from tyranny, coalitions that are now helping the Iraqi and Afghan people build democracies in the heart of the Muslim world. And you have worked to widen the circle of prosperity and progress in every corner of the world. I look forward, with the consent of the Senate, to pursuing your hopeful and ambitious agenda as Secretary of State."[10]

Both Bush and Rice made a point of praising Powell. "It is humbling to imagine succeeding my dear friend and mentor, Colin Powell," said Rice. "He is one of the finest public servants our nation has ever produced. Colin Powell has been a great and inspirational Secretary of State." Rice's voice sounded a genuine note of sorrow. But President Bush hadn't paid Powell the respect of asking for his resignation; he had had his chief of staff do it[11] and then had waited impatiently for Powell's letter to arrive.[12]

The *Washington Post*'s Pulitzer Prize–winning fashion reporter Robin Givhan noted, "Rice accepted her nomination in a butter yellow suit with her distinctive halo of hair and its perfect, immovable, taunting flip."[13] Clara had suggested to Condi that now that she was going to have a new job, it was time to get rid of "that flip." Clara spent almost as much time defending the hair as she did Condoleezza; lots of black women in particular criticized it for being "immovable."[14]

As much as Rice's ascension marked a milestone for Condoleezza and the nation—making her the most powerful black woman in the history of American government—the press noted that it said even more about George W. Bush. Typical of the reaction was a column by David Gergen, a former adviser to three presidents. "Give the man his due," wrote Gergen. "George W. Bush is emerging as one of the boldest, most audacious presidents in modern history . . . Woodrow

Wilson once wrote that 'the president is at liberty, both in law and conscience, to be as big a man as he can.' President Bush comes Texas-sized . . . [He] is centralizing power in the White House in ways not seen since Richard Nixon . . . By closing down dissent and centralizing power in a few hands, he is acting as if he truly believes that he and his team have a perfect track record, that they know best, and that they don't need any infusion of new heavyweights. He has every right to take this course, but as he knows from his Bible, pride goeth before . . . "[15]

From Washington to Europe, observers believed Rice's substitution for Powell at State would mean an even more unilateral foreign policy, destined to further offend America's allies and roil the world.[16] And two things were certain. First, Rice was taking on the most challenging job of her life: Her four-year agenda included containing the nuclear ambitions of North Korea and Iran, shepherding a peace deal between the Israelis and the Palestinians, and continuing the global war on terror—America could address none of those challenges alone. Not to mention the war in Iraq. "I can't think of a time in the past three decades where the foreign policy plate is so full with complex, difficult, and important issues," said former Powell aide Richard Haass, president of the Council on Foreign Relations.[17]

Second, the State Department would speak with new authority, both in Washington and abroad. In Oval Office meetings in the coming months, President Bush would often tell visiting heads of state, "She's like my sister. Whatever she says, it's like talking to me."[18]

But first Rice had to get through her confirmation hearing.

On January 18, she walked into Room 216 of the Hart Senate Office Building, wearing a tailored black suit and pearls, her gait the pinched walk of the precocious little girl Julia Emma Smith remembered from Westminster Presbyterian. The rap on Rice's four years as national security adviser was not flattering. The Washington echo chamber, for so long so laudatory, had turned ugly and condemnatory. The foreign policy establishment couldn't figure out whether she had actually drunk the neocon Kool-Aid or had opportunistically gone along to get along in an administration, it believed, that wasn't as smart as Rice was but whose ideological orientation was clear and intractable.

Official Washington's criticism was more elemental—it was about power. Rice had been weak. She had been "a disaster" as national security adviser because the titans, especially Rumsfeld, had rolled her. And now, having helped plunge America into a war that it looked more and more like we were losing, she was, like her president, out of her depth.

Some of the criticism was not deserved. "She didn't succeed in bridging the differences between Rumsfeld and Powell," said a former senior administration official who was close to Rice, "[but] I don't know who could have succeeded." Iraq, on the other hand, was her failure almost as much as Bush's, he said. "One . . . we didn't have enough troops. Certainly, she was part of the decision making. [But] the president relied on the secretary of defense, who told the generals what they were meant to think.[19]

"[Two], the insight she didn't have and I didn't either was . . . it's more dangerous to try to run this political process than it is to take the risk of turning it back over to the Iraqis [immediately after the invasion]. She made a mistake, a *big* mistake."

Nearly two years after "shock and awe," though the outside world didn't know it, Rice was doubting the wisdom of American tactics in Iraq, too—not the decision to remove Hussein but the tactics for winning the peace.[20] Why was the United States of America, the mightiest military power in history, fighting its most important war since Vietnam without a military strategy?

And that was what the senators wanted Rice to explain to them as she took her seat before the Foreign Relations Committee. Barbara Boxer, a California Democrat, had thrown down the gauntlet as soon as Rice was nominated, telling the Associated Press, "My one issue that I must get at is did she mislead the American people knowingly on many issues surrounding the Iraq war . . . It's caused me to lose sleep at night. She has been out front on this since day one. . . . I have chapter and verse, and especially on television shows, talking right to the American people, making statements that were contradicted before she made them."[21]

In her opening remarks, Rice praised President Bush; pledged that, if confirmed, she would "work with members of Congress, from both sides of the aisle, to build a strong bipartisan consensus . . . strengthen our alliances . . . support our friends, and to make the world safer, and better."[22] And then she moved to Martin Luther King and Birmingham:

[This week] America celebrates the life and legacy of Dr. Martin
Luther King Jr. It is a time to reflect on the legacy of that great man,
on the sacrifices he made, on the courage of the people he led, and on
the progress our nation has made in the decades since. I am especially
indebted to those who fought and sacrificed in the civil rights movement so that I could be here today. . . .

For me, this is a time to remember other heroes as well . . . I grew
up in Birmingham, Alabama—the old Birmingham of Bull Connor,
church bombings, and voter intimidation . . . the Birmingham where
Dr. King was thrown in jail for demonstrating without a permit. Yet
there was another Birmingham, the city where my parents—John and
Angelena Rice—and their friends built a thriving community in the
midst of the most terrible segregation in the country. It would have
been so easy for them to give in to despair, and to send that message of
hopelessness to their children. But they refused to allow the limits and
injustices of their time to limit our horizons. My friends and I were
raised to believe that we could do or become anything—that the only
limits to our aspirations came from within. We were taught not to listen to those who said to us, "No, you can't."

While Rice was acknowledging her debt to King and his followers, she was
also acknowledging that King's Birmingham had not been hers. And it was her
parents' world, she implied, that held the promise of freedom for billions.

The story of Birmingham's parents and teachers and children is a
story of the triumph of universal values over adversity. And those values—a belief in democracy, and liberty, and the dignity of every life,
and the rights of every individual [provide] a source of hope to men
and women across the globe . . . One of history's clearest lessons is
that America is safer, and the world is more secure, whenever and
wherever freedom prevails. It is neither an accident nor a coincidence
that the greatest threats of the last century emerged from totalitarian
movements. Fascism and Communism differed in many ways, but they
shared an implacable hatred of freedom, a fanatical assurance that
their way was the only way, and a supreme confidence that history was
on their side. At certain moments, it almost seemed to be so.

To make her point, Rice listed the "setbacks" of the first half of the twentieth century—Communism's being imposed in Eastern Europe, Soviet dominance
in East Germany, the crushing of the Prague Spring in Czechoslovakia, the victory of the Communists in China, the Soviet nuclear test five years before the
United States predicted it. The moral of Rice's historical analogy was that
"America and the free world are once again engaged in a long-term struggle
against an ideology of tyranny and terror, and against hatred and hopelessness.
And we must confront these challenges with the same vision, courage, and boldness of thought demonstrated by our post–World War Two leaders."

She listed "three great tasks" of American diplomacy: to "unite the community of democracies," "strengthen the community of democracies," and "spread
freedom and democracy." Rice spoke of using international forums to confront
Iran and North Korea; then she quoted Bush's National Security Strategy, a
document that she had edited: "America 'is guided by the conviction that no
nation can build a safer, better world alone. Alliances and multilateral institutions can multiply the strength of freedom-loving nations.' If I am confirmed,
that core conviction will guide my actions."

She promised everything from freedom and democracy in Iraq and Afghanistan, to increased foreign student exchanges, to seizing the opportunity for Mideast peace. And then she declared, "Our interaction with the rest of the world
must be a conversation, not a monologue . . . The time for diplomacy is now."

> Democrats and Republicans united around a vision and policies
> that won the Cold War. The road was not always smooth, but the basic
> unity of purpose and values was there—and that unity was essential to
> our eventual success. No president, and no secretary of state, could
> have effectively protected American interests in such momentous times
> without strong support from the Congress, and from this committee.
> And the same is true today . . . America's co-equal branches of govern-
> ment must work together to advance freedom and prosperity.[23]

It was a virtuoso performance. Rice's eloquence hit all the right notes, very
different notes from Bush's first term. But her confirmation hearing was the
senators' first opportunity without an election staring them in the face to hold
someone accountable for the administration's mistakes in Iraq, and they intended
to use it.

Boxer said, "One of the things that matters most to my people in California and the people in America is this war in Iraq. I personally believe—this is my personal view—that your loyalty to the mission you were given, to sell this war, overwhelmed your respect for the truth.[24]

"You don't seem to be willing to (a) admit a mistake, or give any indication of what you're going to do to forcefully involve others. As a matter of fact, you've said more misstatements, that the territory of the terrorists has been shrinking, when your own administration says it's now expanded to 60 countries. So I am deeply troubled."[25]

"Senator," said Rice, pausing two beats. "I have to say that I have never, ever, lost respect for the truth in the service of anything. It is not my nature. It is not my character. And I would hope that we can have this conversation and discuss what happened before and what went on before and what I said, without impugning my credibility or my integrity." Unlike Boxer, who looked down at the papers in front of her when leveling the charge, Rice looked straight at the senator when responding.

"Well," said Boxer, "you should read what we voted on when we voted to support the war, which I did not, but most of my colleagues did. It was WMD— period. That was the reason . . . [for that] vote. But, again, I just feel you quote President Bush when it suits you, but you contradicted him when he said, 'Yes, Saddam could have a nuclear weapon in less than a year.' You go on television nine months later and said, 'Nobody ever said it was—'"

"Senator, that was just a question of pointing out to people that there was an uncertainty. No one was saying that he would have to have a weapon within a year for it to be worth it to go to war."

"Well, if you can't admit to this mistake, I hope that you'll—"

"Senator, we can have this discussion in any way that you would like. But I really hope that you will refrain from impugning my integrity. Thank you very much."

During two days of testimony, Rice held up remarkably well. Boxer, meanwhile, was criticized in much of the mainstream media—for being partisan and snippy. Even straight news accounts called Rice "forceful" and noted her "singular vigor."[26] The *Atlanta Journal-Constitution* reported the surreal scene of Lincoln Chafee, Republican of Rhode Island, asking Rice if her father knew Martin Luther King. Condi smiled and said, "He did and everyone admired him," considerably simplifying the divisions of black Birmingham over King's movement and John Rice's opposition to his tactics.

Republicans cherished the image of a white female Democrat essentially calling the nominee for the highest post a black woman ever held in government a liar; they knew it wouldn't sit well with African Americans. And it didn't. *Washington Post* columnist Colbert I. King compared what he deemed Boxer's insinuation that Rice was Bush's puppet to political cartoonist Pat Oliphant's recent cartoon of Rice as a "big-lipped, bucktooth" parrot on Bush's shoulder screeching, "Awwrk!! OK Chief. Anything you say, Chief. You bet, Chief. You're my HERO, Chief," as well as to Rice's being called "Aunt Jemima" by a white radio host in Madison, Wisconsin.[27]

Prominent black Democrats like former Atlanta mayor Andrew Young and C. Delores Tucker, chair of the National Congress of Negro Women, spoke up for Rice, and black and white conservatives charged that Boxer's attack was racially motivated.[28]

Watching on television, Rice's family and friends worried that Condoleezza was going to betray the famous Ray woman's temper.[29] Her eyes flashed and narrowed and her back and voice tensed like cords pulled taut, but Rice never lost her cool. The same couldn't be said for some of her relatives. "I was like, somebody turn me loose with this Boxer woman," recalled her cousin Yvonne German. "How *dare* she. [Condoleezza] is not going to sacrifice her integrity for anybody! And they want to blame her. She *has* a boss!"[30]

The Rays had had the same reaction when the media reported in 1990 that a Secret Service agent had shoved Rice while she stood in a line of White House staffers bidding farewell to Soviet leader Mikhail Gorbachev at the San Francisco airport. Ironically, Rice had played a major role in planning the summit meeting between Gorbachev and the first President Bush. She reportedly reacted calmly, but a white staffer had to vouch for her. The president himself was said to be upset by the incident, and the Secret Service launched an investigation.[31] "The phone lines were burning up that night," remembered German. "We were asking, 'Do we need to come there?'"[32]

Watching the confirmation hearing, Clara Rice was anxious, too; Condi's voice had quivered for an instant. "When she gets mad she has—I tell her—the look of Satan," said Clara. "[Her eyes] focus right in and sometimes they go under . . . Barbara Boxer got on her *last nerve*. I said, 'Oh, I hope this hurries up and is over, because I don't want to see her go *off*! Because she can get tough and mean and vicious, like a little pit bull. And she was looking so intensely at [Boxer]. I didn't know if she was gonna cry, or if she was gonna go off!"[33]

Showing rage—or any other emotion that showed a loss of control—was uncharacteristic of Condoleezza. "I made her cry once," said Clara. "And it shocked me . . . She went from furiousness to boo hoo. Then, out at Stanford Hospital [when Clara's gallbladder had burst], she told the nurses or doctors to do something, and they snapped back at her . . . And she cried then. I guess because, whatever it was she was requesting, they were like, 'Back off.' And telling her to back off was just a no-no."

An official in the first Bush administration remembered a tale of Rice letting loose on a fellow staffer who had made the mistake of calling her "honey" during a meeting, but even then Rice's reaction was more icy than hot. "She didn't say anything, but when the meeting was over, she walked up to him and she looked at him and said, 'Reg, if you ever call me 'honey' or anything like that again, I'll tell you what I'm going to do. I'm going to walk out of this office. I'm going to walk down to the Oval Office and I'm going to tell the president' . . . his knees buckled."[34]

But usually Rice was so controlled that the joke among staffers when she ran the NSC was that the only way to know she disapproved of something or someone was when she crinkled her nose. "She never lost her temper," said a former staffer. "We'd have meetings with her, and then we'd come back and somebody would say, 'What happened?'[35]

"Condi crinkled her nose.

"Shit, we have to rewrite that paper!

"When the [real] anger happens," said the staffer, "an amazing kind of stillness takes over, and rigidity."

The Foreign Relations Committee approved Rice's nomination eighteen to two, with only Boxer and John Kerry opposing it. The place Rice would occupy in history as secretary of state had been lost on none of the committee members, and it was as plain as the color of her skin when the full Senate debated her nomination. Majority Leader Bill Frist of Tennessee said, "Dr. Rice has said that while growing up, her dad John and her mother Angelena taught her that in a country where racial segregation and Jim Crow were an ugly fact of life, she had to be twice as good to get ahead. I think it is fair to say she has surpassed this high charge."[36]

Later Senator Richard Lugar, chairman of the Foreign Relations Committee, placed into the *Congressional Record* a *Washington Post* op-ed by Dorothy Height, a pioneer of women's and civil rights. "When Condoleezza Rice is sworn in as secretary of state," it read, "she will be following in the footsteps of Mary McLeod Bethune . . . Sojourner Truth . . . Constance Baker Motley . . . [and] Shirley Chisholm . . . Ms. Rice's appointment is a time for women of color to smile. Our nation finally will put forward a face that reflects the hopes of generations of black women to sit at the table of national and global affairs and participate as equals."[37]

But over two days of floor debate, the criticism of Rice and the part she played in Iraq was blistering. Ted Kennedy of Massachusetts's speech was typical.

> There is no doubt that Dr. Rice has impressive credentials. Her life story is very moving, and she has extensive experience in foreign policy. In general, I believe the president should be able to choose his cabinet officials, but this nomination is different because of the war in Iraq. Dr. Rice was a key member of the national security team that developed and justified the rationale for war, and it has been a catastrophic failure, a continuing quagmire. In these circumstances, she should not be promoted to secretary of state . . . There is a critical question about accountability . . . [38]
>
> In fact, as we now know, there was significant disagreement in the Intelligence Community that Iraq had a nuclear weapons program, but Dr. Rice spoke instead about a consensus in the Intelligence Community that the infamous aluminum tubes were for the development of nuclear weapons. On the eve of the war, many of us argued that inspectors should be given a chance to do their job and that America should share information to facilitate their work.
>
> In a March 6, 2000 [*sic*], letter to Senator Levin, Dr. Rice assured the Congress that the United Nations inspectors had been briefed on every high- or medium-priority weapons of mass destruction missile and [unmanned aerial vehicle]-related site the U.S. Intelligence Community has identified. In fact, we had not done so. Dr. Rice was plain wrong.

The Intelligence Committee report on the prewar intelligence at page 418 stated:

Public pronouncements by Administration officials that the Central Intelligence Agency had shared information on all high and moderate priority suspect sites with United Nations inspectors were factually incorrect.

Had Dr. Rice and others in the administration shared all of the information, it might have changed the course of history. We might have discovered that there were no weapons of mass destruction. The rush to war might have been stopped. We would have stayed focused on the real threat, kept faith with our allies, and would be safer today . . . Instead, as the National Intelligence Council recently stated, the war has made Iraq a breeding ground for terrorism that previously did not exist. . . .

Before we can repair our broken policy, the administration needs to admit it is broken. Yet in two days of confirmation hearings, Dr. Rice categorically defended the president's decision to invade Iraq, saying the strategic decision to overthrow Saddam Hussein was the right one. She defended the president's decision to ignore the advice of Gen. Eric Shinseki, the Army Chief of Staff, who thought that a large number of troops would be necessary if we went to war.

She said:

I do believe that the plan and forces that we went in with were appropriate to the task.

She refused to disavow the shameful acts of torture that have undermined America's credibility in Iraq and the world. When Senator Dodd asked her whether in her personal view, as a matter of basic humanity, the interrogation techniques amounted to torture, she said:

I'm not going to speak to any specific interrogation techniques . . . The determination of whether interrogation techniques are consistent with our international obligations and American law are made by the Justice Department.

. . . Dr. Rice also minimized the enormous challenge we face in training a competent Iraqi security force. She insisted 120,000 Iraqis now have been trained, when the quality of training for the vast majority of them is obviously very much in doubt.

There was no reason to go to war in Iraq when we did, the way we did, and for the false reasons we were given. As a principal architect of our failed policy, Dr. Rice is the wrong choice for secretary of state.

Senator Mark Dayton of Minnesota went even further, calling Rice a liar. Dayton accused Republicans of having the attitude of "our president, regardless whether he is wrong, wrong, or wrong, they defend him, they protect him, and they allow his top administration officials to get away with lying: lying to Congress, lying to our committees, and lying to the American people. It is wrong. It is immoral. It is un-American. And it has to stop. It stops by not promoting top administration officials who engage in the practice, who have been instrumental in deceiving Congress and the American people and, regrettably, that includes Dr. Rice."[39]

To a person, Republicans—and a few Democrats, like Rice's friend Dianne Feinstein—defended Rice's integrity. But even many of those who supported her nomination said they did so with reservations because of her apparent unwillingness to admit that mistakes were made in Iraq.[40]

But Rice was not one to admit mistakes and certainly not in a Senate hearing where her boss's policies were under attack. "She's very good at—not hiding—but keeping from public view whatever doubts she does have," said Blacker. "I think that is a function of her personal experience. All the expectations that are laid on as a consequence of her being so successful, so female, and so black. That if you manifest [doubt], it's like blood in water; it'll draw the sharks. She really believes that. And she has reason to believe it. If all aspects of life are at some level political and all encounters are in some sense political, Condi's have been more political than your average person's . . . And to the extent that you expose any vulnerability, it can have devastating consequences."[41]

Senator John Warner of Virginia upbraided his Senate colleagues. "[Dr. Rice] is as capable and qualified a candidate as has ever been appointed in my lifetime to this position. The personal attacks on her character and integrity . . . I find them somewhat astonishing . . . particularly as it relates to her lifetime dedication to what we call here in the Senate the standards for truthfulness."[42]

Then Warner recalled a committee meeting before the war in Iraq at which he had asked then CIA director George Tenet, "[When] the battles have reached a position where the television cameras of the world can come in and photograph what is there, will those photographs, the television pictures, carry clearly evidence of the existence of weapons of mass destruction? And his acknowledgment was, without a doubt. Now that testimony reflects the best judgment within our government of the situation with regard to weapons of mass destruction."

In the end, the vote wasn't even close: eighty-five to thirteen in favor of Rice. But, significantly, Condi was the first nominee for secretary of state in nearly twenty-five years—since Alexander Haig in 1981—to receive any "no" votes, and she received more than any nominee for the office in the last 180 years, since Henry Clay in 1825.[43]

After her first day of grilling by the Foreign Relations Committee, Rice had returned to the White House "clearly down."[44] But she had performed well before the committee and then, in absentia, had endured serious attacks on her character. Nonetheless, the situation in Iraq was not as simple as Rice made it seem. Nor was her support of the administration's current course as unyielding as she suggested. But like the family and community that bred her, Rice was determined to show a hostile world a face of strength and resolve. What she actually believed was more nuanced, a fact that was already apparent inside the administration and would become clear to the world once she assumed her new post.

Rather than revisit the mistakes of the first term, Rice focused on bringing Bush's bold democratization vision to fruition—or at least putting its building blocks in place over the course of the second. In her first full day on the job, she announced that she was going to Europe and the Middle East, highlighting her desire to repair the transatlantic alliance and to tackle the Gordian knot of the Israeli–Palestinian conflict, which the Bush administration had mostly avoided for four years because George Bush hadn't trusted Yassir Arafat to be a "partner for peace."

It was a heady time to be secretary of state. Despite the long slog of nearly two years of war in Iraq and the challenges posed by Korean and Iranian nuclear ambitions, the world seemed to be moving ever more deliberately toward freedom. Even the Israeli–Palestinian problem was showing signs of a thaw. After the death of Arafat, his successor, Mahmoud Abbas, had deployed Palestinian security forces to quell violence in the Gaza Strip. Abbas and Israeli prime minister Ariel Sharon agreed to a cease-fire in principle and started planning the first high-level meeting between Israelis and Palestinians in more than a year.[45]

It was no wonder, then, that as Rice took her victory lap around the Sunday news talk shows, her excitement was palpable. And in between in-studio interview shots of Condi and the various hosts, the networks aired live images of Iraqis waiting in long lines to vote for their temporary parliament, putting flesh and bone on the president's "Freedom Agenda." At the same time, Sharon announced that the next day Israel would pull troops out of some Palestinian towns in the West Bank.[46]

"This is a good time," enthused Rice as she left her CBS interview. "We've fought two wars. We've been through difficult times, but the future is one of opportunity, and I look forward to trying to explore that . . . We have a lot of work to do in training Iraqi security forces, although I will note that they performed well today in support of their own democracy . . . We have great allies around the world and I hope to visit with them, consult with them, and see how we can move forward on the real opportunities before us." During her ABC interview, she had been even more optimistic: "There hasn't been a time like this, really, I think, since the late 1940s . . . We have a great opportunity to spread freedom and democracy as an antidote to this ideology of terror."[47]

On her plane to London three days later, it was as if Condi was starting where her 2000 *Foreign Affairs* article had left off, performing a diplomatic do-over of Bush's first-term foreign policy. "I think it is fair to say that in everything we do, the allies with whom I'm going to be visiting, and some with whom I will not have a chance to visit, are among our most important partners in facing global challenges. And that's the message that I'll be taking. This is an alliance that has faced down threats before, has seized opportunities before, and has always done so on the basis of common values. That is really the purpose of this trip."[48]

Rice presented an image of American diplomacy the world had never known, under Bush or any other president, and not because of her race. Her fast-talking communications director, Jim Wilkinson, had a strong grasp of history and stage-managed her airport arrivals to look like those of a head of state. As Rice's global notoriety grew, so would the images; instead of meeting with nameless bureaucrats, she would be greeted by local celebrities—athletes or actors or a falconer in Kyrgyzstan[49]—or children offering bouquets of flowers. So, as Rice descended the stairs from her Boeing 757 on her first trip as secretary, the seal of the secretary of state shone on the hatch behind; the words UNITED STATES OF AMERICA roared across the fuselage. Rice wore a black coat trimmed in fur and black leather gloves. The tableau à la Wilkinson was worthy of the president emerging from Air Force One, with the addition of the Ray-family fashion sense.

Rice's twenty-four hours in Paris were dominated by references to "la séduction" she had unleashed on France. The headline on the leftist daily *Libération* read *"Bush sous son meilleur sourire"* ("Bush puts on his best face")[50] beneath a photo of a demurely smiling Rice that called to mind Princess Diana. More important, the French embraced Rice's declaration at the prestigious Political Science Institute that "it is time to turn away from the disagreements of the past. It is time to open a new chapter in our relationship and a new chapter in our alliance."[51]

Even the press back home wasn't immune to Condi's new international allure. At the end of the month, during her second trip to the Continent, Rice's appearance at the U.S. Army airbase in Wiesbaden, Germany, wearing knee-high boots and a long black coat, moved the *Washington Post*'s Robin Givhan to write, "Rice challenges expectations and assumptions . . . If there is any symbolism to be gleaned from Rice's stark garments, it is that she is tough and focused enough for whatever task is at hand.

"She was not hiding behind matronliness, androgyny, or the stereotype of the steel magnolia. Rice brought her full self to the world stage—and that included her sexuality. It was not overt or inappropriate. If it was distracting, it is only because it is so rare."[52]

But there was substance behind all the style; after Rice's first trip, the German government promised to do more to help the U.S. effort in Iraq, and Paris made up with Washington. Still, Rice wasn't as flawless as the image that was growing around her. During a question-and-answer period at the Political Science Institute, for instance, she said Greece and Turkey had fought civil wars in 1947. Only Turkey hadn't. Then, in a private dinner with leading French intellectuals, she said Iran was a totalitarian state. It was a radical argument. Totalitarian states are absolutely controlled from the top. The conventional wisdom was that Iran was authoritarian—highly controlled but not completely controlled from the top. As a Soviet specialist, Rice was well aware of the difference; the debate over whether the regime in Moscow could be considered totalitarian was a central question of Soviet studies. In other words, she knew better. The only answer had to be, the intellectuals reasoned, that Rice was so ideological that she could not clearly see the nature of the Iranian regime.[53]

In Israel, Rice met with Sharon, who had once famously remarked that he couldn't concentrate in a meeting with her in 2000 because her shapely legs distracted him.[54] And then she traveled to Ramallah to meet with Abbas. That part of her inaugural trip swiftly yielded results, too: she came home with the Israelis and the Palestinians having agreed to formalize their cease-fire. Rice called it "the most promising moment of progress between Palestinians and Israelis in years."[55] She had offered the Palestinians $40 million in aid and announced the appointment of a "security coordinator" to help the two sides in their tentative steps toward peace as Sharon pledged to remove Jewish settlers from all of Gaza that summer.

As was often the case in the Middle East, the optimism wouldn't last. Eleven months later, Sharon would lie in a coma following a massive stroke, and the Palestinian people would have democratically elected Hamas, a group the West classified as terrorist, vividly illustrating one of the pitfalls of Bush's freedom agenda: Sometimes elections didn't lead to liberal democracy.

Nonetheless, Rice's eight-day, nine-country tour was "a coming-out season second to none,"[56] said Tom Friedman of the *New York Times*. Over the next two years, she would become arguably the most visible secretary of state in history, traveling nearly half a million miles in 2005 and 2006.[57]

Everywhere she went in his first year, Rice preached Bush's gospel of liberation, from Eastern Europe to Latin America to Asia. In China, she attended a Palm Sunday church service, underscoring the importance Washington placed on religious freedom—though she went to a state-sanctioned church.[58] In South Korea, she met with Internet journalists and for an hour held forth on the merits of democracy in Asia.[59] And when Egyptian authorities arrested opposition member of parliament Ayman Nour on trumped-up charges, Rice canceled a planned trip to Cairo. Rarely had America's top diplomat sent such an undiplomatic message to one of Washington's closest Middle Eastern allies.

Diplomats said Rice's democracy stump speech was more effective than Bush's, in part because she could argue—as she did in a long debate at Beijing University with students critical of America trying to impose its political system on the world—that America hadn't gotten it right in the beginning. "When the Founding Fathers said, 'We the people,' they didn't mean me," said Rice. It became one of her signature lines, allowing Condi to promote Washington's agenda from a place of humility rather than arrogance. "She went through all the mistakes the Founding Fathers made and the Civil War and all the difficulties we have, and she said it is not the perfect form of government, but it is better than all the others," said an official who attended Rice's talk in Beijing. "She really had them . . . and the Chinese students switched to 'How can we become rich like Bill Gates? Are you going to be rich? How are you going to be rich?' It was all about the money."[60]

Six weeks into Rice's term, the Bush doctrine was demonstrated to powerful effect. On February 14, Lebanon's popular prime minister Rafiq Hariri had been assassinated. Certain of Syrian complicity, in less than twenty-four hours Rice had recalled Washington's ambassador to Damascus. Then, on the one-month anniversary of Hariri's assassination, up to a million protestors poured into Beirut's Martyr's Square, demanding an end to fifteen years of Syrian occupation of Lebanon and thirty years of Syrian domination. In the weeks before the protest, Arab media had carried Rice's bluntly anti-Syrian and prodemocracy speeches; now they retroactively linked Washington to the cause of Lebanese freedom.[61]

Perhaps the Bush administration, with its eyes fixed on the ideals of democracy rather than the cynical "realism" of stability, might actually be able to move history, said the pundits. "Across New York, Los Angeles, and Chicago—and probably Europe and Asia as well—people are nervously asking themselves a question: 'Could [Bush] possibly have been right?'" wrote Fareed Zakaria in *Newsweek*. "The short answer is yes . . . As the new secretary demonstrated, a heightened concern for democratization can coexist with traditional U.S. interests and pragmatic alliances."[62] In other words, Zakaria suggested, in her new job Rice was finally getting to do more than translate Bush's idealistic rhetoric into real-world policy, she was proving that the generations-old debate between realism and idealism was passé.

The Rice doctrine was "practical idealism." Its long-term goal was the same as the first term's foreign policy: the spread of democracy, which President Bush had outlined in characteristically bodacious language at his second inauguration in January. "It is the policy of the United States to seek and support the growth of democratic movements and institutions in every nation and culture, with the ultimate goal of ending tyranny in our world," Bush had said.[63] But Rice's rise to power as a principal and not just a staffer brought an end to reflexive unilateralism. There was a new willingness to consult with allies and to engage enemies—whether by recommitting to multilateral negotiations (the Six Party Talks on North Korea) or supporting the efforts of allies (Europe's negotiations with Iran). Rice would prove crucial, administration officials said, to riding herd on the first and gaining the president's backing for the second.

Critics had worried that the departure of Powell, the righteous voice of dissent, and the arrival of Rice, Bush's closest confidant, would effectively make the State Department an extension of the White House. But the opposite seemed to be happening.

And Rice created a State Department that looked much more like the first George Bush presidency, where the litmus test had been brainpower, not ideology. "We're going to need ideas, intellectual capital," she had told the department's employees in her welcome address. "The president has set forth a really bold agenda for American foreign policy, and the State Department has got to be in the lead in this period in which diplomacy will be so important to solidifying the gains of the last few years and to pressing forward an agenda for a freer and more prosperous world . . . Please, understand that this is a time when the history is calling us."[64]

Given the stakes, Rice wanted the most powerful thinkers she could find. Significantly, she chose realists as her top lieutenants.[65] The men (and they were all men) set about helping Rice restore a pragmatic balance to Bush foreign policy, walking a line between ideals and the realities of the world as they found it: America was overstretched in Iraq, the public had no appetite for more military engagements, and Washington needed the world's help to tackle the biggest outstanding problems. Whether Rice or those realities was the stronger impetus to Bush's tactical change was unclear. Phil Zelikow, who became Rice's counselor at State, believed it was both.[66]

That Rice had the ear of the president, putting State back into the game, was a much-needed tonic to the frustrated ranks of the State Department; though they admired Powell, his weak stock at the White House had largely frozen them out of four years of policymaking. Now they had power—Rice's power. "You could feel the power flow back to this side of the Potomac" from the Pentagon, said a former State Department official.

The new balance of power inside the administration was clear early in her tenure, when Condoleezza Rice invited Donald Rumsfeld and their Japanese counterparts to the State Department. When Rumsfeld started to speak, Rice gently cut him off.[67] She had put the supposedly indomitable secretary of defense in his place. The war between State and Defense went on, said State and NSC officials, but State won increasingly often. With Rice firmly in control of foreign policy, Rumsfeld concentrated on internal Pentagon politics and transforming the military.[68]

The foreign policy establishment breathed a sign of relief, while Washington buzzed about how Rice had thrown out the neocons and brought in the realists. The conventional wisdom was that Rice had even deflected the vice president's choice for her deputy at State, John Bolton, and shunted him off to be ambassador to the United Nations instead.[69]

The realists' impact on Bush's foreign policy was clear in Rice's first months. In March, Rice convinced the president to support European efforts to negotiate an end to Iran's nuclear program, reversing the opposition the administration had expressed from the beginning to the European talks. In exchange for Washington's support, Rice received public acknowledgment from the Europeans that they shared American concerns about Tehran's record on human rights, democracy, and terrorism[70] and the implicit understanding that if the Europeans didn't make progress on their diplomatic track, they would join Washington in seeking sanctions against Iran. At the same time, Rice talked tougher than Powell had, declaring, "States that don't recognize that the Middle East is changing, and, indeed, try to halt that change . . . need to be isolated and condemned."[71]

A little more than four months into Rice's tenure, even the *New York Times*'s liberal editorial page noted, in what amounted to high praise for a Bush administration official, "In some areas, at least, American foreign policy seems to be changing for the better, and Ms. Rice can take some of the credit."[72]

Being a woman required a certain toughness, too; Rice encountered prejudices that Powell hadn't, nowhere more so than in the Middle East and Asia. Most Asian leaders had never met an African American woman, much less negotiated with one representing the last superpower. Some of the men were simply starstruck, since Rice's outreach to local TV journalists often made her foreign arrivals a national event. "For a lot of people . . . frankly, it was a little bit 'Wow, it's that person, not like any I've ever dealt with who is constantly on TV and who was on our variety show this morning because she is so popular and I'm not,'" said a former Rice staffer.[73]

It was widely speculated that the former Chinese president Jiang Zemin had a crush on Condi. When they first met, during her term as NSA, Jiang had been wary of Rice and Bush. His advisers had told him that American adventurism in oil-rich Iraq and Bush's global saber rattling were meant to impede China's development so that it wouldn't challenge American supremacy. To alleviate those concerns, the first thing Rice said when she sat down with Jiang was, "The U.S. is not interested in seeing a weak China. We want to see a China that succeeds and is a good partner, based on being confident."[74]

It was a winning statement. Jiang, who otherwise spoke entirely through an interpreter, paused and said in English, "I like your talking."

When he was visiting Crawford for a summit with President Bush on the eve of the 2002 midterm elections, Jiang, a fan of ballroom dancing, had asked Rice to dance. On the floor he looked her over and asked, "Waltz—or tango?"

"Waltz!" said Rice.[75]

The White House staff, especially Bush, liked to tease her about the Crawford hoedown, but being an attractive woman had its disadvantages, too. On Rice's first trip to South Asia, for instance, in March 2005, Rice had serious items on her agenda—from Pakistan's weak efforts to root out the Taliban and al-Qaeda to bolstering Afghanistan's young democracy. Then there were perpetual Pakistan–India tensions, with Pakistan being a nuclear power that faced its own radical Islamists, as well as having its own "freedom deficit," General Pervez Musharraf having come to power in a coup before being elected in widely boycotted elections.

Yet, when Rice sat down with Prime Minister Shaukut Aziz, who fancied himself a ladies' man, Aziz puffed himself up and held forth in what he obviously thought was his seductive baritone. (He bragged—to Western diplomats, no less—that he could conquer any woman in two minutes.) "[He tried] this Savile Row–suited gigolo kind of charm: 'Pakistan is a country of rich traditions,' staring in [Rice's] eyes," a participant at the meeting recalled. "There was this test of wills where he was trying to use all his charms on her as a woman, and she just basically stared him down.

"By the end of the meeting, he was babbling. He was a blithering idiot . . . It was palpable in the room for the Americans. The Pakistanis were shifting uncomfortably. And his voice visibly changed." Some of the foreign men, the American official said, "They don't get it . . . She has a *really* strong will, and I think people sometimes 'misunderestimate' her."[76]

Like China's senior diplomat Tang Jiaxuan. When Rice arrived in Beijing on July 9, American ambassador Clark T. Randt begged her to go see State Counselor Tang. But Tang, a former foreign minister and the dean of the Chinese diplomatic corps, had infuriated Rice when they first met when she was national security adviser. Tang had lectured Rice like a student about Taiwan being a part of China—for fifty minutes of an hour-long meeting, looking at the ceiling instead of looking at her as he held forth. "He treated her as a woman, as a minority, basically from an old Chinese man's sexist, racist, and communist patronizing point of view," said an administration official.[77]

Rice sat motionless for the entire fifty minutes, her legs crossed, her body slightly forward, looking at the floor. When Tang was done he harrumphed, "Well, I've spoken too long. . . ."

Rice sat back in her chair and agreed, "You have spoken too long. And I have to go to see your president, Jiang Zemin. So I'm not going to spend any more time on this. But I would say . . . " Then, Rice fired off three points and got up and left.

Now that she was secretary of state, the Chinese were anxious to have her meet with State Counselor Tang. But Rice refused to schedule the meeting. Back at her hotel suite, Ambassador Randt begged her to reconsider; for Tang to be snubbed by the American secretary of state would be a significant loss of face— and Randt had to work with the Chinese. Knowing full well that her suite was bugged, Rice replied, "No, he's insufferable. I'm not going to do it."

Soon a buffet of Chinese fruits and sweets was delivered to the room. "Compliments of State Counselor Tang," read the card. As her entourage nibbled on the snacks, Rice said, "All right, I'll meet with him." Her Ray-woman pride had bent him to her will.

In the Middle East, it was more a question of the tight strictures on women.

So while she usually didn't cover herself, she did have a treadmill brought to her room since the hotel gym was for men only. And when the Saudi king presented her with a gift of an *abaya*, the modesty garment Saudi women were required to wear in public, Rice graciously accepted it and even wore it later on a visit to a madrassa, an Islamic religious school, in another country.[78]

Despite the challenges, or perhaps because of the consistent underestimation of her in some parts of the world, Rice was able to effect change where Secretary Powell hadn't been. She convinced Beijing to strengthen its antipiracy laws, arguing that as China became a global economic power, curbing the counterfeiting of DVDs and CDs would be increasingly in China's interests. She also convinced Chinese leaders to step up to their global responsibilities on issues they had long ignored, like Darfur and Burma. And while her efforts on the Six Party Talks hadn't yielded the results Washington wanted—a Korean peninsula free of nuclear weapons—Rice succeeded in getting China's new president, Hu Jintao, to start thinking about a common U.S.–China strategy in the event that North Korea conducted a nuclear test.

As it turned out, Rice was far better suited to running a department than to trying to coordinate many. "A lot of the challenge of a national security adviser, especially in this administration, is the adjudication of disputes and sorting out of personality conflicts and other kinds of struggles," said State Department Counselor Phil Zelikow, who's known Rice for nearly twenty years. "This is a task which she can perform, but for which she has little taste.

"She is more naturally a strategist and conceptual manager of policy, trying to point broad directions [and] make judgments about priorities," said Zelikow. "She's a strong public persona, one of those people who flourish in the public eye, much better suited for the kind of job she has now than a job as a White House staffer."[79]

While she needed the practical experience that being NSA had provided, the job had not been the best fit.

Just a week after Rice returned from her first Asia trip as secretary of state, the advantages of "practical idealism" became obvious. On March 31, North Korea declared itself a nuclear power. The administration had invaded Iraq on the mere suspicion Saddam had WMD—and here was a despotic regime that posed an immediate threat to its neighbors, openly declaring that it had nuclear weapons. With the North's ability to strike South Korea, military action was out of the question. The only viable option the administration had to confront Pyongyang was the multilateral Six Party Talks. The Americans redoubled their diplomatic efforts with their Asian allies to get North Korea back in line.

But great-power diplomacy proved less effective in the mess in Iraq, where 130,000 U.S. troops were still fighting. On May 14, Rice flew secretly to Baghdad. The Bush team had reveled in the success of the January 30 elections, but the Shiites, Sunnis, and Kurds still had not managed to form a government. Rice's task was to make them.

For almost a year, the belated understanding had been growing in the administration that the insurgency threatened the political opening that toppling Saddam had created. For months, analysts debated whether the insurgency was fueled by former Baathists, by other Sunnis opposed Shiite-majority rule, or by foreign jihadists, including some loyal to al-Qaeda and bin Laden. But by the time Rice took her first trip to Baghdad as secretary, it was clear that the Sunnis were the biggest problem; the lion's share of Iraq's insurgency was indigenous.

Rice used her twelve-hour visit to tell the Shiite and Kurdish leaders, once more, that the Sunnis must be brought into the political process, even if they had largely boycotted or been too intimidated to vote in January's parliamentary elections. Then, just after she left Iraq, U.S. generals in Baghdad and Washington told reporters that the security situation was getting worse, not better.[80] Even more ominous, Rice's plane had barely taken off when Iran sent its own foreign minister to Baghdad. "The party that will leave Iraq is the United States, because it will eventually withdraw," said Iranian foreign minister Kamal Kharrazi in English, standing beside Iraqi prime minister Ibrahim al-Jaafari. "But the party that will live with the Iraqis is Iran, because it is a neighbor to Iraq."[81]

The message Iraq's democratically elected government was sending to Washington with the Iranian's visit was summarized by Jaafari himself: "We will build relationships between Iraq and other countries according to Iraqi standards and Iraqi national interests." It was just one sign of the vexing complexities that would trouble American policy in Iraq for the rest of Rice's term. In June, Rice made another trip to the Middle East, affirming for the first time on Arab soil the end of an American compact with oppressive regimes. At Cairo University, she told an audience of six hundred invited Western-oriented intellectuals, "We are all concerned for the future of Egypt's [democratic] reforms when peaceful supporters of democracy—men and women—are not free from violence. The day must come when the rule of law replaces emergency decrees—and when the independent judiciary replaces arbitrary justice."[82]

The Egyptian government must fulfill the promise it has made to its people—and to the entire world—by giving its citizens the freedom to choose. Egypt's elections, including the parliamentary elections, must meet objective standards that define every free election.

Opposition groups must be free to assemble, and to participate, and to speak to the media. Voting should occur without violence or intimidation. And international election monitors and observers must have unrestricted access to do their jobs . . .

Throughout the Middle East, the fear of free choices can no longer justify the denial of liberty. . . .

There are those who say that democracy leads to chaos, or conflict, or terror. In fact, the opposite is true: Freedom and democracy are the only ideas powerful enough to overcome hatred and division and violence. For people of diverse races and religions, the inclusive nature of democracy can lift the fear of difference that some believe is a license to kill.

Singling out Washington's other chief ally in the region, Rice said, "In Saudi Arabia, brave citizens are demanding accountable government. And some good first steps toward openness have been taken with recent municipal elections. Yet many people pay an unfair price for exercising their basic rights. Three individuals in particular are currently imprisoned for peacefully petitioning their government. That should not be a crime in any country."

It was a historic speech. As Rice said, "For sixty years, my country . . . pursued stability at the expense of democracy . . . here in the Middle East—and we achieved neither. Now, we are taking a different course. We are supporting the democratic aspirations of all people." And it was delivered with a passion and intelligence that seemed to affirm the rightness of the Bush doctrine and the sincerity of a woman who believed, as Chip Blacker put it in another context, that she was "a change agent."[83]

But the audience's tepid reception should have been a cause for concern. The

Egyptians were divided between those who wanted Rice to go farther—by, say, withholding some of the more than one billion dollars in aid that Washington gave Cairo each year—and those who were insulted by her moralistic lecturing.[84]

In the end, Rice's stirring words would ring hollow anyway. President Hosni Mubarak would leave in place the emergency decree under which he had ruled since 1981, stifling free speech and free assembly. The opposition, including Ayman Nour—over whose arrest Rice had delayed her originally planned trip to Egypt—would be given only three weeks to campaign, and the election monitors that Rice had said "must" come would be barred. And Washington would do nothing.

Neocon Robert Kagan would write a column highlighting the apparent hypocrisy of Rice and Bush. "Perhaps there is concern that too much pressure on Mubarak might produce a victory by the Muslim Brotherhood, the most popular Egyptian opposition party that has been outlawed by the government. That's a risk, of course, but if the Bush administration isn't willing to let Islamists, even radical Islamists, win votes in a fair election, then Bush officials should stop talking so much about democracy and go back to supporting the old dictatorships."[85] It was the old neocon critique of realism—too much attention to "interests" and not enough to "values." Operationally, "practical idealism" didn't seem all that different from realism.

That's because it wasn't. In one week in July, for instance, Rice traveled to the Sudanese capital, Khartoum, to pressure the government to end the genocide in the Darfur region. Then she visited a refugee camp and listened to women tell harrowing stories of being raped by government-backed militiamen.[86] But the administration sought no greater involvement in the continuing humanitarian disaster. Earlier in the week, Rice had telephoned Pakistan's President Musharraf[87] to explain that Washington was signing a new nuclear pact with Pakistan's rival, India. The move reversed a prohibition on the transfer of civilian nuclear technology that had gone into effect when India declared itself a nuclear state in 1998. The deal with Delhi, like Washington's limited moves to stop the killing in Darfur, was a profoundly realist accommodation to the world as it was (the reality of a nuclear India) rather than as it should be (the ideal of nonproliferation.)

Meanwhile, Iraq hit another bump. Rice's demands that Shiite and Kurdish leaders include Sunnis in the political process had gone nowhere. In fact, when the Iraqis sent a draft constitution to the transitional parliament in August, it only further marginalized the Sunni minority. The constitution would create a highly decentralized state where the Shiites would have a superstate in the south and the Kurds would have virtual autonomy in the north, leaving the Sunnis with basically the western desert.[88] President Bush personally called Shiite cleric Abdul Aziz al-Hakim, the leader of the Supreme Council for the Islamic Revolution in Iraq, to argue for the inclusion of Sunni interests in the new constitution and was rebuffed.

The constitution would come up for a vote in October. If it was defeated, the political transition would be dealt a serious setback; even if it passed, with the Sunnis shut out, representative democracy would arrive stillborn. Understandably, Americans were growing more sour on the adventure in Iraq; there was little sign of the stability that would allow U.S. soldiers to come home, and deaths were mounting.

But Rice had more immediate worries in the region. Israeli soldiers were clashing with Jewish settlers as they forcibly evicted them from Gaza, and, capitalizing on the chaos, Palestinian militants stepped up cross-border attacks into Israel. Rice worked to save the possibility of peace talks that had greeted her when she took office. Then came even more disturbing news: Iran rejected the European offer of incentives in exchange for ending its nuclear program and immediately tore the UN inspection seals from its nuclear facilities and started reprocessing uranium.

The glow of Condi's "coming-out season" and Lebanon's Cedar Revolution had faded. In fact, despite all her charm, grit, and power, the world seemed to be sliding backward rather than advancing.

And even greater storms were gathering.

CHAPTER TWELVE

STORMS

It is one thing to have a limited political goal and to fight decisively for it; it is quite another to apply military force incrementally, hoping to find a political solution somewhere along the way. A president entering these situations must ask whether decisive force is possible and is likely to be effective and must know how and when to get out.[1]

CONDOLEEZZA RICE
Foreign Affairs
January/February 2000

C ondoleezza Rice had been working flat out since becoming secretary of state in January, delaying her vacation until the last days of August. The president had been on his vacation for weeks. In fact, Bush was on the way to setting a presidential record, surpassing Ronald Reagan for time spent away from Washington.[2] When her holiday finally came, Rice embraced it with the same intensity she brought to her job. Escaping from work was one of the ways she maintained balance—like her daily workouts, her sessions with her chamber music group, and her Sunday calls to friends and family.

She left Washington for her vacation in New York on Wednesday, August 31. That afternoon she hit some balls with Monica Seles, and that night she took in the sold-out Monty Python musical, *Spamalot*, on Broadway. On Thursday morning she indulged her shoe obsession, shopping at Ferragamo on Fifth Avenue. While Rice was out, her communications chief, Jim Wilkinson, back in his room at the Palace Hotel at Fifth and Madison, came across an item on the *Drudge Report*:

Eyewitness: Sec of State Condi Rice laughs it up at 'Spamalot' while Gulf Coast lays [*sic*] in tatters. Theatergoers in New York City's Great White Way were shocked to see the President's former National Security Adviser at the Monty Python farce last night—as the rest of the cabinet responds to Hurricane Katrina . . . [3]

Wilkinson's heart sank. The thirtysomething aide was so attentive to Rice's image that before she gave speeches in drab hotel conference rooms abroad, he fussed with the backdrop and podium to make sure the pictures would show what the city she was in. And it was Wilkinson who stage-managed her airport arrivals to make them look presidential. It was no secret that he hoped Rice would run for president some day. And now this. Hurricane Katrina had made landfall early Monday morning. Initially, weather forecasters thought New Orleans had dodged a bullet; when the storm hit sixty-five miles southeast of the city, it had been downgraded to a Category Three hurricane from a potentially cataclysmic Category Five. But by 8 a.m. on Monday, one of the city's central canals had been breached. The nearby Lower Ninth Ward, largely black and poor, was under six to eight feet of water, and soon eighty percent of New Orleans was flooded. Mayor Ray Nagin reported "significant" loss of life; bodies could be seen floating in the floodwater. Looting erupted.

Fifteen to twenty thousand residents took shelter in the Superdome, which was a designated "refuge of last resort." Another nearly twenty thousand crowded into the Convention Center, even though it wasn't a designated shelter and had no food or water.[4] On Tuesday morning, Louisiana governor Kathleen Blanco ordered the evacuation of the city, but no transportation was available to move anyone. By Wednesday, when Rice left for her vacation, the media was reporting that thousands were dead in New Orleans, and television screens filled with the images of the survivors. They were almost all African American, their eyes desperate, many carrying babies and what possessions they could grab as the waters rose. Reporters who had covered the Third World compared the scenes to refugee crises they had seen.

By Thursday, the situation had gotten even worse. Every hour, the cable news channels showed a dead woman in a wheelchair outside the Convention Center, covered with a sheet, under the now clear skies of New Orleans. Despite what *Drudge* reported, no one seemed to be responding to Katrina.

Wilkinson—a native of East Texas, whose family had supported civil rights before it was fashionable for whites to do so—was concerned enough about the images of African Americans stranded, begging for water from camera crews, that he conferred with Rice's other top advisers about whether Condi needed to return to Washington. "That woman needs a vacation," said one of Rice's advisers who was also a friend. In fact, all of Rice's staff agreed: She had set travel records jetting around the globe, and she deserved her downtime. And besides, she was secretary of *state*, not the interior.

But within hours, they regretted the decision. The *New York Post*'s gossip column ran a piece reporting that Rice was working on her backhand with Monica Seles.[5] Then the gossip and news Web site *Gawker* posted a story headlined "Breaking: Condi Rice Spends Salary on Shoes."

> . . . So the Gulf Coast has gone all Mad Max, women are being raped in the Superdome, and Rice is enjoying a brief vacation in New York. We wish we were surprised.
>
> What does surprise us: Just moments ago at the Ferragamo on 5th Avenue, Condoleeza [*sic*] Rice was seen spending several thousands of dollars on some nice, new shoes (we've confirmed this, so her new heels will surely get coverage from the [*Washington Post*'s] Robin Givhan). A fellow shopper, unable to fathom the absurdity of Rice's timing, went up to the Secretary and reportedly shouted, "How dare you shop for shoes while thousands are dying and homeless!" Never one to have her fashion choices questioned, Rice had security PHYSICALLY REMOVE the woman.
>
> Angry Lady, whoever you are, we love you. You are a true American, and we'll go shoe shopping with you anytime.[6]

On Friday, the *New York Daily News* would report that *Spamalot* audience members had booed Rice when the lights came up. Then, the paper would ask, "Did New Yorkers chase Condoleezza Rice back to Washington yesterday?"[7]

Rice says that no one chased her anywhere: "On Thursday morning I got up, I had breakfast, and I went down to Ferragamo. I came back. Things had gotten pretty bad, and plus I learned that the State Department had a problem; our New

Orleans Passport Center was down. And . . . the pictures were really ugly. I called the president and I said, 'I think I should come back.'"[8]

Rice insists the alleged encounter with the angry woman at Ferragamo never happened. "Absolutely not . . . this stuff just gets out there."

And in a country outraged by the tragedy unfolding in New Orleans, the tale of the angry shopper did get out there. And—like CNN anchor Anderson Cooper's verbal lashing of Senator Mary Landrieu for politicians' diddling while rats ate dead bodies in the streets[9]—shot around the Internet. Later director Spike Lee would try to find the irate Ferragamo shopper, unsuccessfully. But in Lee's searing 2006 documentary, *When the Levees Broke*, African American social commentator Michael Eric Dyson took Rice to task: "While people were drowning in New Orleans, she was going up and down Madison Avenue buying Ferragamo shoes. Then she went to see *Spamalot!*"[10]

Dyson muddled Ferragamo's address and the chronology of Rice's holiday, but he captured the sense of anger, even betrayal, that many African Americans felt toward the administration in general and Condoleezza in particular in the days after Katrina.

The criticism took Rice by surprise. "These are not my accounts," she protested to Chip Blacker, referring to domestic issues.[11]

"I was watching on the news what was going on with Katrina. I wasn't getting the reports of what the hurricane was going to do or anything like that," says Rice. "And so I responded like the secretary of state, which is [to] worry about the foreign contributions, worry about the [New Orleans] passport center. But it was less than twenty-four hours before I realized it was time to get back.[12]

"Look, I'd be the first to say I learned something from that. I thought of myself as secretary of state; my responsibility is foreign policy. I didn't think about my role as a visible African American national figure. I just didn't think about it."

That Rice hadn't realized that she had a role to play as a black leader was a result of how she saw the world. John and Angelena's efforts to invest their daughter with a limitless sense of possibility, to make her unconquerable, had made her both less confined by race and less conscious of it.

By the time Rice returned to Washington on Thursday afternoon, President Bush was facing a public furor of his own, centered around the photo the White

House had released of Bush peering out the window of Air Force One, surveying Katrina's damage on his way back to Washington from Crawford. Presumably, the White House intended to show a concerned commander in chief; instead, Bush had looked detached and powerless.

Watching the disaster coverage in her seventh-floor office at the State Department, Rice decided she had to go home to Alabama to show that the administration cared. An aide phoned the White House to clear the trip, but the White House resisted; the president should travel to the gulf first, and he was planning to go early next week. But Rice's office was adamant: The secretary needed to be down South "with her people." They reminded the White House that they had their own planes. The White House called back three hours later; Rice had been cleared to go.[13] The president would go earlier.

On Friday morning, CNN anchor Soledad O'Brien, who was in New Orleans, interviewed Michael Brown, director of the Federal Emergency Management Agency (FEMA), by satellite from Baton Rouge. O'Brien was flabbergasted when Brown told her that FEMA had been unaware of the evacuees at the Convention Center until Thursday.[14] "How is it possible that we're getting better intel than you're getting?" O'Brien asked. "We had a crew in the air. We were showing live pictures of the people outside of the Convention Center. We had a National Guardsman who was talking to us, who was telling us he estimated the crowd at 50,000 people. That was at 8 o'clock in the morning yesterday."

> **O'BRIEN:** FEMA has been on the ground for four days, going into the fifth day. Why no massive airdrop of food and water? In Banda Aceh, in Indonesia, they got food dropped two days after the tsunami struck.
>
> **BROWN:** That's what we're going to do here, too. And I think . . .
>
> **O'BRIEN:** But, sir, forgive me . . .
>
> **BROWN:** Soledad, just a moment, please. We're feeding those people in the Convention Center. We have fed over 150,000 people as of last night. That is happening.
>
> **O'BRIEN:** But I guess the point is, as of last night—sir, forgive me, I have to stop you here.

BROWN: What we're hearing, is that we're hearing people's frustrations. There are people that are beginning to manifest themselves out of the community that we didn't know that were there, and we're doing everything we can to find those individuals, case by case to get them help as quickly as possible.

O'BRIEN: But it begs the question, why are you discovering this now? It's five days that FEMA has been on the ground. The head of police says it's been five days that FEMA has been there. The mayor, the former mayor, putting out SOSs on Tuesday morning, crying on national television, saying please send in some troops. So the idea that, yes, I understand that you're feeding people and trying to get in there now, but it's Friday. It's Friday . . .

Following Cooper's and O'Brien's lead, journalists who usually spoke with the feigned distance of objectivity gave voice instead to the nation's shock; many cried.[15]

At nine o'clock, from the South Lawn of the White House, President Bush announced that he was on his way to the gulf.[16] The political storm in Washington was rising. Even some Republicans started to desert the president. Senate Majority Leader Bill Frist called for congressional hearings. Former House Speaker Newt Gingrich questioned whether the administration could handle a terrorist attack if it couldn't respond to a natural disaster that forecasters had seen coming.

Political analyst Stu Rothenberg said presciently, "It's certainly possible this could become a defining event for people." The president's approval rating fell to a new low—forty-one percent in the CBS Poll, thirty-eight percent in the *Newsweek* Poll[17]—and would never recover. Katrina would mark the moment the American people broke faith with George Bush. The incompetence of the government response cast the two-and-a-half-year-old war in Iraq in a new light.[18] And the government's lack of preparedness led to comparisons with 9/11, particularly when the president said no one had anticipated a top-category hurricane hitting New Orleans; scientists and engineers reported that they had, that FEMA had even run drills on the possibility. A year later, Condi Rice would tell *MTV News* that her father, a Louisiana native, had predicted, "Lake Pontchartrain would rise and it would, literally, engulf New Orleans. And that's effectively what happened."[19]

Before Katrina, Rice had reached out to Bruce Gordon, head of the NAACP, to establish a working relationship. It came in handy now. Gordon had called Rice on Thursday, and when they finally talked early Friday morning,[20] he warned her that if the administration didn't fix the chaos in New Orleans, they'd face race riots. Rice requested a White House briefing for Gordon and other black leaders.[21] When the White House proposed doing the briefing on Tuesday, Rice called Air Force One and talked to the president. The briefing, led by Homeland Security secretary Michael Chertoff, was set for the next day.

By 10:30 a.m., the president was on the ground at Mobile Regional Airport in Alabama. Before leaving Washington, with Chertoff by his side, he had called the response to Katrina "unacceptable." But standing next to FEMA director Brown, Bush now said, "Brownie, you're doing a heck of a job."[22] The comment would come to haunt both men.

After a tour of hurricane-ravaged Mississippi and a flyover of New Orleans, Bush held an evening press conference with Brown, Mayor Nagin, and Governor Blanco at the New Orleans airport. "I believe that the great city of New Orleans will rise again and be a greater city of New Orleans," said the president. "I believe the town where I used to come from Houston, Texas, to enjoy myself—occasionally too much—will be that very same town, that it will be a better place to come to."[23] The reminiscence of his days partying in New Orleans struck a sour note.

Hours later, twenty-eight-year-old rap star Kanye West, who had graced the cover of *Time* magazine days before,[24] said plainly what many African Americans were feeling. During a live Katrina relief telethon on NBC, West veered from the earnest script and, his voice quivering, said, "I hate the way they portray us in the media. If you see a black family, it says they're looting. See a white family, it says they're looking for food. And you know that it's been five days because most of the people are black. And even for me to complain about it, I would be a hypocrite because I've tried to turn away from the TV, because it's too hard to watch. We already realize a lot of people that could help are at war right now, fighting another way, and they have given them permission to go down and shoot us. [National Guardsmen had been authorized to shoot looters in New Orleans.]"[25]

Afterward, a hapless Mike Myers, standing beside West, read his part off the teleprompter. When West's turn to speak came again, he said flatly, "George Bush doesn't care about black people."

As the highest-ranking black cabinet member and a close friend of the president, it fell naturally to Condoleezza Rice to defend George Bush. Rice had already started doing that before West spoke out. During a briefing earlier Friday to announce that sixty countries had offered Katrina assistance, Rice said in response to a question, "We are all going to need to be in this together. I think everybody's very emotional. It's hard to watch pictures of any American going through this. And yes, the African American community has obviously been very heavily affected. But people are doing what they can for Americans. Nobody wants to see any American suffer . . . that Americans would somehow in a color-affected way decide who to help and who not to help, I just don't believe it."[26]

On Sunday, Rice made her trip to the region, attending a black church near Mobile. After the service, she was even more emphatic in her defense of the president. "I don't believe for a minute anybody allowed people to suffer because they are African Americans. . . . Nobody, especially this president, would have left people unattended on the basis of race."[27] Nonetheless, when a local man at a relief center asked Rice's aide Jim Wilkinson if he worked for the federal government, Wilkinson was so ashamed, he lied.[28]

Over the next weeks, Rice expended far more words than West had in her effort to refute his seven-word declaration. It didn't help that the president's mother, former first lady Barbara Bush, who was also like family to Rice, said, when visiting New Orleans evacuees in Houston, "And so many of the people in this arena here, you know, were unprivileged anyway, so this is working very well for them."[29]

On the *Tavis Smiley Show*, a popular black radio program, Smiley asked Rice to respond to the fact that many African Americans blacks were "rallying around" West's statement.[30]

RICE: It's just wrong. And it's wrong for people to say that. This president has cared a great deal about minority populations. That's why he's cared about home ownership. It's why he's cared about black children not being warehoused in our schools, and that's why No Child Left Behind has been important to him.

And look, no president of the United States is going to want any American to suffer, and most especially this president. And the idea that there was some sort of racial test, that we were sitting around thinking, *Well, these are black people, therefore we don't have to get there quickly,* it's just ludicrous. And I can't believe people are saying it. And, you know, if they're saying it, they ought to be made to defend it.

SMILEY: Do you believe that there are race and class dimensions, though, to this tragedy?

RICE: I do believe that we are dealing with the fact that there are pockets of America which are very poor and that some of those pockets of America have a bad combination of race and poverty. I do believe that. I'm from the South, and I know that there are still vestiges of the Old South that have to be dealt with. And one of the questions is going to be, in the longer run, how, when we start to rebuild, do we address what was clearly an underlying social problem. . . . We've always known that race and poverty is a particularly bad witches' brew. We know that. But as we address rebuilding, how do we make certain that we don't rebuild on that basis, but we rebuild on a new basis?

On Fox News's *O'Reilly Factor,* Rice said, "This is a president who has not only cared about minority empowerment, not only cared about equal opportunity for minorities, but he's done more than any president I can think of in recent years."[31]

When O'Reilly asked, "Does it hurt your feelings that most black Americans don't like the president? . . . Do you take it personally?" Rice responded, "I don't take anything personally, no. No. But I do like to have an opportunity to talk to people about what this president has meant for the empowerment of black Americans."

"Does it hurt your feelings when some anti-Bush people say that you're a shill for him and [have] sold out your race?"

"Oh, come on," Rice scoffed, smiling. "Why would I worry about something like that?" And then she repeated her mantra from her days as Stanford provost. "Bill, the fact of the matter is, I've been black all my life. Nobody needs to tell me how to be black."

In the *MTV News* interview in September 2006, Rice would go still further in her defense of Bush. "No president, especially this president, who I know and who's my friend, who I know as well as I know my own family—the thought that he would let Americans suffer because they're black was just a hideous thing to say. But that people were poor and didn't have the means to get out, I think probably that was not accounted for."[32]

What Rice never said in all her interviews was that, like Kanye West, she too had cried over what had happened in New Orleans. When she returned to Washington, she had sat glued to the television absorbing the images. At one point she confided to someone close to her, "There but for the grace of God go I."[33]

It was not a rhetorical comment; Juanita Love Thomas was living proof of what might have been. The daughter of John Rice's only sibling, Dr. Theresa Rice Love, Juanita was Condoleezza's first cousin. And Thomas had not escaped the witches' brew of poverty and race.

Growing up, Thomas had been the anti-Condo (she used her uncle's nickname for her only first cousin.) While Condoleezza personified the Rice family values—she was studious and disciplined—Juanita was rebellious and got into trouble. "The way our family worked, this was acceptable and that wasn't acceptable," said Thomas. So when her mother disapproved of the friends Thomas made as a teenager, Thomas said Dr. Love paid more appropriate children to befriend her. "[We were] not allowed to associate . . . with what my mom and John called 'lower-class' black people," she said. "For the Rices, you had to graduate from this school and have five degrees and be this. And I just wasn't like that."[34]

And her mother would ask her, "Why aren't you like Condoleezza?"

"It was really hard, feeling you were inferior," said Thomas. "Every time we talked it was, 'Condoleezza is doing this . . . ' I wanted my mom to accept me for who I was rather than a replica of someone else. I just went through psychological hell with it, and it made us grow farther apart."

But Thomas and her mother had never really been close. While Condoleezza was Angelena's life, Theresa was an academic pioneer and an activist. "[My mother] wasn't there a lot. She did a lot of counseling and seminars and wrote books," said Thomas, who lived with her mother and Grandmother Rice—and for a time with Condi's Aunt G.

But just as Condo and Juanita were dissimilar, so were John and Theresa. While John disdained the drunken rabble that latched on to Martin Luther King's marches in Birmingham—throwing liquor bottles and goading the police[35]—and kept his daughter a safe distance from the movement, Theresa took Juanita's hand as a little girl and led her in a civil rights march in Norfolk,

Virginia, when they lived there. "All these people and the police. I was like, 'Mom, what are we doing? I'm scared.' And she was like, 'Shut up. Let's march,'" Thomas laughed. Love was a determined woman; she had earned a PhD in 1953 from the University of Wisconsin, where the only room she could find to rent was a porch.

After graduating, she became an English professor and an expert in Charles Dickens. But Dr. Love was also interested in "English as a second language" for African Americans and the study of black dialect.[36] As an adult, Thomas would watch her mother and Condoleezza get into intense debates. "It was like a battle of the minds," recalled Thomas fondly. "They were both pigheaded and wouldn't give in."

When Love fell ill, John brought his sister to Palo Alto, where she was hospitalized. Later she moved to New Orleans, where she died in 2002. When Theresa passed away, Thomas said, Condoleezza, by then national security adviser, didn't contact her, though the Ray aunts and uncle did. "Condoleezza was a mini-Theresa . . . [My mother] worshipped the ground she walked on, was her mentor. And when my mom died, she didn't even send a card." Though the assertion sounded bitter, for the most part, Thomas wasn't. "I give my cousin her props," she said in January 2007. "She has accomplished a great deal."

After overcoming her demons, Thomas went on to earn a degree in criminal justice from Southern University in Baton Rouge, where her mother had once taught. "I thank and praise God," she said. "He brought me through this."

When Katrina hit, Thomas was forty-six years old, living in Baton Rouge with her husband and two children and working in a beauty supply store. By then, Thomas and Rice had been estranged for six years. Rice's Aunt G told me in December 2006 that she didn't know what had happened to Thomas, but Thomas said, "She knows I'm here in Baton Rouge. For some reason, they cut us off. . . . I guess they say, 'We definitely cannot be associated with that lower-class black woman.'"

The estrangement provided a stark contrast to Rice's relationships with her Ray cousins, whom Condoleezza considered "siblings."

Rice believed that it was her parents who rescued her from the "witches' brew" of poverty and race in America. But she also believed that the United States had done a better job of achieving racial harmony than any other nation, despite what Katrina had shown. Yet polls revealed that a sizeable minority of

Americans—and a majority of African Americans—agreed with Kanye West. Gallup put the question to Americans bluntly: "Do you think George W. Bush does—or does not—care about black people?" Seventy-two percent of African Americans said they believed he didn't care. Overall, thirty-one percent of Americans believed the president of the United States didn't care about black people, including more than a one in four whites.[37]

Before Katrina, Republican National Committee (RNC) chairman Ken Mehlman had made reaching out to African American voters an RNC priority, preaching wherever he could that blacks in the twenty-first century should return to the party of Lincoln. Mehlman recruited black candidates to run for statewide offices in the 2006 elections[38] and even produced a *2005 Republican Freedom Calendar: Celebrating a Century and a Half of Civil Rights Achievement by the Party of Lincoln*, with each day devoted to black Republican history.[39] But after the storm, Mehlman's hope of prying African Americans from the Democrats lay in tatters, too. A much-publicized NBC/*Wall Street Journal* Poll found that only two percent of African Americans approved of the president's job performance, down from nineteen percent five months earlier and fifty-one percent after 9/11.[40]

Rice disputed those numbers. But even she had had a disagreement with some people in the White House that was tied to race—though she rarely talked about it. It had happened in early 2003. The administration was considering what stance to take on two affirmative action cases coming before the Supreme Court that challenged the University of Michigan's awarding of points to racial minorities when deciding whom to admit. The president had asked Rice's opinion, and Condi had given it. Then, on January 17, the *Washington Post* ran a front-page article headlined "Rice Helped Shape Bush Decision on Admissions." The administration had decided to file two "friend of the court," or amicus, briefs arguing that Michigan's point system was tantamount to racial quotas.[41]

> National security adviser Condoleezza Rice took a rare central role in a domestic debate within the White House and helped persuade President Bush to publicly condemn race-conscious admissions policies at the University of Michigan, administration officials said yesterday.
>
> The officials said Rice, in a series of lengthy one-on-one meetings with Bush, drew on her experience as provost at Stanford University to

help convince him that favoring minorities was not an effective way of improving diversity on college campuses.

Officials described Rice as one of the prime movers behind Bush's announcement on Wednesday that he would urge the Supreme Court to strike down Michigan's affirmative action program.

"I was furious," says Rice. "Not too much has made me more furious. Because not only was that not the advice I had given the president, it was 160 degrees, if not 180, but 160 degrees from what I said to the president."[42] In reality, Rice told Bush, as she had argued at Stanford, that race should be a factor in admissions. "And I actually thought I had had a good effect on where we [came] out as an administration." The White House's briefs addressed only Michigan's point system, rather than arguing that affirmative action was unconstitutional, and the briefs supported diversity as a goal in college admissions.

Rice told friends, "Nobody is going to look to me for cover on this one."[43]

She called George Bush. "Mr. President, I never want to put you in a position of having a member of your administration, particularly one like me who's known to be so close to you, contradict something in policy, but I have to do it," she said. And she asked his permission to issue a five-sentence statement:

> When the President decided to submit an amicus brief, he asked for my view on how diversity can be best achieved on university campuses. I offered my view, drawing on my experience in academia and as provost of a major university. I agree with the President's position, which emphasizes the need for diversity and recognizes the continued legacy of racial prejudice, and the need to fight it. The President challenged universities to develop ways to diversify their populations fully. I believe that while race neutral means are preferable, it is appropriate to use race as one factor among others in achieving a diverse student body.[44]

Rice would insist in the coming days that there was no daylight between her position and the president's—although Bush's other aides emphasized that he had actually not taken a position on whether race should be considered in admissions at all, and neither had the brief. Bush had merely said that schools should seek diversity by considering "a student's potential and life experiences."[45] In an interview with the only black-owned radio network in the country, Rice asserted, "It is hard to talk about life experiences . . . without recognizing that race is part of that."[46]

Two months after Katrina, Rice was welcomed home to Alabama again. The stated goal of her trip to Birmingham and Tuscaloosa with British foreign minister Jack Straw was to show Straw America beyond New York and Washington; but Rice's trip was good for President Bush, too. From a partisan point of view, Rice was a living, breathing rebuttal of charges of racism against the president. When she walked onto the football field of the University of Alabama to toss the coin, the roars were deafening. "She's received . . . as the face of the New South," said Chip Blacker. "She is comfortable both [being] that and being a catalyst for that."[47] In the end, the public adulation during her trip earned Rice more points than it did the president. As she waved to the throngs and made speeches, the talk of Rice as a potential presidential candidate grew exponentially.

Only she was still secretary of state and her "accounts" were international. And while the administration was suffering its post-Katrina hangover, better news was coming from, of all places, Iraq.

On October 15, 2005, Iraqis voted to approve their new constitution. The doomsday scenario—that the Sunni-majority provinces would vote no—didn't come to pass. Deft negotiating by U.S. ambassador Zalmay Khalilzad won a last-minute addition to the constitution allowing a parliamentary committee to suggest changes later, encouraging Sunnis to both approve the document in October and to come out again in December to vote in parliamentary elections. On polling day, some stations in Sunni areas were deserted, but others—including some in the once blood-steeped city of Falluja—saw long lines. Rice noted that Sunni participation in the political process jumped in places from twenty-nine percent in January's elections for a temporary government to more than sixty percent in October's referendum.[48]

But the impressive demonstration of Iraqi democracy only fed the growing impatience of the American public. And with Bush politically weakened after Katrina, Congress demanded to know—with a new constitution and elections for a permanent government in the offing—when the 130,000 U.S. troops would be coming home.

During another three-and-a-half-hour grilling before the Senate Foreign Relations Committee, Rice had explained in October, in answer to a question from freshman senator Barack Obama, "I understand that, yes, [our plans for Iraq] might not work. But every day we have to get up and work at our hardest to make it work."[49] Though Rice didn't say so, making Bush's agenda "work" was why she had stayed on for the second term in a job she had told friends she didn't want.

In November, Rice made her second trip to Iraq as secretary of state. On the way to Baghdad, she stopped in Mosul, a northern city in a largely Sunni province that had defeated the constitution (but not by the two-thirds majority required to count as a "no"). Rice chose Mosul to show solidarity with the State Department's own employees; a roadside bomb a month earlier had killed four security officers there. But Rice also wanted to highlight Mosul as a place where the new U.S. strategy of "clear, hold, and build" had turned back the insurgency and rebuilt infrastructure. In Mosul and later in Baghdad, she once again talked to Shiite and Kurdish leaders about the need to welcome disaffected Sunnis into the political process.

On the eve of the December 15 election for a permanent government, President Bush held what was for him a rare meeting with Democratic congressional leaders. It included all of the war cabinet and Khalilzad. In the meeting, Bush took the more chastened and realistic tone he was increasingly assuming in public. He admitted that mistakes had been made in Iraq but insisted that the war had to be won. And in a final acknowledgment that Rice had won the interagency power struggle in the administration, the White House announced that a week earlier Bush had signed a new national security directive giving the State Department the lead in postwar reconstruction efforts; $200 million that the Pentagon had set aside for "stabilization and reconstruction" in Iraq and elsewhere would be moved to State. In the future, at least in theory, battles the likes of those between Rumsfeld and Powell after the invasion of Iraq would be avoided.

As usual, Rice spun the news magnanimously. "Don Rumsfeld and I have been friends for more than a decade, and we are really good friends," she told Fox's Brit Hume with a smile. "We have an excellent working relationship. We work through problems. Are there some times when we disagree? Of course, but we always do so with the greatest respect and, indeed, the greatest friendship. And he is a really good secretary of defense. He has managed two wars. He has transformed the Pentagon in quite remarkable ways. And he's not only my colleague, but he's my good friend."[50]

In December, the Iraqis voted again in massive numbers, and Rice declared, "I believe that Iraq is going to be a great nation again because, first and foremost, the Iraqi people have shown their commitment to the democratic enterprise against really great odds. There are posters in Iraq today that say 'Vote and you will die' from the terrorists. There are threats and intimidation to the Iraqi people. And yet, as they did in January and as they did in October and as they're doing today, they are showing [their] desire for freedom burns very deep."[51]

The alliance of Shiite parties won a majority in the permanent parliament, with the Kurdish parties' alliance placing second. Together they would have the two-thirds supermajority needed to pass any legislation. So, though the Sunnis had participated in the vote, they had failed to capture enough seats to be indispensable to governing; they were still marginalized.

Despite the trio of seemingly successful plebiscites in Iraq, as the year drew to a close, pundits—and some Republicans—proclaimed 2005 George W. Bush's "lost year." The president's second term had begun with characteristic boldness: a declaration that the aim of the United States was to ultimately wipe out tyranny abroad and a historic plan to remake Social Security at home. Less than twelve months later, Bush's domestic agenda was all but dead; the public and Congress had rejected his idea of private Social Security investment accounts, and an even more ambitious plan to revamp the federal tax code hadn't even made it to the starting block.

Meanwhile, Bush's political guru, Karl Rove, and Cheney's chief of staff, I. Lewis "Scooter" Libby, were under investigation for revealing the identity of CIA agent Valerie Plame, allegedly in retaliation for her husband, Joe Wilson, having publicly blasted the administration's claim that Saddam had sought to buy uranium in Africa. And the *New York Times* reported that Bush had authorized secret wiretaps of Americans on U.S. soil suspected of terrorist-related activities without court approval or oversight.

Even as the administration seemed to lose it bearings, Condi Rice remained Bush's greatest defender. On the *Today* show, she vowed, "The president has always lived within the law."[52]

Then, when fury erupted in Europe over U.S. treatment of terror suspects—clandestine CIA prisons, secret renditions of suspects by European Union governments to the United States and then to countries practicing torture—Rice led the American rebuttal. She had been so successful in reestablishing transatlantic relations over the past year that not a single government minister questioned her directly about the CIA prisons.[53] European MPs and the public were unconvinced by Rice's carefully parsed quasi-denials that the United States practiced or condoned torture, but her mission was damage control, not persuasion, and her P.R. campaign decreased the pressure on Washington as well as on European leaders. Austrian chancellor Wolfgang Schuessel, on a visit to the White House, admitted, "I'm quite happy Condoleezza Rice went to Europe. She took the heat."[54]

Tellingly, Rice was defending policies she had been fighting for months to change from inside the administration.[55] The greatest concession she would make publicly was that innocent people had been snared in the net meant to catch terrorists. Those mistakes will be rectified, she said.[56] Otherwise, her public mask prevailed; she gave no indication that the administration's policies might be morally suspect or counterproductive—she argued the latter inside the administration—and she betrayed no hint of doubt.

It was the same with Iraq. Though Rice had misgivings about the administration's tactics, that was not for the world to know; outside the private counsels of the White House, winning the debate was everything. So at Davies Symphony Hall in liberal San Francisco, Rice answered criticism of Iraq's new constitution by saying, "[The Iraqis] haven't made a compromise as bad as the one in 1789 that made my ancestors three-fifths of a man."[57]

Then on February 22, 2006, the progress Rice had made in overseeing the political reconstruction of Iraq was dealt a potentially fatal blow. At 6:45 a.m. local time in Samarra, sixty-five miles north of Baghdad, Sunni insurgents destroyed the golden dome of the Askariya mosque, one of the holiest places of Shi'a Islam. "This is as 9/11 in the United States," an Iraqi Shiite told a reporter.[58] Seyyed Hossein Nasr, a professor at George Washington University, said, "To see this before your eyes is like the world crumbling."[59] The destruction of the Golden Mosque set off the bloodiest wave of sectarian violence since the American invasion and, just as the insurgents had planned, torpedoed political talks. Iraq's most powerful cleric, the Grand Ayatollah Ali al-Sistani, while appealing for calm, issued a statement saying, "If [the government's] security institutions are unable to provide the necessary security, the faithful are able to do that by the will and blessings of God." In the five days following the bombing, the Baghdad morgue reported 1,300 deaths.[60] A holy war had begun—Muslim against Muslim—and American troops were in the middle of it.

In the end, Rice and U.S. ambassador Khalilzad succeeded in convincing the Sunnis to rejoin the talks to form a unity government, averting what appeared to be a rush to all-out civil war. But as the administration breathed a sigh of relief, a Sunni politician drew a more ominous conclusion from the days of unrest: "Next time [the Sunnis] will try to buy weapons to face these kinds of developments."[61]

In April, Rice returned to Iraq, this time with Jack Straw in tow, to make her usual points about the need for political reconciliation. (On the plane ride to Iraq, Rice had given the bunk in her cabin to Straw, who was sick, and she slept on the floor.) For months, Rice had been insisting that once the new unity government was formed, the sectarian militias would be disbanded.[62] But once again her hopes proved false.

Weeks after the Rice–Straw mission, Prime Minister Nouri al Maliki, a Shiite, formed a government, ending five months of political deadlock. Rice had succeeded in riding herd on the political process and willing Iraq to a constitutional democracy. But the violence didn't subside. The government didn't disband the militias, and the UN estimated an average of more than one hundred Iraqis were still being killed every day.

Americans told pollsters they had more faith in the Democrats to deal with the situation in Iraq than they did in Republicans and the White House. At the same time, in the "forgotten war" America was still fighting in Afghanistan, the defeated Taliban appeared newly resurgent, battling U.S. and NATO forces and gaining territory.

Attempting to recapture the initiative for Washington somewhere in the world, Rice had made a dramatic proposal that only became public in May. She suggested the United States offer to join the Europeans in their nuclear negotiations with Iran. Coming more than twenty-four years after Washington broke ties with Tehran following its Islamic revolution and the hostage crisis, and in the midst of President Mahmoud Ahmadinejad's belligerent rhetoric, the proposal was—as Rice had called it in a private memo to Bush—a "bold" initiative.[63] For the neocons, it was closer to treasonous, the ultimate in appeasement, exactly what the realists of Bush's father's team would have done and, in fact, were advocating.[64]

But a meeting with European and Chinese foreign ministers in Berlin at the end of March had convinced Rice that rather than isolating Iran, the administration's strategy was isolating Washington; if the Bush team didn't do something soon, the anti-Iran coalition would collapse. If Rice couldn't hold the Europeans, Chinese, Russians, and Americans together to pursue diplomacy—and, if that failed, sanctions—then the only option for trying to prevent Tehran from acquiring a nuclear weapon would be military action, perhaps unilateral—Iraq II.

Over a period of weeks, Condi Rice convinced a reluctant George Bush to agree to offer Iran the carrot of direct talks as long as there was a stick if Iran refused: UN sanctions strong enough to impact the regime. Rice had mapped it all out. The precondition for Tehran getting to sit down with Washington was that Iran suspend all nuclear activity. When Bush wanted to leave the final details to Rice, the secretary told the president, according to the *Times*, "Only you can nail this down." Rice had Bush call the presidents of Russia and Germany to do just that. The Europeans agreed; if the Iranians refused to negotiate, then the Europeans would support sanctions.[65]

The neocons were appalled. "[Rice] is now in the midst of—and increasingly represents—a diplomatic establishment that is driven to accommodate its allies even when (or, it seems, especially when) such allies counsel the appeasement of our adversaries," wrote former Vulcan Richard Perle. "It is not too late for us . . . to redeem our honor."[66] The *Weekly Standard* compared Bush to Clinton, charging that the genuinely bold ideals of the administration to reshape the world had been bartered for the "affirmation of the foreign policy elite here and abroad."[67] Gingrich told the right-wing newsletter *Insight* in a piece titled "Dump Condi," "We are sending signals today that no matter how much you provoke us, no matter how viciously you describe things in public, no matter how many things you're doing with missiles and nuclear weapons, the most you'll get out of us is talk."[68]

In the end, Iran rejected Washington's preconditions. Whether Rice's historic offer would later prove the basis for a diplomatic compromise, or—as the neocons suspected—a naive distraction on the road to military confrontation was unknowable. But by convincing the president and Cheney to give her plan a try, Rice had likely saved the international coalition. She had also demonstrated her ability to move her boss in a bold direction of her own, not just to mirror his views. Abroad, the offer proved that America was willing to talk to its adversaries, and at home it showed that Rice had not drunk the neocon Kool-Aid.

Rice's standing inside the administration was bolstered by the political reality that she was the only member of the Bush team with a positive approval rating; a Harris poll in June found her approval rating twenty points higher than Bush's. Surprisingly, a *Washington Post* poll the same month found that only one in ten Americans believed Rice bore "a lot" of responsibility for the war in Iraq; forty-three percent said she bore little or no responsibility. Among those who approved of her performance as secretary of state, fifty-eight percent said it was mostly because of her professional abilities; only twenty percent said it was because of her policy views, and only nine percent said it was because of her personal qualities.[69] But an *Esquire* survey of one thousand men found that Rice was the woman they would most like to take as a date to a dinner party, ahead of Angelina Jolie, Julia Roberts, Oprah Winfrey, and Jennifer Aniston.[70]

The contradictions of the Rice doctrine of "practical idealism" revealed themselves on July 12, when Hezbollah guerillas fired two short-range missiles from their stronghold in southern Lebanon into northern Israel. The missiles were a diversion to allow guerillas to steal across the border, kill three Israeli soldiers, and kidnap two others. The ambush followed months of rising tensions in the region. Hamas, democratically elected to govern the Palestinian territories in January, had kidnapped an Israeli soldier in Gaza three weeks earlier. Israeli prime minister Ehud Olmert declared the Hezbollah abductions an "act of war," and, in a move that surprised Israel's allies and enemies alike, he ordered the bombing of southern Lebanon and sent Israeli troops across the border for the first time since 2000. But Israel's forces troops encountered unanticipated resistance from Hezbollah and five more Israeli soldiers were killed. In response, Olmert called up the reserves.

Rice issued a statement giving relatively short shrift to the Lebanese civilian casualties, epitomizing the tension Hans Morgenthau had noted between idealism and the less "morally satisfying" imperatives of realism.

I condemn today's kidnapping by Hezbollah, a terrorist organization, of two Israeli soldiers. Hezbollah's action undermines regional stability and goes against the interests of both the Israeli and Lebanese people.

I have spoken with UN Secretary General [Kofi] Annan, Lebanese
Prime Minister [Fouad] Siniora, and Israeli Foreign Minister [Tzipi]
Livni.

We are united in our determination to achieve the release of the
Israeli soldiers. Syria has a special responsibility [given its support of
the Hezbollah guerillas] to use its influence to support a positive outcome. All sides must act with restraint to resolve this incident peacefully and to protect innocent life and civilian infrastructure.[71]

But neither side acted with restraint, and within days, Israel and Hezbollah
were waging a full-scale war. While the UN and the Europeans called for an
immediate cease-fire, Rice insisted, "We have to deal with the underlying causes
here, and the underlying cause is that extremist forces . . . have determined that
it is time now to try and arrest the move toward moderate democratic forces in
the Middle East, like the young state of Lebanon or the movement toward a two-
state solution in the Palestinian territories."[72] On day ten of the war, Rice called
the conflict "the birth pangs of a new Middle East."[73]

Only the roots of the conflict between Israel and Hezbollah were much older
than Bush's Freedom Agenda—just like Iraq's sectarian divisions. And Rice's
reasoning seemed to ignore that Hezbollah was part of Lebanon's democratically
elected government, just as Hamas were the elected rulers of the Palestinian territories. In fact, the extremists were doing pretty well under the Freedom Agenda.
And the longer this war went on, killing Lebanese civilians, the more "the Arab
street" backed the extremists.

Washington's agendas were working at cross-purposes. On the one hand, the
administration was taking a classic realist view: Let Israel degrade Hezbollah as
much as possible before calling for a cease-fire. But on the other hand, the
administration's idealist agenda dictated that it support the democratic government in Lebanon. To square the circle, the White House hoped for an Israeli
victory that would weaken Hezbollah both militarily and politically inside the
Beirut government.

State Department counselor Phil Zelikow advised Rice to go to Israel, not to
start work on a cease-fire, but to show solidarity with the Israelis who were
under constant missile attack and to ascertain Israel's military strategy and goals.
"We were already uneasy about what their strategy was," said Zelikow.[74]

But Rice and Bush believed she should wait, so instead she accompanied Bush to a G8 summit in Russia, did a quick stopover in Jerusalem and Beirut afterward, and then headed for a regional summit in Asia. As a result, the United States didn't learn until it was too late that Prime Minister Olmert didn't have a military strategy. By the time Rice traveled to the region to start real cease-fire talks, three weeks into the war, Zelikow said, "it was already at a point where the Israeli operation seemed to lack strategic focus. Yet, at the same time, it was causing tremendous damage in Lebanon that had now undermined the position of the [Lebanese] government and the Arab center."[75]

In other words, Bush and Rice's Morgenthauian gamble—to let Israel seize the opportunity presented by the kidnappings to weaken Hezbollah—had become a runaway train. The administration still believed that military might could create "a balance of power that favors freedom," remaking the political landscape into one where democracy could take root. But it was a simplistic calculation: Remove Saddam, degrade Hezbollah, and voilà. The logic ignored the political realities and the histories of nations and assumed that because all peoples yearned to be free, democracy would flower if given the opportunity.

In the case of the Israeli-Hezbollah war, the argument failed for an even simpler reason: Israel was not winning. In fact, Hezbollah was proving surprisingly resilient and was still killing Israeli civilians after three weeks of war. From a realist's point of view, both the Americans and the Israelis had committed the cardinal sin: Rather than demonstrating their power in what they believed would be quick, low-cost wars—in Iraq and in Lebanon, respectively—they had revealed the limits of their might.

On the second day of Rice's negotiations, as she talked with the Israeli defense minister, an Israeli missile attack killed dozens of civilians in a bomb shelter in the southern Lebanese town of Qana. Original estimates placed the dead at more than sixty. Now U.S.-allied Arab leaders from Cairo to Amman who had quietly supported the attack on Hezbollah voiced outrage. All day that Sunday, images of dead children being pulled from the rubble in Qana, their faces caked with blood and debris, dominated Arab television.

One of Rice's aides received the news on his BlackBerry in a message from the U.S. ambassador in Beirut. Rice ended her meeting and went to the hotel conference room where her traveling press corps was holed up. She extended her condolences to the Lebanese people and said she would not go to Lebanon to

continue the negotiations as she had planned, insisting that it had been her decision and she had not been disinvited by the Beirut government. Though the
United States still wasn't calling for an immediate cease-fire and blocked efforts
at the UN to do so, Rice said, "We are pushing for an urgent end to the current
hostilities. But the views of the parties on how to achieve this are different."[76]

It was the first public acknowledgment that the United States and its Israeli
allies were not on the same page. And Rice's stress was starting to show.

> The United States has been working harder, and harder and hard-
> er . . . I would remind [everyone] that it is because the United States
> pressed and worked with Israel to get the airport open so that human-
> itarian flights could get in that that got done. It is because the United
> States pressed for humanitarian corridors, that that got done . . .
>
> We want the Security Council to take [the cease-fire issue] up
> soon, and we want the Security Council to take it up with as much
> concrete progress toward a real cease-fire, as is humanly possible by
> the time that that meeting takes place. So, I will continue to work, and
> work and work; that is what we can do. If there is any way humanly,
> to accelerate our efforts, I would do it. But we are already doing really
> what is of the human limitation to try to get to an end of this con-
> flict.

After negotiating with the Israelis all day, Rice finally convinced them to
suspend their air campaign for forty-eight hours. Back home, the neocons dis-
paraged her cold-then-hot diplomacy, pointing out that the real problem was
Syria and, increasingly, Iran, which was supplying Hezbollah with missiles and
equipment through Syrian territory. You couldn't remake the Middle East with
Iran, the ultimate spoiler, sitting in the region and about to acquire nuclear
weapons. It was the same case Rice had made to her friend Chip Blacker about
Saddam Hussein.

As Rice left the region on Monday, July 31, she said she had an "emerging
consensus" that would end the war and leave Lebanon in control of all its territory and Israel free of the Hezbollah threat. But the root cause of the conflict, the
reason the Americans and Israelis had given for not halting the fighting sooner—
the disarmament of Hezbollah—would be left to the Lebanese government.[77]

Clara Rice had been reading the blistering criticism of Condoleezza for not traveling to the Middle East sooner, the first widespread disapproval of the job she was doing as secretary of state. Clara was appalled by an article someone sent her that called for Condoleezza's resignation. Though she never told Condi, Clara worried about her. She would ask Condoleezza if she was getting enough rest, and Condi, like her father, would insist, "'Oh, I'm fine. I'm great. This is wonderful. I *love* what I'm doing.' But I don't believe it," said Clara Rice. "Sometimes she looks like she really can use some rest."[78]

Rice called her stepmother the day she returned to Washington.

"Did you make any headway over there this time?" Clara asked.

"Yeah, I think by the end of the week we might get these people to stop shooting," said Condi, "because too many people are dying." Clara told Condoleezza that Clara's church was praying for her: "Just keep doing what you're doing. You're doing great."

Rice's Aunt G knew better than to fret. "I used to worry about Condoleezza, but I turned that over to the Lord," said McPhatter. "I would be a nut case if I worried about Condoleezza."[79]

Back in Washington and then New York, Rice led U.S. and French efforts to hammer out a UN resolution. Israel objected to using the same ineffectual UN force that had been in southern Lebanon before the war and had allowed Hezbollah's attacks in the first place. The Arabs and the Lebanese wanted the resolution to call for the immediate withdrawal of Israeli troops, but Israel wanted to remain in Lebanon until an international force arrived. French president Jacques Chirac was leery about committing French troops, which everyone assumed would be the backbone of an international force.

Rice and UN secretary general Kofi Annan worked to overcome the roadblocks. They would strategize and decide who needed to agree to what, then Annan would call a foreign capital and come back with the necessary agreement; then they would start the process over again. Rice was a skillful negotiator. She had brokered a crucial border crossing deal between the Israelis and Palestinians the previous November in the Bush administration's first foray into Mideast peace efforts. In a formidable demonstration of will and endurance, Rice had worked straight through, staying up one night until 4 a.m. to force concessions from the two sides.[80] Unfortunately, two months later, Hamas's election would once again squelch hopes for peace. Rice's excellence as a tactician couldn't redress the administration's flawed strategic vision—that extremists could come to power through democratic elections, for instance—inevitably limiting her ability to effect real progress.

The cease-fire between Israel and Hezbollah began at 8 a.m. local time on August 14. In thirty-four days of war, twelve hundred Lebanese had been killed, mostly civilians, and 156 Israelis were dead, mostly soldiers. An arms embargo was imposed to keep Hezbollah from being resupplied by Syria and Iran, but the group didn't disarm, and the Beirut government was too weak to force it to.

Rice turned her attention back to Iraq, returning to Baghdad in October. Progress on the political track had not improved security, but Rice still believed it could: "The ability to get a national reconciliation plan, to get [the various sectarian and ethnic groups] to understand precisely how their interests are going to be represented and how their interests are going to be served in this political process, to pull more people into the political process and out of the insurgency, more people into the political process and out of connections with militias, that's why the political process is so central." Though she linked politics and security, Rice emphasized that the immediate security issue—where there had been no progress—was not her responsibility; it was Don Rumsfeld's.[81]

In congressional testimony in August, General John Abizaid, the U.S. commander in the Middle East, had conceded that Iraq could spiral into civil war, but on her fifth trip to Iraq as secretary of state, Rice gave that possibility no quarter, insisting that the world had to give Bush and Maliki's new troop surge "a chance to work."

"What the American people see on their television screens is the struggle. It is harder to show the political progress that is going on at local levels, at provincial levels, and indeed at the national level," said Rice. But a major reason for her trip was that the Iraqis were making insufficient progress on outstanding political issues: how the sectarian and ethnic groups would divide oil revenues, what degree of autonomy the provinces would have, and how militias would be disbanded.[82] And it didn't help the secretary's argument that after listening to her praise Iraq's progress, the reporters traveling with her experienced its instability firsthand. Their plane had to circle Baghdad International for close to an hour because the airport was under attack.[83] Then, while Rice met with President Jalal Talabani, the electricity went out.[84] But the Bush administration had a two-pronged message on Iraq for the fall congressional campaign: Admit that the situation is difficult so the president doesn't look out of touch or in denial, but at the same time project confidence that the mission will succeed. Only the American public had grown deeply skeptical of the adventure in Iraq, and the more Rice insisted progress was being made, however nuanced her statements, the more she jeopardized her credibility, just as the administration had diminished its own over the course of the war. In fact, the ultimate risk of Rice's tenure in George Bush's Washington was the creeping belief that her loyalty to the president and his policies had overwhelmed either her judgment, her perception, or both. Or, as Barbara Boxer had charged, her loyalty to the truth.

The last charge wasn't fair; Rice believed what she said. But her determination to not show doubt or vulnerability, her unsurpassed discipline at staying on message, her need to win every argument, her faith in her own skills of persuasion, and her ability to convince herself of reality as she chose to see it—all traits that had contributed to her historic rise—conspired against the transparent frankness of, say, a Colin Powell. Condoleezza Rice didn't do confessions.

When Rice returned to Washington, she reprised the controversial role she had played as a partisan spokesperson in the campaign in 2000 with her rousing address to the RNC and in 2004 with her speeches in swing states just before the election. During "Radio Day" at the White House on October 24, Rice gave interviews to a succession of mostly conservative talk radio hosts invited to Washington to get the president's message out to his base. Even more controversially, in an interview with *Essence* magazine—for their Power Issue, though Rice still hadn't made the cover—she compared those calling for the withdrawal of U.S. troops from Iraq to Northerners who wanted to end the Civil War before the slaves were freed.[85]

That tough talk about the need to stay in Iraq now was meant to complement Bush's new modesty about the mistakes of the past. When the president had been asked in July, for instance, what mistakes he most regretted, he said his bravado—daring the insurgents to "bring it on" in 2003[86] and slogans like "wanted dead or alive," referring to Osama bin Laden. "I learned some lessons about expressing myself maybe in a little more sophisticated manner," said Bush.[87] Until then, acknowledging any mistakes had been rare. When Bush was asked the same question during the second presidential debate in 2004, he had said he couldn't think of a single mistake he had made on the "big questions."[88]

Having run in 2000 on a platform of humility and competence—a platform constructed largely by Condoleezza Rice—Bush had come full circle. But the president found contrition too late. When voters went to the polls on November 7, they handed Bush and congressional Republicans one of the harshest rebukes in recent political history. According to the final exit polls, the Democrats won an outright majority of votes nationwide and fifty-seven percent of Independent voters, compared with thirty-nine percent who supported Republican candidates. The Democrats even captured a majority of male voters, a rarity in elections over the last forty years. In the end, the Democrats gained thirty-one seats in the House and six in the Senate, giving them their first majority in both houses since the Republican Revolution of 1994.[89]

President Bush declared it a "thumpin'" and the next day announced Donald Rumsfeld's resignation. (The secretary of state wasn't able to make it to Rumsfeld's farewell ceremony; she was hosting a luncheon for outgoing UN secretary general Kofi Annan.)

On the heels of the thumping, the Iraq Study Group (ISG), the bipartisan panel led by Bush's father's secretary of state, James Baker, released its long-awaited report. Baker conceded the commission had held off until after the mid-term elections to avoid the taint of electoral politics, unlike the 9/11 commission. Declaring the situation in Iraq "grave and deteriorating," the ISG stated categorically, "Current U.S. policy is not working . . . Making no changes in policy would simply delay the day of reckoning."[90]

Bush called the report constructive but seemed to reject out of hand two of its key proposals: threatening to withhold economic and military support from the Baghdad government unless it made progress cracking down on militias and death squads, and talking to Iran and Syria to enlist their help in stabilizing Iraq. The president pointed out that he was awaiting parallel reviews from the State Department, the NSC, and the Pentagon before deciding on a new course in Iraq, a course he would unveil in the weeks before Christmas.

For her part, the secretary of state was uncharacteristically silent for two days. When she finally spoke, she was both respectful and aloof, a study in velvet forcefulness. "I think it's a very good report, and it's done by people that I admire and have known for a very long time," Rice said. "None of us see the situation in Iraq as favorable. We all see it as extremely difficult . . . But I also recognize that the Iraqis have made a commitment to a unified Iraq in the political leadership, that they have a number of structures at their disposal to try to address this, and that we need to give them better tools including particularly on the security side."[91]

When it came to talking to Iran and Syria, Rice took a hard line. "[If] Iran . . . does not want an unstable Iraq [or] Syria does not want an unstable Iraq . . . they will act on that, because it's in their interest to do so."

Rice was still a realist, but a realist who had been mugged by 9/11. "One of the most important fundamentals to get right is that the Middle East has suffered for sixty years from a freedom deficit. It has suffered from the absence of legitimate channels for political expression. It has suffered from the absence of democratic change at a time when the entire rest of the world . . . moved to [democracy]. And the absence of that democratization in the Middle East led . . . to the maturation of extremist political forces at the expense of moderate political forces who had no legitimate channels." In other words, it led to September 11.

That was why, Rice said, "as we address the future of the Middle East, the importance of the democratic reforms . . . will continue to be a centerpiece, or perhaps the centerpiece, of the administration's foreign policy. [And] in both Syria and Iran you have states that have chosen to be on the side of the divide that is fueling extremism, not moderation."

Rice's analysis was the opposite of Baker's. The ISG report had pointedly made no mention of the administration's goal of spreading democracy in the Middle East, other than to state, "Most of the region's countries are wary of U.S. efforts."[92] When he released the report, Baker had gone even further. Mocking the idealists who had dreamed that Iraq could be the fulcrum of a democratic Middle East, he said flatly, "Struggling in a world of fear, the Iraqis themselves dare not dream. They have been liberated from the nightmare of a tyrannical order only to face the nightmare of brutal violence."[93] Baker and his fellow commissioners were not merely critiquing "Junior's" handling of Iraq; they were repudiating the naïveté that animated it. And Rice was fighting back, insisting that the democratization agenda would continue to dictate the administration's actions because until the region was free America wouldn't be safe. It was the crux of the Republican foreign policy civil war: Bush 43 vs. Bush 41. Realists vs. idealists. Cut a deal to stabilize Iraq or fight on to change the Middle East. It was the same "unresolved tension" that, like the music of Brahms, had raged inside

Rice since she had first learned the name of Hans Morgenthau. It was the fight in which Rice had seemingly switched sides after September 11. But she hadn't; she had found her "practical idealism." The ISG report would end up a political orphan, with neither Democrats nor Republicans backing it, but the divisions that it illustrated within the Republican foreign policy establishment would endure.

Armed with a sense of the Baker group's recommendations, Bush had taken a preemptive swipe at the realists the week before, insisting, "It's in our interest to help liberty prevail in the Middle East, starting with Iraq. And that's why this business about graceful exit just simply has no realism to it at all."[94] After the ISG report was released, Tony Blair made Bush's point better than the president had: "The only realistic path to security is by ensuring the spread of liberty . . . In my view, the only modern form of realism is one that has ideals at the center of it."[95]

Then Bush quoted Blair to explain why the situation in Iraq was so dire. "The prime minister put it this way. He said, 'The violence is not the result of faulty planning. It is a deliberate strategy. It is the direct result of outside extremists teaming up with internal extremists—al-Qaeda with the Sunni insurgents, and Iran with the Shia militia—to foment hatred and to throttle, at birth, the possibility of a nonsectarian democracy.'"[96]

That was what Rice believed, too: The violence in the region came from extremists fighting to make sure the new political forces supporting democracy—in Iraq, in Lebanon, in the Palestinian territories—didn't take root. Rice couldn't believe otherwise. To do so would suggest that her decision to stay on for the second term had been futile, and that the region had nonetheless taken "turns and directions that [weren't] very good."[97]

CHAPTER THIRTEEN

HISTORY

I've always felt that I've gotten where I am because I follow what interests me instead of worrying about the job market or what I ought to do. I'm also a very religious person and believe it's God's will to do certain things. You can't be rigid about your life. You can't have it all planned out far ahead of time.[1]

CONDOLEEZZA RICE
Stanford Magazine
Winter 1985

After postponing the announcement of his new strategy for stabilizing Iraq until after Christmas, President Bush went on national television on January 10 to unveil his plan. The centerpiece of Bush's "New Way Forward" was increasing security in Baghdad. He would send more than twenty-one thousand additional U.S. troops to Iraq. The United States would also increase funding and oversight of reconstruction teams, accelerate the training of Iraqi police and military, and embed American military advisers in Iraqi units, which, the president noted, the Iraq Study Group had recommended. Once the violence was reduced and the government in Baghdad was secure, U.S. troops would withdraw, Bush said.

> The changes I have outlined tonight are aimed at ensuring the survival of a young democracy that is fighting for its life in a part of the world of enormous importance to American security . . .
> Times of testing reveal the character of a nation. And throughout our history, Americans have always defied the pessimists and

seen our faith in freedom redeemed. Now America is engaged in a
new struggle that will set the course for a new century. We can, and
we will, prevail.[2]

Despite the force of his closing words, the president appeared discomfitingly
sober, even morose. "With his knitted brow and stricken features, he looked,
well, scared," observed *Newsweek*'s Howard Fineman.[3] MSNBC aired a chron-
ological succession of clips from the president's past speeches on Iraq, and the
evolution was startling. Bush's mien went from boldly confident to visibly uncertain. After watching the clips, conservative commentator Pat Buchanan said they
depicted "the death of ideology."[4] Coming from the man who had declared at the
1992 Republican National Convention that America was fighting a culture war,
it was a significant statement. "Ideology is like religion," said Buchanan. "You
could see the president speaking out of a devout faith that we shall prevail in
those earlier clips. And the last clips are like someone who has lost his faith, who
no longer believes in that god."

More than two-thirds of Americans opposed the latest "surge," including
General John Abizaid, the longtime U.S. commander in the Middle East. Critics
said it was as if the president had taken no notice of the election two months
earlier or of Jim Baker's Iraq Study Group, though Bush seemed to acknowledge
his differences with Baker's commission when he said, "In the long run, the most
realistic way to protect the American people is . . . by advancing liberty across a
troubled region."

Condoleezza Rice agreed. Testifying before the Senate Foreign Relations
Committee the next day, she faced unrelenting skepticism about the new plan,
from Democrats and Republicans alike. But Rice fought back as determinedly as
ever, giving no quarter to the skeptics and arguing that the surge was not a military "escalation" but an "augmentation." The president's ability to project confidence might have withered, but Rice's had not. Whatever Bush's state, his
"sister" was undiminished.

For all their similarities, Rice and Bush differed in one essential aspect.
Bush had never had to overcome obstacles as fundamental or as formidable as
those overcome by Rice. She had spent the most formative years of her life willing away realities she did not want to see. She still believed America could
change the world. We had done it during Bush's father's term—she had been

there. And we could do it again. In fact, we must do it again, because until we did America would not be safe. And should Condoleezza Rice ever lose faith in the administration's course in Iraq, she had the force of will to ensure that no one would see it.

That discipline could prove to be her greatest service yet to George W. Bush, even greater than the foreign policy credibility she had given him in 2000, which transformed him into a plausible world leader. For the final two years of Bush's term, whatever course he pursued in Iraq, Rice would be the unfailing avatar of his faith.

In reality, the administration's ability to influence Iraq's future was limited. Washington could increase security in Baghdad temporarily, but the United States could not produce an enduring political settlement between Shiites, Sunnis, and Kurds; Rice had been trying to encourage just that for most of her time in Washington. But like Bush, she believed that withdrawing from Iraq before it was stable would haunt America for generations, potentially creating an oil-rich failed state that would harbor Islamic terrorists likely to launch the next 9/11. That was a legacy neither Bush nor Rice was willing to live with. And to keep it from happening, Bush would pay any price, including watching his presidency end in a hail of recriminations. If there was no way to withdraw without Iraq falling apart, then he was unlikely to withdraw at all and Rice's unflappable discipline would be more crucial than ever.

But the ultimate judgment of the public face of Condoleezza Rice would depend not on her impressive performances but on what she accomplished in her last two years as secretary of state. Just as Kissinger's tactics and motives in the Nixon administration had been overshadowed by his strategic legacy, particularly the decision to establish relations with "Red China," Rice's stature as "a world historical figure," as her friend Chip Blacker put it, would be determined by what kind of world she left behind.

Bush had announced in his speech that Rice would be traveling to the Middle East to bolster support for the Baghdad government and to "continue the urgent diplomacy" to end the Palestinian–Israeli conflict. If Rice could pave the way for a historic accord between Arabs and Israelis, accomplishing what no other secretary of state had been able to, then that would be her legacy, the headline of her obituary. But the obstacles to realizing a lasting peace had not disappeared. And Iran, as well as Iraq, would complicate Rice's mission.

As U.S forces surged into Baghdad, an additional aircraft carrier group moved to the Persian Gulf. Bush pledged that the United States would "work with others to prevent Iran from gaining nuclear weapons," but speculation exploded in Washington that Iran could be the administration's next war of choice. Rice had skillfully shepherded the Europeans toward imposing UN sanctions in December, sanctions that by January were already putting pressure on Iran's economy. But if those sanctions failed to stop Tehran's march toward nuclear weapons, military action before the end of Bush's term seemed more likely than not.

Then there was North Korea. In February 2007, Rice and her chief negotiator Christopher Hill managed to get a deal that would freeze North Korea's nuclear activities and allow weapons inspectors back into the country. The agreement was immediately criticized for allowing Pyongyang to keep an estimated half-dozen bombs—most of which it had built in the years the Bush administration had refused to negotiate—and for being no better than the 1994 agreement the Clinton administration had reached with North Korea, the terms of which Bush's team had been rejecting for more than four years. Nonetheless, if the deal held, it would be one of Rice's undisputable victories. She had pushed it forward, refusing to let it get bogged down in the normal interagency process, where the vice president's office and the Pentagon had derailed past attempts at a deal, and she had convinced Bush to sign off on it.[5] It was a long way from the role she had played as national security adviser in the first term.

Rice will be judged on all these issues, though none more so than Iraq. Her former boss and employee Bob Blackwill called it the sad and poignant part of Rice's tenure. "Her diplomacy in a classic Metternichian sense is quite skillful—and not up to the task," said Blackwill, "because the correlation of forces are against us." He believed the war in Iraq was a handicap that even Rice couldn't overcome.

"What is Condi as secretary of state and national security adviser without the Iraq War? It's different," Blackwill sighed. "It's different."

If Rice completes her term as secretary of state, she will step down on January 20, 2009, almost exactly twenty years after she came to Washington as a member of Brent Scowcroft's NSC. She will be fifty-four years old. She will have spent more than half of her adult life in leadership positions, including ten years in senior jobs in Washington. Ironically, power had not been her initial goal. Success had been. Power was a happy coincidence.

In fact, after the one pursuit in which Rice had invested most of her young life evaporated—a career as a concert pianist—she never set another long-term goal. And once it was clear that she lacked the disciplined abandon to become a pianist, all that was left was the discipline. It was that "home training" imparted by her parents that led Rice to the limitless boundaries they had promised were her birthright. She spent the rest of her life plunging into work, passing from one set of short-term objectives to the next, from one performance to the next. Each performance led to accomplishment, and each accomplishment led to further opportunity.

But what drove her was drive. And with no defined destination, Rice followed the true north of the men who inspired her: Hans Morgenthau, Josef Korbel, George W. Bush. And, before them all, John Rice.

But in a sense, Rice seems to have stopped dreaming, at least as most of us dream: for the distant, the transcendent, the impossible. If she didn't dream, then she couldn't be denied. Hope—whether for a political office, a changed world, or a relationship—usually depends on external forces. Discipline, on the other hand, depends solely on the will of the self.

Rice's future will undoubtedly be one of still more accomplishments. As opportunities inevitably present themselves, her résumé will lengthen with new titles—all impressive, some probably history making—but she will likely never attain the greatness that comes from setting one's sites on a far horizon and trudging toward it.

Of course, Condoleezza Rice already has led a life of significance, touching and changing important institutions—not to mention, as a teacher, inspiring untold numbers of young men and women to try to understand the world. She enhanced undergraduate education at Stanford and righted the university's finances. At the State Department, she steered American foreign policy from the unilateralism of George Bush's first term to engagement and alliance management in the second, and she restructured the diplomatic corps.[6]

In leading each institution, Rice had her faults. For instance, however the ledger of her tenure as Stanford provost balances—fiscal and academic health on one side, community dissension and fear on the other—the situation for women faculty in particular in the post-Casper–Rice years attests to what was—and is—possible. Under Rice's successor, John Hennessy, women became deans of schools in greater numbers, and Hennessy raised funds for women in science years before Larry Summers's controversial tenure at Harvard focused national attention on the issue.

Of course, the Department of Labor investigation hanging over Stanford may have encouraged Hennessy's gender outreach. And perhaps it was more politics and perception than reality—the numbers of tenured women and minorities have not increased significantly, for, as Rice said, change in faculty makeup is endemically slow—but professors and administrators alike describe an atmosphere at Stanford where, as one official put it, "the sun has come out after the long night."[7] Inarguably, the female faculty's morale has improved.[8]

Rice's transformational diplomacy makeover of the State Department will likely be a less checkered success. Her decision to move positions from First World to developing nations and to emphasize diplomats getting into the field holds at least the possibility that the world may come to know the United States by more than the often negative stereotypes of power and avarice it now holds. And then there's the first factor. Rice has attained far more than the circumstances of her birth ever suggested possible. And in that sense, the lessons her life teaches are universal: No circumstance can conquer the individual dedicated to achievement—admittedly, somewhat ironically, since Rice for all her storied history faced relatively little personal adversity. But for millions of African Americans, and not just African Americans but all Americans; and not just women, but also men—Rice's life demonstrates the power of inner will in overcoming external constraints.

By virtue of her sex and her race, the lessons do carry a special significance. Rice has allowed millions to see themselves in places of power where they might not have had the vision to see themselves before. And, as important, she has taught others to see them there, too; as Rice's friend and Stanford colleague Lucius Barker put it, "World leaders have to meet [with] this black woman."[9]

From a realist's point of view, Rice's greatest success has been her ability to accrue personal power. That had not been her initial goal; but nonetheless, she never let ideology or even consistency get in the way of fulfilling whatever she judged to be in her interest at a given time. As important, Rice was unencumbered by a "personal myth structure," as Chip Blacker called it, which cast her as an outsider, unlike many women, people of color, and members of other minority groups. Condoleezza Rice never conceived of herself as a stranger to the corridors of power. She believed she belonged.

But Rice's story suggests there also is a price to be paid. For just as her life is a powerful lesson on the rewards of being phenomenally prepared and the virtues of being open to possibilities, it is also a cautionary tale of how an intensely centered will can obscure circumstances, perspectives, and people outside one's purview. Said Harry Elam, another Rice friend and Stanford professor, "In terms of the things that [Condi] did, yes, I would like my daughter to feel incredibly good about herself, that she as a black person can achieve in this country, that she can be an ice skater, or a musician, or whatever she wants to be." But as a road map to success, at least for black people, Elam said Rice's example is limited "because of the way she talked about [her accomplishments]. It's an individual success."

But so far, Rice's firsts are her most significant legacies: not what she has accomplished but what she has attained. There is nothing small in being first. But this is a different world from civil rights–era America, and just being the first is no longer enough. Even being twice as good is not necessarily good enough; black and female leaders, like all leaders, are judged by what they achieve.

And in that mundane sense, Rice has so far fallen short. The Middle East, for instance, may emerge tomorrow as a more stable, more democratic group of polities than it was yesterday. But in the short-term it seems a long way from here to there. Indeed, the government's own analyses, from the Intelligence Community and from the military, judge the world to be no safer than it was on September 11. And while the war in Iraq, in particular, was meant to be a rapid demonstration of American power, in the end the experience has sapped the nation's will and resources, and instead exposed the limits of American might. From a realist perspective, then, while Rice has succeeded in increasing her own personal power, she has failed to enhance America's internationally.

There is plenty of time for Rice to raze new barriers; her story is still being written. In addition to what she accomplishes with the remainder of her term as secretary of state, her legacy will depend on what she achieves afterward, whether those accomplishments are in corporate America, in academia, or in politics. Given her phenomenal will and capabilities, she may yet become not just the first, not just the only, but the best.

Rice herself had not decided in the winter of 2007 what she would do after January 20, 2009. Her friends and family suspect Condoleezza will spend her post-Bush years in business or academia. They are certain she will not seek a university presidency, since Rice turned down multiple offers while she was provost at Stanford. "If I had to guess," said her friend Randy Bean, "I would say CEO of a multinational. That would put her in the place where she could recoup the financial sacrifice she [will have] made over the last eight years and she'd be running something. . . . She could run JP Morgan Chase and make a lot of money in a year.[10]

"But I also think there is this thing that she can't control, which is Bush basically. . . . She cannot say no to that guy. I think that's the only variable."

John McCain, one of the 2008 GOP front-runners, likes Condi Rice. And she also would make a formidable pair with Rudy Giuliani, the other Republican favorite. If either of the early Democratic leaders for 2008, Hillary Clinton or Barack Obama, captures their party's nomination, Rice may come under considerable pressure to join the Republican presidential ticket, depending on the state of Iraq in 2008. "She has said repeatedly that she has no desire to run for president," said a Washington friend, "but she wouldn't mind being recruited [for vice president]."[11]

Said veteran Republican strategist Charles Black, "I would be surprised if whoever the Republican nominee is does not offer [her] the vice presidency . . . With a Condi Rice on the ticket—with somebody at the top of the ticket that [black] people were comfortable with—maybe you'd get an extra ten percent of the African American vote, which could be decisive in the election. But again I premise it on that comfort level [with] the top. Somebody needs to be known and have something of a track record" with African Americans.[12] Many of Rice's friends and close colleagues believe she would find the vice presidency hard to turn down if it were offered. But as usual, that is a decision Rice will make only when faced with it; she won't plan on it.

While those close to Rice say they couldn't see her in the U.S. Senate—merely one of one hundred—they say she could run for governor of California. Politics have beckoned Rice since her early days at Stanford, when friends said she briefly considered a run for Congress. Twenty years later, while she was serving as national security adviser, California Republicans approached her about challenging then-Governor Gray Davis before Arnold Schwarzenegger stepped forward and defeated Davis in the 2003 recall election. Should Rice decide to run for governor of California in 2010, when Schwarzenegger's term ends, she will be fifty-five years old. Rice has never said publicly that she wants the job, but she hasn't excluded the possibility privately. As a pro-choice, pro–gay rights, pro-gun Republican, she would be well positioned for a California run.

Chip Blacker, who told a student more than a decade ago, "Mark my words, she's going to be president," believes Rice doesn't know herself whether she will pursue a political career. In a real sense, the decision is out of her hands. "She is a genuine Calvinist, in the sense that it's not about God's plan—because that has an arrogant quality to it—it's God's will," said Blacker. "It's this notion that there is an all-knowing, all-seeing, all-caring God whose will will determine the course of our lives. And we're not smart enough because we're limited human beings to have access to that. But in Condi's case, she knows it when she sees it.[13]

"I believe that Condi's view is if it's going to happen, it's going to happen. If it doesn't, it's no big deal. 'I've led a life of consequence and I have no regrets.'"

If, as the pundits predicted in the aftermath of the 2006 elections, the future of the Republican Party lies in its ability to appeal not just to Southern conservatives, now its regional base, but to Western libertarians[14] and traditional moderate Republicans, then Condoleezza Rice may be the candidate of the future. Her politics are better suited to the new age of Republicanism—assuming that it has arrived, which will likely be one of the debates of the 2008 primaries—than to the old. As Rice explains, for example, on the issue of same-sex marriage, "I believe marriage is between a man and a woman, but I've been of the view that this is something society will work out over time. And I certainly believe that gay people can be as good friends, as good citizens as anybody. Two of my *best* friends are gay. And I have never wanted to see any sense that somehow these were people who were *lesser* citizens. [The] Defense of Marriage Act, I guess, is one thing. The Constitution to me is something you change *rarely*."[15]

On her stance on abortion rights, Rice says she is mildly pro-choice, "or largely pro-life. Put it either way. . . . I think the country isn't ready for a change in the law [to outlaw abortion], but I am *really* conflicted, particularly as it becomes clearer and clearer that life can be sustained earlier and earlier."

Rice's stepmother, Clara, doesn't believe Rice will run for office—for one reason: "It is very difficult for Condoleezza to lose. She doesn't want to hear the word! And if she thinks she's going to lose something she doesn't go near it—because [of] just the thought of 'I wasn't good enough. I lost.'"[16]

Should Rice run for elective office—especially for president some day—more would be at stake than just the possibility of failure. With few exceptions, her very closest friends are Democrats, and on social issues they are liberal Democrats. Should she have to take a political stance opposing her best friends, the contradictions of the public Condi and the private Condi would clash as never before. As Randy Bean put it, "I'd hate to see what the gaping jaws of politics would do to her."[17] Both Bean and Blacker said there were points beyond which Rice's public pronouncements might place an unendurable strain on their relationships. In essence, that line was opposition to equal rights for lesbians and gays. "The true test of her character will be if and when that moment comes," said Blacker.[18]

"This is where the danger is, it just cracks . . . and she has to choose." His voice revealed a dread clearly more profound than politics. "It's hard. Politicians, like professional athletes, are a species apart. And she's not a natural politician. She's charismatic. She's a natural leader. But she's not a politician. I just don't know how she would handle that. And I don't think she's eager to find out. This isn't someone who goes home and in the privacy of her bedroom whistles 'Hail to the Chief.' She doesn't do it."

Adds Bean—who's still holding Rice's Stanford football season tickets—"You know there's something that just aches [inside her]. She just wants to make a home for herself and settle and be a normal person and not be the star of the world."

Or maybe that's just a "sister's" wishful thinking.

Whatever she does in 2009, for the next two years Condoleezza Rice will remain on message. She says George W. Bush has made the world freer. The oppressive Taliban theocracy has been toppled in Afghanistan. Iraq is under a democratically elected government. After thirty years of dominance, Syria is out of Lebanon, Hezbollah is not firing missiles into Israel, and the Palestinians and Israelis are talking. And women are voting in Kuwait, Saudi Arabia is holding municipal elections, and from Bahrain and Oman to Morocco and Jordan, political reform is alive in the Arab world.

When a *Washington Post* reporter pointed out to Rice in December 2006 that Richard Haass, president of the Council on Foreign Relations and a former top aide to Colin Powell, says the United States is in a more vulnerable position than it's been in decades, and that another international analyst calls this "the worst position we have been in as a nation since December 8, 1941," Rice didn't miss a beat. "When the international system starts rearranging itself the way that it is rearranging itself currently," she said, "it's turbulent and it's often violent." Rice compared events in Iraq and the Middle East to the end of World War II, when America's role was to be the promoter and protector of freedom. "The old bargains in the Middle East have really collapsed," she said.[19]

> There is a new relationship brought about largely by Iraq that is going to have to emerge between Sunnis and Shia . . . There is a debate that is going on within Islam . . . about the role of politics and religion . . . There is a freeing up of political systems that has exposed the relative weakness of moderate political forces vis-à-vis more extreme political forces which were organized. Those are all emerging. But of course with any challenge of that kind, there also comes certain opportunities. And as the Middle East is rearranging itself, it's also creating new alliances and new opportunities. On the one side of the divide you have Iran, Hezbollah, Hamas, and Syria, which has chosen to throw its weight on that side of the ledger. On the other you have the so-called moderate Arab states, I'll call them mainstream states—Saudi Arabia, Jordan, Egypt, the Gulf states. And strangely, they then find themselves in support of fledgling democratic forces in Lebanon and in the Palestinian territories and in Iraq.

As Rice saw it, this was Bush's legacy. The Arab nations allied with the United States, once given a pass on oppressing their people at home—and still not pushed to the wall as Bush had suggested they would be in his second inaugural—were supporting democracy, if not at home then at least in the neighborhood: "These mainstream states [provide] a whole different strategic context in the Middle East than five years ago." Rice did not explicitly note the risk that this new strategic context could lead to regional conflagration, but she did warn,

"You have to be very careful in trying to deal with the difficult circumstances [in Iraq] that you don't unravel this new and much more favorable strategic context in the Middle East."

Another positive result of Bush's bold foreign policy, the secretary of state said, was that it had "given room . . . for a potential new push on the Israeli–Palestinian issue because the mainstream states also, I think, would actually really like to see a resolution of this conflict now. You have more energy with people saying, 'Well, we ought to be able to resolve these issues.'"

Resolving those issues will keep Rice more than occupied for the next two years. And as is her wont, she won't think about what comes next until she has done the best she can with the tasks at hand. Her energies will be focused on safeguarding Bush's vision, even as it seems to many that that vision has already died in the alleys of Baghdad and the deserts of western Iraq. None of that will deter Rice, no matter how bad the correlation of forces becomes.

Then, when her term is over, she will follow the path that the Lord has already set for her, though she can't know where that path will lead. And however history judges her, as both George Bush's teacher and his pupil—the skillful tactician who translated a bold foreign policy vision into the birth of a new Middle East, or the too-loyal consigliere who failed to save an inexperienced and irresponsible president—she will move on, she'll get over it.

NOTES

A NOTE ON NOTES:

Interviews were conducted in person unless otherwise stated. Though I talked to many sources more than once, only the date of the first on-the-record interview is listed. Many Washington sources, as is common in the capital, would only consent to be interviewed if their names were not used. In those cases, the source is listed as "senior administration official," "NSC staffer," or some similar general title. Occasionally, to protect confidentiality, a source is listed simply as anonymous.

In addition, following are some abbreviations that are commonly used within the notes: DU: University of Denver; NPR: National Public Radio; NSC: National Security Council; NSA: national security adviser; SUNS: Stanford University News Service.

FOREWORD

1. Christian Methodist Episcopal
2. Bonds, Mattie Ray, interview with the author, Sept. 9, 2006.
3. National Weather Service Forecast Office, Birmingham, AL, "Apr. 4, 1977, Smithfield Tornado," undated, http://www.srh.noaa.gov/bmx/significant_events/1977/smithfield/index.php.
4. Rice, Clara, interview with the author, Aug. 1, 2006.

INTRODUCTION

1. Stokes, Donald, "How a Young Black Girl from Birmingham Studied Music, Czech, Russian—and Arms," *Campus Report,* (Dec. 7, 1983), 3. The article was reprinted in its entirety with a new headline the next year: Donald Stokes, "Illogical Steps to a Logical Life: Condoleezza Rice, Specialist in International Security," *Stanford Observer,* Oct. 1984, 7
2. Davis, Michaela, interview with the author, Feb. 28, 2006.
3. *Essence* claims a monthly circulation of 1,063,000 and a readership of more than seven million.
4. Cooper, Anna Julia, "Womanhood: A Vital Element in the Regeneration and Progress of a Race," delivered to a meeting of the Protestant Episcopal Church, 1886. The entire quote, probably one of the most famous in all of African American scholarly literature (the speech from which it came became the first chapter of Cooper's seminal *A Voice from the South*) is: "Only the Black woman can say 'when and where I enter, in the quiet, undisputed dignity of my womanhood, without violence and without suing or special patronage, then and there the whole Negro race enters with me.'" See Charles Lemert and Esme Bhan, eds., *The Voice of Anna Julia Cooper* (Lanham, MD: Rowman & Littlefield, 1998), 53–71.
5. *Essence,* Oct. 2003.
6. Davis interview.
7. "President's Job Ratings Fall to Lowest Point of His Presidency," Table 2, Harris Poll #28, Apr. 14, 2005, http://www.harrisinteractive.com/harris_poll/index.asp?PID=557.

8. "Oprah's Cut with Condoleezza Rice," *O, The Oprah Magazine,* Feb. 2002, http://www.oprah.com/omagazine/200202/omag_200202_ocut.jhtml. Andrew Card, then chief of staff to the president, informed Bush that a second plane had hit the World Trade Center in a now-famous scene as the president was reading to schoolchildren in Florida.

9. Davis interview. The secretary of state is actually the fourth in the line of presidential succession, after the vice president, the speaker of the House of Representatives, and the president pro tempore of the Senate.

10. For details on Angela Davis's experience as a girl in "Bombingham," see *Angela Davis: An Autobiography* (New York: International Publishers, 1988), 78–79.

11. Davis interview.

12. Solomon, Akiba, interview with the author, Mar. 2, 2006.

13. *Essence,* May 2005.

14. Solomon interview.

15. Villarosa, Linda, interview with the author, Mar. 7, 2006.

16. Solomon interview.

17. Robinson, Eugene, "What Rice Can't See," *Washington Post*, Oct. 25, 2005, A21.

18. Churchill, Winston, "A World Broadcast" Oct. 1, 1939. See Charles Eade, *Winston Churchill War Speeches, 1939–45* (London: Cassell, 1951), 108–12.

19. MacDonald, Elizabeth, and Chana R. Schoenberger, "The 100 Most Powerful Women," *Forbes*, Aug. 15, 2005, 46; and MacDonald and Schoenberger, "Power Women," *Forbes*, Sept. 6, 2004, 68.

20. Kettman, Steve, "Bush's Secret Weapon," *Salon,* Mar. 20, 2000, http://archive.salon.com/politics2000/feature/2000/03/20/rice/.

21. Collins, Amy Fine, "Best-Dressed List 2006," *Vanity Fair*, Sept. 2006, 323.

22. *Sunday Morning*, CBS, May 14, 2006.

23. Former Bush administration official, interview with the author.

24. Haygood, Will, "Honored to Have the Chance," *Boston Globe,* Dec. 21, 2000, A1.

25. "Interview with Condoleezza Rice," *Late Edition*, CNN, Sept. 8, 2002, 12:00 p.m. ET, http://transcripts.cnn.com/TRANSCRIPTS/0209/08/le.00.html.

26. Amber, Jeannine, "Being Condoleezza," *Essence*, Oct. 2006, 184.

27. Rutenberg, Jim, and Robert Pear, "Bush, at Low Point in Polls, Will Push Domestic Agenda," *New York Times*, Jan. 23, 2007, 1.

28. Dowd, Ann Reilly, "Is There Anything This Woman Can't Do?" *George*, June 2000, 88.

29. Americans for Dr. Rice, May 13, 2006, http://4condi.com/.

30. Sammon, Bill, "2008 Run, Abortion Engage Her Politically," *Washington Times*, Mar. 12, 2005, http://washingtontimes.com/national/20050311-115948-2015r.htm.

31. Tumulty, Karen, "Is This the Race for 2008?" *Time,* Aug. 29, 2005, 24.

32. CNN Poll, conducted by Opinion Research Corporation, Dec. 15–17, 2006, http://www.pollingreport.com/P-Z.htm. See also "Public Sours on Government and Business," Pew Research Center, Oct. 25, 2006, http://people-press.org/reports/display.php3?ReportID=261. According to the Pew Research Center poll, taken from Oct. 12–24, 2006, of registered votes, ninety-three percent of Republicans, fifty-three percent of Democrats, and sixty-three percent of Independents had a favorable view of Rice. Rice received the highest positive rating from Republicans of any potential 2008 GOP presidential nominee, ninety-three percent compared to seventy-four percent for John McCain and ninety-two percent for Rudy Guiliani. The poll was taken when the president's approval rating was at forty percent and while the administration was smarting from widespread disappointment at its response to Katrina. Clearly, for most Americans, those errors did not affect their views of Rice. Democratic consultant Donna Brazile, Al Gore's campaign manager, noted the poll on NPR on Oct. 27, 2005, on "Political Insider" predicting that as a presidential candidate, Rice would garner "like traditional Republicans . . . up to fifteen to twenty percent of the African American vote."

33. Jones, Jeffrey M., "George W. Bush, Hillary Clinton Most Admired Again," Gallup News Service, Dec. 29, 2006, http://brain.gallup.com/content/default.aspx?ci=25996.

34. Schoeneman, Deborah, "Armani's Exchange . . . Condi's Slip . . . Forget the Alamo," *New York*, Apr. 26, 2004, http://nymetro.com/nymetro/news/people/columns/intelligencer/n_10245/.

CHAPTER ONE

1. Rice, Condoleezza, Class Day Speech, *Campus Report,* Jun. 19, 1985, 12. Each Stanford graduating class selects professors they would like to have address them before they leave. Rice was selected four times, by the classes of 1985, 1988, 1993, and 1999.

2. Smith, Julia Emma, interview with the author, Mar. 27, 2005.

3. Scowcroft, Brent, interview with the author, Oct. 6, 2005.

4. Just over four percent of RNC delegates were black, a sixty-three percent increase over 1996. See Lori Rodrigues and Lisa Teachey, "Parade of Diversity No Sign GOP Has Changed, Foes Say; Supporters Say It's a Step in the Right Direction," *Houston Chronicle,* Aug. 4, 2000, 26.

5. Geyer, Georgie Anne, "Bush Understands Tenor of His Time," Universal Press Syndicate, *Chicago Tribune,* Aug. 4, 2000, 25.

6. For a study of Bush's appeal at this time to moderates, see the Pew Research Center's "The Political Typography," undated, http://people-press.org/reports/display.php3?PageID=77.

7. Gigot, Paul, "Race Card: GOP Finally Antes Up," *Wall Street Journal,* Aug. 4, 2000, A10.

8. Ibid.

9. According to a *Los Angeles Times* poll conducted June 8–13, 2000, though Bush was leading Gore by ten points overall, Gore was beating Bush among moderates forty-nine to forty percent; Mar. 10, 2006, http://www.latimes.com/news/nationworld/timespoll/la-000615abortpoll442pa1an,1,3962162.htmlstory?coll=la-news-times_poll-nation.

10. "Featured Republican Speakers: Weighing In on Renewing America's Purpose," Election 2000: Republican National Convention, NPR, Mar. 8, 2000, http://www.npr.org/news/national/election2000/conventions/speakers.monday.html.

11. Rice, Condoleezza, address to the 2000 Republican National Convention, Philadelphia, Aug. 1, 2000, PBS, transcribed by author. Compared to disseminated text, http://www.npr.org/news/national/election2000/conventions/speech.crice.html.

12. Milbank, Dana, "A Political Gathering That's Nice and Nasty," *Washington Post,* Aug. 3, 2000, C01; and Mark Jurkowitz, "Convention's Lack of Contention Tests Pundits," *Boston Globe,* Aug. 3, 2000, D1.

13. Apple, R. W., Jr., "Promises of Changes, But Unspoken Details," *New York Times,* Aug. 3, 2000, A27; and Howard Kurtz, "Making a Little News Go a Long Way," *Washington Post,* Aug. 3, 2000, C01.

14. Cynthia Tucker, "General's Orders: Colin Powell Gives GOP Lesson on Outreach," *Atlanta Journal-Constitution,* Aug. 2, 2000, 16A; and Adrian Walker, "Up Front, But Still Tokens," *Boston Globe,* Aug. 3, 2000, B1.

15. Marinucci, Carla, "Conventional Wisdom: Who Won, Who Lost," *San Francisco Chronicle,* Aug. 5, 2000, A8.

16. Mondics, Chris, and Jackie Koszczuk, "A Showcase for Fresh New Faces in GOP," *Philadelphia Inquirer,* Aug. 5, 2000, A3.

17. Will, George, "The GOP of Powell and Rice," *Washington Post,* Aug. 6, 2000, B07.

18. Carl, William J., III, "Rice Wows 'Em," *Dallas Morning News,* Aug. 3, 2000, 33A.

19. "Republicans Offer Agenda of Promise," unsigned editorial, *Atlanta Journal-Constitution,* Aug. 4, 2000, 20A.

20. Cohen, Richard, "Diversity: It's Not All Phony," *Washington Post,* Aug. 3, 2000, A29.

21. Bunch, William, "RNC Gives Bush a Bigger Bounce Over Al," *Philadelphia Daily News,* Aug. 5, 2000, 8.

22. Berke, Richard L., "For Republicans a Night to Bolster Bush, *New York Times,* Aug. 2, 2000, 1. Pat Robertson complained at a Christian Coalition rally in Philadelphia the day of Rice's speech that "this convention is all sweetness and light."

23. Ibid.

24. Weyrich, Paul M., "A Ploy to Evangelical Voters," Renew America, Sept. 23, 2004, http://www.renewamerica.us/columns/weyrich/040923.

25. Stricherz, Mark, "Born Again," *Weekly Standard,* Jan. 26, 2004. Rove made his observation at a speech to the American Enterprise Institute, a conservative think tank.

26. Unsigned editorial, "Bush's Savvy Foreign Policy Team," *Chicago Tribune,* Aug. 3, 2000, 24.

27. Education, Social Security, and health care were the three top voter concerns throughout 2000.

28. See the compendium of polling at http://www.pollingreport.com/wh2cand.htm.

29. Cohen, "Diversity."

30. Wooten, Jim, "The Republican National Convention: Steering Clear of Potholes Adds to Upbeat Mood," *Atlanta Journal-Constitution,* Aug. 6, 2000, 7B.

31. Leonard, Mary, "McCain Character Loyal to a Fault," *Boston Globe,* Mar. 4, 2000, A1.

32. Silva, Mark, "Fighting to Finish in S.C., Bush, McCain Rally Forces," *Miami Herald,* Feb. 19, 2000, 3A.

33. On March 4, 2000, in the wake of widespread controversy caused by Bush's visit, the president of Bob Jones University, Bob Jones III, said on CNN's *Larry King Live* that "as of today, we have dropped the rule" against interracial dating.

34. "Bob Jones University Ends Ban on Interracial Dating," CNN, Mar. 4, 2000, http://archives.cnn.com/2000/US/03/04/bob.jones/.

35. "Candidates George W. Bush, Alan Keyes, and John McCain Squared Off Thursday Night, Sharing Their Visions of America's Future," transcript, *Los Angeles Times,* Mar. 3, 2000, S1.

36. See note 1 in this chapter.

37. The university was carved out of the Stanford family's farm to serve the "children of California," Leland and Jane Stanford's living memorial to their son Leland Stanford Jr., who died of typhoid just before his sixteenth birthday in Florence, Italy, on March 13, 1884. Leland Stanford Sr., who served as Governor of California, was one of the original organizers of the Republican Party in the state.

38. "American Dream Must Be Delivered to All People, Rice Says," *Campus Report,* Jun. 19, 1985, 12.

39. "'Will to Succeed' Called Potent Weapon in Battle Against Prejudice, Bigotry," *Campus Report,* Jun. 15, 1988, 13.

40. Ibid.

41. Warren, James, "Windy City Ex Robert Conrad Hangs Out with GOP Elite," *Chicago Tribune,* Aug. 6, 2000, C2.

42. Hence the enthusiasm over Barack Obama's speech to the Democratic National Convention in 2004. Though not a product of American segregation, Obama having a black and a white parent also has a privileged place in American society from which to comment on race.

43. Haygood, Will, "Honored to Have the Chance," *Boston Globe,* Dec. 21, 2000, A1.

44. Hamberry-Green, Brenda, interview with the author, Apr. 19, 2006.

45. Thomma, Steven, and Mark Bowden, "Bush: Put Prosperity to Use 'We Will Confront the Hard Issues,'" *Philadelphia Inquirer,* Aug. 4, 2000, A01.

CHAPTER TWO

1. Moore, Geraldine, *Behind the Ebony Mask: What American Negroes Really Think* (Birmingham, AL: Southern University Press, 1961), 16.

2. Information panels at the Vulcan Exhibition Center, Birmingham, AL. Viewed on Mar. 24, 2005.

3. Atkins, Leah Rawls, *The Valley and the Hills: An Illustrated History of Birmingham and Jefferson County* (Woodland Hills, CA: Windsor Publications, 1981), 49.

4. Huntley, Horace, interview with the author, Mar. 28, 2005.

5. Vulcan Exhibition Center, Mar. 24, 2005.

6. Atkins, *The Valley and the Hills*, 58–61.

7. Leighton, George R., "Birmingham, Alabama: The City of Perpetual Promise," *Harper's,* Aug. 1937, 225–42, as cited in Diane McWhorter's *Carry Me Home: Birmingham, Alabama, The Climatic Battle of the Civil Rights Movement* (New York: Touchstone, 2001).

8. Moore, *Behind the Ebony Mask*, 25.

9. Ibid, 211.

10. Ibid, 30–31.

11. Ibid, 206.

12. United States Supreme Court, *Brown v. Board of Education of Topeka et.al.,* 347 U.S. 483 (1954).

13. McWhorter, Diane, *Carry Me Home: Birmingham, Alabama, The Climatic Battle of the Civil Rights Movement* (New York: Touchstone, 2001), 86–87.

14. Moore, *Behind the Ebony Mask*, 29; Glenn T. Eskew, *But for Birmingham: The Local and National Movements in the Civil Rights Struggle* (Chapel Hill, NC: The University of North Carolina Press, 1997), 106–8.

15. Branch, Taylor, *Pillar of Fire: America in the King Years 1963–65,* (New York: Simon & Schuster, 1998), 26.

16. Hunter, George "Third," III, interview with the author, Mar. 26, 2005.

17. Tommasini, Anthony, "And on Piano, Madame Secretary," *New York Times,* Apr. 9, 2006, sec. 2, 1.

18. Smith, Julia Emma, interview with the author, Mar. 27, 2005. In an interview with Dale Russakoff for her article "Lessons of Might and Right" in the *Washington Post,* Condoleezza Rice's second cousin Connie Rice said, "The Rices were kind of joyless except for Condi's dad."

19. Condoleezza Rice has spoken very rarely about the difference in treatment that her parents' appearances generated. It is likely she was referring obliquely to "colorism" when she told Steven Weisman in a *New York Times* interview, "I wish that I had more time to talk to my mother . . . I think [my mother's] experiences and my father's experiences were in many ways very different, and it had to do with my mother's physical beauty and elegance and her ability to bridge in some ways—and it was, it's something I wish I had more time to talk about"; "Interview with Steven Weisman of the *New York Times*," U.S. Department of State, Oct. 20, 2005, http://www.state.gov/secretary/rm/2005/55437.htm. It is far more likely that Ann Rice's light skin, which may have been one aspect of her beauty, engendered a different response from whites than her elegance or her general aspect. Rice's mother, for instance, registered to vote without incident.

20. Maxwell, Bill, "The Paper Bag Test," *St. Petersburg Times,* Aug. 23, 2003, http://www.sptimes.com/2003/08/31/Columns/The_paper_bag_test.shtml. For a penetrating discussion of "colorism," the prejudice of blacks toward other blacks based on the lightness or darkness of their skin, see Marita Golden's *Don't Play in the Sun: One Woman's Journey Through the Color Complex* (New York: Doubleday, 2004).

21. Smith interview.

22. Rice, Condoleezza, address to the 2000 Republican National Convention, Philadelphia, Aug. 1, 2000, PBS, transcribed by author.

23. Gordon, Tom, and Mary Orndorff, "Condoleezza Rice: Defying the Stereotypes," *Birmingham News,* Jan. 22, 2001, 01-A.

24. Russakoff, Dale, "Lessons of Might and Right," *Washington Post,* Sept. 9, 2001, W23.

25. Gordon and Orndorff, "Defying the Stereotypes." This story, attributed to "family members" by Gordon and Orndorff, has been widely repeated since they reported it. From what I can discern, their article is always the

original source for the subsequent reports. In one of our interviews, Condoleezza Rice said she had been told the story many times, with no narrative context about the family or its values.

26. Gordon and Orndorff, "Defying the Stereotypes."

27. Rice, Condoleezza, interview with the author, Nov. 2, 2006.

28. Spencer, Thomas, "Bush Aide Criticizes Clinton Policy," *Birmingham News*, Apr. 11, 2000, 01-B.

29. Gordon and Orndorff, "Defying the Stereotypes."

30. Rice, RNC address.

31. Flynt, Wayne, *Alabama in the Twentieth Century* (Tuscaloosa, AL: The University of Alabama Press, 2004), 320–21.

32. Stillman College, "Our History," undated, http://www.stillman.edu/stillman/stillhist/history.html.

33. Rice, Condoleezza, interview.

34. Rice, Condoleezza, "Transform America, One by One," *Birmingham News*, May 22, 1994, 01-01; Ann Reilly Dowd, "Is There Anything This Woman Can't Do?" *George*, June 2000, 88.

35. Dowd, "Is There Anything?"

36. Rice, Condoleezza, interview.

37. Rice, John Wesley, Jr., *Vita*, undated, University of Denver, Penrose Library, Archives, Rice, John Wesley folder 2 of 2.

38. Gordon and Orndorff, "Defying the Stereotypes."

39. Stillman College, "Our History."

40. Thomas, Clarence, interview with the author, Sept. 12, 2006.

41. Thomas interview.

42. Rice, *Vita*.

43. Thomas interview; Smith interview; Geneva Williams, interview with the author, Sept. 8, 2006.

44. Rice, Clara, interview with the author, Aug. 1, 2006.

45. See "Deaths," Palo Alto Weekly Online, Jan. 2, 2001, http://www.paloaltoonline.com/weekly/morgue/community_pulse/2001_Jan_3.OBITS03.html

46. Garrison, Greg, "Bush Advisor Rice Slated to Attend Westminster Memorial for Father," *Birmingham News*, Mar. 18, 2001, 15-A.

47. Rice, *Vita*.

48. Smith interview.

49. Rice, *Vita*, and *Polk's Birmingham City Directory*, 1952, 811.

50. McPhatter, Genoa, interview with the author, Dec. 12, 2006; Rice, Clara, interview.

51. Dowd, "Is There Anything?"; Tommasini, "And on Piano."

52. German, Yvonne, phone interview with the author, Sept. 20, 2006.

53. Bonds, Mattie Ray, interview with the author, Sept. 9, 2006.

54. Ibid.

55. Rice, Condoleezza, interview; see also Russakoff, "Lessons of Might and Right."

56. Rice, "Transform America, One by One."

57. Bonds interview.

58. Bonds interview; *Polk's Birmingham City Directory*, 1949, 692; for full name of Republic Steel, as listed in the directory; see Lynne B. Feldman, *A Sense of Place: Birmingham's Black Middle-Class Community, 1890–1930* (Tuscaloosa, AL: The University of Alabama Press, 1999), 33.

59. Bonds interview.

60. Rice, Condoleezza, interview.

61. Bonds interview.

62. Ibid.

63. Ibid.

64. Russakoff, "Lessons of Might and Right."

65. Ibid.

66. Smith interview.

67. U.S. Census Bureau, *A Half-Century of Learning: Historical Statistics on Educational Attainment in the United States: 1940 to 2000*, Table 12a.

68. U.S. Census Bureau, *A Half-Century of Learning*, Table 11a.

69. U.S. Census Bureau, *A Half-Century of Learning*, Table 8a. (By 2000, 11.5 percent of blacks would have a bachelor's degree or higher in Alabama and 21.2 percent of whites, compared to 14.3 percent of blacks nationally and 26.1 percent of whites nationally.)

70. McPhatter interview.

71. Rice, Condoleezza, interview.

72. McPhatter interview. The Jefferson County Registrar had no record of the marriage. Three times, I requested searches of state records (marriage records are public in Alabama). Each time the State of Alabama's Center for

Health Statistics, Office of Vital Records sent a "Certificate of Failure to Find." The certificates are dated March 31, 2005; April 6, 2005, and January 29, 2007. Each is signed by Dorothy S. Harshbarger, State Registrar and Director. The January 29 certificate states that "for the years 1949–1959 . . . no record of marriage was found to exist for JOHN WESLEY RICE and ANGELENA RAY." I found no record of the Ray's marriage in the relevant marriage and birth "books" housed in the Jefferson County administrative buildings in downtown Birmingham and divided by race until the 1960s; there was also no record of Condoleezza Rice's birth. The latter was not uncommon for Negro births, but the former is an oddity.

73. Rice, Condoleezza, interview.

74. Ibid.

75. Smith interview.

76. Gordon and Orndorff, "Defying the Stereotypes."

77. Moore, *Behind the Ebony Mask*, 45.

78. See also State Department transcript, "Remarks with United Kingdom Foreign Secretary Jack Straw at the Blackburn Institute's Frank A. Nix Lecture," Oct. 21, 2005, http://www.state.gov/secretary/rm/2005/55423.htm. In the speech Rice calls Shuttlesworth a "great friend of my father."

79. *Birmingham News*, Dec. 26, 1956; *Birmingham World*, Dec. 29, 1956; as cited in Eskew, *But for Birmingham*: 134.

80. Eskew, *But for Birmingham*, 129–35.

81. As Eskew reports in *But for Birmingham*, pages 74–75, a typical case was the battle over public golf courses. Instead of fighting for the elimination of Jim Crow links, Negro leaders fought for the establishment of a colored golf course.

82. Russakoff, "Lessons of Might and Right."

83. This account is reconstructed from McWhorter's and Eskew's works, most of the dialogue is taken directly from McWhorter's, which is based on extensive examination of Klan files; McWhorter, *Carry Me Home*, 124–25, and Eskew, *But for Birmingham*, 114–15.

84. Eskew, *But for Birmingham*, 140.

85. *Birmingham News*, Sept. 9, 1957; *Birmingham Post-Herald*, Sept. 10, 1957; interviews with Fred Shuttlesworth; Fredericka "Ricky" Shuttlesworth oral history in Ellen Levine's *Freedom's Children* (New York: Avon, 1993), 43–44; *Chicago Defender*, Sept. 28, 1957; Spike Lee's documentary, *4 Little Girls*; all as cited in McWhorter, *Carry Me Home*, 127.

86. McWhorter, *Carry Me Home*, 127.

87. Wigginton, Russell, "Louisville and Nashville Railroad," *The Tennessee Encyclopedia of History and Culture*, 1998, http://tennesseeencyclopedia.net/imagegallery.php?EntryID=R004 (accessed Mar. 28, 2006).

88. Hunter, Third, interview.

89. Smith interview; Hunter, Third, interview.

90. Dowd, "Is There Anything?"

91. Stokes, Donald, "How a Young Black Girl from Birmingham Studied Music, Czech, Russian—and Arms," *Campus Report*, 7 (Dec. 1983), 3.

92. De Lama, George, "Academic Style: Stanford's New Provost Brings a Different Perspective to Campus," *Chicago Tribune*, Aug. 15, 1993, CN-5.

93. Von Kreisler-Bomben, Kristin, "Condoleezza Rice: Balancing Act," *Stanford* magazine, Winter 1985, 16.

94. Ibid.

95. Russakoff, "Lessons of Might and Right."

96. Hunter, Carolyn, interview with the author, Mar. 21, 2005.

97. Hunter, Carolyn, interview; Smith interview.

98. *Polk's Birmingham City Directory*, 1965.

99. Gordon and Orndorff, "Defying the Stereotypes."

100. Anonymous interview.

101. Hunter-Beavers, Vanessa, interview with the author, Mar. 21, 2005.

102. Reed, Julia, "The President's Prodigy," *Vogue*, Oct. 2001, 396.

103. Hunter-Beavers interview; Smith interview.

104. Dowd, "Is There Anything?"

105. Smith interview.

106. Dowd, "Is There Anything?"

107. Rice, Clara, interview.

108. Hunter, Third, interview.

109. Smith interview; Hunter, George Jr., interview with the author, Mar. 21, 2005.

110. Smith interview.

111. German interview.

112. Ibid.

113. Ibid.

114. Hunter, George, Jr., interview.

115. Hunter, Third, interview.

116. Russakoff, "Lessons of Might and Right."

117. Russakoff, Dale, "Team Rice, Playing Away," *Washington Post*, Mar. 17, 2005, D01.

118. Ibid.

119. McWhorter, *Carry Me Home*, 252.

120. Photograph, viewed by the author.

121. Carter, Eva, interview with the author, Mar. 27, 2005.

122. Hurt, Avery, "Rice Family Values," *Birmingham*, June 2002, 111.

123. Russakoff, "Lessons of Might and Right." Russakoff reports Rice was seven years old and the year was 1961, since Russakoff, unlike some reporters, is careful to coordinate Rice's age, which changes very late in a given year, with the day or days events occurred, it is very likely that this incident occurred between Nov. 14 and Dec. 31, 1961.

124. Russakoff, "Lessons of Might and Right."

125. Dowd, "Is There Anything?"

126. This incident, including all the dialogue, is taken from Russakoff's "Lessons of Might and Right" piece in the *Washington Post*. Blacker confirmed the incident in an interview with the author.

127. Dowd, "Is There Anything?"

128. Rice told the *New York Times'* Weisman in their Oct. 20, 2005 interview, "My parents were in some ways determined to shelter me a little bit from the hard side of Birmingham. And so there were things they didn't talk about that I learned later."

129. Hunter, Carolyn, interview.

130. Reed, "The President's Prodigy."

131. De Lama, "Academic Style."

132. Stokes, "Black Girl."

133. As quoted in "Lessons of Might and Right," Rice tells Russakoff: "Every night I pray and say thank you that You gave me the parents You gave me. How fortunate was I to have these extraordinary people as my parents. I do think they had a sense of wanting to make me special from a very early age."

134. Sciolino, Elaine, "Compulsion to Achieve," *New York Times*, Dec. 18, 2000, A1; Brant, Martha, and Evan Thomas, "A Steely Southern," *Newsweek*, Aug. 6, 2001, 28.

135. Haygood, Will, "Honored to Have the Chance," *Boston Globe*, Dec. 21, 2000, A1.

136. Tommasini, "And on Piano."

137. Ibid.

138. Lemann, Nicholas, "Without a Doubt," *New Yorker*, Oct. 14, 2002, 164.

139. Heyman, J.D., et.al. "The Velvet Hammer," *People*, Dec. 6, 2004, 107.

140. Rice, Condoleezza, interview.

141. Smith interview.

142. "I'm a really religious person," Rice told Oprah Winfrey in the Feb. 2002 issue of *O, The Oprah Magazine* article. "I don't believe that I was put on this earth to be sour, so I'm eternally optimistic about things." Dozens of people who know Rice well confirmed that characterization.

143. Reed, "Prodigy."

144. McWhorter, *Carry Me Home*, 257.

145. Ibid, 259.

146. Ibid, 264–73.

147. Ibid, 288.

148. Ibid, 294.

149. Ibid, 297.

150. Stokes, "Black Girl." Rice told Stokes that she remembered the Cuban Missile Crisis "vividly, though I was barely eight years old." She was, in fact, just weeks shy of her eighth birthday.

151. Reed, "Prodigy."

CHAPTER THREE

1. Rice, Condoleezza, University of Alabama General Commencement, Tuscaloosa, AL, May 15, 1994. Rice was thirty-nine years old, and she was addressing the largest graduating class in Alabama history. Her address, which is particularly inspiring, was reprinted in whole by the *Birmingham News* on May 22, 1994, under the headline, "Transform America, One by One." The speech was also a clear criticism of the ennui and self-doubt that Rice felt plagued the country at that time, midway through Bill Clinton's first term. Her address is a call to action to overcome defeatism and a sense of America's decline, and it offers some indication of what Rice thought a George W. Bush presidency would bring America.

2. FBI interviews with witnesses, FBI investigative file on the Sixteenth Street Baptist Church bombing (FBI file no. 157–352), Birmingham Public Library, as cited in Diane McWhorter's *Carry Me Home: Birmingham, Alabama, The Climatic Battle of the Civil Rights Movement* (New York: Touchstone, 2001), 522.

3. McWhorter, *Carry Me Home*, 520.

4. Branch, Taylor, *Pillar of Fire: America in the King Years 1963–65* (New York: Simon & Schuster, 1998), 138.

5. Report of Special Agent James R. Logan Jr., Oct. 4, 1963, and memo on damage, Sept. 17, 1963, FBI investigative file on the Sixteenth Street Baptist Church bombing (FBI file no. 157-352), Birmingham Public Library; Aaron Rosenfeld testimony, Chambliss trial transcript, p. 496; all as cited in McWhorter, *Carry Me Home*, 670n.

6. Dowd, Ann Reilly, "Is There Anything This Woman Can't Do?" *George*, June 2000, 88.

7. Most often Rice has described her relationship with Denise McNair as friends. At other times she has said they "attended the same parties." Denise's father, Chris McNair, described the two girls' relationship merely as "they were in the same kindergarten" to me. Rice herself described their relationship that way in an interview with the *Washington Post*, Mar. 12, 1989. However, in an interview with *Ebony* magazine, Dec. 2005, Rice described McNair as a "good friend" she knew "very well." This seems to be a less common characterization.

8. Russakoff, Dale, "Lessons of Might and Right," *Washington Post,* Sept. 9, 2001, W23.

9. Dowd, "Is There Anything?"

10. Russakoff, "Lessons of Might and Right."

11. Dowd, "Is There Anything?"

12. Bombings file, Birmingham Public Library.

13. Dowd, "Is There Anything?" There are many other accounts of John Rice taking part in the armed neighborhood watch, though no others say he organized it, including Evan Thomas, "The Quiet Power of Condi Rice," *Newsweek*, Dec. 16, 2002, 24; Russakoff, "Lessons of Might and Right."

14. Hunter, George "Third," III, interview with the author, Mar. 26, 2005.

15. Woolfolk, Odessa, interview with the author, Mar. 24, 2005. See also Glenn T. Eskew's *But for Birmingham: The Local and National Movements in the Civil Rights Struggle* (Chapel Hill, NC: The University of North Carolina Press, 1997), 318, on the cause of the bombing; and McWhorter, *Carry Me Home*, 510, on the Klansmen's motivation and preparations.

16. Frady, Marshall, *Wallace* (New York: World, 1968), 142.

17. McWhorter, *Carry Me Home*, 502–9.

18. Eyewitness account of Rev. Irvin Cheney Jr., attached to NAACP report from Ruby Hurley to Gloster Current, Sept. 26, 1963, III-H-213, papers of the National Association for the Advancement of Colored People, Library of Congress, as cited in Branch, *Pillar of Fire,* 142n.

19. Audiotapes, 112.6, 113.1, John F. Kennedy Library, Boston, as cited in Taylor Branch's *Pillar of Fire*, 138–43.

20. Eskew, Glenn T., *But for Birmingham: The Local and National Movements in the Civil Rights Struggle* (Chapel Hill, NC: The University of North Carolina Press, 1997), 219.

21. McWhorter, *Carry Me Home*, 323–24; Eskew, *But for Birmingham*, 218.

22. *New York Times*, Apr. 5, 1963, as cited in Eskew, *But for Birmingham*, 223n.

23. *New York Times*, Apr. 5, 1963, as cited in Branch, *Pillar of Fire*, 46n.

24. Branch, *Pillar of Fire,* 46.

25. Ibid, 47.

26. Ibid, 47.

27. Ibid, 48–49.

28. Woolfolk interview.

29. The eighteenth-century French philosopher and writer's classic *Candide, Or Optimism* ends with the lead character saying, *"Il faut cultiver notre jardin."* "We must cultivate our [own] garden." For centuries philosophy and literature students have debated whether the message of *Candide*, which traces a naïve young man through adventure and hardship in a dangerous and horrid world, is that we should attack the outside world's horrors with no illusions that this is "the best of all possible worlds" or that we should improve the world by minding our own little corner of it, without worrying what destiny or grand designs. Or that the human condition is essentially tragic and we foolishly attempt to change it. Rev. Rice's philosophy was probably closest to the second; only he might have added that as we succeed in bettering our small plot of earth, we are in fact advancing the broader "human condition."

30. Smith, Julia Emma, interview with the author, Mar. 27, 2005.

31. Hunter, Third, interview.

32. Smith interview.

33. Rice, John Wesley, Jr., *Vita*, undated, University of Denver, Penrose Library, Archives, Rice, John Wesley folder 2 of 2, Apr. 15, 2005; Rice, Condoleezza, interview with the author, Nov. 2, 2006.

34. Haygood, Will, "Honored to Have the Chance," *Boston Globe*, Dec. 21, 2000, A1.

35. Jenkins, Jimmi, Jr., interview with the author, Mar. 21, 2005. Jenkins was a member of Ullman High School's class of 1966 and Rice's across-the-street neighbor.

36. Smith interview.

37. Ibid.

38. Ibid.

39. Hunter, Third, interview.

40. Branch, *Pillar of Fire,* 76.

41. Branch, *Parting the Waters: America in the King Years 1954–63* (New York: Simon & Schuster, 1988) 747–55. On King's resistance, see also McWhorter, *Carry Me Home,* 361; SCLC leader Andy Young had also told the kids they were too young to get arrested; they should go to the library instead and read.

42. Branch, *Pillar of Fire,* 77.

43. Martin Luther King, *Why We Can't Wait,* 9; *New York Times,* May 3, 1963; *Birmingham News,* May 3, 1963; all as cited in McWhorter, *Carry Me Home,* 366n.

44. Branch, *Pillar of Fire,* 77.

45. WRVR-FM radio documentary, "Testament of Nonviolence," 1963, Michigan State University Library, East Lansing, Part 1, Side 2; Martin Luther King, *Why We Can't Wait,* 98; Ralph David Abernathy, *And the Walls Came Tumbling Down,* 262; all as cited in McWhorter, *Carry Me Home,* 367n.

46. Hunter, Carolyn, interview with the author, Mar. 21, 2005.

47. Hunter, Third, interview.

48. Ibid.

49. McWhorter, *Carry Me Home,* 371–75.

50. Branch, *Pillar of Fire,* 78.

51. Smith interview.

52. Russakoff, "Lessons of Might and Right."

53. Rice, Condoleezza, interview.

54. Ibid.

55. Branch, *Pillar of Fire,* 80.

56. Branch, *Parting the Waters,* 825, as cited in Branch, *Pillar of Fire,* 84.

57. Branch, *Parting the Waters,* 107–8.

58. Kennedy speech, transcript in *New York Times,* Jun. 12, 1963, as cited in McWhorter, *Carry Me Home,* 464. The immediate precipitating event to the president's television address was the federal government's clash with Alabama Gov. George Wallace after his famous "stand in the schoolhouse door," when he refused to obey a federal court order to allow Deputy Attorney General Nicholas Katzenbach to register two black students, James Hood and Vivian Malone, at the University of Alabama. In response, the Kennedys finally found the courage to do what they had been avoiding, take the nation's racial demons head on. In doing so, they understood, as Johnson would in signing the legislation, that they may have severely handicapped, or even sacrificed, their party's ability to carry enough states to win electoral-college majorities in presidential elections.

59. Branch, *Pillar of Fire,* 234, 388; see also Branch, *Pillar of Fire,* 90–95, on Johnson's early role as vice president.

60. Russakoff, "Lessons of Might and Right."

61. "Oprah's Cut with Condoleezza Rice," *O, The Oprah Magazine,* Feb. 2002, http://www.oprah.com/omagazine/200202/omag_200202_ocut.jhtml.

62. Branch, Taylor, *At Canaan's Edge: America in the King Years 1965–68* (New York: Simon & Schuster, 2006), 423.

63. Eskew, *But for Birmingham,* 327–28.

64. Haygood, "Honored."

65. Eskew, *But for Birmingham,* 326–40. Eskew goes into great depth about the limited victories of the Movement in Birmingham and the enormous problems that still faced—and face—the poor African American majority in the city. He argues, from a left-of-center perspective, that the Movement's narrow goals, which white intransigence made seem grander than they were and the entrenched Negro leadership class, which maintained its hold over the masses throughout the changes of the 1960s and later decades, stifled what could have been more meaningful social change benefiting the majority of blacks rather than a slim middle class. See also McWhorter, *Carry Me Home,* 599–602, on the limits of the Movement's gains and the reality of life for the majority of Birmingham blacks, as well as class relations in the city.

66. Author's reporting, downtown Birmingham, March 2005. See Eskew, *But for Birmingham,* 329–31, for U.S. census data on income and poverty in the 1980s and 1990s.

67. Rice, Condoleezza, interview.

68. "Condoleezza Rice: True Believer," interview with Katie Couric *60 Minutes,* CBS News video, Sept. 24, 2006, http://www.cbsnews.com/stories/2006/09/21/60minutes/main2029782.shtml?source=RSSattr=Politics_2029782.

69. Stokes, Donald, "How a Young Black Girl from Birmingham Studied Music, Czech, Russian—and Arms," *Campus Report,* Dec. 7, 1983, 3.

70. Thomas, "Quiet Power."

71. Dowd, "Is There Anything?"

72. Reed, Julia, "The President's Prodigy," *Vogue*, Oct. 2001, 396.

73. Stokes, "Black Girl."

74. Rice, Condoleezza, interview.

75. Rice, Condoleezza, interview.

76. Dowd, "Is There Anything?"

77. Rice, Condoleezza, interview.

78. See Stokes, "Black Girl," and Russakoff, "Lessons of Might and Right."

79. Russakoff, "Lessons of Might and Right."

80. Eskew, *But for Birmingham*, 231. See also Branch, *Parting the Waters* and *Pillar of Fire*, and McWhorter, *Carry Me Home*.

81. Russakoff, "Lessons of Might and Right."

82. *New York Times*, Mar. 4, 1965, Branch, *Pillar of Fire*, 600; Charles E. Fager, *Selma, 1965*, 85–86; all as cited in Branch, *At Canaan's Edge*, 24n.

83. Rice, Condoleezza, interview.

84. Dowd, "Is There Anything?" Rice's aunt Connie Ray also said the little girl was anguished by not being able to attend the State Fair, see Tom Gordon and Mary Orndorff, "Condoleezza Rice: Defying the Stereotypes," *Birmingham News*, Jan. 22, 2001, 01-A.

85. Russakoff, "Lessons of Might and Right."

86. Ibid.

87. Rice, Condoleezza, interview.

88. Branch, *Pillar of Fire*, 522.

89. Rice, Condoleezza, interview.

90. Russakoff, "Lessons of Might and Right."

91. Robinson, Eugene, "What Rice Can't See," *Washington Post*, Oct. 25, 2005, A21.

92. Russakoff, "Lessons of Might and Right." The full Russakoff quote reads: "Connie Rice, the civil rights lawyer, says white people's attraction to her cousin is more complex than they realize. 'Our parents knew black people faced a presumption of inarticulateness,' she says, 'and what they did was they programmed us to know: These folks have a disability, they think they're better than you, but here's how to deal with it. Condi and I speak the King's English to the Queen's taste. We're fluent in all kinds of white cultures. We float right through them . . . I'll have a meeting with white people and they'll say, 'I love Connie.' And I'm thinking, 'You have no idea what I've done to make you feel comfortable, to neutralize your racist expectations.' Condi does it to a tee. And white people don't notice. Condi won't agree. She'll think it's too race-centric. But the endgame is the same: She neutralizes it." Rice's friend Coit Blacker told Russakoff that Rice "instinctively" holds her head up to "preempt" bigoted presumptions of black ignorance from being projected on her.

93. This was a recurrent theme in Ray relative interviews.

94. Smith interview; "Connie Rice Commentary: 10 Things Condi Didn't Say," *The Tavis Smiley Show*, NPR, Apr. 13, 2004, http://www.npr.org/templates/story/story.php?storyId=1835007&ft=1&f=4117735.

CHAPTER FOUR

1. Reed, Julia, "The President's Prodigy," *Vogue*, Oct. 2001, 396.

2. Rice, Condoleezza, interview with the author, Nov. 2, 2006.

3. Williams, Geneva, interview with the author, Sept. 8, 2006.

4. In an interview with Katie Couric of CBS News on *60 Minutes* on Sept. 24, 2006, Rice told Couric that it was after she took the "Preliminary SATs" that a teacher reviewing her results said she was not college material.

5. Baenan, Judith, president, St. Mary's Academy, interview with the author, Apr. 13, 2005. Baenan said Rice earned "solid scores" on her PSATs and "excellent" scores on her SATs.

6. Turnbull, Louise, interview with the author, Apr. 13, 2005.

7. Turnbull interview; Rogers McCallister, interview with the author, Apr. 13, 2005; Dr. Fred Holmes interview with the author, Apr. 15, 2005.

8. Turnbull interview; Holmes interview.

9. McCallister interview.

10. Holmes interview.

11. University of Denver memorandum from Vice Chancellor Wilbur C. Miller to Dean John W. Rice Jr., Jul. 6, 1970, in John Wesley Rice file, University of Denver Archives, folder 2 of 2.

12. In a letter to Rice, another assistant dean calls him "a proper prima donna"; see letter from Assistant Dean of Student Life Mary E. Choury to Assistant Dean John W. Rice, Dec. 31, 1970, in John Wesley Rice file, University of Denver Archives, folder 2. Choury's letter is a blistering complaint to Rice for missing a meeting with her scheduled for 9:30 a.m. on Dec. 30, 1970. The letter does not explain what the purpose of the meeting was, but is vitriolic, calling Rice's "deliberate failure" to keep their appointment "not only . . . unprofessional, but cruel."

13. Gilbert, Alan, interview with the author, Apr. 15, 2005. Gilbert, a professor of political science, would later instructed Condoleezza Rice as a graduate student at DU.

14. Holmes interview.

15. Mitchell died in 1996.

16. Hill, Dr. Albert Fay, interview with the author, Apr. 13, 2005.

17. Rice, Condoleezza, interview.

18. Ibid.

19. Ibid.

20. Pamphlet, *The Black Experience in America 1970*, undated, in John Wesley Rice file, University of Denver Archives, folder 2.

21. Berlet, Chip, "Condi's Dad and the Lessons of War," PublicEye.org, Oct. 27, 2004, http://www.publiceye.org/frontpage/OpEds/berlet_condi_dad.html.

22. Ibid.

23. Rice, Condoleezza, interview.

24. Dowd, Ann Reilly, "Is There Anything This Woman Can't Do?" *George*, June 2000, 88.

25. Baenan interview.

26. Bryant, Phyllis, interview with the author, Apr. 16, 2005.

27. Greiser, Thomas, e-mail interview with the author, Feb. 12, 2007.

28. Rice, Condoleezza, interview.

29. McNatt, Rosemary Bray, "My Mother Was My Fierce Defender," *Good Housekeeping*, May 2006, 91.

30. Rice, Condoleezza, interview.

31. Ibid.

32. Williams interview.

33. Ibid.

34. Ibid.

35. Rice, Condoleezza, interview.

36. Hill interview; Lydia McCollum, interview with the author, Apr. 13, 2005.

37. Montview Centennial Book Committee, *The Spirit of Montview 1902–2002: A History of Montview Boulevard Presbyterian Church* (Denver: Walsworth Publishing Company, 2001), 27.

38. Ibid, 25.

39. Ibid.

40. Hill interview.

41. Ibid.

42. Murayama, Dr. Allen, interview with the author, Apr. 14, 2005.

43. Hill interview.

44. Ibid.

45. Murayama interview.

46. Hill interview.

47. Murayama interview.

48. Rice, Condoleezza, interview.

49. Holmes interview; Dr. Bernard Gibson, interview with the author, Apr. 15, 2005.

50. Rice, Condoleezza, interview.

51. Holmes interview.

52. Rice, Clara, interview with the author, Aug. 1, 2006.

53. Felix, Antonia, *Condi: The Condoleezza Rice Story* (New York: Pocket Books, 2002), 79.

54. University of Denver appointment notice, John W. Rice Jr., Mar. 21, 1972, in John Wesley Rice file, University of Denver Archives, folder 2.

55. Rice, Condoleezza, interview.

56. Reed, "Prodigy."

57. Dowd, "Is There Anything?"; Elaine Sciolino, "Compulsion to Achieve," *New York Times,* Dec. 18, 2000, A1.

58. Rice, Condoleezza, interview.

59. St. Mary's Academy, *Ave 71'*[sic] (Englewood, CO: St. Mary's Academy, 1971).

60. Rice, Condoleezza, interview.

61. Lichtmann, Theodor, phone interview with the author, May 2, 2005.

62. While Lichtmann emphasized that this was just his opinion, Condoleezza Rice would say much the same thing in an interview with Oprah Winfrey in the Feb. 2002 issue of O.

63. Lichtmann interview.

64. Ibid.

65. Rice, Condoleezza, interview.

66. Lichtmann interview.

67. Sciolino, "Compulsion to Achieve."

68. Dowd, "Is There Anything?"

69. Rice, Condoleezza, interview.

70. Ibid.

71. Letter from Wilbur C. Miller to John W. Rice, Jr., Jun. 2, 1972, in John Wesley Rice file, University of Denver Archives, folder 2.

72. University of Denver press release, Apr. 13, 1973.

73. See letter of recommendation from William T. Driscoll, PhD, associate dean of the College of Arts and Sciences, Mar. 9, 1971, in John Wesley Rice file, University of Denver Archives, folder 2; McCallister interview; Holmes interview.

74. Driscoll, letter of recommendation.

75. Rice finally received a significant raise in the middle of the 1973–74 school year, from $17,200 to $21,000, after the paltry $700 increase that came with his promotion; see University of Denver appointment notice, John W. Rice, Jr., Jul. 1, 1973, and University of Denver appointment notice, John W. Rice, Jr., Jul. 1, 1974, both in John Wesley Rice file, University of Denver Archives, folder 2. There is no record in the file of the 27.9 percent raise from $17,200 to $21,000; however, the two regular annual appointment letters make it clear that Rice had received an intermediate increase in the course of the 1973–74 academic year.

76. See memos to John Rice from Edward Lindell, Jun. 14, 1973, and Vice Chancellor Carl York, Jun. 26, 1973, in John Wesley Rice file, University of Denver Archives, folder 2.

77. In the 1974–75 school year, the question of Rice's academic title was still racing around the administration. The move to give Rice an academic title was set in motion by a memo from Vice Chancellor for University Resources John L. Blackburn, his immediate boss, in a letter to Dean Lindell dated Sep. 4, 1974: "It has come to my attention that with the move of John Rice from your office to my area we failed to indicate, by any academic designation, his tie with one of your departments for the teaching of the Black Experience course. "I believe it appropriate for you to make some academic designation appropriate with his classroom responsibilities." In the end, Rice was given the title of adjunct professor.

78. Cory, Ruth, "Rice, Lindell Research Plan for Complete Minority Library," *The Clarion*, Feb. 22, 1971, in John Wesley Rice file, University of Denver Archives, folder 1.

79. Chancellor Maurice B. Mitchell letters to Assistant Vice Chancellor John Rice, Sept. 30, 1974, and Oct. 24, 1974, in John Wesley Rice file, University of Denver Archives, folder 2.

80. Russakoff, Dale, "Team Rice, Playing Away," *Washington Post*, Mar. 17, 2005, D01.

81. Rice, Condoleezza, interview.

CHAPTER FIVE

1. "American Dream Must Be Delivered to All People, Rice Says," *Campus Report*, Jun. 19, 1985, 12.

2. Korbel's childhood and family history from Michael Dobbs's *Madeleine Albright: A Twentieth-Century Odyssey* (New York: Owl, 2000), 24–25.

3. Dobbs, *Madeleine Albright*, 14–15.

4. Albright, Madeleine, with Bill Woodward, *Madam Secretary: A Memoir* (New York: Miramax, 2003), 7. Edvard Beneš was the Czech president and a hero to Josef Korbel.

5. Dobbs, *Madeleine Albright*, 41.

6. Ibid, 45–47.

7. Ibid, 2–6. Dobbs's biography of Albright, which spends about a third of its length detailing the horrors that her ancestors' suffered, ranks among the most chilling Holocaust literature I have ever read.

8. Rice said this in her interview with me and has repeated the comment in many other interviews.

9. Blacker, Coit "Chip," interview with the author, Jul. 10, 2006. When I was an undergraduate at Stanford, Blacker served as my academic adviser in my international relations major. The academic adviser approves a student's course schedule. We were not personally close.

10. Lemann, Nicholas, "Without a Doubt," *The New Yorker*, Oct. 14, 2002, 164.

11. Nordlinger, Jay, "Star-in-Waiting," *National Review*, Aug. 30, 1999, 35.

12. Korbel had been a Social Democrat in Europe and became a Democrat in the United States, as Dobbs details at great length.

13. Dobbs, *Madeleine Albright*, 220.

14. Dowd, Ann Reilly, "Is There Anything This Woman Can't Do?" *George*, June 2000, 88.

15. Prussian soldier and intellectual Carl Phillip Gottfried (or Gottlieb) von Clausewitz (1780–1831) in his opus *On War*, as cited by Antulio J. Echevarria II, "War and Politics: The Revolution in Military Affairs and the Continued Relevance of Clausewitz," undated, http://www.clausewitz.com/CWZHOME/ECHEVAR/ECHJFQ.htm.

16. Morgenthau, Hans, and Kenneth J. Thompson, *Politics Among Nations: The Struggle for Power and Peace,* 6th ed. (New York: Knopf, 1985), 31.

17. Ibid, 13.

18. Ibid, 12.

19. Blacker interview.

20. Rice, Condoleezza, interview with the author, Nov. 2, 2006.

21. Russakoff, Dale, "Team Rice, Playing Away," *Washington Post*, Mar. 17, 2005, D01.

22. Rice, Condoleezza, interview.

23. Russakoff, Dale, "Lessons of Might and Right," *Washington Post,* Sept. 9, 2001, W23.

24. German, Yvonne, phone interview with the author, Sept. 20, 2006.

25. Rice, Clara, interview with the author, Aug. 1, 2006.

26. Rice, Condoleezza, University of Alabama General Commencement, Tuscaloosa, AL, May 15, 1994.

27. Sammon, Bill, "2008 Run, Abortion Engage Her Politically," *Washington Times*, Mar. 12, 2005, http://www.washtimes.com/national/20050311-102526-8899r.htm.

28. Anonymous interview.

29. Picture from the 1974 *Kynewisbok*, the yearbook of the University of Denver, in Condoleezza Rice folder, DU Archives.

30. "Talking Fitness with Condoleezza Rice," NBC4, Washington, DC, Mar. 1, 2006, http://www.nbc4.com/health/7570624/detail.html.

31. "Hesburgh Biography," University of Notre Dame, Jul. 23, 2006, http://www.nd.edu/aboutnd/about/history/hesburgh_bio.shtml.

32. Mitchell, Maurice B., letter to Condoleezza Rice, Mar. 7, 1974, in Condoleezza Rice folder, DU Archives.

33. Robinett, Jane, interview with the author, Sept. 27, 2006.

34. Ibid.

35. Ibid.

36. Ibid. Rice would not comment on her personal life.

37. Ibid.

38. Ibid.

39. The author could not locate Michelle, but Robinett distinctly recalled the incident back on campus where Rice's words were rehashed.

40. Robinett interview. Rice did not dispute dating either Notre Dame football player, though she said she would correct secondary sources where their information was wrong.

41. Rice, Condoleezza, interview.

42. Lemann, "Without a Doubt."

43. Moore, J. Michael, "Spanning the Decades: Rick Upchurch," DenverBroncos.com, http://www.denverbroncos.com/page.php?id=334&storyID=5680.

44. "Rick Upchurch," Pro Football Reference.com, undated, http://www.pro-football-reference.com/players/UpchRi00.htm.

45. "About Rick," Rick Upchurch.com, undated, http://www.rickupchurch.com/About%20Rick.htm.

46. Robinett interview. Rice would not comment on her personal life except to correct inaccuracies when they were presented to her. She did not say this was incorrect.

47. Carson, Deborah, interview with the author, Sept. 6, 2006.

48. Robinett interview. Rice would not comment on her personal life but did not dispute Robinett's account.

49. "About Rick," Rick Upchurch.com.

50. Sanchez, Rene, "Black Women Earning College Degrees at Twice the Rate of Black Men," *Washington Post*, Feb. 27, 1997.

51. U.S. Census Bureau, Current Population Survey, Table 1. According to the census document released on the Internet in March 2005, as of 2004 there were a total of 431,000 black women between forty and fifty-nine, like Rice, with advanced or professional degrees, compared to 265,000 black men.

52. Dobbs, Michael, "Albright, Rice Share 'Korbelian' Outlook," *Houston Chronicle*, Jan. 7, 2001, A-6.

53. Ibid.

54. With no real interest in law school, Rice had only applied to the schools at the University of Denver, the University of Colorado, the University of Michigan, and Notre Dame.

55. Gilbert, Alan, interview with the author, Apr. 15, 2005.

56. Ibid.

57. CARE (College Acquaintance and Recruitment Experience) brochure, undated, though since the brochure refers to Rice as a nineteen-year-old senior, it was evidently published in the winter or spring of 1974.

58. Moore, Gordon, "The Time 100: William Shockley," Mar. 29, 1999, http://www.time.com/time/time100/scientist/profile/shockley.html.

59. Russakoff, "Lessons of Might and Right."

60. Rice, Condoleezza, Curriculum Vitae, Jan. 1984, SUNS Archive, Condoleezza Rice folder 1. See also Kristin Von Kreisler-Bomben, "Condoleezza Rice: Balancing Act," *Stanford* magazine, Winter 1985, 16.

61. Blacker interview.

62. Blacker interview; Bean, Randy, interview with the author, Aug. 4, 2006. Rice has made this point often, as she did to me.

63. Rice, Condoleezza, interview.

64. Ibid.

65. Ibid.

66. Stanford has seven "schools" that are responsible for teaching and research: Graduate School of Business, School of Earth Sciences, School of Education, School of Engineering, School of Humanities and Sciences (H&S), School of Law, and School of Medicine. Each school has its own dean, who operates as its chief, and each has numerous departments that concentrate on specialized areas of interests. Political Science is one of the departments in the School of Humanities and Sciences, which graduates eighty percent of Stanford undergraduates.

67. Kennedy, David, interview with the author, Aug. 3, 2006.

68. Blacker interview.

69. Kennedy, David, interview.

70. Ibid.

71. Ibid.

72. Ashmore, Harry S., "The End of the Hutchins Era at the Center for the Study of Democratic Institutions," reprinted from *The Center Magazine,* Nov.–Dec. 1984, The School of Cooperative Individualism, http://www.cooperativeindividualism.org/ashmore-harry_on-the-center-for-study-of-democratic-instns.html.

73. University of Denver, Notice of Appointment, Apr. 14, 1978, DU Archives, John W. Rice folder 2 of 2.

74. Blackburn, John L., Vice Chancellor for University Resources, and Kenneth Purcell, Dean, College of Arts and Sciences, University of Denver; letter to John W. Rice, Jr., Mar. 31, 1978, DU Archives, John W. Rice folder 2 of 2.

75. Purcell memo to Rice, Mar. 23, 1979, DU Archives, John W. Rice folder 2 of 2.

76. Morgan, Douglas, Controller, letter to John Rice, Sept. 27, 1978, DU Archives, John W. Rice folder 2 of 2.

77. Purcell memo.

78. Ibid.

79. Rice, Condoleezza, interview.

80. See Purcell memo, May 5, 1979; letter from Dean of Students Robert L. Burrell, May 21, 1982; and letter from Vice Chancellor Tom Goodale, June 9, 1982; DU Archives, John W. Rice folder 2 of 2.

81. Rice, Condoleezza, interview.

82. Burrell, Robert L., confidential letter to Dr. John W. Rice, Jr., May 21, 1982, DU Archives, John W. Rice folder 2 of 2.

83. Griesser, Thomas, e-mail interview with the author, Feb. 12, 2007.

84. Birkeland, John H., letter to Victor Quinn, Cockrell, Quinn & Creighton (DU counsel), Jul. 13, 1982, DU Archives, John W. Rice folder 2 of 2.

85. Memo to Chancellor Ross Pritchard, Sept. 30, 1982, DU Archives, John W. Rice folder 2 of 2.

86. Rice, Condoleezza, interview.

87. Frazer, Jendayi, interview with the author, Aug. 31, 2006. Other Rice protégés such as Sharon Holland, a junior professor at Stanford when Rice was provost, made the same point.

CHAPTER SIX

1. Rice, Condoleezza, memo to Blackwill, "Thinking About Germany," Jan. 12, 1990, as cited in Philip Zelikow and Condoleezza Rice, *Germany Unified and Europe Transformed: A Study in Statecraft* (Cambridge, MA: Harvard University Press, 2002), 158–60.

2. Schwartz, Mark, "Fifteen Years after Loma Prieta Earthquake," *Stanford Report,* Oct. 13, 2004, http://news-service.stanford.edu/news/2004/october13/Quakes-1013.html.

3. Casper, Gerhard, interview with the author, Jul. 31, 2006.

4. Rice, Condoleezza, curriculum vitae, Jan. 1992, SUNS Archives, Condoleezza Rice folder.

5. In 1984 Rice won the Walter J. Gores Award for Excellence in Teaching and in 1993, a Dean's Teaching Award.

6. Former Stanford administrator interview; two Harvard sources interviews.

7. Kennedy, David, interview with the author, Aug. 3, 2006.

8. Bean, Randy, interview with the author, Aug. 4, 2006.

9. Dowd, Ann Reilly, "Is There Anything This Woman Can't Do?" *George,* June 2000, 88.

10. In 2005, Rice told *New York Times'* Steven Weisman in an interview, "you know right away when somebody is either patronizing or when—which is the one [response] that I dislike most, by the way, which is kind of, you know, the 'poor minorities.' No matter who you are or what you've achieved or how you've achieved it, that's the one that I find most disturbing." See "Interview with Steven Weisman of the *New York Times,*" State Department Web site, Oct. 20, 2005, http://www.state.gov/secretary/rm/2005/55437.htm.

11. Russakoff, Dale, "Lessons of Might and Right," *Washington Post,* Sept. 9, 2001, W23.

12. Rice, Condoleezza, interview with the author, Nov. 2, 2006.

13. German, Yvonne, phone interview with the author, Sept. 20, 2006.

14. Dallin, Alexander, and Condoleezza Rice, *The Gorbachev Era* (Palo Alto, CA: Stanford Alumni Association, 1986).

15. Bean interview; Rice, Clara, interview with the author, Aug. 1, 2006.

16. Rice, Clara, interview.

17. Lemann, Nicholas, "Without a Doubt," *The New Yorker*, Oct. 14, 2002, 164.

18. Scowcroft, Brent, interview with the author, Oct. 6, 2005.

19. Rice, Condoleezza, interview.

20. Scowcroft interview.

21. In October 1986 Reagan sat down with Mikhail Gorbachev in Reykjavik, Iceland, and offered drastic reductions in U.S. nuclear armaments, even envisioning the eventual elimination of such weapons, provided Reagan's Strategic Defense Initiative, or Star Wars, was allowed to go forward and the Anti-Ballistic Missile Treaty scrapped.

22. Bean interview.

23. "Interview with Dr. Condoleezza Rice," The National Security Archive, George Washington University, Dec. 17, 1997, http://www.gwu.edu/~nsarchiv/coldwar/interviews/episode-24/rice1.html.

24. Rice had interned in 1977 at the State Department's education and culture bureau and had been a Council on Foreign Relations International Affairs Fellow, assigned to the Pentagon in the '86–'87 school year, working for the director of the Joint Chiefs of Staff (the principal uniformed military advisers to the president) while Colin Powell was chairman of the Joint Chiefs under Reagan.

25. Almond, Mark, *Uprising: Political Upheavals That Have Shaped the World* (London: Mitchell Beazley, 2002).

26. "Man of the Year," *Time*, Jan. 4, 1998.

27. For excerpts from Gorbachev's speech see "Address by Mikhail Gorbachev at the 43rd U.N. General Assembly Session, Dec. 7, 1988 (Excerpts)," *The Cold War Files*, Cold War International History Project, http://www.coldwarfiles.org/index.cfm?fuseaction=documents.details&thisunit=0&documentid=110.

28. See Bush, George, and Brent Scowcroft, *A World Transformed* (New York: Knopf, 1998), 39.

29. Zelikow and Rice, *Germany Unified*, 24. See also Robert Gates, *From the Shadows* (New York: Touchstone, 1996), 459–62.

30. Bush and Scowcroft, *A World Transformed*, 40.

31. Scowcroft interview.

32. In their book, Zelikow and Rice credit the report to Rice and her boss Blackwill. In his interview with the author, however, Scowcroft named the document as specifically an accomplishment of Condoleezza Rice.

33. Zelikow and Rice, *Germany Unified*, 27.

34. Ibid., 26.

35. Bush, George, "A Europe Whole and Free: Remarks to the Citizens in Mainz. President George Bush. Rheingoldhalle. Mainz, Federal Republic of Germany, May 31, 1989," U.S. Diplomatic Mission to Germany, http://usa.usembassy.de/etexts/ga6-890531.htm. See also Bush and Scowcroft, *A World Transformed*, 45–55.

36. Scowcroft interview.

37. Daalder, Ivo, interview with the author, May 16, 2005.

38. Zelikow and Rice, *Germany Unified*, 64–65.

39. Ibid., 75.

40. Ibid., 82.

41. Ibid., 98–101.

42. Reagan, Ronald, "Remarks at the Brandenburg Gate," Jun. 12, 1987, http://www.reaganfoundation.org/reagan/speeches/wall.asp.

43. Zelikow and Rice, *Germany Unified*, 20–21, 104, 255, 364–69. Zelikow and Rice's book, a masterpiece of diplomatic history that provides a virtual day-by-day account of the calculations, interests, and discussions that led to Germany's reunification, both inside the U.S. administration and among the keys players, including Kohl and Gorbachev, can also be read as a reasoned yet passionate defense of the style and legacy of George Bush. One of its central conceits is that had Bush not been Bush—a leader who avoided taking credit even when he deserved it, a president dedicated to quiet diplomacy rather than fiery challenges to his adversaries—then the Soviet Union might have awaken much sooner to the loss of its European empire, and instead of conciliation the end of the Cold War might have been marked by chaos.

44. Scowcroft, Brent, memo to President Bush, "The Soviets and the German Question," Nov. 29, 1989, as cited in Zelikow and Rice, *Germany Unified*, 125–26.

45. Rice, Condoleezza, memo to Blackwill, "Thinking About Germany," Jan. 12, 1990, as cited in Zelikow and Rice, *Germany Unified,* 158–60.

46. Ross, Dennis, interview with the author, May 17, 2005.

47. Zelikow and Rice, *Germany Unified*, 167–68, 172.

48. Baker, James, interview with the author, May 24, 2005.

49. Zelikow and Rice, *Germany Unified*, 193–94.

50. "[P]ersonal relationships, though strained, did not break," wrote Zelikow and Rice, *Germany Unified*, 195.

51. Zelikow and Rice, *Germany Unified*, 227.

52. See Zelikow and Rice, *Germany Unified*, 437, n67.

53. Zelikow and Rice, *Germany Unified*, 228.

54. Ibid., 281–82.

55. Elaine Sciolino, "Compulsion to Achieve," *New York Times*, Dec. 18, 2000, A1.

56. "Modest Bush Approval Rating Boost at War's End," Pew Research Center, Apr. 18, 2003, http://people-press. org/reports/display.php3?ReportID=182.

57. Bush, George H. W., e-mail interview, December 2006.

58. Zelikow and Rice, *Germany Unified*, 207.

59. For a detailed explication of the role his national security adviser played in the smooth running of the national security process, see Bush and Scowcroft, *A World Transformed*, 35.

60. See Zelikow and Rice, *Germany Unified*, 22–23.

61. Zelikow and Rice, *Germany Unified*, 367–68.

62. Rice curriculum vitae, Jan. 1992, SUNS Archives.

63. The quote is widely repeated, but one reference is found in "Condi Rice Can't Lose," by *Time*'s Romesh Ratnesar, Sept. 27, 1999, 51.

64. Frazer, Jendayi, interview with the author, Aug. 31, 2006.

65. Rice's RNC address, transcribed by author.

66. Shultz, George, interview with the author, Apr. 20, 2005. The members, according to the former secretary of state were himself; physicist Sid Drell, who had been a supporter of Rice from her arrival at Stanford; and Lucy Shapiro, "a first-rate biologist."

67. Shultz interview.

68. Ibid.

69. Rice curriculum vitae, Jan. 1992, SUNS Archives.

70. Rice, Condoleezza, White House biography.

71. Mann, James, *Rise of the Vulcans: The History of Bush's War Cabinet* (New York: Penguin Books, 2004), 226.

72. Rice curriculum vitae, Jan. 1992, SUNS Archives.

73. Shultz interview.

74. Blacker, Coit "Chip," interview with the author, Jul. 10, 2006.

75. Casper interview.

76. Committee member interview with the author.

77. A list of university appointments and promotions dated Jun. 11, 1993, shows Rice was "promoted to full professor effective May 1, 1993"; SUNS, Condoleezza Rice folder, general and bio.

78. Thomas, Ewart, interview with the author, Jul. 31, 2006.

79. Bean interview.

80. Ibid.

81. Former Rice colleague, interview with the author.

82. Blacker interview.

83. State Department security guard, interview with the author.

84. Frazer interview.

85. See Cose, Ellis, and Alison Samuels, "The Black Gender Gap," *Newsweek*, Mar. 3, 2003, 46.

86. Bean interview.

87. Ibid.

88. Rice, Clara, interview.

89. "San Francisco 49ers Draft History," databaseFootball.com, undated, http://www.databasefootball.com/draft/ draftteam.htm?tm=SFO&lg=nfl.

90. "Interior Secretary Gale Norton Appoints Three to National Park Foundation Board," National Park Foundation press release, Mar. 31, 2003, http://www.nationalparks.org/AboutUs/AboutUs-PR_3.31.03.shtml.

91. Russakoff, Dale, "Team Rice, Playing Away," *Washington Post*, Mar. 17, 2005, D01.

92. Bean interview.

CHAPTER SEVEN

1. Rice, Condoleezza, interview with the author, Nov. 2, 2006.

2. Ledezma, Mirabel, "Chicano Students Go on Hunger Strike!" Movimiento Estudiantil Chicano de Atzlan listserve post, http://seas.stanford.edu/diso/articles/chicanohungerstrike.html.

3. Guzman, Ed, and Adam Kemezis, "Six Eventful Years—Highlights of Rice's Term," *Stanford Daily*, Dec. 11, 1998, http://daily.stanford.edu/article/1998/12/11/sixEventfulYearsHighlightsOfRicesTerm.

4. Ledezma, "Chicano Students."

5. Lemann, Nicholas, "Without a Doubt," *The New Yorker*, Oct. 14, 2002, 164.

6. Frazer, Jendayi, interview with the author, Aug. 31, 2006.

7. Casper, Gerhard, interview with the author, Jul. 31, 2006.

8. Jackson, Michael, interview with the author, Aug. 24, 2006.

9. Guzman and Kemezis, "Six Eventful Years."

10. "Provost Challenges Managers to Work Hard, Adapt to Change," SUNS press release, Nov. 11, 1993, SUNS Archives, "Condoleezza Rice, speeches, text" folder.

11. Stanford professor, interview with the author.

12. Former Stanford administration official, interview with the author.

13. Barabak, Mark Z., "Condoleezza Rice at Stanford," *Los Angeles Times*, Jan. 16, 2005.

14. Former Stanford employee, interview with the author.

15. Elam, Harry, interview with the author, Jul. 31, 2006.

16. Stanford professor, interview with the author.

17. Former Stanford student interview with the author.

18. Thomas, Ewart, interview with the author, Jul. 31, 2006.

19. Former administration official, interview with the author.

20. Bartholomew, Karen, "Senate Off to Rousing Start," *Campus Report*, Oct. 6, 1993.

21. See SUNS press releases, Sept. 22, 1993 and Dec. 6, 1993; SUNS Archives, Condoleezza Rice folder.

22. "Report of the Provost's Committee on the Recruitment and Retention of Women Faculty," November 1993, http://universitywomen.stanford.edu/reports/SU-reportofprovost.pdf#search=%22stanford%20report%20on%20r ecruitment%20and%20retention%20of%20women%20faculty%20%22.

23. SUNS press release, "Myra Strober: Other Institutions Better at Recruiting," Dec. 1, 1993, SUNS Archives, Condoleezza Rice folder.

24. Faculty Senate minutes from the May 14, 1998, meeting, http://news-service.stanford.edu/news/1998/may20/minutes520.html.

25. Ibid.

26. Ibid.

27. Ibid.

28. Manuel, Diane, "Hiring, Tenuring of Women Faculty Topic of Reports to Faculty Senate," *Stanford Report*, May 13, 1998, 1.

29. Manuel, Diane, "Senators, Others Debate Status of Women Faculty," *Stanford Report*, May 20, 1998, 1.

30. Manuel, "Senators"; see also Michelle Levander, "Teacher on Trial: An Inside Look at Tenure," *San Jose Mercury News*, Jan. 6, 1999, 1B; Levander, "Tenure Fight Rocks Stanford," *Mercury News*, May 30, 1997; and Jennifer Kong, "Fulfilling Stanford's Commitment to Diversity: Eliminating Gender Bias and Increasing the Number of Tenured Women Faculty," *The Boothe Prize Essays 2003*, 38–57, http://pwr.stanford.edu/publications/Boothe_0203/PWR%20Boothe-Kong.pdf; and Yvonne Daley, "Wanted: Female Faculty," *Stanford* magazine, Mar./Apr. 1999, http://www.stanfordalumni.org/news/magazine/1999/marapr/articles/female_faculty.html.

31. Stanford professor, interview with the author. The minutes of the Senate meeting and the *Stanford Report* article do not detail the exchange between Rice and Okin. The minutes report part of the exchange as follows: "Professor Okin (Political Science) questioned the Provost's standard of 'reasonableness' based on campus news reports about a specific, recent grievance, to which Provost Rice replied that she would not comment on a specific case, and that the press reports had been erroneous."

32. Lemann, "Without a Doubt."

33. Manuel, "Senators."

34. May 14, 1998, Faculty Senate minutes.

35. Rice, Condoleezza, letter to the editor, *Stanford Report*, Jun. 10, 1998, 4.

36. Thomas, Ewart, interview with the author, Aug. 2, 2006.

37. Kennedy, Donald, interview.

38. Daley, "Wanted: Female Faculty."

39. Ibid.

40. Blacker, Coit "Chip," interview with the author, Jul. 10, 2006.

41. Rice, Condoleezza, *World Politics* 40, no. 1 (Oct. 1987), 55–81.

42. Odom, William E., interview with the author, May 22, 2005.

43. Anonymous interview with the author.

44. Stanford source, interview with the author.

45. Blacker interview.

46. Elam interview.

47. Brant, Martha, and Evan Thomas, "A Steely Southern," *Newsweek*, Aug. 6, 2001, 28.

48. Croal, Ngai, interview with the author, May 23, 2005. Croal, a writer for *Newsweek*, is a colleague and friend of the author.

49. Background interview with the author.

50. "Condoleezza Rice," *Mad About Music*, WNYC New York Public Radio, Jan. 2, 2005, http:www.wnyc.org/shows/mam/episodes/2005/01/02.

51. Brest, Paul, interview with the author, Aug. 1, 2006.

52. Rice, Clara, interview with the author, Aug. 1, 2006.

53. All educational and census bureau statistics from "The Center for a New Generation Overview," Jul. 12, 2005, http://www.bgcp.org/Linked%20documents/CNG/CNG%20Overview4.pdf.

54. Holland, Sharon, interview with the author, August 23, 2006.

55. Ibid.

56. Manuel, Diane, "Memorial Scheduled for English Professor," Oct. 20, 1997, SUNS, press release, http://www.stanford.edu/dept/news/pr/97/971022romero.html.

57. SUNS press release, May 9, 1994.

58. Jackson interview.

59. Barker, Lucius, interview with the author, Aug. 4, 2006.

60. Anonymous interview.

61. Elam interview.

62. Thomas, Ewart, interview.

63. Stanford professor, interview with the author.

64. Croal interview. Rice confirmed this quote, although she remembers saying it to a female student.

65. Rice, Condoleezza, "Reflect not on what you learned but on how you have learned it," *Stanford Report*, Jun. 16, 1999.

66. "Rice Steps Down to Pursue Her Passion," *Stanford* magazine, Jan./Feb. 1999, 23. Rice made her announcement on December 8, 1998.

67. Cohn, Bob, "Rice on Students, Tough Decisions and Her Oil Tanker," *Stanford* magazine, May/Jun. 1999, 30.

68. Ibid.

69. Robinson, James, "'Velvet-Glove Forcefulness,'" *Stanford Report*, Jun. 9, 1999. The *Stanford Daily* pronounced the change in undergraduate education "[Rice's] most important impact." (Guzman and Kemezis, "Six eventful years.")

70. According to a former Rice colleague, Rice eliminated "Central Supplies," the Soviet-sounding department that existed solely to fulfill office supply needs and had asked, "Why do we own a barbershop?"

71. Rice, Condoleezza, interview.

72. Levander, Michelle, "U.S. Probes Stanford Promotion Policies," *San Jose Mercury News*, Feb. 2, 1999, 1A.

73. Rafferty, Carol, "Top Scholar Encourages Race-Sensitive Admissions," *San Jose Mercury News*, Mar. 6, 1999, 1B.

74. Krieger, Lisa M., "University Under Scrutiny," *San Jose Mercury News*, Oct. 10, 2005, 1B.

75. Former Stanford employee, interview with the author.

76. Women's Caucus member, interview with the author.

77. Rice, Condoleezza, interview.

78. Blacker interview; interviews with Rice's Stanford friends.

79. Blacker interview.

80. Holland interview.

81. Bean, Randy, interview with the author, Aug. 4, 2006.

82. Blacker interview.

83. Mann, James, *Rise of the Vulcans: The History of Bush's War Cabinet* (New York: Penguin Books, 2004), 227.

84. Rice, Clara, interview.

85. Stanford administrator interview.

86. Brest interview.

87. Blacker interview.

CHAPTER EIGHT

1. Allen, Mike, "Bush Taps Rice for Security," *Washington Post*, Dec. 18, 2000, A01.

2. Rice, Clara, interview with the author, Aug. 1, 2006.

3. Rice, Clara, interview. Condoleezza Rice confirmed this conversation in an interview with the author.

4. "Texas Governor George W. Bush Wins in a Landslide," CNN allpolitics.com, Nov. 3, 1998, http://www.cnn.com/ALLPOLITICS/stories/1998/11/03/election/governors/texas/index.html.

5. Rice, Condoleezza, interview with the author, Nov. 2, 2006.

6. Ibid.

7. Ibid.

8. Sciolino, Elaine, "Bush's Foreign Policy Tutor," *New York Times*, Jun. 16, 2000, A1.

9. Swanson, Doug J., "Brain Power," *Dallas Morning News*, Aug. 11, 1999, 1A.

10. Ibid.

11. Shultz remembered Michael Boskin, President George H. W. Bush's chief economic adviser; former Shultz chief speechwriter Robert Kagan; and Abe Sofaer, a specialist in diplomacy, national security, and separation of powers. Mann's *Vulcans* provides a slightly different list than Shultz's account: Sofaer, John Cogan, John Taylor, and Martin Anderson, p. 248. Rice said in an interview that she thought the gathering was in the fall. Shultz remembered it being in the spring. *Dallas Morning News*'s Swanson reported in August 1999 that it occurred in April.

12. Shultz, George, interview with the author, Apr. 20, 2005.

13. DeYoung, Karen, *Soldier: The Life of Colin Powell* (New York: Knopf, 2006), 285.

14. Woodward, Bob, *State of Denial: Bush at War: Part III* (New York: Simon & Schuster, 2006), 6.

15. Rice, Condoleezza, interview.

16. Rice Stanford colleague, interview with the author.

17. Rice, Condoleezza, interview.

18. Sciolino, "Tutor."

19. Rice, Condoleezza, interview.

20. Reed, Julia, "The President's Prodigy," *Vogue*, Oct. 2001, 396.

21. Sciolino, "Tutor."

22. Carson, Deborah, interview with the author, Sept. 6, 2006.

23. Many of Rice's friends and family members made this point very strongly, as did, more delicately, some of her Washington colleagues.

24. Rice, Condoleezza, interview.

25. Ibid.

26. Hamberry-Green, Brenda, interview with the author, Apr. 19, 2006.

27. Kristof, Nicholas D., "How Bush Came to Tame His Inner Scamp," *New York Times*, Jul. 29, 2000, A1.

28. Robinson, Walter V., "1-Year Gap in Bush's Guard Duty No Record of Airman at Drills in 1972–73," *Boston Globe*, May 23, 2000, A1.

29. Alexander, Paul, "Alabama Getaway," *Rolling Stone*, Oct. 14, 2004, 51.

30. Rice, Connie, phone interview with the author, Oct. 3, 2006. German, Yvonne, phone interview with the author, Sept. 20, 2006.

31. Rice, Condoleezza, interview.

32. The literature on the president's former life is extensive, both in mainstream newspapers and magazines, as well as biographies of Bush. The president has never denied his aimless pre-midlife. For a synopsis of Bush's undisciplined youth from an anti-Bush viewpoint, see Paul Alexander, "All Hat, No Cattle," *Rolling Stone*, Aug. 5, 1999, 36; and especially Alexander, "Alabama Getaway." For a neutral bias, see Kristof, "Scamp"; and Evan Thomas's profiles in *Newsweek*: "The Road to Resolve," Sept. 6, 2004, 32; and "A Son's Restless Journey," Aug. 7, 2000, 32.

33. For Bush's decision to stop drinking, see Bill Minutaglio's *First Son: George W. Bush and the Bush Family Dynasty* (New York: Crown, 1999); Kristof, "Scamp"; and Jill Lawrence, "The Evolution of George Bush, *USA Today*, Jul. 28, 2000, 8A.

34. Woodward, *State of Denial*, 15.

35. Milbank, Dana, "Dispelling Doubts with the Rangers," *Washington Post*, Jul. 25, 2000, A01.

36. Ignatius, David, "Groomed at the Ballpark," *Washington Post*, Jun. 18, 2000, B07.

37. See Thomas, "Road to Resolve," and "A Son's Restless Journey."

38. Blacker, Coit "Chip," interview with the author, Jul. 10, 2006.

39. In his anti-Iraq examination of the uniformed military's diminished role in the Bush administration, *Fiasco*, the *Washington Post*'s Thomas Ricks presents a plausible case for Bush taking on more of the values of the sixties than is commonly assumed or apparent from his behavior or rhetoric.

40. Rice, Condoleezza, interview.

41. Andy Hiller of WHDH-TV asked Bush to name the leaders of Pakistan, India, Chechnya, and Taiwan, the candidate knew only "Lee," Taiwan's Lee Teng-hui of Taiwan.

42. Sciolino, "Tutor."

43. Ibid.

44. Ibid.

45. Rice, Condoleezza, "Promoting the National Interest," *Foreign Affairs* 79, no. 1 (Jan./Feb. 2000), 45–62.

46. Ibid.

47. Blacker interview.

48. Former Bush campaign aide, interview with the author.

49. Dowd, Ann Reilly, "Is There Anything This Woman Can't Do?" *George*, June 2000, 88.

50. Ibid.

51. Ibid.
52. Rice, Clara, interview.
53. Ibid.
54. Ibid.
55. Pederson, Rena, "Condoleezza on the Go," *Dallas Morning News*, Oct. 22, 2000, 2J.
56. Zeleny, Jeff, and Sabrina L. Miller, "Bush Sends Adviser to Court Undecideds on North Shore," *Chicago Tribune*, Nov. 1, 2000, N3.
57. CNN *Inside Politics* transcript, Oct. 18, 2000, http://transcripts.cnn.com/TRANSCRIPTS/0010/18/ip.00.html.
58. Sciolino, "Tutor."
59. Blacker interview.
60. Buchanan, Pat, 1992 Republican National Convention address, Aug. 17, 1992, PBS recording, Vanderbilt University Television News Archives.
61. Edsall, Thomas B., "Bush Lost 9 to 1 Among Blacks," *Washington Post*, Dec. 12, 2000, A01.
62. Carson interview.
63. Edsall, "Bush Lost 9 to 1."
64. Hamberry-Green said in an interview that Rice told her and the other women in her Palo Alto saloon that she was certain Bush would win in the end.
65. Carson interview.
66. The split decision from the court was among the most controversial of its history. The judges issued six separate opinions totaling sixty-five pages just hours before the deadline that would have allowed a congressional challenge to a state's electors, and just three days before the Electoral College was to meet. Unlike the other four dissenting justices, who said they dissented "respectfully," Justice Ruth Bader Ginsburg—who would later become a friend of Rice and swear her in in Rice's ceremonial swearing-in as secretary of state—wrote only, "I dissent." See Linda Greenhouse of the *New York Times*' "Bush Prevails," Dec. 13, 2000, A1.
67. Raum, Tom, "Bush Camp, Republican Candidate Hails Rulings," *Miami Herald*, Dec. 5, 2000.
68. Oppel, Richard A., and Frank Bruni, "Bush Adviser Gets National Security Post," *New York Times*, Dec. 18, 2000; Mike Allen, "Bush Taps Rice for Security Adviser," *Washington Post*, Dec. 18, 2000, A01.
69. Allen, "Bush Taps Rice." The other advisers were Karen Hughes and Alberto Gonzales, longtime Bush aides in Texas, and, in the case of Gonzalez, also a Bush appointee to the state supreme court.
70. Oppel, "National Security Post"; Allen, "Bush Taps Rice."
71. Oppel, "National Security Post."
72. Finn, Peter, "Allies Reassured by Old Hands in Bush's Circle," *Washington Post*, Dec. 14, 2000, A37.
73. Allen, "Bush Taps Rice."
74. Ibid.
75. Rice, Clara, interview.
76. Ibid.
77. Ibid.
78. Ibid.
79. Blacker interview.
80. Rice, Clara, interview.
81. Rice, Condoleezza, interview.
82. Ibid.
83. Rice, Clara, interview.

CHAPTER NINE

1. Blacker, Coit "Chip," interview with the author, Jul. 10, 2006.
2. Ibid.
3. Blacker interview; Bean, Randy, interview with the author, Aug. 4, 2006.
4. DeYoung, Karen, *Soldier: The Life of Colin Powell* (New York: Knopf, 2006), 299.
5. DeYoung, Karen, and Mufson, Steven, "A Leaner and Less Visible NSC," *Washington Post*, Feb. 10, 2001, A01.
6. Blackwill, Robert, interview with the author, Oct. 25, 2006.
7. Blackwill interview.
8. DeYoung, *Soldier*, 314.
9. Ibid., 315.
10. Ibid., 315.
11. Ibid., 316.
12. Ibid., 316–18.
13. Ibid., 317.
14. Ibid., 324–25.

15. Mufson, Steven, "U.S. Will Resume Talks with N. Korea," *Washington Post*, Jun. 7, 2001, A01.

16. Perlez, Jane, "Divergent Voices Heard in Bush Foreign Policy," *New York Times*, Mar. 12, 2001, A8.

17. For the example of pulling Powell back on suggesting the U.S. would come up with an alternative to the Kyoto Protocol on global climate change, see Thom Shanker, "White House Says the U.S. Is Not a Loner, Just Choosy," *New York Times*, Jul. 31, 2001, A1. And see DeYoung, *Soldier*, p. 326 and throughout.

18. Former NSC staffers, interviews with the author.

19. Mann, James, *Rise of the Vulcans: The History of Bush's War Cabinet* (New York: Penguin Books, 2004), 282.

20. Shanker, "Not a Loner."

21. DeYoung, *Soldier*, 327–28.

22. Sipress, Alan, "Aggravated Allies Waiting for U.S. to Change Its Tunes," *Washington Post*, Apr. 22, 2001, A04.

23. Slavin, Barbara, and Judy Keen, "Bush Trusts Foreign Policy Tutor with World," *USA Today*, Jun. 11, 2001, 7A.

24. For a representative sampling, see William Pfaff, "Is Bush Capable of Pulling Off a 'New American Unilateralism'?" *Chicago Tribune*, Jun. 19, 2001, N19; R.C. Longworth, "U.S. Walks Alone on World Stage," *Chicago Tribune*, Jun. 24, 2001, C1; Anthony Lewis, "Bush the Radical," *New York Times*, Jul. 21, 2001, A15; Jim Hoagland, "The Danger of Bush's Unilateralism," *Washington Post*, Jul. 29, 2001, B07; and from earlier in the administration, Jonathan Clarke, "May Powell Win the GOP Slug Fest Over Foreign Policy," *Los Angeles Times*, Feb. 6, 2001, B9.

25. Wright, Robin, "Bush Trip to Europe Will Air U.S. View," *Los Angeles Times*, Jun. 10, 2001, A1.

26. Wright, Robin, "Colin Powell: At the Policy Helm," *Los Angeles Times*, Sept. 9, 2001, M3.

27. Ratnesar, Romesh, "Condi Rice Can't Lose," *Time*, Sept. 27, 1999, 51.

28. Pederson, Rena, "Condoleezza on the Go," *Dallas Morning News*, Oct. 22, 2000, 2J.

29. For a defense of the administration's policies, see Mann's argument in *Vulcans* (p. 287–88) that the Clinton administration—in its refusal to join the International Criminal Court, to send the Kyoto Protocol to the Senate and rejection of the international treaty to ban landmines—had started a post–Cold War trend toward unilateralism. Rice could convincingly argue that the administration's actions sprung solely from a hard-eyed calculation of America's interests on a case-by-case basis. (And she did: see Warren P. Strobel of the *Philadelphia Inquirer*'s "Leading U.S. Foreign Policy, Rice Confounds Doubters," Aug. 12, 2001, E03.) She would also dispute the view that a wide-range of voices went unheard or unacknowledged in the administration.

30. Ratnesar, "Condi Rice Can't Lose." Powell, Rice, and most of the Vulcans, were longtime Council members; the careers of some had even benefited from it, like the fellowship that had given Condi her first important exposure to Washington (and to Powell) from 1986 to 1987 working for the Joint Chiefs of Staff at the Pentagon. Powell's director of policy planning at the State Department, Richard Haass, would go on to head the Council after his time in the Bush administration. The author is also a member of the CFR and a former fellow.

31. Kagan, Robert, and William Kristol, "A National Humiliation," *Weekly Standard*, Apr. 16, 2001, 11, as cited in Mann, *Vulcans*, 284.

32. See Krauthammer, Charles, "The New Unilateralism," *Washington Post*, Jun. 8, 2001, A29.

33. The vice president's belief that Congress robbed the presidency of power has been widely written about, see, for example, Evan Thomas and Richard Wolffe's "Bush in the Bubble," *Newsweek*, Dec. 19, 2005, 30.

34. Thomas, Evan, "The Rescue Squad," *Newsweek*, Nov. 20, 2006, 38.

35. In *State of Denial*, Bob Woodward came to much the same conclusion, writing on page 16, that "despite all the tutoring, Bush had no plan for foreign affairs. He held no 'so-help-me-God' convictions." In fact Bush did have such convictions, only they amounted to broad philosophies rather than specific policies. The end result, however, was that there was no plan, just goals and priorities, in no specific order.

36. Hart said that Rice had told him this when they saw each other at the CFR in the spring of 2001. Rice volunteered as a student on Hart's 1974 Senate campaign and advised him in 1980.

37. Hart, Gary, interview with the author, Apr. 29, 2005.

38. "President Nixon and Bob Haldeman Discuss Donald Rumsfeld, Mar. 9, 1971," Conversation number 464-12, WhiteHouseTapes.org, Miller Center of Public Affairs, University of Virginia, http://www.whitehousetapes.org/clips/rmn_rumsfeld.html.

39. Interviews with administration officials; DeYoung, *Soldier*, 334.

40. CIA director George Tenet offers what seems to be a rarely held contrarian view that Rice was actually disorganized in her job. See Woodward, *Denial*, 79.

41. DeYoung, *Soldier*, 334.

42. In addition to the many books on the Bush foreign policy team, see Evan Thomas and Roy Gutman, "See George. See George Learn Foreign Policy," *Newsweek*, Jun. 18, 2001, 20.

43. Woodward, *Denial*, 33; Mann, *Vulcans*, 285; for praise of the president's boldness, and the suggestion that it was not a gaffe, see "The End of Strategic Ambiguity," editorial, *Washington Times*, Apr. 27, 2001.

44. Many Rice colleagues both in Washington and California made this point. See also Evan Thomas, "The Quiet Power of Condi Rice," *Newsweek*, Dec. 16, 2002, 24.

45. Scowcroft, Brent, interview with the author, Oct. 6, 2005.

46. In addition to many friends who were also colleagues, who worked with Rice at Stanford or in Washington, who made this point in interviews, so did *National Journal*'s Paul Starobin in his cover profile of Rice "On Her Own," Jan. 29, 2005, and *Newsweek*'s Evan Thomas, "Quiet Power."

47. Rice friend and colleague interview.

48. Perlez, "Divergent Voices"; Warren P. Strobel, "Leading U.S. Foreign Policy, Rice Confounds Doubters," *Philadelphia Inquirer,* Aug. 12, 2001, E03; Thom Raum, Associated Press, "Top Bush Team Changes: Rice Gains, Cheney Falls," *Miami Herald,* Jul. 29, 2001, 25A; Dave Montgomery, and Warren P. Strobel, "U.S., Russia Still Differ on Defense Ideas," *Philadelphia Inquirer,* Jul. 27, 2001, A02.

49. Thomas and Gutman, "See George Learn."

50. Perlez, "Divergent Voices."

51. Strobel, "U.S., Russia Still Differ."

52. Reed, Julia, "The President's Prodigy," *Vogue,* Oct. 2001, 396.

53. "Oprah's Cut with Condoleezza Rice," *O, The Oprah Magazine,* Feb. 2002, http://www.oprah.com/omagazine/200202/omag_200202_ocut.jhtml.

54. "Rice in 'Vogue': Interview of Writer Julia Reed on National Security Adviser's Photo Spread," CNN transcript, Oct. 31, 2001, http://transcripts.cnn.com/TRANSCRIPTS/0110/31/ltm.01.html.

55. "Oprah's Cut with Condoleezza Rice."

56. Ibid.

57. Ibid. In his book *Against All Enemies: Inside America's War on Terror* (New York: Free Press, 2004), Richard Clarke describes the sequence of events somewhat differently, but his account is not materially different from Rice's.

58. Clarke, *Against All Enemies,* 3.

59. Ibid. In *Against All Enemies,* Clarke would write that Rice was later "criticized in the press by unknown participants for 'just standing around,'" but that "she had shown courage by standing back. She knew it looked odd, but she also had enough self-confidence to feel no need to be in the chair."

60. "Remarks by the President Upon Arrival at Barksdale Air Force Base," White House Press Office release, Sept. 11, 2001, http://www.whitehouse.gov/news/releases/2001/09/20010911-1.html#.

61. See David Frum's *The Right Man* (New York: Random House, 2002), 124–51; as cited in Mann, *Vulcans,* 296.

62. Author's transcription of White House video, White House News Archives for Sept. 14, 2001, http://www.whitehouse.gov/news/releases/2001/09/#.

63. Colombani, Jean-Marie, editorial, *Le Monde,* "*Nous sommes tous Americains,*" Sept. 13, 2001, 1. Later critics of Colombani, like Middle East scholar Fouad Ajami, would assail him for what they considered his anti-American views following 9/11.

64. Woolfolk, Odessa, interview with the author, Mar. 24, 2005.

65. Carson, Deborah, interview with the author, Sept. 6, 2006.

66. German, Yvonne, phone interview with the author, Sept. 20, 2006.

67. Thomas, Evan, et.al., "Their Faith and Fears," *Newsweek,* Sept. 9, 2002, 36.

68. Carson interview.

69. Rice Washington colleague interview.

70. Blacker interview.

71. See Mann, *Vulcans,* 308.

72. Bush speech to the American Enterprise Institute, Feb. 26, 2003, as cited in Mann, *Vulcans,* 352.

73. See Mann, *Vulcans,* 326–27.

74. Blacker interview.

75. Haass, Richard, interview with the author, Jun. 19, 2006.

76. Woodward, Bob, *Plan of Attack,* (New York: Simon & Schuster, 2004), 149–51.

77. Woodward, *Attack,* 151.

78. Jehl, Douglas, "British Memo on U.S. Plans for Iraq War Fuels Critics," *New York Times,* May 20, 2005, A10.

79. See Mann, *Vulcans,* for detailing of Bush I secretaries of State James Baker and Lawrence Eagleberger public objections to going to war in Iraq, 337–38.

80. See *Face the Nation,* CBS News, Aug. 2, 2004 and Brent Scowcroft, "Don't Attack Saddam," *Wall Street Journal,* Aug. 15, 2002, A12.

81. Mann, *Vulcans,* 337. Mann writes that Scowcroft had actually sent Rice a copy of the oped, but that it hadn't reached her until the morning the *Journal* ran the piece.

82. Kessler, Glenn, and Pincus, Walter, "Advisers Split as War Unfolds," *Washington Post,* Mar. 31, 2003, A01.

83. Bumiller, Elisabeth, "Bush Aides Set Strategy to Sell Policy on Iraq," *New York Times,* Sept. 7, 2002, A1.

84. "Interview with Condoleezza Rice," *Late Edition,* Sept. 8, 2002, 12:00 p.m. ET, http://transcripts.cnn.com/TRANSCRIPTS/0209/08/le.00.html.

85. Ibid.

86. Ibid.

87. Mann, *Vulcans,* 316–17.

88. *The National Security Strategy of the United States of America*, Sept. 2002, unnumbered introduction, first page of report, http://www.whitehouse.gov/nsc/nss.pdf.

89. "Remarks by National Security Adviser Condoleezza Rice on Terrorism and Foreign Policy," speech to Paul H. Nitze School of Advanced International Studies, Johns Hopkins University, Apr. 29, 2002, as cited in Mann, *Vulcans*, 316.

90. *The National Security Strategy*, 15.

91. See Mann, *Vulcans*, 345–47.

92. Mann, *Vulcans*, 349.

93. Blacker interview.

94. Pluckhahn, Charles, letter to the editor *New York Times*, Feb. 6, 2003. Pluckhahn captured the general effect of Powell's speech: "I am one of those who has been ambivalent about going to war with Iraq over the issues cited by the Bush administration. The president has offered far too much bombast and triumphalism and far too little evidence and sober assessment to satisfy me. All this changed with Secretary of State Colin L. Powell's presentation to the United Nations. It was long on facts, short on rhetoric and logically irrefutable. He made the case beyond a shadow of doubt. If Saddam Hussein does not yield completely and immediately, the United States should—and will, either alone or with allies—do what must be done. The evidence is complicated, but the conclusion is not: We've got another Hitler out there, and it's our job to stop him now."

95. Barabak, Mark Z., "The Times Poll," *Los Angeles Times*, Feb. 9, 2003, 1.

96. Keller, Bill, "The I-Can't-Believe-I'm-a-Hawk Club," *New York Times*, Feb. 8, 2003, 17.

97. Bumiller, Elisabeth, "War Public Relations Machine Is Put on Full Throttle," *New York Times*, Feb. 9, 2003, 17.

98. Wright, Robin, "'Game Is Over' for Baghdad, Bush Declares," *Los Angeles Times*, Feb. 7, 2003, 1.

CHAPTER TEN

1. Rice, Condoleezza, "Acknowledge That You Have an Obligation to Search for the Truth," 2002 Stanford Commencement Address, *Stanford Reports*, June 16, 2002, http://news.service.stanford.edu/news/2002/june19/comm_ricetext-619.html.

2. Rice, Condoleezza, interview with the author, Nov. 2, 2006.

3. Tyler, Patrick, E., "U.S. Forces Take Control in Baghdad," *New York Times*, Apr. 10, 2003, A1.

4. DeYoung, Karen, "Bush Proclaims Victory in Iraq," *Washington Post*, May 2, 2003, A01.

5. See Bash, Dana, "White House Pressed on 'Mission Accomplished' Sign," CNN, Oct. 29, 2003, http://www.cnn.com/2003/ALLPOLITICS/10/28/mission.accomplished.

6. Mann, James, *Rise of the Vulcans: The History of Bush's War Cabinet* (New York: Penguin Books, 2004), 358.

7. Kristof, Nicholas D., "Cheers to Jeers," *New York Times*, Jun. 17, 2003, A27.

8. Rice, Condoleezza, interview.

9. Finn, Peter, "Iraqi Ambushes Beset Troops," *Washington Post*, Jun. 27, 2003, A20.

10. Former NSC staffer, interview with the author.

11. Miller, Franklin, interview with the author, Oct. 25, 2006.

12. DeYoung, Karen, "U.S. Sped Bremer to Iraq Post," *Washington Post*, May 24, 2003, A01.

13. Deans, Bob, "U.S. 'Leaned on Us,' Arms Monitor Says," *Atlanta Journal-Constitution*, Jun. 12, 2003, 3A.

14. In May former House Speaker Newt Gingrich said openly what neocons had been saying privately for months. Speaking at the American Enterprise Institute, Gingrich, a close friend of Rumsfeld, alleged that while Bush (and DoD) were focused on "facts, values, and outcomes" in Iraq, State was all about "process, politeness, and accommodation." Powell and his troops were guilty of a "deliberate and systematic effort to undermine" President Bush's policies, Gingrich charged. Powell was incensed enough to respond in congressional testimony the next week that finding diplomatic solutions was what diplomats were supposed to do. "We do it damn well, and I am not going to apologize to anyone," Powell said. His deputy, Armitage, told *USA Today*, "Mr. Gingrich is off his meds and out of therapy."

15. Reynolds, Maura, "Rice, a Puzzle to Some, Has a Place at Bush's Table," *Los Angeles Times*, May 30, 2003, 36; see also Evan Thomas, "The Quiet Power of Condi Rice," *Newsweek*, Dec. 16, 2002, 24.

16. Reynolds, "Rice a Puzzle."

17. For an analysis of the subsequent reports from British intelligence and the U.S. Senate on the origins of the claims and Bush having reason to believe they were true—and the argument that they were true, see "Bush's '16 Words' on Iraq and Uranium: He May Have Been Wrong but He Wasn't Lying," FactCheck.org, Annenberg Political Fact Check, Annenberg Public Policy Center of the University of Pennsylvania, Jul. 26, 2004, modified Aug. 23, 2004, http://www.factcheck.org/article222.html.

18. "Newsmaker: Condoleezza Rice," *NewsHour with Jim Lehrer*, PBS, Jun. 30, 2003, http://www.pbs.org/newshour/bb/white_house/july-dec03/rice_7-30.html#.

19. "President Bush Discusses Top Priorities for the U.S., Press Conference of the President," White House release, Jul. 30, 2003, http://www.whitehouse.gov/news/releases/2003/07/20030730-1.html.

20. Ibid.

21. "Newsmaker: Condoleezza Rice," *NewsHour*.

22. Ibid.

23. A former White House staffer, as well as Rice, confirmed that the president referred to her as being "like my sister."

24. Rice colleague and friend, interview with the author.

25. Woodward, Bob, *State of Denial: Bush at War, Part III* (New York: Simon & Schuster, 2006), 245–46.

26. Rothkopf, David, *Running the World: The Inside Story of the National Security Council and the Architects of American Power* (New York: Public Affairs, 2005), 393.

27. Reynolds, "Rice a Puzzle."

28. With surprising consistency, current and former administration officials tell of this duplicity in numerous instances and across issue-areas.

29. NSC staffer, interview with the author.

30. Miller interview.

31. Former NSC staffer, interview with the author.

32. Former White House staffer, interview with the author.

33. DeYoung, Karen, *Soldier: The Life of Colin Powell* (New York: Knopf, 2006), 477–78.

34. Rice, Condoleezza, interview.

35. Former State Department official, interview with the author. For an in-depth examination of Cheney's role, see Rothkopf, *Running the World*, 419–28.

36. Ibid., 421–22.

37. Blacker, Coit "Chip," interview with the author, Jul. 10, 2006.

38. More than a half-dozen administration and former administration officials made this argument in interviews. Rice, however, in the run-up to the prewar at least, presented a different view to *Newsweek*, saying she saw her job as to sharpen debate among the principals and then take the options to the president. She said the principals, if anything, played down their differences before the president. See Evan Thomas's "Chemistry in the War Cabinet," *Newsweek*, Jan. 28, 2002, 26, and Thomas's "Their Faith and Fears," *Newsweek*, Sept. 9, 2002, 36.

39. Thomas, Evan, and Richard Wolffe, "Bush in the Bubble," *Newsweek*, Dec. 19, 2005, 30.

40. For a longer discourse on the tangible effects on the postwar in Iraq, see Rothkopf, *Running the World*, particularly page 420.

41. Administration official, interview with the author.

42. Former administration official, interview with the author.

43. Scowcroft, Brent, interview with the author, Oct. 6, 2005.

44. Miller interview.

45. Allen, Mike, "Iraq Shake-up Skipped Rumsfeld," *Washington Post*, Oct. 8, 2003, A10.

46. Dinmore, Guy, et.al., "It's Business as Usual on Iraq, Insists Rumsfeld," *Financial Times*, Oct. 10, 2003, 8.

47. Sanger, David E., "White House to Overhaul Iraq and Afghan Missions," *New York Times*, Oct. 6, 2003, A1.

48. Senior NSC staffer, interview with the author.

49. See DeYoung, *Soldier*, 374, 463.

50. Rice, Condoleezza, interview.

51. Barry, John, and Michael Hirsh, "A Warrior Lays Down His Arms," *Newsweek*, Nov. 20, 2006.

52. Woodward, *Denial*, 240–41.

53. Ibid., 274.

54. Ibid., 264–65.

55. Bumiller, Elisabeth, "A Partner in Shaping an Assertive Foreign Policy, Jan. 7, 2004, A1.

56. Frazer, Jendayi, interview with the author, Aug. 31, 2006.

57. Diamond, Larry, interview with the author, Aug. 5, 2006.

58. NSC staffer, interview with the author.

59. Blacker interview.

60. "Excerpts from the Tower Commission's News Conference," *New York Times*, Feb. 27, 1987, A8.

61. Blacker interview. For an excellent discussion of Bush's impulses to "to seize the opportunity to do achieve big goals," see Bob Woodward's *Plan of Attack* (New York: Simon & Schuster, 2004), 162.

62. Woodward, *Denial*, 136–38.

63. Gordon, Michael R., "The Strategy to Secure Iraq Did Not Foresee a 2nd War," *New York Times*, Oct. 19, 2004, A1.

64. Rice, Condoleezza, interview.

65. Woodward, *Denial*, 301.

66. Diamond, Larry, *Squandered Victory: The American Occupation and the Bungled Effort to Bring Democracy to Iraq* (New York: Owl, 2006), 240–42.

67. See Rothkopf, *Running the World;* Woodward, *Denial;* DeYoung, *Soldier*.

68. Rose, David, "Neo Culpa," *Vanity Fair*, Jan. 2007, 82.

69. See Ibid.

70. Schoeneman, Deborah. "Armani's Exchange . . . Condi's Slip . . . Forget the Alamo," *New York*, Apr. 26, 2004, http://nymag.com/nymetro/news/people/columns/intelligencer/n_10245/.

71. Rice, Condoleezza, interview.

72. Baker, James, interview with the author, May 24, 2005.

73. Rice friend, interview with the author.

74. Rose, "Neo Culpa."

75. Blacker interview.

76. For an excellent discussion of the differences between Bush and his immediate predecessors in this regard, see Evan Thomas, and Richard Wolffe, "Bush in the Bubble," *Newsweek*, Dec. 19, 2005, 30.

77. Pillar, Paul R., "Intelligence, Policy, and War in Iraq," *Foreign Affairs* 85, no. 2 (Mar./Apr. 2006), 15–28.

78. Woodward, *Denial*, 144–45.

79. Ibid.

80. Former NSC official, interview with the author.

81. Blacker interview; former NSC staffers and State Department official interviews. On the CIA and State, see Rothkopf, *Running the World,* especially page 407; Woodward, *Denial*; and Evan Thomas, et.al., "(Over)selling the World on War," *Newsweek*, Jun. 9, 2003, 24. On State, see DeYoung, *Soldier*. On CIA, see Michael Isikoff, and David Corn, *Hubris: Inside the Story of Spin, Scandal, and the Selling of the Iraq War* (New York: Crown, 2006), especially pages 3–6, 356–58. On Army Chief of Staff General Eric Shinseki, who said that "several hundred thousand" troops would be needed to occupy Iraq, see all Peter Slevin, "Bush to Cast War as Part of Regional Strategy," *Washington Post*, Feb. 28, 2003, A19; and Ann Scott Tyson and Josh White, "A Soldier's Soldier, Outflanked," *Washington Post*, Dec. 21, 2006, A14. On the Air Force Secretary Jim Roche and his army counterpart, Thomas White, telling Rumsfeld Iraq could become another Vietnam, see John Barry, and Michael Hirsh, "A Warrior Lays Down His Arms," *Newsweek*, Nov. 20, 2006.

82. Baker interview.

83. Former administration official, interview with the author.

84. Carson, Deborah, interview with the author, Sept. 6, 2006.

85. Rice, Clara, interview with the author, Aug. 1, 2006.

86. Woodward, *Denial*, 226. In this passage Woodward describes the extraordinary second and last meeting that Jay Garner had with the president. Garner does not share his profound misgivings with Bush over what's happening in Iraq, but instead engages in happy talk and colorful stories. Garner's explanation to the journalist was that he was "a military guy" and that he had done his job and reported all these feelings to his boss, Don Rumsfeld.

87. Blacker interview.

88. Frazier interview.

89. "Rice Admits Multiple Iraq Errors," BBC.com, Mar. 31, 2006, http://news.bbc.co.uk/2/hi/americas/4865344.stm.

90. Former Rice colleague, interview with the author.

91. Rice, Clara, interview.

92. Rice, Condoleezza, interview.

93. Diamond, John, "'We Were Almost All Wrong,'" *USA Today*, Jan. 28, 2004, 1A.

94. Kessler, Glenn, "Powell Says New Data May Have Affected War Decision," *Washington Post*, Feb. 3, 2004, A01.

95. Woodward, *Denial*, 281

96. Stevenson, Richard A., "Powell and White House Get Together on Iraq War," *New York Times*, Feb. 4, 2004, A11.

97. "Post New Hampshire Primary/John Kerry," *Newsweek* Poll/Princeton Survey Research Associates, Jan. 31, 2004.

98. Woodward, *Denial*, 278–81.

99. Rice, Condoleezza, interview.

100. Transcript, "Hearing of the National Commission on Terrorist Attacks upon the United States. Witness: Dr. Condoleezza Rice, Assistant to the President for National Security Affairs. Chair: Thomas H. Kean; Vice Chair: Lee H. Hamilton, Room 216, Hart Senate Office Building, Washington, DC, 9:03 A.M. EDT, Thursday, April 8, 2004," http://www.9-11commission.gov/archive/hearing9/9-11Commission_Hearing_2004-04-08.pdf.

101. "Richard Clarke interview," *60 Minutes* transcript, CBS, Mar. 21, 2004, www.cbsnews.com/stories/2004/03/19/60minutes.

102. Canellos, Peter S., "Rice Plays Key Role, But with Few Lines," *Boston Globe*, Mar. 30, 2004, A3.

103. "Dr. Condoleezza Rice Discusses the War on Terror on '60 Minutes,'" White House transcript, Mar. 28, 2004, http://www.whitehouse.gov/news/releases/2004/03/print/20040328.html.

104. Ibid.

105. "Hearing on Terrorist Attacks," Rice Testimony, transcript, 17.

106. When she was first told in the Faculty Senate that the policy of the previous administration had been to decide borderline tenure cases in favor of women and minorities, Rice's answer had been, basically, "Well, I'm provost now." But in a letter to *Stanford Report* shortly after, she said the previous administration had had no such policy.

107. "Hearing on Terrorist Attacks," Rice Testimony, transcript, 23.

108. Hamberry-Green, Brenda, interview with the author, Apr. 19, 2006. See note 44 in chapter 1.

109. Brownstein, Ronald, "The Briefing on Bin Laden," *Los Angeles Times*, Apr. 11, 2004, A1.

110. "Condi's Testimony/Iraq" Poll. *Newsweek*/Princeton Survey Research Associates, Apr. 10, 2004.

111. Ibid.

112. "President's Daily Brief, 'Bin Laden Determined to Strike in US; 6 August 2001," The National Security Archive, The George Washington University, Apr. 10, 2004, http://www.gwu.edu/~nsarchiv/NSAEBB/NSAEBB116/pdb8-6-2001.pdf.

113. Brownstein, "The Briefing on Bin Laden."

114. Milbank, Dana, and Mike Allen, "Bush Gave No Sign of Worry in August 2001," *Washington Post*, Apr. 11, 2004, A01.

115. Miller, Greg, "A Call to Action," *Los Angeles Times*, Jul. 23, 2004, A1.

116. Von Drehle, David, "The 567-Page Story of a Humbled America," *Washington Post*, Jul. 23, 2004, A01.

117. Connolly, Ceci, "Relatives Praise Commission and Push for Changes," *Washington Post*, July 23, 2004, A21.

118. May, Ernest R., "When Government Writes History," *New Republic,* May 23, 2005, 30.

119. Ibid.

120. National Commission on Terrorist Attacks upon the United States, *The 9/11 Commission Report*, Jul. 22, 2004, 339–44.

121. *9/11 Commission Report*, 400–401.

122. Former commission staffer, interview with the author.

123. "Hearing on Terrorist Attacks," Rice Testimony, transcript, 39.

124. 9/11 commission biographies, "Timothy J. Roemer," undated, http://www.9-11commission.gov/about/bio_roemer.htm.

125. "Hearing on Terrorist Attacks," Rice Testimony, transcript, 68.

126. Former commission staffer, interview with the author.

127. Woodward, *Denial*, 79.

128. Ibid., 79–80.

129. Ibid., 49–50.

130. Ibid., 80.

131. Shenon, Philip, "Rice Questions Account of Qaeda Warning," *New York Times.com*, Oct. 2, 2006, 1:30 p.m., http://www.nytimes.com/2006/10/02/washington/03ricecnd.html?hp&ex=1159848000&en=5de194832d554019&ei=5094&partner=homepage; see also Robin Wright, "Rice Disputes Report CIA Warned Her about Attack," *Washington Post*, Oct. 2, 2006, 3:34 p.m., http://www.washingtonpost.com/wp-dyn/content/article/2006/10/02/AR2006100200187.html.

132. Woodward, *Denial*, 80.

133. *9/11 Commission Report*, 359.

134. Zelikow, Philip, interview with the author, Nov. 2, 2006.

135. *9/11 Commission Report*, 399.

136. Ibid., 134.

137. Ibid., 402.

138. "Bush Administration's First Memo on al-Qaeda Declassified," The National Security Archive, Feb. 10, 2005, http://www.gwu.edu/~nsarchiv/NSAEBB/NSAEBB147/index.htm.

139. *9/11 Commission Report*, 260.

140. Blacker interview.

141. Ibid.

142. "Dr. Condoleezza Rice on '60 Minutes,'" White House transcript.

143. Rice, Connie, phone interview with the author, Oct. 3, 2006.

144. Rice, Clara, interview.

145. Hylton, Wil S., "Casualty of War," *GQ*, June 2004, 226.

146. Woodward, *Denial*, 303.

147. Blacker interview. The commission report chronicled repeated threat reports circulated within the government in the late 1990s raising the explicit possibility of an attack using airliners as missiles: One circulated in September 1998, based on information provided by a source who walked into an American consulate in East Asia, that mentioned "a possible plot to fly an explosives-laden aircraft into a U.S. city." A month earlier an intelligence agency received information that Libyans sought to crash a plane into the Trade Center. The North American Aerospace Defense Command had developed exercises aimed at countering the threat, and the report said a DoD memo planned a drill in April 2001 that would have simulated a terrorist crash into the Pentagon.

148. Milbank, Dana, and Mike Allen, "For the Bush Camp, a Well-Cushioned Blow," *Washington Post*, Jul. 23, 2004, A20.

149. "The Plain Truth," unsigned editorial, *New York Times*, Jun. 17, 2004, 28.

150. *9/11 Commission Report*, 367.

151. Woodward, *Denial*, 275–76.

152. Ibid., 312.

153. "Iraq Transition of Power," U.S. Department of Defense, Jun. 2005, http://www.defenselink.mil/home/features/2005/IraqTransition.

154. Filkins, Dexter, "U.S. Transfers Power to Iraq Two Days Early," *New York Times*, June 29, 2004, 1.

155. Woodward, *Denial*, 331.

156. See David E. Sanger, "Two Iraq Views, Two Campaigns," *New York Times*, Sept. 22, 2004, 1.

157. Sanger, David E, "Rice Says Iran Must Not Be Allowed to Develop Nuclear Arms," *New York Times*, Aug. 9, 2004, 3.

158. Shenon, Philip, "Former Iraq Arms Inspector Faults Prewar Intelligence," *New York Times*, Aug. 19, 2004, A20.

159. Woodward, *Denial*, 330.

160. White House 2004: General Election, PollingReport.com, Nov. 1–2, 2004, http://www.pollingreport.com/wh04gen.htm.

161. Woodward, *Denial*, 339.

162. Rice, Condoleezza, interview.

163. Bean, Randy, interview with the author, Aug. 4, 2006.

164. 2004 Ohio election results, *Washington Post*, Nov. 24, 2004, http://www.washingtonpost.com/wp-srv/elections/2004/oh/?flashpage=map.

165. Carson interview.

166. More than a dozen friends and relatives said Rice had told them she was coming home at the end of the first term and that she was tired.

167. Rice, Condoleezza, interview.

168. Ibid.

169. Rice, Clara, interview; Condoleezza Rice friends interview.

170. Rice, Condoleezza, interview.

CHAPTER ELEVEN

1. "Interview on ABC's *This Week* with George Stephanopoulos and Peter Jennings," State Department transcript, Jan. 30, 2005, http://www.state.gov/secretary/rm/2005/41375.htm.

2. McPhatter, Genoa, interview with the author, Dec. 12, 2006.

3. Reed, Julia, "The Great Divide," *Vogue*, Nov. 2006, 332.

4. Ibid.

5. McPhatter interview.

6. Reed, "The Great Divide."

7. Former Bush administration official, interview with the author.

8. Bean, Randy, interview with the author, Aug. 4, 2006.

9. "President Nominates Condoleezza Rice as Secretary of State," White House press release, Nov. 16, 2004, http://www.whitehouse.gov/news/releases/2004/11/20041116-3.html#.

10. Ibid.

11. DeYoung, Karen, *Soldier: The Life of Colin Powell* (New York: Knopf, 2006), 6–9.

12. Woodward, Bob, *State of Denial: Bush at War, Part III* (New York: Simon & Schuster, 2006), 363–65.

13. Givhan, Robin, "President Bush's Kissing Cabinet," *Washington Post*, Nov. 19, 2004, C19.

14. Rice, Clara, interview with the author, Aug. 1, 2006.

15. Gergen, David, "The Power of One," *New York Times*, Nov. 19, 2004, 27.

16. See Schofield, Matthew, "Rice Seen as Bad News for U.S.-European Ties," *Miami Herald*, Nov. 17, 2004, 10A; H.D.S. Greenway, "The Purge at C.I.A.," *Boston Globe*, Nov. 19, 2004, A19; and Steve Chapman, "A Doctrine That's Looking a Lot Better," *Chicago Tribune*, Nov. 18, 2004, C31.

17. Marshall, Tyler, and Sonni Efron, "Bush Plans Effort to Mend Key Alliances," *Los Angeles Times*, Nov. 20, 2004, A01.

18. Administration official interview. Confirmed by Condoleezza Rice.

19. Former senior administration official interview.

20. Senior NSC official interview.

21. Schweid, Barry, Associated Press, "Kudos and Caution Follow Naming of Rice for State," *Philadelphia Inquirer*, Nov. 18, 2004, A17.

22. Rice testimony, as prepared before the Senate Foreign Relations Committee, Confirmation Hearing, Part I, Jan. 18, 2005, http://www.senate.gov/~foreign/testimony/2005/RiceTestimony050118.pdf.

23. Ibid.

24. Lochhead, Carolyn, "Rice Defends Bush's Iraq Policies in Testy Exchange with Boxer," *San Francisco Chronicle*, Jan. 19, 2005, A1.

25. Excerpts from Rice testimony, "Rice's Day: Sharp Views of Senators, and Nominee's Replies, Focusing on the War," *New York Times*, 19 Jan. 2005, 8.

26. See Lochhead, Carolyn, *San Francisco Chronicle*, Jan. 19, 2005, A1; Steven R. Weisman, and Joel Brinkley, "The Condoleezza Rice Hearing," *New York Times*, Jan. 19, 2005, 1; and Bob Deans, "Rice Defends Iraq War in Senate Showdown," *Atlanta Journal-Constitution*, Jan. 19, 2005, 1A.

27. King, Colbert I., "Why the Crass Remarks about Rice?" *Washington Post*, Jan.22, 2005, A17.

28. Groening, Chad, and Jody Brown, "Black Conservatives Take On Rice's Liberal Democratic Opposition," *Christian.com*, Jan. 27, 2005, http://www.christian.com/ArticlesDetail.asp?id=1465.

29. German, Yvonne, phone interview with the author, Sept. 20, 2006; Bean interview; Clara Rice interview.

30. German interview.

31. See Gerstenzang, James, "Agent's Shoving of Black Bush Aide Probed," *Los Angeles Times*, Jun. 7, 1990, A22.

32. German interview.

33. Rice, Clara, interview.

34. Senior George H. W. Bush administration official, interview with the author.

35. Former NSC staffer, interview with the author.

36. *Congressional Record*, 109th Congress, 1st sess., vol. 151, no. 5, Jan. 25, 2005, S374.

37. Ibid., S382.

38. Ibid., S383.

39. Ibid., S383–84.

40. See Colorado Senator Ken Salazar's speech, *Congressional Record*, S390–91; and Virginia Senator John Warner, *Congressional Record,* S408–09.

41. Blacker, Coit "Chip," interview with the author, Jul. 10, 2006.

42. *Congressional Record*, S408–09.

43. Stolberg, Sheryl Gay, "Rice Is Sworn In as Secretary after Senate Vote 85 to 13," *New York Times*, Jan. 27, 2005, 3. Rice fared better than Clay percentage-wise.

44. Woodward, *Denial*, 377.

45. "Reuters Report, Sharon and Abbas to Meet within 2 Weeks," *New York Times*, Jan. 30, 2005, 8.

46. *This Week* interview.

47. Ibid.

48. "Remarks to the Press en Route London," State Department transcript, Feb. 3, 2005, http://www.state.gov/secretary/rm/2005/41785.htm.

49. "Secretary Rice Arrives in Kyrgyzstan," State Department Web site, Oct. 11, 2005, http://www.state.gov/r/pa/ei/pix/2005/54679.htm.

50. *"Bush sous son meilleur sourire," Libération*, Feb. 9, 2005, 1.

51. Rice, Condoleezza, "Remarks at the Institut d'Etudes Politiques de Paris-Sciences Po," Feb. 8, 2005, http://www.state.gov/secretary/rm/2005/41973.htm.

52. Givhan, Robin, "Condoleezza Rice's Commanding Clothes," *Washington Post*, Feb. 25, 2005, C01.

53. Sciolino, Elaine, "The French Are Charmed and Jarred by 'Chere Condi,'" *New York Times*, Feb. 10, 2005, A6.

54. Hockstader, Lee, "Israel's Sharon Met U.S.'s Rice, and Their Encounter Had Legs," *Washington Post*, Feb. 4, 2001, A27.

55. Greenberg, Joel, and Cam Simpson, "Sharon, Abbas to Declare Truce, *Chicago Tribune*, Feb. 8, 2005, C1.

56. Friedman, Thomas L., "Rice's Poker Hand," *New York Times*, Mar. 31, 2005, 27.

57. "Countries Visited and Mileage: 2006," http://www.state.gov/secretary/trvl/c16690.htm.

58. Mangier, Mark, "China and Vatican Make No Secret of Thaw," *Los Angeles Times*, Jun. 25, 2005, A1.

59. "Well-Spoken," unsigned editorial, *Washington Post*, Mar. 22, 2005, A16.

60. Administration official, interview with the author.

61. See *Washington Post* editorial, Mar. 22, 2005.

62. Zakaria, Fareed, "What Bush Got Right," *Newsweek*, Mar. 14, 2005, 22.

63. Bush, George W., Second Inaugural Address, Jan. 20, 2005, http://www.whitehouse.gov/inaugural.

64. Rice, Condoleezza, "Welcome Remarks to Employees," Jan. 27, 2005, http://www.state.gov/secretary/rm/2005/41261.htm.

65. Rice convinced Robert Zoellick, Jim Baker's lieutenant during Bush I, to resign his post as the U.S. trade representative and become her deputy. She brought in Phil Zelikow, the University of Virginia professor who had recently been the executive director of the 9/11 commission and who had coauthored with Rice *Germany Unified and Europe Transformed*, as her special counselor; and R. Nicholas Burns as undersecretary for political affairs,

the office in charge of the regional bureaus and the embassies. He too had worked with Rice in Bush I and had more recently served as U.S. ambassador to NATO in Brussels. And she placed Stephen Krasner, her old friend and former political science department chair at Stanford, in the Office of Policy Planning, the shop tasked with crafting strategies for current and future challenges. Krasner was a famous realist who had been one of four Harvard graduate students who in the sixties had created essentially a new subfield in international relations theory called international political economy.

66. Zelikow, Philip, interview with the author, Nov. 2, 2006.

67. Kessler, Glenn, "At State, Rice Takes Control of Diplomacy," *Washington Post*, Jul. 31, 2005, A01.

68. Richter, Paul, "Rice Reshaping Foreign Policy," *Los Angeles Times*, Mar. 15, 2005, A1.

69. Many State and NSC officials argued that Rice had blocked Bolton's becoming her deputy.

70. See David Jackson, "Bush: U.S., EU of 'One Voice' on Iran Administration Agrees to Carrot-Stick Approach to Nuclear Program," *Dallas Morning News*, Mar. 12, 2005, 20A.

71. Richter, "Rice Reshaping Foreign Policy."

72. "Signs of Life at State," unsigned editorial, *New York Times*, Jul. 4, 2005, A12.

73. Former Rice staffer, interview with the author.

74. Ibid.

75. Former administration official, interview with the author.

76. Ibid.

77. Ibid.

78. State Department official, interview with the author.

79. Zelikow interview.

80. See Burns, John F. "Generals Offer Sober Outlook on Iraqi War," *New York Times*, May 19, 2005, 1.

81. Burns, John F., "Registering New Influence, Iran Sends a Top Aide to Iraq," *New York Times*, May 18, 2005, A10.

82. "Remarks at the American University in Cairo," State Department transcript, Jun. 20, 2005, http://www.state.gov/secretary/rm/2005/48328.htm.

83. Blacker interview.

84. See Marshall, Tyler, "Cairo Audience Cool to Rice's Call for Democratic Reform, *Los Angeles Times*, Jun. 21, 2005, A3.

85. Kagan, Robert, ". . . And American Paralysis," *Washington Post*, Aug. 29, 2005, A15.

86. See Kessler, Glenn, "Rice Visits Darfur Camp, Pressures Sudan," *Washington Post*, Jul. 22, 2005, A19.

87. Linzer, Dafna, "Bush Officials Defend India Nuclear Deal," *Washington Post*, Jul. 20, 2005, A17.

88. Weisman, Steven R., "Smaller Goals for U.S. in Iraq," *New York Times*, Aug. 29, 2005, A1.

CHAPTER TWELVE

1. Rice, Condoleezza, "Promoting the National Interest," *Foreign Affairs* 79, no. 1 (Jan./Feb. 2000), 45–62.

2. VandeHei, Jim, and Baker, Peter, "Vacationing Bush Poised to Set a Record," *Washington Post*, Aug. 3, 2005, A04.

3. As posted on Gawker.com. "Breaking: Condi Rice Spends Salary on Shoes," Gawker.com, Sept. 1, 2005, http://gawker.com/news/weather/breaking-condi-rice-spends-salary-on-shoes-123467.php.

4. Haygood, Wil, and Ann Scott Tyson, "It Was as If All of Us Were Already Pronounced Dead," *Washington Post*, Sept. 15, 2005, A01.

5. "Rice Spends Salary on Shoes," Gawker.com.

6. Ibid.

7. Rush, George, and Joanna Molloy, "As South Drowns, Rice Soaks in N.Y.," *Daily News*, Sept. 2, 2005, 32. "Condi Rice Leaves NYC High and Dry," Gawker.com, Sept. 2, 2005, http://gawker.com/news/weather/condi-rice-leaves-nyc-high-and-dry-123626.php.

8. Rice, Condoleezza, interview with the author, Nov. 2, 2006.

9. *Anderson Cooper 360 Degrees*, CNN transcript, Sept. 1, 2005, http://transcripts.cnn.com/TRAN-SCRIPTS/0509/01/acd.01.html.

10. Lee, Spike, *When the Levees Broke*, 40 Acres and a Mule Productions, 2006.

11. Blacker, Coit "Chip," interview with the author, Jul. 10, 2006.

12. Rice, Condoleezza, interview.

13. Administration official interview.

14. *American Morning*, CNN transcript, Sept. 2, 2005, http://transcripts.cnn.com/TRANSCRIPTS/0509/02/ltm.01.html.

15. See Stanley, Alessandra, "Reporters Turn from Deference to Outrage," *New York Times*, Sept. 5, 2005, A14.

16. "President Heads to Hurricane Katrina Affected Areas," White House transcript, Sept. 2, 2005, http://www.whitehouse.gov/news/releases/2005/09/20050902.html.

17. Milligan, Susan, "As Criticism Mounts, Bush Tours Gulf Coast," *Boston Globe*, Sept. 3, 2005, A1; for *Newsweek* Poll, see Mabry, Marcus, "Eye of the Political Storm," *Newsweek.com*, Sept. 10, 2005, http://www. msnbc.msn.com/id/9280375/site/newsweek.

18. Bush archnemesis *New York Times* columnist Frank Rich wrote, "You could almost see Mr. Bush's political base starting to crumble at its very epicenter, Fox News, by Thursday night. Even there it was impossible to ignore that the administration was no more successful at securing New Orleans than it had been at pacifying Falluja." (Rich, Frank, "Fallujah Floods the Superdome," *New York Times*, Sept. 4, 2005, sec. 4, 10.)

19. "Interview with Gideon Yago from MTV News," State Department transcript, Sept. 12, 2006, http://www. state.gov/secretary/rm/2006/73362.htm. Author amended by listening to video in MTV RAW News video archive, MTV Overdrive, "Unprepared for Hurricane Katrina," undated, http://www.mtv.com/overdrive/?id=1542158.

20. "International Relief Activities Related to Hurricane Katrina," State Department transcript, Sept. 2, 2005, http://www.state.gov/secretary/rm/2005/52478.htm.

21. Administration official interview.

22. "President Arrives in Alabama, Briefed on Hurricane Katrina," White House transcript, Sept. 2, 2005, http:// www.whitehouse.gov/news/releases/2005/09/20050902-2.html#.

23. "President Remarks on Hurricane Recovery Efforts," White House transcript, Sept. 2, 2005, http://www. whitehouse.gov/news/releases/2005/09/20050902-8.html.

24. Tyrangiel, Josh, "Hip Hop's Class Act," *Time*, Aug. 29, 2005.

25. "Kanye West: 'Bush Doesn't Care about Black People,'" *Democracy Now!* video, Sept. 5, 2005, http://www. democracynow.org/article.pl?sid=05/09/05/1453244.

26. "International Relief Activities," State Department transcript.

27. Daily, Matt, Reuters News Service, "Rice Denies Race Affected Relief Effort," *Houston Chronicle*, Sept. 5, 2005, A19.

28. Wilkinson, James, interview with the author, Sept. 25, 2006.

29. Unsigned news report, "Barbara Bush Calls Evacuees Better Off," *New York Times*, Sept. 7, 2005, A22.

30. "Interview on the Tavis Smiley Show," State Department transcript, Sept. 8, 2005, http://www.state.gov/ secretary/rm/2005/52835.htm.

31. "Rice Talks to O'Reilly," Fox News transcript, Sept. 12, 2005, http://www.foxnews.com/ story/0,2933,169421,00.html.

32. "Interview with Gideon Yago from MTV News," State Department transcript; "Unprepared for Hurricane Katrina," MTV video archive.

33. Source close to Rice, interview with the author.

34. Thomas, Juanita Love, phone interview with the author, Jan. 14, 2007.

35. Frazer, Jendayi, interview with the author, Aug. 31, 2006.

36. "Theresa Rice Love" obituary, *Times-Picayune*, Sept. 26, 2002, Metro, 04.

37. Froomkin, Dan, "Was Kanye West Right?" *TheWashingtonPost.com*, Sept. 13, 2005, http://www.washington-post.com/wp-dyn/content/blog/2005/09/13/BL2005091300884.html.

38. The candidates were: Michael Steele, lieutenant governor of Maryland, who would be running for the U.S. Senate in 2006, football great Lynn Swann and Ohio Secretary of State Ken Blackwell, who would running for the governorships of Pennsylvania and Ohio, respectively. All three candidates would lose.

39. See http://www.carnellknowledge.com/pdfs/2005_calendarSM.pdf. See also Wallsten, Peter, "Recasting Republicans as the Party of Civil Rights," *Los Angeles Times*, Jan. 29, 2005, A17.

40. Froomkin, Dan, "A Polling Free-Fall among Blacks," *TheWashingtonPost.com*, Oct. 13, 2005, http://www. washingtonpost.com/wp-dyn/content/blog/2005/10/13/BL2005101300885.html. Other polls showed the president with a twelve-percent approval rating among blacks.

41. Allen, Mike, and Charles Lane, "Rice Helped Shape Bush Decision on Admissions," *Washington Post*, Jan. 17, 2003, A01.

42. Rice, Condoleezza, interview.

43. Ibid.

44. "Statement by the National Security Advisor Dr. Condoleezza Rice," Office of the Press Secretary, The White House, Jan. 17, 2003, http://www.whitehouse.gov/news/releases/2003/01/20030117-1.html.

45. Allen, Mike, "Rice: Race Can Be Factor in College Admissions," *Washington Post*, Jan. 18, 2005, A01.

46. Ibid.

47. Blacker interview.

48. "On-the-Record Briefing, London, England," State Department transcript, Oct. 16, 2005, http://www.state. gov/secretary/rm/2005/55172.htm.

49. Weisman, Steven R., "Rice, in Testy Hearing, Cites Progress in Iraq," *New York Times*, 20 Oct. 2005, A1.

50. "Secretary of State Condoleezza Rice on Fox News with Brit Hume," State Department transcript, Dec. 15, 2005, http://www.state.gov/secretary/rm/2005/58184.htm.

51. Ibid.

52. "Interview on NBC Today Show with Katie Couric," State Department transcript, Dec. 16, 2005, http://www.state.gov/secretary/rm/2005/58190.htm.

53. Kessler, Glenn, "Rice Wins Over E.U. Counterparts," *Washington Post*, Dec. 10, 2005, A16.

54. Ibid.

55. See, for example, Golden, Tim, and Schmitt, Eric, "Detainee Policy Sharply Divides Bush Officials," *New York Times*, Nov. 2, 2005.

56. See Bernstein, Richard, "Skepticism Seems to Erode Europeans' Faith in Rice," *New York Times*, Dec. 7, 2005.

57. Marinucci, Carla, and Wildermuth, John, "Rice Goes to Bat for Bolton," *San Francisco Chronicle*, May 28, 2005, A1.

58. Knickmeyer, Ellen, and K. I. Ibrahim, "Bombing Shatters Mosque In Iraq, *Washington Post*, Feb. 23, 2006, A01.

59. Kennicott, Philip, "What Was and Never Shall Be," *Washington Post*, Feb. 23, 2006, C01.

60. Knickmeyer, Ellen, and Bessam Sebti, "Toll in Iraq's Deadly Surge: 1,300," *Washington Post*, Feb. 28, 2006, A01.

61. Hernandez, Nelson, "Diplomacy Helped to Calm the Chaos," *Washington Post*, Feb. 28, 2006, A11.

62. "Remarks with British Foreign Secretary Jack Straw," State Department transcript, Apr. 3, 2006, http://www.state.gov/secretary/rm/2006/64036.htm.

63. Cooper, Helene, and David E. Sanger, "With a Talk Over Lunch, a Shift in Bush's Iran Policy Took Root," *New York Times*, Jun. 4, 2006, 1.

64. Blumenthal, Sidney, "The Neocons' Next War," *Salon.com*, Aug. 3, 2006, http://www.salon.com/opinion/blumenthal/2006/08/03/mideast/index_np.html.

65. Cooper and Sanger, "Shift in Iran Policy."

66. Perle, Richard, "Why Did Bush Blink on Iran? (Ask Condi)," *Washington Post*, Jun. 25, 2006, B01.

67. Rubin, Michael, "Bubba Dubya?" *Weekly Standard*, Jun. 19, 2006.

68. Unsigned, "Dump Condi: Foreign Policy Conservatives Charge State Dept. Has Hijacked Bush Agenda," *insightmag.com*, Jul. 25–31, 2006, http://www.insightmag.com/Media/MediaManager/Condi2.htm.

69. Unsigned, "Washington Post-ABC News Poll," Jul. 5, 2006, http://www.washingtonpost.com/wp-srv/politics/polls/postpoll_condoleezzarice_070506.htm.

70. Kessler, Glenn, "Defining Her Own Sphere of Influence," *Washington Post*, Jul. 4, 2006, A03.

71. "Statement by Secretary of State Condoleezza Rice," State Department release, Jul. 12, 2006, http://www.state.gov/secretary/rm/2006/68902.htm.

72. "Interview on ABC *This Week* with George Stephanopoulos," State Department transcript, Jul. 16, 2006, http://www.state.gov/secretary/rm/2006/69026.htm.

73. "Special Briefing on Travel to the Middle East and Europe," State Department transcript, Jul. 21, 2006, http://www.state.gov/secretary/rm/2006/69331.htm.

74. Zelikow, Philip, interview with the author, Nov. 2, 2006.

75. Ibid.

76. "Briefing on Efforts to Stop Violence in Lebanon," State Department transcript, Jul. 30, 2006, http://www.state.gov/secretary/rm/2006/69720.htm.

77. "Statement on Three-Part Comprehensive Settlement," State Department transcript, Jul. 31, 2006, http://www.state.gov/secretary/rm/2006/69726.htm.

78. Rice, Clara, interview with the author, Aug. 1, 2006.

79. McPhatter, Genoa, interview with the author, Dec. 12, 2006.

80. For a more detailed report, see Weisman, Steven R., "For Rice, Risky Dive into Mideast Storm, *New York Times*, Nov. 16, 2005; and Weisman, "In Personal Move, Rice Pushes Mideast Talks into a 2nd Day," *New York Times*, Nov. 15, 2005.

81. "Briefing En Route Baghdad, Iraq," State Department transcript, Oct. 5, 2006, http://www.state.gov/secretary/rm/2006/73648.htm.

82. Ibid.

83. Wright, Robin, "Rice Pushes Iraqis to Defuse Violence," *Washington Post*, Oct. 6, 2006, A18.

84. Shenon, Philip, "Rice, in Baghdad, Insists That Iraqis Are 'Making Progress,'" *New York Times*, Oct. 6, 2006, A12.

85. Amber, Jeannine, "Being Condoleezza," *Essence*, Oct. 2006, 184.

86. Bush had actually said, "bring 'em on," though the official White House transcript reads "bring them on." See "President Bush Names Randall Tobias to Be Global AIDS Coordinator," White House transcript, Jul. 2, 2003, http://www.whitehouse.gov/news/releases/2003/07/20030702-3.html#.

87. "President Bush and Prime Minister Tony Blair of the United Kingdom Participate in Joint Press Availability," White House transcript, May 25, 2006, http://www.whitehouse.gov/news/releases/2006/05/20060525-12.html.

88. "Debate Transcript: The Second Bush-Kerry Presidential Debate," Commission on Presidential Debates, Oct. 8, 2004, http://www.debates.org/pages/trans2004c.html.

89. "U.S. House of Representatives / National / Exit Poll," *CNN.com*, undated, http://www.cnn.com/ELEC-TION/2006/pages/results/states/US/H/00/epolls.0.html.

90. Baker, James A., III, and Lee A. Hamilton, cochairs, et.al., *The Iraq Study Group Report* (New York: Vintage Books, 2006), xiii–xiv, 38.

91. "Remarks with German Foreign Minister Frank-Walter Steinmeier after Meeting," State Department transcript, Dec. 8, 2006, http://www.state.gov/secretary/rm/2006/77543.htm.

92. Baker and Hamilton, *The Iraq Study Group Report,* 28.

93. "The Iraq Study Group News Conference," transcript, *New York Times*, Dec. 6, 2006, http://www.nytimes.com/2006/12/06/world/middleeast/06isg_transcript.html?n=Top%2fNews%2fWorld%2fCountries%20and%20Territories%2fIraq.

94. "President Bush Participates in Joint Press Availability with Prime Minister Maliki of Iraq," White House transcript, Nov. 30, 2006, http://www.whitehouse.gov/news/releases/2006/11/20061130-1.html.

95. "President Bush and Prime Minister Blair," White House transcript.

96. Ibid.

97. Rice, Condoleezza, interview.

CHAPTER THIRTEEN

1. Von Kreisler-Bomben, Kristin, "Condoleezza Rice: Balancing Act," *Stanford* magazine, Winter 1985, 16.

2. "President's Address to the Nation," White House transcript, Jan. 10, 2007, http://www.whitehouse.gov/news/releases/2007/01/20070110-7.html.

3. Fineman, Howard, "A Crisis of Confidence," *Newsweek.com*, 10 Jan. 10, 2007, http://www.msnbc.msn.com/id/16568507/site/newsweek/.

4. "*Scarborough Country* for Jan. 10, 11 p.m.," MSNBC transcript, http://www.msnbc.msn.com/id/16579097/. Dates of speeches from White House transcripts for each date.

5. Cooper, Helene, and Jim Yardley, "Pact with North Korea Draws Fire from a Wide Range of Critics in U.S.," *New York Times*, Feb. 14, 2007, 10.

6. For greater detail, see Transformational Diplomacy briefings at State.org, including Fact Sheet, Jan. 18, 2006, http://www.state.gov/r/pa/prs/ps/2006/59339.htm.

7. Stanford official, interview with author.

8. See Rhode, Deborah, "How We Tackle the 'Woman Problem'" *Stanford Report*, May 24, 2006, http://news-service.stanford.edu/news/2006/may24/rhode-052406.html.

9. Barker, Lucius, interview with the author. Aug. 4, 2006.

10. Bean, Randy, interview with the author, Aug. 4, 2006.

11. Rice friend, interview with the author.

12. Black, Charles, interview with the author, Jun. 26, 2006.

13. Blacker, Coit "Chip," interview with the author, Jul. 10, 2006.

14. See Tierney, John, "Can This Party Be Saved?" *New York Times*, Sept. 2, 2006, A15; and Goldberg, Jonah, "A Label We Can All Claim," *Chicago Tribune*, Jun. 30, 2006, C31.

15. Rice, Condoleezza, interview with the author, Nov. 2, 2006.

16. Rice, Clara, interview with the author, Aug. 1, 2006.

17. Bean interview.

18. Blacker interview.

19. "Interview with the Washington Post Editorial Board," State Department transcript, Dec. 14, 2006, http://www.state.gov/secretary/rm/2006/77856.htm.

BIBLIOGRAPHY

ARCHIVES

Birmingham Public Library Archives, George Bush Presidential Library, Miller Center of Public Affairs (University of Virginia), The National Archives, The National Security Archive (The George Washington University), Stanford University News Service Archives, University of Denver Archives, Vanderbilt Television News Archives (Vanderbilt University).

BOOKS

Of invaluable use to me were Diane McWhorter's *Carry Me Home: Birmingham, Alabama, The Climatic Battle of the Civil Rights Movement*, which detailed the history of Birmingham but especially the events of 1963 and 1964; and Taylor Branch's monumental biographies of the Reverend Dr. Martin Luther King Jr. As I relied on McWhorter's book for detailed scenes of the Birmingham atrocities, I also relied on the singular reporting of Bob Woodward, particularly his *State of Denial*, for many of the scenes inside the Bush administration, as well as Karen DeYoung's *Soldier: The Life of Colin Powell*. Finally, the work of Geraldine Moore, a black woman employed by the *Birmingham News* in the 1950s, provided crucial insights into Birmingham's "Negro" middle class, a community whose richness I could not have imagined.

Albright, Madeleine, with Bill Woodward. *Madam Secretary: A Memoir*. New York: Miramax, 2003.

Almond, Mark. *Uprising: Political Upheavals That Have Shaped the World*. London: Mitchell Beazley, 2002.

Atkins, Leah Rawls. *The Valley and the Hills: An Illustrated History of Birmingham and Jefferson County*. Woodland Hills, CA: Windsor, 1981.

Branch, Taylor. *At Canaan's Edge: America in the King Years 1965–68*. New York: Simon & Schuster, 2006.

———. *Parting the Waters: America in the King Years 1954–63*. New York: Simon & Schuster, 1988.

———. *Pillar of Fire: America in the King Years 1963–65*. New York: Simon & Schuster, 1998.

Bush, George, and Brent Scowcroft. *A World Transformed*. New York: Knopf, 1998.

Chandrasekaran, Rajiv. *Imperial Life in the Emerald City: Inside Iraq's Green Zone*. New York: Knopf, 2006.

Clarke, Richard. *Against All Enemies: Inside America's War on Terror*. New York: Free Press, 2004.

Daalder, Ivo H., and James M. Lindsay. *America Unbound: The Bush Revolution in Foreign Policy*. Washington, DC: Brookings Institution, 2003.

Dallin, Alexander, and Condoleezza Rice. *The Gorbachev Era*. Palo Alto, CA: Stanford Alumni Association, 1986.

Davis, Angela Y. *Women, Race & Class*. New York: Vintage, 1983.

DeYoung, Karen. *Soldier: The Life of Colin Powell*. New York: Knopf, 2006.

Diamond, Larry. *Squandered Victory: The American Occupation and the Bungled Effort to Bring Democracy to Iraq*. New York: Owl, 2006.

Dobbs, Michael. *Madeleine Albright: A Twentieth-Century Odyssey*. New York: Owl, 2000.

Duzdiak, Mary L. *Cold War Civil Rights: Race and the Image of American Democracy*. Princeton, NJ: Princeton University Press, 2000.

Eade, Charles. *Winston Churchill War Speeches, 1939–45*. London: Cassell & Co., 1951.

Eskew, Glenn T. *But for Birmingham: The Local and National Movements in the Civil Rights Struggle*. Chapel Hill, NC: The University of North Carolina Press, 1997.

Feldman, Glenn. *Before Brown: Civil Rights and White Backlash in the Modern South*. Tuscaloosa, AL: The University of Alabama Press, 2004.

Feldman, Lynne B. *A Sense of Place: Birmingham's Black Middle Class Community, 1890–1930*. Tuscaloosa, AL: The University of Alabama Press, 1999.

Felix, Antonia. *Condi: The Condoleezza Rice Story*. New York: Pocket Books, 2002.

Flynt, Wayne. *Alabama in the Twentieth Century*. Tuscaloosa, AL: The University of Alabama Press, 2004.

Frady, Marshall. *Wallace*. New York: World, 1968.

Gaddis, John Lewis. *Strategies of Containment: A Critical Appraisal of American National Security Policy During the Cold War*. Rev. ed. Oxford: Oxford University Press, 2005.

Gates, Robert. *From the Shadows*. New York: Touchstone, 1996.

Haass, Richard N. *Intervention: The Use of American Military Force in the Post–Cold War World*. Washington, DC: Carnegie Endowment for International Peace, 1994.

———. *The Opportunity: America's Moment to Alter History's Course*. New York: PublicAffairs, 2005.

Height, Dorothy. *Open Wide the Freedom Gates: A Memoir*. New York: PublicAffairs, 2003.

Horne, Gerald. *Black & Red: W.E.B. DuBois and the Afro-American Response to the Cold War, 1944–1963*. Albany, NY: State University of New York Press, 1986.

Isikoff, Michael, and David Corn. *Hubris: The Inside Story of Spin, Scandal, and the Selling of the Iraq War*. New York: Crown, 2006.

Lemert, Charles, and Esme Bhan, eds. *The Voice of Anna Julia Cooper*. Lanham, MD: Rowman & Littlefield, 1998.

Mann, James. *Rise of the Vulcans: The History of Bush's War Cabinet*. New York: Penguin Books, 2004

McWhorter, Diane. *Carry Me Home: Birmingham, Alabama, The Climatic Battle of the Civil Rights Movement*. New York: Touchstone, 2001.

Montview Centennial Book Committee. *The Spirit of Montview, 1902–2002: A History of Montview Boulevard Presbyterian Church*. Denver: Walsworth, 2001.

Moore, Geraldine. *Behind the Ebony Mask: What American Negroes Really Think*. Birmingham, AL: Southern University Press, 1961.

Morgenthau, Hans. *Politics Among Nations: The Struggle for Power and Peace*. 1948. Sixth edition revised by Kenneth J. Thompson. New York: Knopf, 1985.

Morris, Dick, and Eileen McGann, *Condi vs. Hillary: The Next Great Presidential Race*. New York: Regan, 2005.

Packer, George. *The Assassins' Gate: America in Iraq*. New York: Farrar, Straus and Giroux, 2005.

Parker, Inez Moore. *The Rise and Decline of the Program of Education for Black Presbyterians of the United Presbyterian Church U.S.A., 1865–1970*. San Antonio, TX: Trinity University Press, 1977.

Phillips, Kevin P. *The Emerging Republican Majority*. New Rochelle, NY: Arlington House, 1969.

Rice, Condoleezza. *The Soviet Union and the Czechoslovak Army, 1948–1983*. Facsimile of the 1st ed. Princeton, NJ: Princeton University Press, 1984.

Ricks, Thomas E. *Fiasco: The American Military Adventure in Iraq*. New York: Penguin, 2006.

Rosen, Gary, ed. *The Right War? The Conservative Debate on Iraq*. Cambridge: Cambridge University Press, 2005.

Rothkopf, David. *Running the World: The Inside Story of the National Security Council and the Architects of American Power*. New York: PublicAffairs, 2005.

St. Mary's Academy. *Ave 71' [sic]*. Englewood, CO: St. Mary's Academy, 1971.

Suskind, Ron. *The Price of Loyalty: George W. Bush, the White House, and the Education of Paul O'Neill*. New York: Simon & Schuster, 2004.

University of Denver. *Kynewisbok*. Denver: University of Denver, 1974.

Walton, Hanes, Jr. *Black Republicans: The Politics of the Black and Tans*. Metuchen, NJ: Scarecrow, 1975.

Woodward, Bob. *Bush at War*. New York: Simon & Schuster, 2002.

———. *Plan of Attack*. New York: Simon & Schuster, 2004.

———. *State of Denial: Bush at War: Part III*. New York: Simon & Schuster, 2006.

Wright, Lawrence. *The Looming Tower: Al-Qaeda and the Road to 9/11*. New York: Knopf, 2006.

Young, Alford A., Jr., Manning Marable, Elizabeth Higginbotham, Charles Lemert, and Jerry G. Watts. *The Souls of W.E.B. DuBois*. Boulder, CO: Paradigm, 2006.

Zelikow, Philip, and Condoleezza Rice. *Germany Unified and Europe Transformed: A Study in Statecraft.* Cambridge, MA: Harvard University Press, 2002.

CONGRESSIONAL HEARINGS AND DEBATE

Senate Foreign Relations Committee. Confirmation Hearing of Dr. Condoleezza Rice. 109th Cong., 1st sess., Jan. 18, 2005.

———, Iraq in U.S. Foreign Policy. Witness: The Hon. Condoleezza Rice. 109th Cong., 1st sess., Oct. 19, 2005.

———, Securing America's Interests in Iraq: The Remaining Options, the Administration's Plan for Iraq. Witness: The Hon. Condoleezza Rice. 110th Cong., 1st sess., Jan. 11, 2007.

U.S. Congress. *Congressional Record.* Floor Debate on the Nomination of Condoleezza Rice for Secretary of State. 109th Cong., 1st sess., Jan. 25, 2005. Vol. 151, no. 5.

DOCUMENTARIES

Lee, Spike. *When the Levees Broke.* 40 Acres and a Mule Productions. 2006.

GOVERNMENT DOCUMENTS

U.S. Census Bureau. *A Half-Century of Learning: Historical Statistics on Educational Attainment in the United States: 1940 to 2000.* Washington, DC, Apr. 2006.

———. *Current Population Survey.* Washington, DC, Mar. 2005.

The White House. *The National Security Strategy of the United States of America.* Washington, DC, Sept. 2002.

INDEPENDENT REPORTS

The Iraq Study Group. Baker, III, James A., and Lee A. Hamilton, co-chairs, et.al. *The Iraq Study Group Report.* New York: Vintage, 2006.

National Commission on Terrorist Attacks upon the United States. *The 9/11 Commission Report.* Jul. 22, 2004.

JOURNALS

Blinken, Antony J. "The False Crisis Over the Atlantic." *Foreign Affairs* 80, no. 3 (May/Jun. 2001): 35–49.

Pillar, Paul R. "Intelligence, Policy, and War in Iraq." *Foreign Affairs* 85, no. 2 (Mar./Apr. 2006): 15–28.

Rice, Condoleezza. "Promoting the National Interest." *Foreign Affairs* 79, no. 1 (Jan./Feb. 2000): 45–62.

———. "The Party, the Military, and Decision Authority in the Soviet Union." *World Politics* 40, no. 1 (Oct. 1987): 55–81.

PUBLIC REMARKS

Buchanan, Pat. 1992 Republican National Convention address. Houston, TX, Aug. 17, 1992. PBS recording. Vanderbilt Television News Archives.

Bush, George, H. W. "A Europe Whole and Free." Mainz, Federal Republic of Germany, May 31, 1989. U.S. Diplomatic Mission to Germany transcript.

Bush, George W. "Debate Transcript: The Second Bush-Kerry Presidential Debate." St. Louis, MO, Oct. 8, 2004. Commission on Presidential Debates transcript.

———. "President Arrives in Alabama, Briefed on Hurricane Katrina." Mobile, AL, Sept. 2, 2005. White House transcript.

———. "President Bush and Prime Minister Tony Blair of the United Kingdom Participate in Joint Press Availability." Washington, DC, May 25, 2006. White House transcript.

———. "President Bush Discusses Top Priorities for the U.S., Press Conference of the President." Washington, DC, Jul. 30, 2003. White House transcript.

———. "President Bush Meets with British Prime Minister Tony Blair." Washington, DC, Dec. 7, 2006. White House transcript.

———. "President Bush Names Randall Tobias to be Global AIDS Coordinator." Washington, DC, Jul. 2, 2003. White House transcript.

———. "President Bush Participates in Joint Press Availability with Prime Minister Maliki of Iraq." Amman, Jordan, Nov. 30, 2006. White House transcript.

———. "President Heads to Hurricane Katrina Affected Areas." Washington, DC, Sept. 2, 2005. White House transcript.

———. "President Nominates Condoleezza Rice as Secretary of State." Washington, DC, Nov. 16, 2004. White House transcript.

———. "President Remarks on Hurricane Recovery Efforts." Kenner, LA, Sept. 2, 2005. White House transcript.

———. "President's Address to the Nation." Washington, DC, Jan. 10, 2007. White House transcript.

———. "Remarks by the President Upon Arrival at Barksdale Air Force Base." Barksdale, LA, Sept. 11, 2001. White House transcript.

———. Second Inaugural Address. Washington, DC, Jan. 20, 2005. White House transcript.

Gorbachev, Mikhail. "Address by Mikhail Gorbachev at the 43rd U.N. General Assembly Session (Excerpts)," New York, Dec. 7, 1988. Cold War International History Project transcript.

Reagan, Ronald. "Remarks at the Brandenburg Gate." West Berlin, Federal Republic of Germany, Jun. 12, 1987. Reagan Foundation transcript.

Rice, Condoleezza. "Address to the Republican National Convention." Philadelphia, Aug. 1, 2000. Vanderbilt Television News Archives.

———. "Briefing En Route Baghdad, Iraq." Oct. 5, 2006. State Department transcript.

———. "Briefing on Efforts to Stop Violence in Lebanon." Jerusalem, Israel, Jul. 30, 2006. State Department transcript.

———. Commencement Address, University of Alabama General Commencement, Tuscaloosa, AL, May 15, 1994.

———. "Dr. Condoleezza Rice Discusses the War on Terror on *60 Minutes*." Washington, DC, Mar. 28, 2004. White House transcript.

———. "Hearing of the National Commission on Terrorist Attacks upon the United States. Witness: Dr. Condoleezza Rice, Assistant to the President for National Security Affairs." Washington, DC, Apr. 8, 2004. National Commission on Terrorist Attacks upon the United States transcript.

———. "International Relief Activities Related to Hurricane Katrina." Washington, DC, Sept. 2, 2005. State Department transcript.

———. "Interview on ABC *This Week* with George Stephanopoulos." St. Petersburg, Russia, Jul. 16, 2006. State Department transcript.

———. "Interview on ABC's *This Week* with George Stephanopoulos and Peter Jennings." Washington, DC, Jan. 30, 2005. State Department transcript.

———. "Interview on NBC *Today* Show with Katie Couric." Washington, DC, Dec. 16, 2005. State Department transcript.

———. "Interview with Gideon Yago from MTV News." New York, Sept. 12, 2006. State Department transcript.

———. "Interview with Steve Weisman of the *New York Times*." Washington, DC, Oct. 20, 2005. State Department transcript.

———. "Interview with the *Washington Post* Editorial Board." Washington, DC, Dec. 14, 2006. State Department transcript.

———. "On-the-Record Briefing, London, England." London, Oct. 16, 2005. State Department transcript.

———. "Remarks at the American University in Cairo." Cairo, Egypt, Jun. 20, 2005. State Department transcript.

———. "Remarks at the Institut d'Études Politiques de Paris—Sciences Po." Paris, Feb. 8, 2005. State Department transcript.

———. "Remarks to the Press en Route London." Feb. 3, 2005. State Department transcript.

———. "Remarks with British Foreign Secretary Jack Straw." Baghdad, Iraq, Apr. 3, 2006. State Department transcript.

———. "Remarks with German Foreign Minister Frank-Walter Steinmeier after Meeting." Washington, DC, Dec. 8, 2006. State Department transcript.

———. "Remarks with United Kingdom Foreign Secretary Jack Straw at the Blackburn Institute's Frank A. Nix Lecture." Tuscaloosa, AL, Oct. 21, 2005. State Department transcript.

———. "Rice Talks to O'Reilly." New York, Sept. 14, 2005. FOX News transcript.

———. "Secretary of State Condoleezza Rice on Fox News with Brit Hume." Washington, DC, Dec. 15, 2005. State Department transcript.

———. "Special Briefing on Travel to the Middle East and Europe." Washington, DC, Jul. 21, 2006. State Department transcript.

———. "Statement by the National Security Advisor Dr. Condoleezza Rice." Washington, DC, Jan. 17, 2003. White House press release.

———. "Statement by Secretary of State Condoleezza Rice." Paris, Jul. 12, 2006. State Department release.

———. "Statement on Three-Part Comprehensive Settlement." Jerusalem, Israel, Jul. 31, 2006. State Department transcript.

———. "Welcome Remarks to Employees." Washington, DC, Jan. 27, 2005. State Department transcript.

PRINT, BROADCAST, AND ONLINE MEDIA

Articles published by the *New York Times*, followed by the *Washington Post*, and then *Newsweek* were an essential help, as well as the seminal article by Ann Reilly Dowd in *George* magazine.

Magazines: *Birmingham*; *Christianity Today*; *Essence*; *Forbes*; *George*; *Good Housekeeping*; *GQ*; *Harper's*; *Look*; *National Review*; the *New Republic*; *New York*; the *New Yorker*; *Newsweek*; *O, The Oprah Magazine*; *People*; *Rolling Stone*; *Stanford* magazine; *Time*; *Today's Christian*; *Vanity Fair*; *Vogue*; the *Weekly Standard*.

Newspapers: *Atlanta Journal-Constitution*, *Birmingham News*, *Boston Globe*, *Campus Report* (Stanford University), *Chicago Tribune*, the *Clarion* (University of Denver student newspaper), *Daily News* (New York), *Dallas Morning News*, *Detroit Free Press*, *Financial Times* (London), *Globe*, *Houston Chronicle*, *Libération* (Paris), *Los Angeles Times*, *Miami Herald*, *Le Monde* (Paris), *New York Times*, *Palo Alto Weekly*, *Philadelphia Daily News*, *Philadelphia Inquirer*, *St. Petersburg Times*, *San Francisco Chronicle*, *San Jose Mercury News*, *Stanford Daily* (Stanford University independent student newspaper), *Stanford Reports*, *USA Today*, *Wall Street Journal*, *Washington Post*, *Washington Times*.

News Agencies: Associated Press, Reuters News Service.

Polling Organizations: Gallup, The Harris Poll, Pew Research Center, pollingreport.com, Princeton Survey Research Associates.

Television/Radio Programs: ABC (*This Week* with George Stephanopoulos); BBC; CBS (*Face the Nation, 60 Minutes, Sunday Morning*); CNN (*American Morning, Anderson Cooper 360 Degrees, Inside Politics, Larry King Live, Late Edition*); FOX News (*The O'Reilly Factor*); MSNBC (*Scarborough Country*); MTV (*MTV News*); National Public Radio (*Political Insider*); NBC (*Today*); NBC4, Washington, DC; PBS (*African American Lives, NewsHour with Jim Lehrer*); WNYC New York Public Radio (*Mad About Music*).

Web sites: Carnell Knowledge (www.carnellknowledge.com), Christian.com, databaseFootball.com, DenverBroncos.com, FactCheck.org, Gawker (www.gawker.com), Insight (www.insightmag.com), Pro-Football-Reference.com (www.profootballreference.com), PublicEye.org, RenewAmerica (www.renewamerica.us), Rick Upchurch (www.rickupchurch.com), Salon.com.

ACKNOWLEDGMENTS

This would have been a very different book without the cooperation of Secretary of State Condoleezza Rice. I thank Secretary Rice for sitting down with me for three interviews without demanding any editorial control over the book. I also thank her for opening the doors to her friends, family, and colleagues. I am forever grateful to them for sharing with me the Condoleezza Rice that they know, especially Mattie Ray Bonds, Genoa McPhatter, and Yvonne German. I owe a special debt to Clara Rice, Randy Bean, and, in particular, Chip Blacker, whose guidance, insight, and multiple lengthy interviews shaped my thinking on everything from Rice's relationships to the inner workings of the Washington bureaucracy.

I am very grateful for the friendship and invaluable advice that my *Newsweek* colleague Richard Wolffe provided at the beginning of this project, and the impressions of my colleague and friend Martha Brant, as well as Sarah Lenti and James Wilkinson, both of whom have worked for Rice and acted as early emissaries on my behalf. On that score, I extend a very special thank you to Blacker, Lenti, and Fareed Zakaria for pleading my case to Condi Rice. And I would not have been able to complete the many aspects of this project without Secretary Rice's chief of staff Brian Gunderson, and especially his deputy Brian Besanceney. I thank them for their patient assistance.

In Birmingham, in addition to Miss Mattie, I owe a great debt to the people of Titusville, especially Julia Emma Smith, Deborah Carson, the Hunters, Eva Carter, and Horace Huntley and Odessa Woolfolk of the Birmingham Civil Rights Institute. Virginia Volker and Leah Atkins, as well as Jim Baggett of the Birmingham Public Library Archives, were the embodiment of Southern Hospitality. There were a host of others who facilitated my work in Denver, Palo Alto, and Washington. My thanks to Judith Baenen, the former president of St. Mary's Academy, and Louise Turnbull, who were particularly helpful; and Dr. Fay Hill and Lydia McCullom of Montview Boulevard Presbyterian Church. I was also assisted by the archivists and library personnel at the University of

Denver as well as the journalists and archivists at Stanford University News Service.

There is no place like Stanford. And I am grateful to its faculty, staff, administrators, and students—present and former—for their generosity and help. I thank them for their perspectives and remembrances, which were often painful for them to recall. The incomparable "Dean Jean" Fetter Chu was a particular help early on in directing me around my old campus, as was Professor Ewart Thomas.

For almost twenty years, across three continents, *Newsweek* has been my professional home. The good humor, brains, and hard work of my friends there are unmatched in journalism. I thank all of my colleagues for their encouragement and support over the past two years, especially the correspondents who so ably took the helm while I was on leave: David Jefferson, Arian Campo-Flores, Christopher Dickey, Brad Stone, Rod Nordland, Keith Naughton, Dan McGinn, Karen Breslav, Mark Starr, and Stryker McGuire. And a very special thanks to my editors for allowing me to take my sabbatical—and then some—though the news never stopped; the generosity of Mark Whitaker and Jon Meacham have been overwhelming. I am also especially grateful to Mark Miller for sitting in for me when I needed it most, to Tom Manning for keeping the paper flowing, and to Evan Thomas for asking me the hard questions early on. Finally, thanks to my friends Nisid Hajari and Jeff Bartholet for being constant intellectual soul mates now and always.

Like Condoleezza Rice, I have been blessed with extraordinary friends and family. Randy Shapiro and Jeanne Sakas, who are so much more than colleagues, kept me sane and on an even keel for the last two years; as did a virtual bevy of assistants: Raina Kelley, Roisin Timoney, and Deborah Millan. Thank you all for keeping me from losing my day job as I worked on this book and for keeping me smiling.

My researchers on the book, Chris Toward and Lisa Helem, were an essential help. Chris read and reread drafts. But this book would have never been possible without the gentle strength and endless wisdom of my agent, Charlotte Sheedy. My editor, Leigh Haber, worked extraordinarily hard and remained good-humored throughout the process. I am honored that *Twice as Good* is the inaugural title of her new imprint. I also thank the good people of Rodale for making miracles a daily occurrence when it came time to finish the project, and a special thanks to project editor Karen Neely and her team.

Jon Rosenwasser, Bob Cohn, and Hamilton Cain, were the best readers any writer could ask for. I am grateful for their insightful advice on how to make the book better.

My best friend, Sam Crews, provided my West Coast lodging and, as always, his levelheaded constancy and support. My sister, Traciana Graves, was a source of love and courage; and my other Grace, Saskia Reilly-Corsano, provided an important intellectual sounding board. And my brother, Frankie Edozien, was my rock.

My father, Maurice Hall, has been a source of strength and love to me. I thank my father for that, and I thank God that he's still here with us.

There is no one on earth like my mother, Jerilynn Mabry, who for almost forty years has set her clock by my and my brother's lives. She taught us early on that there are no limits to what we can do. I am grateful to her every day for her boundless love, her fierce pride, and her ceaseless encouragement. I thank her, particularly, for the roles she's played in making this book a reality, from her time as my personal assistant to her (unsolicited) hawking of the book on the buses and subways of New York.

Finally, I especially thank my partner, Christopher Hubis, for being understanding and supportive, and for forgiving me for virtually disappearing for more than a year. Even when I was physically present, I often wasn't there. Chris sacrificed a piece of our life together in service to this book. And yet he was gracious enough to be a reader, a cheerleader, a skeptic, and a fan; and I owe him so much more than six months of dog walking.

CREDITS

Page 1: (top), Courtesy of Clara Rice; (bottom) Courtesy of Julia Emma Smith
Page 2: Courtesy of Condoleezza Rice
Page 3: (top left) Courtesy of Condoleezza Rice; (bottom left) Courtesy of Clara Rice; (top right, bottom right) Courtesy of Condoleezza Rice
Page 4: (top) Courtesy of Clara Rice; (bottom) © Chris McNair
Page 5: (top left) Courtesy of Condoleezza Rice; (top right, bottom right) Courtesy of Clara Rice
Page 6: (top left) Courtesy of Condoleezza Rice; (bottom left) University of Denver Special Collections & Archives; (top right) Courtesy of University of Notre Dame Sports Information; (bottom right) Courtesy of Condoleezza Rice
Page 7: (top) © Chuck Painter/Stanford News Service, (center, bottom) George Bush Presidential Library
Page 8: (top, bottom) © Linda A. Cicero/Stanford News Service
Page 9: (top) © Laura Camden/Reuters, (bottom left) © Mandel Ngan/AFP/Getty Images; (bottom right) © Mark Wilson/Getty Images
Page 10: (top) © Mark Wilson/Getty Images; (bottom) © 2005 by Khue Bui
Page 11: (top) © Charles Platiau/AFP/Getty Images; (bottom) © Alberto Pizzoli-Vatican Pool/Getty Images
Page 12: (top) © Faleh Kheiber/Getty Images; (center) State Department Photo; (bottom) © Charles Ommanney/Contact Press
Page 13: (top left, bottom) State Department Photo; (top right) © Vyacheslav Oseledko/AFP/Getty Images
Page 14: (top) © Mandel Ngan/AFP/Getty Images; (bottom) AP Photo/J. Scott Applewhite
Page 15: (top left, top right) © AFP/Getty Images; (bottom left) © Asif Hassan/AFP/Getty Images; (bottom right) © Getty Images
Page 16: (top) © Awad Awad/AFP/Getty Images, (bottom) © Charles Ommanney/Contact Press

INDEX